THE POLITICS OF PUBLIC MONEY

Spenders, Guardians, Priority Setters,
and Financial Watchdogs
inside the Canadian Government

Public money is one of the primary currencies of influence for politicians and public servants. It affects the standards by which they undertake the nation's business and it impacts on the standard of living of the nation's citizens. *The Politics of Public Money* examines the extent to which the Canadian federal budgetary process is shifting from one based on a bilateral relationship between departmental spenders and central guardians to one based on a more complex, multilateral relationship involving a variety of players.

In this innovative work, David A. Good examines this shift in terms of a broader societal change from an 'old village,' conditioned by old norms of behaviour, to a 'new town,' which brings with it new ideas about how public money should be managed and spent. Organized into four parts, the book opens with 'The Changing Politics of Public Money,' which sets out a revised and expanded framework for analysing the politics and management of public money. Part 2, 'The Public Money Players,' looks at the motivations, interdependence, and independence of the four budget players. The third part, 'The Public Money Processes,' deals with the central functions of budgeting – determining fiscal aggregates, making budget allocations, and ensuring effective financial management. Finally, 'New Prospects for Public Money' looks ahead to the future and considers ways to strengthen the interaction among the players, and in so doing reshape the politics and management of public money.

An insightful and incisive study of the changing budgetary process, *The Politics of Public Money* examines the promises and pitfalls of budgetary reform and sheds new light on the role insiders play in influencing government spending.

DAVID GOOD is a professor in the School of
University of Victoria.

The Institute of Public Administration of Canada Series in Public Management and Governance

Editor: Donald Savoie

This series is sponsored by the Institute of Public Administration of Canada as part of its commitment to encourage research on issues in Canadian public administration, public sector management, and public policy. It also seeks to foster wider knowledge and understanding among practioners, academics, and the general public.

For a list of books published in the series, see page 371.

DAVID A. GOOD

The Politics of Public Money:

Spenders, Guardians, Priority Setters,
and Financial Watchdogs
inside the Canadian Government

UNIVERSITY OF TORONTO PRESS
Toronto   Buffalo   London

© University of Toronto Press Incorporated 2007
Toronto Buffalo London
Printed in Canada

Reprinted 2008

ISBN 978-0-8020–9341-7 (cloth)
ISBN 978-0-8020–9503-9 (paper)

Printed on acid-free paper

Library and Archives Canada Cataloguing in Publication

Good, David A.
The politics of public money: spenders, guardians, priority setters,
and financial watchdogs inside the Canadian government / David A. Good.

(Institute of Public Administration of Canada series in public management
and governance)
Includes bibliographical references and index.
ISBN 978-0-8020-9341-7 (bound)
ISBN 978-0-8020-9503-9 (pbk.)

1. Government spending policy – Canada. 2. Budget – Political aspects –
Canada. 3. Expenditures, Public – Canada. 4. Budget process – Canada.
I. Title. II. Series.

HJ793.G65 2007   352.40971   C2007-901896-3

University of Toronto Press acknowledges the financial assistance to its publishing
program of the Canada Council for the Arts and the Ontario Arts Council.

University of Toronto Press acknowledges the financial support for its publishing
activities of the Government of Canada through the Book Publishing Industry
Development Program (BPIDP).

For Gilda

Contents

Preface

In writing this book about public money I have incurred many private debts. I owe a debt of deep personal thanks and enormous gratitude to my many friends and colleagues – academics and practitioners – who read early versions of the manuscript and provided me with a host of perceptive comments and suggestions for improvement. I thank Peter Aucoin, Herman Bakvis, Sandy Borins, Barry Carin, David Dewar, Rod Dobell, Mike Joyce, Joanne Kelly, Arthur Kroeger, Evert Lindquist, Michael Prince, Jim Quinn, Donald Savoie, Allen Schick, Harry Swain, and David Zussman. I thank the two anonymous reviewers selected by the University of Toronto Press for their comments and helpful suggestions. I also thank André Blais and Louis Imbeau who reviewed and commented on an early draft of chapter 1. I want to acknowledge and thank Jim McDavid and the students in Sandy Borin's graduate seminar in public management at the University of Toronto for critiquing my research proposal and suggesting improvements when I was in the early stages of my work. I am grateful to my own graduate students in the School of Public Administration at the University of Victoria who listened to and critiqued my concepts about the politics of public money in our classes and discussions.

I thank Janet Milne and the Conference Board of Canada for the opportunity to prepare a paper on expenditure reallocation as part of their work on financial leadership in government and to exchange ideas on public money with a large group of senior financial executives as part of the conference on Public Sector Financial Leadership in 2006. I thank the Institute of Public Administration of Canada for its support and encouragement. I thank Tim Feng of the Parliamentary Centre for invitations to explain Canadian budgeting to several delegations of senior officials of the Budget Affairs Commission of the National People's Congress and

Provincial People's Congresses of China. There is nothing like the discipline of explaining to a group of knowledgeable foreign budget officials, in simple terms and through a translator, the seeming complexity and nuance of an important domestic governmental process.

This book could not have been written without a host of co-authors – the many public servants and politicians who extended to me more than the normal level of cooperation and consideration. They patiently listened to my simple and naive questions, thought deeply about their responses, and brought an honesty and candour to a subject matter that is sometimes prone to exaggeration and unreality. I am deeply indebted to them all. I hope that in this book they recognize something of the reality of the world in which they work and that it can stimulate productive discussions for bringing about improvements to the politics and management of public money.

Like much research, this project was supported by public money. I am grateful to the Social Sciences and Humanities Research Council of Canada for their financial support. More specifically, I am thankful to the anonymous peer-review panel members who, after several attempts on my part, were able to conclude that this project might be worthwhile when compared to the severely limited resources available and the seemingly limitless requests on the table. If I learned anything about public money, it was that persistence can have its own rewards.

I was blessed with the support of two top-notch research assistants – Steven Emery and Marion Brulot. Not only did they deliver, but we had fun along the way. I thank Jennifer Guest for her efficient and ever responsive administrative support. I am grateful to Milton Wani and Carolyn Yakel for their assistance in preparing the index for the book. It is often said that every writer needs a good editor – mine was better than good. I owe a special thank you to my copy editor, Beth McAuley, who was not only a pleasure to work with but contributed significantly to improving the manuscript. I thank Virgil Duff of the University of Toronto for his early and enthusiastic encouragement for the project and for his ongoing support and advice throughout the entreprise.

As always my deepest debt goes to my wonderful wife, Gilda, for her steadfast love, support, and encouragement. Her skill in managing the private money in our household budget allowed me to study the politics of public money in our nation's budget.

Needless to say, even with this enormous support and these outstanding debts, the errors of commission and omission that remain are my responsibility.

"Gentlemen, the fact that all my horses and all my men couldn't put Humpty together again simply proves to me that I must have <u>more</u> horses and <u>more</u> men."

THE POLITICS OF PUBLIC MONEY

Spenders, Guardians, Priority Setters,
and Financial Watchdogs
inside the Canadian Government

Introduction

This book is about the politics and management of public money inside the Canadian government. It explores how decisions about public money – how much to spend, where it should be spent, and how it is to be managed – are changing in the Canadian federal government.[1] To be sure, important questions about how government deals with public money have been explored before, but the process is changing in fundamental and significant ways. Just as there is great debate over how government is changing and should change, so too there is controversy about how the government actually manages public money and how it should be done. This is because matters of public money are central to government. Indeed, public money talks. It speaks to the great public purposes of society – where governments place their priorities and what they decide to ignore. It affects the standards of living in the nation and it reflects standards by which politicians and public servants undertake the nation's business. Public money speaks to promises and aspirations. It also speaks to deep concerns – both real and sometimes fabricated – of citizens, taxpayers, and members of Parliament about the way public money is spent. Inside and outside government, matters of public money are filled with great promises and fraught with bitter disappointments.

Much of our understanding about the politics and management of public money has been derived from our understanding of budgeting, and much of that understanding has come from studies by academics and articles by practitioners.[2] In 1964, Aaron Wildavsky's book *The Politics of the Budgetary Process* was published. It set out the spenders and guardian framework, which for that period and for the remainder of the twentieth century defined not only the way in which most academics thought about the budgetary process but also described how most practitioners experienced budgeting. Like some budgets, the early drafts of his manuscript received 'unusually negative response (nine publishers rejected it).'[3] According to Wildavsky, 'readers found it too critical of government (if they were in it) or too tolerant of bad practices (if they suffered from them) ... At first the reaction in the old BOB (Bureau of the Budget) was that none of it was true. After about two years the word was that some of it was true. By the time four years had elapsed the line was that most of it was true, but wasn't it a shame.'[4] It seemed that budgeting by spenders and guardians was what it was, not what some might wish it to be.

That there are both spenders and guardians in budgetary processes surprises no one. Parents know it when they deal with the competing demands in their young families while trying to juggle the household budget to meet emerging and changing needs. Business people know it when they listen to the competing plans of their finance, research, and marketing organizations as they put together the company's budget for the markets they expect to face. Public officials know it when they struggle to balance a multiplicity of public needs against a limited pool of public means. Similarly, few are surprised that the relative influence and circumstances of spenders and guardians not only shape the way budget decisions are made but also what budget decisions are actually taken. Different types of families make different budget choices and they arrive at their decisions through different means. Different companies take different risks and make different investments in their spending plans. Rich governments arrive at different budget decisions through different processes than do poor ones. Understanding the exercise of influence between spenders and guardians in government has told us much about how the budgetary process actually works. But, do spenders and guardians and their interactions tell us enough and will they continue to do so in the future?

The central focus of this book is to examine the extent to which the exercise of influence in the Canadian federal budgetary process is shifting from a simple bilateral relationship between departmental spenders and central guardians (the Department of Finance and Treasury Board Secretariat) within an 'old village' conditioned by old norms of behaviour, to a more complex multilateral relationship among spenders, guardians, priority setters (the Prime Minister's Office and the Privy Council Office) and financial watchdogs (the Office of the Auditor General) within a 'new town' conditioned by new norms of behaviour.

Posing this central question about the changing nature of influence and relationships within the budgetary process is one thing; getting answers is quite another. Indeed, at the beginning of this research, it was not readily apparent how to get reliable answers to the question. Despite all the talk about government being more open and transparent, for those on the outside who look in on 'the town,' the actual behaviour of Ottawa insiders appears obscure and opaque, inextricably tied to the conventions of cabinet secrecy and cabinet solidarity. Indeed, secrecy of cabinet proceedings is 'one of the cornerstones of the Westminster system of government.'[5] To be sure, 'access to information' legislation has dramatically increased the volume of government information that is now publicly available. However, that information, often sought and secured by outsiders – the media, the opposition parties, or interest groups – contains little by way of the specific context within which decisions are actually made and actions taken. On the one hand, the subsequent media stories are often incomplete and partial and sometimes even erroneous. It is not uncommon for government insiders when provoked about a particular media report to simply observe that there is much more to it than what has been publicly reported. On the other hand, while governments are finding it in their interests to release more information (even in the absence of external requests), the underlying contextual information surrounding an actual decision is invariably omitted and, typically, much of what the outsider sees or hears is the rhetorical 'spin' carefully crafted to ensure that a simple message is communicated with the minimal of media and opposition distortion. While the public buzz and gossip about what actually goes on inside government has increased, it has rarely served to provide clearer pictures, only more confused ones.

In Ottawa, all important information about important matters, and especially about public money, still flows through private channels – inaccessible and closely guarded briefing notes, secret memoranda to cabinet and records of decision, private telephone calls, quiet and confidential corridor chats, and unrecorded meetings and discussions. Decisions are taken in private, in the sanctity of the departmental or ministerial office, behind the closed doors of the cabinet room, in the seclusion of the prime minister's personal office, in the 'in camera' sessions of the federal-provincial-territorial meeting, or over 'working dinners' in the privacy of the executive boardroom. Both public servants and ministers are sworn to their oaths of secrecy, protecting each others' confidences in an effort to maintain cabinet solidarity and retain a semblance of public service anonymity. The few outsiders who, through years of ongoing effort, have gained access to insiders carefully nurture their relationships and vigorously protect their sources. When insiders do engage with outsiders, such as with the media or an interest group, and take them into their confidence, the information provided is less likely to be an accurate private reflection of how they actually behaved and why, and more likely a public pronouncement intended to improve their future leverage over others within the town.

When considered in the abstract, the prospects for gaining access to reliable information about the behaviour of participants in the budgetary process inside government does not look good. While the veil of secrecy traditionally surrounding the budgetary process has been lifted in part, some of the most important aspects of decision-making continue, and should continue, to remain hidden. Furthermore, most officials, with extensive experience in the management of public money, are preoccupied with the pressing issues of the day, 'wrapped up' in the crises of the moment, and have little time to talk to outsiders. However, insiders, like most others, step back occasionally and reflect on what they have done, if for no other reason than as a reprieve or refuge from their all-too busy schedules. Indeed, it is surprising just how few opportunities there are for reflection inside government.

An outsider can be a useful sounding board for an insider. Having been a former public servant, as I am, can help an outsider gain access to current budget participants. However, once in the door there is no guarantee that questions posed will be completely answered. Good questions that demonstrate an understanding of the subject matter and an empathy that conveys an appreciation for the complexity and impossibility of the task are important. If things progress well, the public servant, minister, or ministerial aide, over the course of the interview, might go to considerable lengths to illustrate just how his/her particular role in and around the budgetary process relates to others. Finance guardians don't just focus on departmental spenders; they have much to say about the influence of the Prime Minister's Office (PMO) and the Privy Council Office (PCO) on budgets. Priority setters in the PMO and PCO often explain their roles in the budgetary process in relation to, and in contrast with, the Department of Finance and its minister. Guardians themselves – Finance and the Treasury Board Secretariat – when pressed are prepared to explain the changing budgetary relations in terms of their institutional dynamics with each other. It is not just spending departments who are prepared to speak about the Office of the Auditor General, which keeps a watchful eye on them, but guardians and priority setters are commenting on the subtle and indirect influence of financial watchdogs on matters of public money.

Because, like all researchers, my ignorance about the subject matter was the greatest at the beginning of this project, I first interviewed retired officials who had been major budget players and who had left government. The next step was to interview those currently inside government. Not only could I flaunt my initial ignorance on those who had the time and patience to be more tolerant and understanding, but I could also probe deeply into the way things used to be done in the 1970s, 1980s, and 1990s. I generally began interviewing at the lower ranks in the public service and worked the interviews 'up through the levels,' usually beginning with those closer to the outside – departments and agencies – before focusing on those in central agencies.

Those interviewed were selected on the basis of their positions (e.g., a deputy minister in charge of a big spending department or an associate deputy minister of the Department of Finance with extensive budget preparation responsibilities) or because, through their skill and knowledge, they had developed reputations as effective players in the 'budget community.' The interviews ranged from front-line budget analysts in central agencies (Treasury Board Secretariat and Department of Finance) and officials in various departments and offices, through mid-level executives, to deputy ministers, ministers, and political staff. The preponderance of interviews took place with those at the most senior levels. The interviews included 'policy people,' program managers, budget analysts, chief financial officers, auditors and evaluators, ministers, and 'political operatives.' In total, nearly fifty face-to-face interviews were conducted from December 2004 to April 2006 in the quiet security of departmental and ministerial offices. Most interviews lasted about two hours, some only one hour, with a few extending to more than three hours. Some agreed to be reinterviewed to clarify certain points or to deal with new questions that emerged.

The focus of the interviews was primarily on the work people actually did and why, and not on how they conceived the budgetary process to work or not to work. Interviewers were not asked to do the conceptual work – that is the job of the researcher – only to speak from their experience. The questions were invariably short, but the follow-up was extensive and vigorous. For example:

• When it comes to matters of the budget and public money, what do you do in your job? How do you actually do that? Why did you behave that way in that particular circumstance?

- How do you get your way with the Department of Finance, the minister of finance, the minister of (a major department), the Auditor General?
- You, I gather are a person who gets your way on budget matters. What makes some men/women more powerful than others?
- In your job, when it comes to budget matters, what's the biggest mistake you want most to avoid? Why? How do you do it?
- You've been involved in budget-making for some time. What has surprised you most? Why?
- Where does the budget get made? Who is the budget office?
- What one question did I forget to ask that I should have asked?

In almost every case, these questions provoked lengthy and elaborate responses, often raising new issues and explanations that the interviewee believed were important for me as the researcher to understand and appreciate.

Getting straight answers to tough questions is enhanced when public servants and politicians know that what they say will not be attributed directly to them. This was a necessary, but relatively small, concession to make since the focus of this book is on understanding budget behaviour in terms of the roles in the process and not in terms of individual personalities. There is no doubt that in Ottawa personalities embrace the budgetary process, and if we want to understand and explain a specific budget decision, then focusing on personalities may well be the best way. However, if we want to understand the broader pattern of budgetary outcomes over time, then focusing on roles is the better approach.

Similarly, officials and ministers are not likely to be forthcoming and candid in their reflections about their behaviour and that of others when, before questions are even asked, a tape recorder appears on the table. Not only might it lead to the emergence of their own recording device, but more importantly, it will invariably create the impression of a media interview, complete with suspicions, cautions, and a dogged determination to 'stay on message.' This is not conducive to receiving honest answers to probing questions. Instead, to accurately 'record' the information I garnered from the interview, I paid careful attention to the answers provided and the language used. I quickly and discretely scribbled key words, phrases, and sentences onto a small note pad throughout the course of the session. Perhaps most importantly, immediately after completing the session, I used these notes to construct a detailed, line-by-line, written account of the interview. Later, I organized and categorized this information in terms of key concepts, then analysed and compared the information from all of the interviews and from documents and public reports.

There are, no doubt, limitations in using an interview methodology as the principal means to address the research questions set out in this book. While much of the interview information was compared and analysed along with published and accessible government reports and documents and studies by academics and professionals, considerable weight was placed upon the interviews themselves. The interview material cited in the book is extensive and some of the citations are lengthy in order to not only explain a complex point but also to expose the broader context and thinking that surrounds a particular quote. Certain information from some interviews was cross-checked with information from others and in a few cases reverified and clarified with the interviewees. Care was taken to avoid 'leading' the interviewees to conclusions which would necessarily support the underlying research hypothesis – that there were spenders and guardians and that, more recently, priority setters and financial watchdogs were having increasingly direct and indirect influence on the budgetary process. The focus of the questioning was on what participants did and who they did it with, and not on whether they thought there were new roles and whether they thought they were important. Instead, it was on asking recognized individuals to describe their role in the budgetary process and the management of public money. Nonetheless, the mere act of selecting who and who not to interview – there were few junior staff included but no outsiders – and asking particular questions has its limitations.

This book is organized into four parts. The first – 'The Changing Politics of Public Money' – sets out a revised and expanded framework for analysing the politics and management of public money that takes us beyond the spenders and guardians framework. Chapter 1 in this section includes the interaction across the four principal players – spenders, guardians, priority setters, and financial watchdogs – around the three key budget decisions of how much to spend, where it should be spent, and how it is to be managed. It highlights the evolution of budgeting and the management of public money within the Canadian federal government from the 'old village' of a tightly knit expenditure community of spenders and guardians to a 'new town' of more open and visible budgeting facing new pressures and incorporating new players.

The second part – 'The Public Money Players' – contains four chapters and analyses the motivations, interdependence, and independence of the four budget players. It uses the framework from chapter 1 to explore the extent to which the interaction among these players creates a stable pattern of mutual expectations about how they behave towards each other. In chapter 2, the guardians are analysed by examining the changing role of the budget office. It seeks to shed light on the often hidden but critical relationship (sometimes uneasy) between the Department of Finance and the Treasury Board Secretariat. It describes the diverging relationship between these two central guardians as they have struggled to eliminate deficits and maintain balanced budgets while undertaking various public sector reforms under the broad banner of new public management. Chapter 3 describes the motivations and interests of spenders and their changing relationships with the other players. It explores how spenders work, with and through others, to get money, to keep money, and to spend it and analyses the strategies and tactics they use to create expenditure flexibility and how they maintain credibility and reputation. It examines the changing reciprocity between spenders and guardians by focusing on changes in the mixture of their essential currency of information and expenditure allocations.

An examination of the priority setters in chapter 4 takes us to the centre of government – the Prime Minister's Office and the Privy Council Office. Here we explore the most important of all relationships, those between the prime minister and the minister of finance. This chapter examines the increasing influence of priority setters, particularly at the 'front-end' of the budget process, in determining priorities and in shaping new spending initiatives. Chapter 5, the final chapter in this section, considers the increasingly important role played by financial watchdogs, most notably the Office of the Auditor General. It analyses how, through the use of their powerful performance audits, financial watchdogs have built a reputation for independence, credibility, and assumed objectivity. This chapter analyses the indirect and subtle influence that financial watchdogs are having on budgeting, particularly at the 'back-end' of the process and how it has indirectly shaped the behaviour of spenders, guardians, and priority setters.

The third part – 'The Public Money Processes' – is divided into three chapters, each dealing with one of the central functions of budgeting – determining fiscal aggregates, making budget allocations, and ensuring effective financial management and promoting efficiency. Chapter 6 analyses the determination of fiscal aggregates and the setting of the fiscal framework – expenditures, revenues, and the fiscal balance. It explores the 'balanced budget mentality,' how fiscal targets and objectives are set, how fiscal prudence gets built into budgets in order to hedge against uncertainty, and the increasing use of harder fiscal rules in the place of softer fiscal principles. In chapter 7, the process of expenditure allocation is analysed in terms of the range of budget items, from the big fixes, to the must dos, to tax expenditures, and to reductions and reallocations. The chapter examines how most allocations are based on priorities, with fewer being justified by performance. It explores the seemingly endless search for expenditure reallocation and the budgetary conflict that it engenders. Chapter 8 deals with financial management and efficiency and explores the important topic of budget implementation. It analyses the degree to which the budget office is struggling to adjust its focus from expenditure control to program performance in the face of the efforts of spenders to secure more flexibility in resources and management, and of auditors and comptrollers to increase accountability and efficiency in government expenditure. The chapter deals with the interaction between the central comptrollers general in the Treasury Board Secretariat and the chief financial officers in departments and agencies.

The fourth part of the book – 'New Prospects for Public Money' – looks ahead and considers budgeting in a 'new town.' Chapter 9 examines the role of Parliament and its committees in matters of public money and assesses the increasing frustration of parliamentarians with the supply process and the limited prospects for change. Chapter 10 provides a backdrop for change by examining the promises and the pitfalls of budgetary reform, where each reform over the last half century has been a reaction to the shortcomings of the previous reforms. The final chapter asks if there is a better way. It examines how the framework of spenders, guardians, priority setters, and financial watchdogs can provide a more complete way for analysing the politics and management of public money in contemporary government. It concludes with a number of suggestions to strengthen the interaction across these players and, in so doing, improve the politics and management of public money.

As this book goes to press in spring 2007, it is not surprising that the Harper Conservative minority government is promising to implement a 'new expenditure management system.' It has been more than a decade since the 1995 'Program Review' cut deeply into the ongoing base of government expenditures, resulting in a level of program spending that, compared to the size of the economy, was similar to that of the immediate post–Second World War period. Since the mid-1990s, direct program spending has more than doubled, to over $95 billion annually. With it has come the political commitment to 'keep the rate of growth of program spending, on average, below the rate of growth of the economy' and the political rhetoric to 'ensure existing spending is effective, efficient, focused on areas of federal responsibility and pro- vides value for money.'[6] The lofty promises of 'a continuous culture of reallocation' by the Martin Liberal government have not been achieved, and the excessive preoccupation with accountability by the Harper gov- ernment has served only to strengthen one part of the overall system – the financial watchdogs – at the expense of others.

What is surprising is the low profile and tentative manner in which the outlines of this new expenditure management system have been publicly released. The entire system is contained to a single page, deeply buried in a voluminous 300-page document supporting the 19 March 2007 budget. Indeed, more words were devoted to the expansion of truckers' meal expenses than to the new system. If the commitment to the new system appears weak, it is matched by the fact that, in the bud- get year, the rate of growth in program expenditures is above the rate of growth in the economy.

The promise of this new system is to rest upon four principles:

- Departments and agencies will manage their programs to clearly defined results, and assess their performance against those results,
- The Treasury Board Secretariat will oversee the quality of these assessments and ensure that departments explicitly address risk as well as cost-effectiveness,
- Building on these assessments, Cabinet will systematically review the funding and relevance of all program spending to ensure that spending is aligned with Canadians' priorities and effectively a nd efficiently delivers on the Government's responsibilities, and
- Cabinet will undertake a rigorous examination of all new spend- ing proposals, taking explicit account of the funding, performance and resource requirements of existing programs in related areas.[7]

According to one Treasury Board Secretariat official, the essence of the new system is to change the focus from 'what the spending is on' to 'what the spending is for.'[8] In short, the performance and results of programs will inform and shape expenditure decisions that are taken through the regular review of new spending proposals and of the existing base of spending. The extent to which this actually happens is dependent upon three conditions. The first is the ability, interest, and incentives for cabinet ministers to regularly review new spending proposals in light of existing programs and to periodically review the ongoing base of existing spending. The second is the extent to which ministers will make use of performance and results information in undertaking such reviews. The third is the extent to which officials – spenders, guardians, priority setters, and watchdogs – can produce performance and results information that can be readily digested by ministers and that is reliable, relevant, and timely to their decisions.

The story that unfolds in this book indicates that putting in place these conditions represents an enormous challenge for ministers and public servants. There is little evidence to suggest that the amount of public money will be replaced by program results and performance as the quintessential currency of influence in the budgetary process. These proposed reforms can not simply be achieved by implementing the operational designs of the Treasury Board Secretariat, however strongly they may be supported by the clerk of the Privy Council. It will also require the active and visible political commitment of the prime minister, working closely with the minister of finance and president of the Treasury Board, to manage effectively the political conflict among ministers and departments that will invariably result from direct challenges to new spending and serious reviews of the ongoing base of existing spending. It will require a new-found tenacity and ingenuity on the part of the public service to rebuild its significantly diminished capacity to ensure that knowledge, information, and advice about programs and expenditures can be systematically assembled, analysed, and communicated. Perhaps most important, it will require the re-establishment of a level of trust and reciprocity among spenders, guardians, priority setters, and financial watchdogs that has been significantly eroded over the past several decades.

PART ONE

The Changing Politics of Public Money

1 Beyond Spenders and Guardians

No matter what the program, to get money you need to show how it helps to achieve the government's priorities.

Spending deputy minister

The minister of finance cannot decide all the budget priorities.

Former top adviser to a prime minister

Finance needs to see us as tough on departments and departments need to see us as tough on Finance and PCO (Privy Council Office).

Treasury Board Secretariat assistant secretary

The job is to help Members of Parliament hold government to account, but this does not exclude relationships with the government.

Former top official, Office of the Auditor General

Budget behaviour is shaped by established norms and practices. It is learned behaviour and there is a need to change it.

Department of Finance associate deputy minister

At 8:00 p.m. on 13 June 1963, Walter Gordon, the freshly minted minister of finance, rose in the House of Commons and delivered the Government of Canada's one hundredth budget since Confederation. He was dressed in a charcoal-grey suit with one button missing. As promised, the budget was developed and presented within sixty days of the election of the new minority Liberal government of Prime Minister Lester Pearson. Prepared in secret within the Department of Finance (with three key external advisers) and unveiled to Parliament and the Canadian public, the budget was to represent a new start. It took nearly everyone by surprise. There was no hint of the proposed changes in the concise Speech from the Throne presented twenty-seven days earlier on 16 May. The budget focused on three main problems: the budgetary deficit, unemployment, and foreign ownership and control of Canadian industry.

Spenders had pushed government expenditures up by 10.5 per cent from the previous year to a level of $8.3 billion in 1963–4, representing 17.3 per cent of the GDP. Guardians, however, were successful in decreasing the budgetary deficit by $350 million to a level of $585 million, albeit largely through tax increases. The minister explained that the government was reviewing the recommendations of the Royal Commission on Government Organization (broadly known as the Glassco Commission) and that 'those recommendations that may be expected to result in greater efficiency in the public service or in useful reductions in expenditures will be implemented as quickly as possible.'[1] To stimulate employment, the finance minister established a special allowance for employers hiring workers over age forty-five who had been out of work for six months and offered corporate income tax benefits in the form of accelerated depreciation for new private sector capital investments in manufacturing in areas of slow economic growth. To begin the process of reversing the American acquisition of Canadian companies, he instituted a 30 per cent takeover tax. To further encourage Canadian ownership, he reduced the withholding tax on dividends paid to non-residents for companies whose shares were at least one quarter Canadian owned and increased it for firms with a lower proportion of domestic ownership.

Hidden behind these major budget items were a host of specific expenditure decisions that emerged through the momentum of annual budgeting and the day-to-day combat between departmental spenders and Department of Finance guardians. Defence expenditures in the army, navy, and air services, representing nearly one-quarter of total expenditures, continued to increase. Large expenditure increases were made in health and welfare for hospital insurance, family allowances, unemployment insurance, and old age benefits reflecting growth in the population. The steady increase in expenditures for veterans' pensions and treatment and welfare services continued, as did those for the national airline, the railway and steamship lines, and canals and marine services. Expenditures for the Post Office and for the Department of

Public Works increased. The Department of Labour continued on an upward track with large expenditure increases on technical and vocational training. Reflecting the increases in government employees and payrolls, the government's contribution to its superannuation account continued on its upward climb.

Not all of this was to be. The disintegration of Finance Minister Gordon's budget began the next day when it was revealed during question period in the House of Commons that significant parts of the budget had been prepared by three 'outside consultants or ghost writers,' two of whom had remained in their companies' employ. Nearly a month later, on 8 July, after constant attacks from the opposition, the media, and the business community, Finance Minister Gordon made significant modifications to his budget.[2] He reneged on his commitment to reduce the budgetary deficit, thereby reinforcing a pattern of deficit financing that had begun in the early 1950s and would continue into the late 1990s.

Over forty years later at 4:00 p.m. on 23 March 2004, Ralph Goodale, the new minister of finance, stood in the House of Commons and delivered the one hundred and fifty-first budget of the Government of Canada. He wore a red tie, matching pocket handkerchief, white shirt, dark suit, and new shoes.[3] The budget was developed and presented 102 days after the swearing in on 12 December of the new government of Prime Minister Paul Martin, who had just won the leadership of the Liberal Party. The budget was intended to set the stage for an election, which was expected shortly. It was to represent a new start and a new way of doing government business. It was prepared within the Department of Finance, but not in secret, since all the major priorities had been signalled fifty days earlier on 2 February in the Speech from the Throne, which had been carefully crafted by the Prime Minister's Office (PMO) and the Privy Council Office (PCO) under the close eye and careful direction of the new prime minister. The budget surprised no one, and it quickly sank from media attention.

The overriding theme of the budget was unprecedented; it was 'sound financial management.' This was an attempt by the Liberal government to cast the maladministration and subsequent corruption that was part of the so-called sponsorship scandal into a problem of poor management that could be addressed in the budget. The budget was in response to the concerns of the public financial watchdog – the auditor general – who on 10 February released her long-awaited scathing report on the misspending of public monies on Liberal- and federalist-friendly advertising firms in the Province of Quebec. The budget speech reflected the intense reaction of the public to the Auditor General's report and to the prime minister's immediate response to establish a commission of inquiry by Mr Justice John Gomery.

Despite the overriding concern with financial management, spenders got their way on many items in the budget. The budget projected total expenditures of $183 billion, representing 14.5 per cent of the GDP, significantly lower than 1963. Program expenditures were expected to grow at 4.4 per cent annually, a rate faster than the forecast growth in the economy. The budget confirmed an additional $2 billion in year-end expenditures for provinces and territories for health care, created the Canada Public Health Agency, established a new learning bond to help low-income families save for post-secondary education for their children, and provided $7 billion in goods and services tax (GST) relief for municipalities. Nonetheless, guardians continued to hold their own. This was the seventh consecutive balanced budget. The budget implemented $1 billion in annual expenditure reallocation from existing spending and created a cabinet Committee on Expenditure Review with a promise to examine all programs and identify at least $3 billion in annual savings over four years for reinvestment in new expenditure priorities.[4]

Two different budgets in two different times, over forty years apart; but is the budgeting really different? Has the budgetary process changed? What, if anything, has changed and what has stayed the same? What is the source of change? To what extent do changes in the budgetary process explain changes in budgetary outcomes? A key for understanding changes in budgeting begins with understanding the changing role of the budget office.[5] When Canadian officials from the budget office meet annually with their counterparts from the thirty member countries of the Organisation for Economic Cooperation and Development (OECD), they talk about the 'functions of the budget office.' Dressed up in the latest language, the two-day agenda for the twenty-fourth annual meeting in June 2003 reflected the basic budget office functions: 'the role of fiscal rules,' 'the political economy of reallocation,' and 'budgeting and managing for performance.'[6] In one sense this emerging perspective goes beyond the traditional notions of budgeting that have tended to focus primarily on matters of allocation – who gets what. Now included in the purview of the budget office officials is an extended set of concerns about public money – how much to spend it, where to spend it, and how it should best be managed. Indeed, as Allen

Schick explains, 'all budget systems – reformed and traditional – have three basic budget objectives: (1) to maintain aggregate fiscal discipline, (2) to allocate resources in accord with government priorities, and (3) to promote the efficient delivery of services.' The story about the changing politics and management of public money is the story about the changing relative importance of these objectives to government and the changing ways in which governments go about pursuing them.

To be sure, when it comes to public money, these three objectives are complementary and interdependent. Without overall fiscal discipline, priorities and allocations cannot be linked. How much to spend on early child development depends on how much of a priority it is and how much there is for spending overall. Without fiscal discipline there is little incentive to promote efficiency and improve management. On the one hand, resource limits at the top help, but they do not guarantee that there is efficient expenditure and prudent management at the bottom. On the other hand, arbitrary expenditure allocations and weak financial management, even with tight overall fiscal discipline, lead to distorted priorities and inefficient service delivery. Public money does not go to the government's priorities; it is simply absorbed into the base of ongoing departmental budgets. Efficient service delivery requires more than just setting and maintaining fiscal limits. Finally, poor financial management and inefficient service delivery erode confidence in the fiscal discipline of government and in its ability to link expenditure allocations and government priorities. If the public detects – or perceives – waste and inefficiency in any program or expenditure, whatever the size, the government's credibility and reputation for fiscal discipline suffers.

Not only are these three objectives complementary, they are also in competition with one another. Governments, like budgets, cannot do everything all at once. Like their budgets, the resources of governments – time, energy, personnel, political capital, leadership, and commitment – are limited. At any point, governments give varying degrees of priority, time, and attention to each objective. Sometimes governments keep these competing objectives in balance; for example, when strong consensus for overall fiscal discipline leads to a tight linking of expenditures to priorities and the cutting of expenditures that are not priorities, or when the fiscal framework expands to meet pressing and important national priorities. Sometimes, however, these competing objectives are out of balance. This can happen when governments are

preoccupied with the flexibility necessary for the allocation and realloc-
cation of expenditures to changing priorities and give little regard to
the need for prudent financial management and efficient service delivery. Or, when governments are too rigidly focused on the imperative
for fiscal discipline and a balanced budget, they may not foresee and
respond to changing economic conditions.[8] Embedded in each budgetary and financial management process and in the seemingly constant
flow of reforms for improvement are implicit assumptions about the
relative importance of each of these objectives.

Spenders and Guardians

Understanding the politics and management of public money has traditionally focused on the budgetary process and the roles of participants and the relationships among them. For many decades the
budgetary process in the Canadian federal government was described
and practised as a bilateral game between two sets of players – spenders and guardians – with their inherent competitive behaviour conditioned by the kinship and culture of 'village life' on the Rideau River.
Budgeting in Ottawa, however, is changing and is being reshaped
through powerful outside forces and influential newcomers who are
penetrating the expenditure community and creating new norms of
behaviour in a new town.

For much of the latter half of the last century, there was a consonance
between the way academics thought about budgeting and the way
practitioners in the federal government did budgeting. The spenders
and guardians framework formulated by Wildavsky defined the way
in which most academics conceptualized government budgeting since
it first appeared in 1964.[9] He argued that budgetary outcomes could
best be described and explained by examining the interaction of budget players performing stylized institutional roles of spenders and
guardians. These roles, or 'expectations of behaviour attached to institutional positions,' were the division of labour among the key participants in the budgetary process.[10]

When 'old budget hands' in Ottawa reminisce about their experiences
and boast about what they got or complain about what they didn't get in
a budget, they use these same roles to describe their behaviour and that
of their counterparts. Spenders speak about their 'smart spending' and
their 'good investments.' They also speak, in less charitable language,
about the 'tight-fisted guardians' of the Department of Finance and the

Treasury Board Secretariat. Guardians speak about the 'tough' decisions they took. They chastise the 'big spenders' in the Departments of Health or in National Defence and the impossibility of meeting their seemingly insatiable appetites at the trough of public expenditure. The spender and guardian framework is widely used throughout the world by practitioners in international agencies such as the OECD, the World Bank, and the International Monetary Fund (IMF) to describe the budgetary process.

In this framework, spenders and guardians interact in a complementary way and their interactions create a stable pattern of mutual expectations, thereby reducing the burden of complex budgetary calculations. As Wildavsky described it:

> Administrative agencies act as advocates of increased expenditure, and central control organs function as guardians of the treasury. Each expects the other to do its job; agencies can advocate knowing that the center will impose limits, and the center can exert control, knowing that agencies will push expenditures as hard as they can. Thus roles serve as calculating mechanisms. The interaction between spending and cutting roles makes up the component elements of budgetary systems.[11]

These mutual expectations between spenders and guardians serve as conventions to guide and condition behaviour. Some of these conventions are explicit and formal, taking the form of codified rules of budget behaviour. But, as Wildavsky found, most are implicit and informal, shaped and nurtured over a long and sustained process of interaction between spenders and guardians. Guardians oversee the budget as a whole to ensure that the total of all budget allocations does not lead to overexpenditure, unwanted deficits, or unsustainable debts. Spenders are preoccupied with providing programs and services of sufficient quantity and quality to meet the increasing demands of the citizens they serve. They are not concerned with the budget as a whole because they know the guardians are, and guardians do not develop and advocate expenditure programs because that is the job of the spenders.

Wildavsky viewed the inherent conflict resulting from the interaction between spenders and guardians as necessary for resolving budget decisions. Separating functions and responsibilities between spenders and guardians and embodying them with institutional form – central control agencies and spending departments – allowed for specialization and reduced the complexity inherent in budget decisions. Spenders could focus their expert knowledge and experience on designing expenditure programs, and guardians could capitalize on information and analysis about the economic, fiscal, and political situation to set limits for overall expenditures and force choices among competing demands. The result? Year after year a multitude of seemingly endless individual and separate budget decisions could be moulded into a single annual budget.

The interaction between spenders and guardians did not mean that budgeting was a 'free-for-all' fight constrained only by the limits of financial resources. Spenders and guardians had to cooperate as well as compete. Without cooperation between spenders and guardians, there would be no agreement and hence no budget. Without cooperation, spenders would not put forward requests for spending and guardians would not push back to constrain overall expenditures. Conflicts had to be managed and agreements struck in order for a budget to be made. Complexities had to be simplified and, at times, egos had to be massaged. In determining how much funding to request and how much to grant, budget players relied upon various 'aids to calculation' to reduce conflict and complexity. Both spenders and guardians depended upon past experience, focused on knowable expenditure inputs rather than on uncertain program outputs and unknowable policy outcomes, made annual incremental changes to the budget, and avoided changes to the ongoing base of budget expenditures

For Wildavsky, understanding budgeting was about understanding what it actually was and how it actually worked, rather than how would-be reformers thought it should be. Although in his writings Wildavsky made little reference to Charles Lindblom and to his classic work on 'the science of muddling through,' he did illustrate why and how budgeting was incremental.[12] As he explains:

> If the present budgetary process is rightly or wrongly deemed unsatisfactory, then one must alter in some respect the political system of which the budget is but an expression. It makes no sense to speak as if one could make drastic changes in budgeting without also altering the distribution of influence. But this task is inevitably so formidable (though the reformers are not directly conscious of it) that most adversaries prefer to speak of changing the budgetary process, as if by some subtle alchemy the intractable political element could be transformed in to a more malleable substance.[13]

The spenders and guardians framework was particularly powerful, and through numerous studies and applications, it accounted for differences in budgetary behaviour across different political systems and for explaining the impact of different budgetary reforms in countries, provinces, or states under different economic circumstances.[14] The framework continues to be widely reflected in the academic literature on budgeting.[15] Through his extensive research, Wildavsky discovered that the roles of spenders and guardians were performed at all levels in both the political and bureaucratic spheres. He also found that these roles were played out at each stage in the budgetary process – the setting of fiscal aggregates, the determination of allocations, and the management of programs.[16] For example, on questions of the overall size of the expenditure budget, he analysed the shifting balance of influence between spenders and guardians, proposing various budget reforms to establish fixed limits and constraints on total expenditures when he thought spenders were too strong and guardians too weak.[17] When it came to matters of expenditure allocation, where Wildavsky focused much of his work and upon which much of his framework is built, he found that the mutual expectations between spenders and guardians shaped the outcomes. How much was available to spend shaped what programs got funded, and what programs had to be pursued shaped how much funding was made available. On matters of program delivery and management, which he formulated as a fundamental issue of budget implementation, he saw spenders focused on ends (programs) and guardians on means (expenditures), observing that 'means and ends can be brought into somewhat closer correspondence only by making each partially dependent on the other.'[18]

From Old Village to New Town

Different political systems have shaped and conditioned the behaviour of spenders and guardians differently.[19] In the American system, with its constitutional separation of powers and its built-in 'checks and balances,' the behaviour of spenders and guardians has been conditioned by the public exposure of conflict and the establishment of numerous laws, formal rules, and explicit procedures at nearly every stage in the budgetary process.[20] When it came to parliamentary systems of government, Wildavsky argued that the behaviour of spenders and guardians was conditioned not so much by formal rules but by the kinship and culture within a tightly knit expenditure community that governed the expectations of spenders and guardians and established their behavioural norms. In Britain and in Canada, budgetary conflict between spenders and guardians has traditionally been privately absorbed and often quietly managed. In the United States, it has been publicly exposed and sometimes not managed at all.

As Heclo and Wildavsky explained, privacy at the centre of government was the defining characteristic of British parliamentary budgeting.[21] This was 'village life' in Whitehall. It was best understood in terms of a combination of four central concepts. None was absolutely unique to Britain; most parliamentary systems contained most if not all of them, perhaps in less powerful combination. These concepts were (1) a community of insiders that was small, private, and closed; (2) mutual confidence as a 'pervasive bond' governing how insiders dealt with each other and, by extension, strangers on the outside; (3) common calculations to help them deal with the complexity of budget decisions; and (4) the assessment of political climate by public servants and ministers before determining expenditure strategy. Together these four concepts explain much of the behaviour of spenders and guardians in parliamentary government.

The kinship and culture of the British expenditure community of Whitehall was not exactly the same in the Canadian federal expenditure community on the Rideau. The 'old tie' and the 'grey suit' were not identical. But when it came to matters of expenditure, the combination of these four concepts has conditioned the behaviour of spenders and guardians in the Ottawa expenditure community. Budget preparation has traditionally been a private and internal affair in government, run by the minister of finance and top officials in the department, with limited tasks assigned to the president of the Treasury Board and the Treasury Board Secretariat, and with the prime minister looking over both their shoulders and intervening with the minister of finance as and when he wished. Only within the last decade have new processes been put in place in an effort to increase outside input and to condition the expectations and reactions of outsiders. Mutual confidence and trust among and between ministers and public servants and between spenders and guardians has been the traditional underlying ingredient that has sustained relationships, ensured coherence, and facilitated difficult choices. Common calculations have helped spenders and guardians to simplify decisions, reduce complexities, and hedge against the inevitable uncertainties of budget making. By chipping away at the margins of the budget, rather than attacking its base, spenders and guardians have mutually agreed to focus their time and energy around budget increments, with the result that each year budget decisions could be made and deeply divisive conflicts avoided. Assessing the political climate and knowing when 'windows of opportunity' open and when they close have been essential intuitive skills for ministers and officials anxious to push through new expenditures or shut down the demands from others. These norms and beliefs about trust, common calculations, and political assessment have been deeply shared by the community of spenders and guardians who work at the centre of government. Indeed, understanding 'village life' has been critical in understanding budgeting in Ottawa.

Donald Savoie, in his prize-winning study over fifteen years ago of federal spending, applied the spenders and guardians framework in his exploration of 'village life' within the expenditure community.[22] Newly appointed practitioners have used the framework in their training, public servants and politicians in their practice, and 'old hands' in retelling their budget tales.[23] The framework is, however, showing signs of wear. Despite the high-profile promises in early 2004 of the first Martin government for 'a politics of achievement' and a 'continuous culture of reallocation,' the seeds of change in the budgetary process were sown years before.[24] Over the past decade, and more recently in the past few years, there has been an accumulation of forces that are changing the way budgeting is being done. The old village has given way to a new town, if not a major city.

These changes got underway some time ago, and were perhaps most visibly manifested in the 1995 'Program Review' budget in which expenditures were significantly reduced and many programs dramatically restructured.[25] The result was that federal program spending in 1996 fell to 12.6 per cent of the GDP, a level that had not been achieved since 1949–50. These changes have been more recently reflected in the growing importance and prominence of external watchdogs as contained in the Federal Accountability Act brought forward by the Harper Conservative minority government in 2006.

Allen Schick, in his tribute to Wildavsky, best describes these important changes in the United States context, some of which ring equally true in Canada:

> The intellectual journey that took Aaron Wildavsky from the old politics of budgeting to the new spanned a quarter century, during which federal spending soared from $100 billion to more than one trillion dollars a year; from small deficits to oversized ones; from ordered conflict to 'in your

face' confrontation; from the measured pace of incremental appropriations to the jagged edges of formula-driven entitlements; from a closed
process to one exposed to the winds of political and economic change. It
is a journey that did not end when we lost the one true giant that the
study of budgeting ever had, and it is a journey that we 'toilers in the
budgetary field' – to borrow V.O. Key's quaintly delightful phrase – must
continue.[26]

The key questions are how best to continue the study of budgeting in
the face of significant and fundamental changes, and how to adjust our
conceptual frameworks to better understand budgetary behaviour and
describe and explain the budgetary process and its outcomes.

Beyond Spenders and Guardians

At the provincial level in Canada, Louis Imbeau has analysed the extent
to which the spenders and guardians framework can be used to explain
the process of deficit elimination in Alberta, Saskatchewan, and British
Columbia. He concludes that 'Wildavsky's conceptualization should be
somewhat amended' to include three major assumptions. First, the program agency that plays the spending or advocacy role also needs to play
the role of guardian within the department. Second, despite the role (i.e.,
the expected behaviour attached to one's institutional position), an actor
may adopt various attitudes with regard to the budget. For example, a
spender can take a 'total view' rather than the traditional 'partial view'
of the budget and thereby have a greater regard for the budget's bottom
line (deficit or surplus). Third, the various roles and attitudes combine to
define different types of budgetary processes. For example, according to
Imbeau there is 'incremental budgeting' when guardians adopt a total
view of the budget and spenders a partial view, 'fiscal crisis budgeting'
when both spenders and guardians adopt a total view of the budget
(e.g., eliminate or reduce the deficit), and 'social crisis budgeting' when
both guardians and spenders adopt a partial view of the budget (e.g., to
support a war effort).[27]

Joanne Kelly and John Wanna, however, pose the essential question in
stark terms in their essay, 'Are Wildavsky's Guardians and Spenders Still
Relevant?' They assess the impact of new public management reforms on
the balance of power and relationships between spenders and guardians
and conclude that their research demonstrates 'the continued relevance of
(the) framework' is still useful for studying budgetary reforms.[28] They

suggest, however, an expanded classification that differentiates between the individual budget actor's *institutional role* and the *functions* they perform in the budgetary process. Like Imbeau, they note that some actors perform multiple functions at the same time. For example, central guardians in the Department of Finance may be, and in fact have been, spenders as they design high-profile direct expenditure and tax expenditure initiatives at the same time as they ration limited funding among a few competing departmental claimants, saying 'no' to other claimants, while cutting still others.[29] Some actors may perform multiple functions at different stages in the process. For example, some departmental heads may be spenders in the early stages of the process as they advocate for funding from central guardians, but become guardians at later stages as they allocate and reallocate funding among competing units within their departments and agencies. The authors hypothesize that the institutional roles are likely to remain relatively constant over time, while the functions performed by budget actors can and will change.

At one level none of this is new or surprising when it comes to the Canadian federal budgetary process. The Department of Finance has a long record of being – or at least seeing themselves as – 'the idea generating department of government,'[30] and has always held considerable sway over important design questions on major policies and programs and not just fiscal matters.[31] Powerful departmental ministers and their deputies with reputations as spenders have jealously guarded the small ministerial and departmental reserves that they have managed to scrape together through difficult reductions to their own programs and services. Like tight-fisted little guardians these spenders have prudently allocated their limited resources to priority initiatives internal to their own departments and, on occasion to helpful external allies after turning away a steady stream of persistent claimants. What is new is the extent to which new public management, with the promise of giving managers increased operating discretion in exchange for the promise of accountability of results, undertaken in a period of sustained fiscal restraint, has contributed to a greater formalization of both the spender and guardian functions within a single role, be it the deputy minister of finance, the secretary of the Treasury Board, or a deputy minister of a spending department. In short, to get one's way today, everyone now claims to take the 'total view' of the budget.

To be sure there are a host of forces in the government that are affecting budgeting and the way it is practised. Although budgeting is a central process of government, not every force will affect budgeting. There are, however, several that are having a fundamental influence on the way in which budgeting is carried out, affecting the determination of fiscal aggregates, the allocation of resources, and the efficient delivery of public services. The necessity for fiscal restraint, particularly the requirement for a balanced budget or better, along with ideas inherent in new public management have brought to the fore two major issues affecting the practise of budgeting. The one major issue can be summed up as priorities, and the other as performance.

With the requirements for restraint and a balanced budget, the government has focused more on strategic planning and priority setting. As long as the economy and budgets were expanding significantly each year there was less need for the government to undertake the difficult and painful task of determining and setting out publicly explicit budget priorities, indicating which programs would receive funding and which would not. In the 1950s and 1960s and for much of the 1970s there was sufficient overall funding to increase the budgets of *all* departments and agencies – the infamous 'fair share' allocation – and the government was spared much of the divisive and conflict-ridden debates over what should increase and what should not. Even when its fiscal flexibility was reduced in the 1980s, the government first minimized conflict and simplified its calculations through the use of across-the-board cuts to all departments – the infamous 'equal sacrifice' treatment – rather than the clear enunciation of specific priorities. However, as more and more of the government's expenditures were being used to finance the increasing costs of carrying the ballooning debt and as many years of across-the-board cuts had significantly reduced the capacity of government to deliver its programs, the government in the 1990s found it necessary to be more selective in where it cut and where it spent. This required that the government define its expenditure priorities more clearly. It required that budgets be driven by explicit priorities rather than implicit norms of 'fair share' and 'equal sacrifice.' Even after budgets had been balanced in the late 1990s, the ongoing strong public commitment to 'a balanced budget or better' required that the government have clear and explicit priorities for the allocation and reallocation of expenditures.

Along with the need for it to set priorities, there were also increasing demands for better performance in government. With more of the expenditure budget being used to pay for the escalating service costs of the increasing debt, the amount of expenditure available to underwrite the costs of programs and services was significantly reduced.

With declining public services and a continued tax bu:
became increasingly focused on the government's dimini
mance. To many citizens it seemed that they were payi
and receiving too little. Starting in the mid-1980s, governi...cnt 10cused
on a series of initiatives to improve performance ranging from the
establishment of service standards to innovations in alternative service
delivery. More recently, these initiatives have broadened to include
results reporting, performance measurement, accountability and financial management, and expanded internal and external audits.

As the issues and ideas concerned with government priorities and
government performance have been brought to the fore, they have had
significant and direct influence on the practice of budgeting and have
affected the functions traditionally carried out by the two major actors in
the budgetary process – spenders and guardians. Perhaps more important, they have affected and changed the roles of the actors in two ways:
one is the expansion of individual institutional roles of both spenders
and guardians to incorporate within each of them new and different
roles and, hence, new and different functions. The other is the gradual
emergence of entirely new institutional roles in the budgetary process,
separate and distinct from the traditional roles of spenders and guardians. Let's examine first the expansion of these roles.

Spenders incorporate guardian functions within their roles and
guardians incorporate spending functions within theirs. Why is this
so? As the forces of change have escalated, the potential for conflict
between spenders and guardians has also increased. As the prospects
for conflict have increased, both spenders and guardians have tem-
pered their mutual demands in order to accommodate the interests of
the other. Spenders have found it in their interests to incorporate
guardian roles and guardians have found it in their interests to incorporate spender roles. Each has found that its relative influence over
the other is a function of the extent to which it can incorporate a part
of the other's role. For example, when departmental spenders can act
like effective guardians within their own departments, they can
achieve greater expenditure flexibility to pursue their primary interest (spending) without recourse to the central guardians. When
guardians in the Department of Finance or the Treasury Board Secretariat can design and develop efficient and effective expenditure programs, they can restrain other departmental spending knowing that
the important spending priorities of government have already been
looked after.[32]

Priority Setters

Whether there are new roles emerging in the budgetary process or
whether spenders and guardians are simply taking on new functions is
an important question. It is not just a matter of semantics. At first blush
it might seem that simply adjusting these roles to include new functions might be sufficient to explain the new outcomes emerging from
the budgetary process. For example, Imbeau has written of 'social crisis budgeting' in which both guardians and spenders adopt a 'partial
view' of the budget that focuses on one priority area of spending, like
supporting a war effort. In reality this is another way of saying that the
government has priorities and that, in periods of fiscal restraint, it
increasingly focuses the expenditure budget, limiting and seeking public support for its priorities, and linking the expenditure budget more
closely and sharply to these priorities.

In the past when there was sufficient 'fiscal room' for many priorities in a budget, with each agency receiving its 'fair share' of the incremental funds, guardians were able to spread the increment to all
departments and agencies, thus maintaining the perception of no
losses to anyone. As budgeting has moved from allocating the increments to all, to cutting everybody (some more than others), and then to
cutting some while benefiting others, priority setting in budgeting has
taken on greater importance. Government is finding that priorities
need to be established upfront and early on and it is less prepared to let
expenditure priorities simply emerge as seeming by-products from the
'argy bargy' of spender and guardian bilateralism. As a consequence, a
new and separate institutional role of priority setters has emerged in
the budgetary process. In the Canadian federal government, it is
embodied in the Prime Minister's Office and the Privy Council Office.
To be sure these important and distinctly different offices have always
played an indirect role in the budget,[33] but in the last decade their roles
have been more significant, more direct, and more involved. Indeed, as
the budget has become more central to the act of governing, these central agencies have become more directly involved in budget-making.[34]

Government has always planned and set priorities.[35] However, as
Schick explains, it has traditionally found that it is not in its interest to
explicitly link priorities and budgets:

> ... the long-standing tendency in budgeting has been for government
> to be inexplicit about its priorities, to have priorities imputed from the

allocations actually made rather than to state them in advance. According to this line of reasoning, explicating priorities generates undue conflict and complicates the task of producing the budget. It is better
therefore, for government to prepare the budget without an explicit
statement of objectives or priorities.[36]

But 'the centre' of government is now giving significant attention to
overall planning, the articulation of government priorities, and the
linking of those priorities to the expenditure budget. In many respects,
the attempt to link formal priority planning with budget planning was
first visible with the introduction of the Policy and Expenditure Management System (PEMS) by Prime Minister Trudeau in 1980.[37] The language of the Privy Council Office publication speaks volumes:

> The often asked question of how much the government should spend
> depends upon what the money is to be spent. Similarly, the question of
> where to spend depends upon how much there is to spend. Objectives
> shape the determination of resource limits and resources in turn shape
> objectives.[38]

For Trudeau, at a time when the National Energy Program (NEP) was a
top priority of his government, the envelope expenditure structure of
PEMS was particularly important to ensure that expenditure and priorities were linked. PEMS allowed him to carve out from the economic
development envelope a separate and distinct energy envelope for a
single department, the Department of Energy, Mines, and Resources.
Not only did this signal the importance of the energy priority but,
more significantly, it also ensured that new expenditure allocations
could be made directly and exclusively to this priority area and that
spending ministers in the economic development area, who had
designs on fortunes for their own departments and priorities, could
not access the expanding energy envelope.

Although PEMS was abolished, or more to the point, quietly faded
away, the link between the setting of government priorities and the
preparation of budgets has become closer and stronger.[39] Political parties are increasingly setting out their priorities along with detailed
expenditure plans in their comprehensive election platforms ('Red-
books,' 'Moving Canada Forward,' 'Demanding Better,' 'Stand Up for
Canada'). Public servants in the PCO and in many departments are
increasingly using these priorities as an integral part of their 'transition

'planning' for new governments. The Speech from the Throne, once described by one minister as 'a one day wonder,' is more and more being used by government to sort, signal, and communicate its priorities, with the budget providing the specific expenditures and programs for implementing these declared government commitments. The establishment in the late 1980s of a regular time each year for budgets (late February) has created greater certainty for linking priorities and expenditures. The use and regularity of 'cabinet retreats' – usually in the late spring to 'take stock' and to launch the 'summer work plan' and in the late fall to 'sort out priorities' in advance of the budget – have served to link priorities more tightly to budget preparation.

We therefore see that a new and important player – priority setters – is now joining the spenders and guardians in the budgetary game. Priority setters in the PMO and the PCO are creating new space and taking over some old space in the budgetary process that has traditionally been occupied by spenders and guardians. For example, as budgets have become important public communications documents for government, PMO and PCO priority setters are focusing on the political and policy messages that are conveyed to voters and citizens. In the face of continuous fiscal restraint and increasing demands for programs and services, the PMO and the PCO are shaping the priorities of the minister of finance's budget. They are working more actively with and on spenders to shape and position expenditure proposals. They are also working with the Department of Finance to turn back unwanted, low-priority expenditure proposals. They are also creating new space within the budgetary process for the consideration and determination of overall government priorities in advance of budget preparation and, in so doing, are changing the traditional interactions between spenders and guardians.

Financial Watchdogs

Priority setters are not the only newcomers to the budget game. Financial watchdogs are now firmly and visibly on the scene. At one time, financial watchdogs only lurked around the edges of the budgetary process, dependent on their bark to effect change. Now with the bite of their public reports and commentary, sharpened by a highly attentive and probing media and a less deferential and more sceptical public, they have become more central to the action.

One way of appreciating the emerging influence of financial watchdogs on the budgetary process and understanding how financial watchdogs think about public money is to examine a theory of budget-ing that is separate from, but related to, the spenders and guardians framework. This is the theory of 'the budget-maximizing bureaucrat.' This provocative and controversial model of bureaucratic and political behaviour, formulated by William Niskanen[40] in 1971, spawned a sig-nificant stream of important new literature and was the subject of widespread and extensive academic debate, often the focus of consid-erable criticism.[41] Although empirical testing of the model produced 'mixed' results,[42] it became required reading for certain politicians and bureaucrats and, as this happened and the concepts took root, it became associated with a particular ideology in support of 'smaller government.'[43] The original central hypothesis of this public choice model was that bureaucrats attempt to maximize their budgets, because it is claimed to be in their interest to do so, and the strategies that they adopt contribute significantly to the overall growth of gov-ernment expenditures.[44]

Twenty years later, in 1991, Niskanen reflected on what he had learned from the many contributors to this new literature, the critiques of his model, and his own experience, and he made an important change. He 'dropped entirely' the assumption that bureaucrats maxi-mize their budgets in favour of the assumption that they act to maximize their discretionary budget, defined as 'the difference between the total budget and the minimum cost of producing the output expected by the political authorities.'[45] What did this change mean and why is it signifi-cant? Niskanen explains:

Since neither the bureaucrats nor the political authorities ... can claim this discretionary budget as personal income, this surplus is spent in ways that serve the interests of the bureaucrats and the political authorities ... The political review agents exercise their authority to threaten more thor-ough monitoring as a means to capture some part of the discretionary budget in types of spending that serve their special interests (such as the relative use of factor inputs and the geographic distribution of employ-ment and contracts). The bureaus, in turn, share some part of the discre-tionary budget with the review agents as the price of spending the remainder in ways that serve the bureau (such as additional staff, capital, and perquisites). The distinctive conclusion of this modified model is that bureaucratic inefficiency is the *normal condition*. Bureaucrats and politi-cians will differ on the distribution of the bureau's surplus, but neither group has sufficient incentive to reduce the excess spending.[46]

If accurate, this would be a fundamental conclusion, because when it comes to inefficiency in government, it points the finger not just at budget-maximizing bureaucrats but also at politicians, the so-called political sponsors of expenditure.[47] It must be emphasized, however, that in the model the uses to which the 'surplus' or the 'discretionary budgets' are put are themselves automatically deemed to be 'inefficient.' The model therefore applies a private sector definition of efficiency to government without consideration as to whether these discretionary budgets might be serving some other beneficial public purpose such as employment or geographical benefits.

Nonetheless, the conclusions from the model, which are particularly pertinent to financial watchdogs, suggest that in the absence of effective incentives and constraints on both bureaucrats and political sponsors, inefficiency (as narrowly defined) in government spending will be the norm. This suggests that reducing inefficiency in government, as defined by the private sector, will be difficult and its elimination likely impossible. It also helps to explain why taxpayers are especially attentive to matters of public money (in essence, their tax dollars) since they have implicitly come to understand that there are underlying forces that invariably lead both bureaucrats and politicians to be inefficient and wasteful in public expenditures. Some may see the problem residing more with bureaucrats than politicians or vice versa, but in general most taxpayers just see it as problem with government in general.

These underlying bureaucratic and political biases within government, which can lead to what taxpayers have come to perceive as inherent inefficiency and waste in public expenditure, have long been recognized if not so neatly articulated and clearly explained by Niskanen in his model. In parliamentary systems of government, the longstanding antidote to these natural biases has been the creation of strong independent monitoring organizations, operating outside the government of the day, not as agents of the government but as agents of Parliament. This independent agent is a clear recognition that inside government both bureaucrats and politicians face incentives that can lead to inefficiency and waste. When the Office of the Auditor General of Canada was created in 1878, the minister of finance of the day, Alexander Mackenzie, told the House of Commons that Canada should follow the English example and 'free the auditing of public accounts from any interference on the part of the administration' (read government).[48] In short, the same person should not act as both deputy minister of finance (a public servant of the government) and legislative auditor. Nor should the chair of the Public Accounts Committee (a politician) be the legislative auditor. A century and a quarter later, we see the creation of the parliamentary budget officer as part of the Harper government's Federal Accountability Act. Established in 2006, it too is premised on the view that 'parliamentary committees should have access to independent, objective analysis and advice on economic and fiscal issues.'[49]

Within the framework developed by Niskanen, the creation of a separate Auditor General (neither a public servant of the government nor a politician) can be seen as an independent check on both the behaviour of political authorities as review agents and bureaucrats as spenders in order to address inherent biases leading to inefficiency and waste in government. The effects of politics on efficiency in government have, of course, been long-standing and universally recognized, although it invariably comes down to a question of whose notions of efficiency will be considered. More recently, however, bureaucratic behaviour has also come to be associated with inefficiency in government. When it comes to budgeting, though, independence comes at cost. In order for the independent agent to remain independent, he/she must not engage directly with the government in the act of budgeting, that is, in determining aggregate fiscal levels, allocating resources to government priorities, or deciding on the appropriate mix of expenditure and program inputs for the efficient delivery of services. Instead, auditors general are to be independent financial watchdogs for Parliament and the public. When it comes to matters of public money, these independent auditors learned long ago, through their experience and training, to keep a particularly close and constant eye on budget-maximizing bureaucrats and their politically minded sponsors.

Over the last twenty-five years the influence and credibility of the auditor general in matters of public money has increased significantly.[50] Lest anyone be doubtful about the increasing influence of the Auditor General's watchdog role on budget-making and on governments, they should look no further than Finance Minister Ralph Goodale's unprecedented pre-election budget of 23 March 2004. He devoted the first three pages of his fifteen-page budget speech to 'strengthening financial management'[51] in government in the aftermath of the Auditor General's report on the 'appalling'[52] sponsorship program. Furthermore, a 'sick and deeply, deeply troubled' Prime Minister Paul Martin, facing what he described as an 'outraged' public, went on his 'mad as hell tour' and vowed to 'get to the bottom of it.'[53]

Priority Setters and Financial Watchdogs

With the exception of the Parliamentary Budget Officer, the institutions that represent these two new roles of priority setters (PMO and PCO) and financial watchdogs (Office of the Auditor General) are, of course, not new. These long-established institutions have played an indirect role in the budgetary process. The Auditor General has traditionally been viewed as aligned with the guardians and is increasingly seen by many taxpayers as a force for smaller government. The PMO and PCO, usually, although not always, have been aligned with the spenders. Indeed, for many, priorities are often a code word for expenditure increases. What is new is that these stylized roles are taking on a larger and more significant part in describing and explaining the budgetary process and its outcomes.

As with spenders and guardians, priority setters and financial watchdogs operate in a complementary way, creating a stable pattern of mutual expectations. However, unlike spenders and guardians, both are concerned with 'all of government' and they rarely interact directly with each other. Priority setters are concerned with the 'what' and 'who' of public expenditure: are the broad visions of government translated into defined priorities, is money going to them, and is the government achieving its political commitments? They take refuge in the belief that they are defining and ordering the priorities of government and, by extension, meeting the needs of all citizens. Financial watchdogs are concerned with the 'how' of public expenditure: is spending done with due regard for economy, efficiency, and the capacity of government to assess effectiveness?[54] They take refuge in the belief that they are protecting the taxpayer from the inevitable inefficiency of government and the possibility of the misuse of public money. Each expects the other to do its job. Priority setters can push priorities and the need to fulfill political commitments to the limit, knowing that watchdogs will invariably report on deficiencies in how things were done, and watchdogs can report regularly on deficiencies and transgressions in how things are done knowing that priority setters are focused on what is being done.

Priority setters and watchdogs rarely interact directly with one another, but there is an underlying and implicit conflict between them.[55] Priority setters are agents of government, more specifically, agents of the prime minister. Financial watchdogs are agents of Parliament and the Public Accounts Committee, chaired by a member of the opposition. While the conflict is not highly visible between these agents, it is highly visible between their respective principals; that is, between the government and the opposition. Indeed, this inherent conflict is fundamental to the exercise of good government and, hence, good budgeting and management. At its best, this is a government that is accountable to Parliament and a Parliament that can hold government to account.

Separating functions and responsibilities between priority setters and financial watchdogs allows for specialization. Priority setters deal with budget issues 'before the fact' and focus on 'the front-end' of the budgetary process to shape budget decisions before they are taken. Priority setters directly shape current budget decisions. In contrast, financial watchdogs deal with budget issues 'after the fact' and focus 'beyond the back-end' of the budget process after budget decisions have been taken. Financial watchdogs indirectly influence future budget decisions. Priority setters focus on ministers, notably the prime minister, in shaping the major priorities to be included in the budget. Financial watchdogs focus on members of Parliament and public opinion, providing reports on whether expenditures are economical, efficient, and effective and made in accordance with those authorized by Parliament. Where the direct influence of priority setters comes from access to the prime minister and the private whisper in his ear, the indirect influence of financial watchdogs comes from their perceived legitimacy in the eye of the public and the public reporting of their independent findings.

New Questions

The central question of this book is the extent to which the exercise of influence, which is fundamental to understanding the budgetary process within the Canadian federal government, is shifting from a simple bilateral relationship between central guardians (Department of Finance and Treasury Board) and departmental spenders (e.g., Health Canada and National Defence) within an 'old village' to a complex multilateral relationship among guardians, spenders, priority setters (PMO and PCO), and financial watchdogs (e.g., the Office of the Auditor General) within a 'new town.'

More specifically, to what extent are priority setters exercising increased influence directly on the budgetary process by focusing on the 'front-end' of the process and linking other central government processes (transition planning, priority setting, campaign commitments, Speech from the Throne preparation, budget planning) directly to budget preparation?[56] To what extent is this direct influence on the budgetary process taking place within the context of an overall shift in influence away from line ministers and their departments to the centre of government and, within the centre, a shift of influence to the prime minister and his advisers at both the political and public service levels and away from cabinet and cabinet committees?[57] To what extent are priority setters increasingly becoming a focal point and a centralized voice within the budgetary process for political and ideological priorities that earlier were expressed through diverse departments speaking for their constituencies? Are the financial watchdogs exercising increased, indirect influence on the budgetary process as they focus on the 'back-end' of the process through the publication of reports about government (mis) management of public expenditures, in an environment of increasing media and opposition scrutiny?[58] Are financial watchdogs becoming a more forceful and publicly credible voice at the edges of the budgetary process, representing the concerns of taxpayers and various organizations that earlier found expression almost exclusively through the central guardians of Finance and Treasury Board? We can begin to address these questions by focusing on the players themselves.

PART TWO

The Public Money Players

2 The Guardians and the Changing Role of the Budget Office

There is no budget office; it's a network of players. It's a process that extends over a long period of time with many players operating at different levels. The different levels are open to a lot of people. Some players are lead players at certain parts in the process and bit players at other points. It's not systematic; unlike the Australians, our system is not clearly defined and well ordered with clear responsibilities between the players.

Senior Treasury Board official

Is there a network? Not really. Sure we get some advice from others, but we in Finance are the budget office.

Senior Department of Finance official

In the Canadian case, it is difficult to consider the CBA (central budget agencies) as a unitary actor; rather, evidence suggests an arena where multiple actors compete and collaborate depending on the circumstances. Decision-making and the budget cycle are fragmented and episodic.

Lotte Jensen and John Wanna, 'Conclusions: Better Guardians'[1]

Understanding the politics and management of public money begins with understanding the budget office. Surprisingly in Ottawa there is no longer a shared view about the budget office, what it is, where it is, and who runs it. For many years the conventional view has been that the budget office was divided between the Department of Finance and the Treasury Board. In a nutshell, the Department of Finance was responsible for management of the macroeconomy and for the overall fiscal policy and the Treasury Board Secretariat for the operating budgets of programs and the general management of government. On paper (more recently on websites), this is the way it still appears.

In the words of the Department of Finance, its budget functions include 'responsibilities for preparing the budget, developing tax and tariff policy and legislation, administering major transfers of federal funds to provinces and territories, and managing federal borrowing on financial markets.'[2] With a certain element of modesty, but considerable degree of truth, the Department also notes that it is 'actively involved in the government's policy and legislative agenda, helping to develop and implement economic, social, and financial policies and programs.'[3]

In its own words, the budget functions of the Treasury Board include responsibilities for 'managing the government's financial, personnel, and administrative responsibilities.' It is 'the general manager and employer of the public service, it sets policy in these areas, examines and approves the proposed spending plans of government departments, and reviews the development of approved programs.'[4] In the words of a former secretary of the Treasury Board, its functions include 'expenditure management oversight,' 'performance management oversight,' and 'responsibilities relating to human resource management.'[5] The Treasury Board Secretariat is the 'administrative arm' of the Treasury Board and is responsible for 'recommendations and advice to the Treasury Board on policies, directives, regulations, and program expenditure proposals with respect to the management of the government's resources.'[6] The Treasury Board includes the Office of the Comptroller General whose responsibilities are 'to provide strategic leadership to government departments, other central agencies and the Treasury Board Secretariat on all matters related to comptrollership.' Comptrollership 'implies vigorous stewardship of public resources, a high standard of ethics, and provision of appropriate parliamentary oversight' and 'involves TBS working with departments and agencies to better integrate financial and non-financial information, to take an integrated approach to managing risks and ensure appropriate control systems are in place.'[7]

The key to understanding what these self-descriptions actually mean is to analyse the interaction among the guardians. Who are they? How do they distinguish themselves from each other? What do they need from each other? How do they take each other into account? Who gets to play on what and who gets ignored? How are they perceived by others, notably spenders, priority setters, and financial watchdogs?

The starting point for addressing these important questions is to examine three perspectives on budgeting: the basic functions of the budget, the component parts of the budget, and the budget process itself. This chapter begins by highlighting the respective roles of Finance and Treasury Board with respect to the major budget functions as set out previously by Schick. It provides an analysis of the changing components of the budget and the implications for the increasing importance of Finance relative to Treasury Board. It provides an overview of the roles of Finance and Treasury Board guardians in the budgetary process. This, however, is only a starting point. To understand the guardians, this chapter takes us inside their respective organizations and examines more closely who they are and why they behave the way they do.

Guardians and Budget Functions

Because budgeting is complex, no single guardian can handle all its aspects. Different guardians therefore come to specialize in one or more of the three main functions of budgeting – determining fiscal aggregates, allocating resources, and ensuring efficiency and sound financial management. The Department of Finance has always had near-exclusive responsibility for the determination of fiscal aggregates and for maintaining overall fiscal discipline. It is the minister of finance who sets the fiscal framework and through his annual budgets carries on his shoulders a government-wide responsibility for overall fiscal management. When the Treasury Board Secretariat was created in 1966, as a separate entity from the Department of Finance, it assumed distinct responsibility for promoting efficiency in the delivery of programs and for sound financial management.[8] The responsibility for resource allocation has traditionally been shared between the Department of Finance and the Treasury Board Secretariat, although over the past decade it has increasingly been assumed by the Department of Finance. We will undertake a more in depth examination of these three functions of budgeting in chapters 6, 7, and 8, respectively.

Guardians and Budget Components

A key to understanding the division of responsibilities among guardians is to examine the budget itself. To outsiders the budget may look like one total budget, but insiders actually view it as an amalgamation of separate parts. Because budgeting is complex, budget office officials break the budget into pieces, with the Treasury Board Secretariat and the Department of Finance each specializing in specific parts. Guardians view the budget as consisting of five distinct components: (1) major transfer payments to individuals; (2) major transfer payments to provincial and territorial governments; (3) operating and other expenditures; (4) public debt charges; and (5) tax expenditures. The Department of Finance has primary responsibility for everything except for operating and other expenditures, which is the general responsibility of the Treasury Board Secretariat and includes operating and capital, payments to Crown corporations, and minor transfer payments and subsidies.[9] In the words of a senior official, these operating and other expenditures are 'really a residual category' and are what officials refer to as the 'small p' programs of government.[10] The Department of Finance has responsibility for the other four components: (1) the 'big P' programs of major payments to individuals (e.g., elderly benefits, employment insurance); (2) transfers to provinces and territories (Canada Health and Social Transfer and fiscal equalization); (3) public debt charges; and (4) tax expenditures.

Table 1 compares the composition of direct expenditures when Ralph Goodale was minister of finance to the situation faced by Walter Gordon when he was minister of finance. The structure of direct expenditures has changed considerably over the last forty years and, with it, the roles and relative influence of the principal guardians in the budget office – the Department of Finance and the Treasury Board Secretariat. The most dramatic change has been in operating and capital expenditures, which are the general responsibility of the Treasury Board Secretariat. In 1963, the government's operating and capital expenditures represented nearly 60 per cent of total direct expenditures. By 2004, this relative share had been reduced to less than 40 per cent of total direct expenditures. Over the forty-year period, operating and capital expenditures as proportion of the GDP declined from 10 per cent to 5.7 per cent.

Over this same period, the area of greatest proportional expansion, from 9.7 per cent to 16.6 per cent of total direct expenditures, has been in major transfers to the provincial and territorial governments, reflecting new and increasing fiscal arrangements for equalization and for health, education, and welfare.[11] The proportion of expenditures for major transfers to individuals also increased, although less significantly – from 20.5 per cent to 23.7 per cent, reflecting new benefits for

Table 1
2003–4 and 1963–4 Direct expenditures by component

| | 2003–4 | | | 1963–4 | | |
	$B	% of Total	% of GDP	$B	% of Total	% of GDP
Major transfers to individuals	42.0	23.7	3.4	1.7	20.5	3.6
Major transfers to provinces and territories	29.4	16.6	2.4	0.8	9.7	1.7
Operating and other expenditures	70.0	39.5	5.7	4.8	57.8	10.0
Public debt charges	35.8	20.2	2.9	1.0	12.0	2.1
Total direct expenditures	177.2	100.0	14.5	8.3	100.0	17.4

Source: Canada, Department of Finance, *Federal Government Public Accounts,* http//:fin.qc.ca/fr/
2004/frt04_le.html.

the elderly in the form of old age security (OAS) and guaranteed
income supplement (GIS) payments, and for the unemployed and
underemployed in the form of employment insurance (EI) benefits.
Public debt charges represented 12 per cent of direct expenditures in
1963 and grew to over 20 per cent in 2004, reflecting increased debt levels. As a percentage of the GDP, in 1963–4 total direct expenditures represented 17.4 per cent of the economy and by 2004 they had been
reduced to 14.5 per cent.

This view of the budget, however, looks only at the 'front door' of
expenditures and ignores important 'back-door spending' in the form
of tax expenditures, that is, tax measures such as exemptions, deductions, rebates, deferrals, and credits that are used to advance a wide
range of economic, social, and other public policy objectives. These tax
expenditures, which are the exclusive responsibility of the Department
of Finance, shape and determine public policy across nearly every area
of government activity from children to health and education, to retirement, farming, and fishing, to federal–provincial fiscal arrangements.
Information on tax expenditures is not found in the annual budget and
estimates documentation, which is widely available and readily recog-
nizable. Instead, tax expenditure reports, which were first provided in
Finance Minister John Crosbie's budget of 1979 and subsequently on

an irregular basis, must be searched out on the Department of Finance website with annual reports dating back to 1995.[12]

While it is not customary to include tax expenditures as part of total expenditures, they are an important element in any budget. When they are included, the actual budget expands to nearly twice the size that it appears in the annual published budget.[13] In 2004, tax expenditures amounted to $154 billion, making up the largest component of total expenditures – 'front and back door.'[14] Tax expenditures include such items as the $9 billion child tax benefit, the $2.5 billion in non-taxation of business-paid health and dental benefits, and the $1.8 billion for the scientific R&D investment tax credit.[15] The 1963 tax expenditures are estimated to be $5.9 billion, once again making up the single largest component of total expenditures.[16]

An additional perspective involves expenditures that require the approval of Parliament on an annual basis and those expenditures that have ongoing legislative approval. The first expenditures, called 'voted appropriations,' require the annual approval of Parliament through an annual appropriation bill. The second expenditures, called 'statutory,' are those that Parliament has authorized on an ongoing basis through enabling legislation. In 1963, 'voted appropriations' represented 58 per cent of all expenditures, thereby giving parliamentarians, ministers, and public servants annual discretion over more than half of all expenditures. By 2004, the situation was nearly reversed with 'voted expenditures' representing only 35 per cent ($65 billion) of total budgetary expenditures and statutory expenditures representing 65 per cent ($118 billion). The annual discretion of parliamentarians, ministers, and public servants over expenditures has been greatly reduced over the past forty years and this in turn has affected the relative roles and influence of the Treasury Board Secretariat and the Department of Finance.

Understanding Canadian federalism is a key to understanding this changing structure of federal expenditures and the changing roles within the budget office.[17] It has often been noted that, under the Canadian constitution, the responsibilities and financial powers of the federal and provincial governments are not well matched. The federal government has a significant array of legislative responsibilities and full powers of taxation. The provincial governments are assigned the costly responsibilities of health, education, and welfare, and slightly more limited powers of taxation. The reasons for the situation find their origins in the circumstances of the mid-nineteenth century when the responsibilities thought to require the most money, like defence or transportation, were assigned to the federal government. In contrast, responsibilities thought to require the least money, such as municipal infrastructure and welfare (then a private matter), were assigned to the provinces.

When it came to public spending, the great change in the later half of the twentieth century was the growth in health, education, and welfare, all areas of provincial responsibility. Since the federal government lacked the jurisdiction in these increasingly important areas, it needed to collaborate with provincial governments. With the exception of unemployment insurance, where the constitution was amended in 1940 to enable the federal government to establish a program, spending in these social areas was a matter of the federal government working out cost-shared arrangements with the provinces. However, the capacity of provinces to shoulder the costs was and continues to be uneven. The question was how to establish comparable levels of social services across provinces in light of large differences in fiscal capacity. The response to the problem has been fiscal equalization, a federal transfer program enabling have-not provinces to provide reasonably comparable programs at reasonably comparable costs.[18]

As a consequence of these federal–provincial fiscal arrangements, coupled with large increases in expenditures for the elderly through old age security (OAS) and guaranteed income security (GIS) payments, an increasing share of the federal budget now takes the form of statutory transfer payments to provinces and individuals. As this change in the structure of expenditures has occurred, the Department of Finance, relative to the Treasury Board Secretariat, has taken on a greater responsibility for the expenditure budget. Looked at differently, the discretionary component of the budget, or the 'small p' programs for which the Treasury Board Secretariat has general responsibility, has declined significantly. In 1964, it represented nearly 60 per cent of the direct expenditure budget. Today, it is less than 40 per cent.[19]

Guardians and the Budgetary Process

The third perspective for understanding the budget office is to examine the budgetary process. It would seem to be an easy task to describe who does what and when. Yet the most recent and most basic public descriptions are incomplete, inaccurate, and, in some cases, misleading.[20] Even the federal government's latest publication on the subject is now over ten years out of date and does not include the supply process of Parliament.[21] Descriptions of bits and pieces of the budgetary process, often along with various assessments are found scattered throughout a host of recent publications.[22] How best, then, to describe the budgetary process in simple terms?

The budgetary process is an annual cycle – a budget is made every year. The process is continuous, extending for more than a single year. Budget plans for the next year are underway while budgets for the current year are being unveiled, and budget results from previous years are being reported and publicly commented on. In a sense, the process has no beginning or end. The budgetary process is continuously evolving, with ongoing changes to its small features and periodically large changes to its central features through major expenditure management reforms. There are many players and pretenders (public servants, ministers, members of parliament, auditors general, interest groups, other levels of government, and citizens), some with considerable influence at critical stages and others with little or no influence even at routine stages. Given this complexity, there is little wonder that the process seems to defy simple description.

When does the minister of finance start to work on his next budget? According to one minister, the day after the last one is tabled in the House of Commons, usually at the end of February.[23] In fact, preliminary planning within the Department of Finance begins before then. Through the regular release of economic data, the Department of Finance economic forecasters are continually monitoring and analysing macroeconomic indicators such as growth, employment, interest rates, and inflation to provide a basis for establishing a set of prudent 'economic assumptions' that will underpin the fiscal forecast for the upcoming budget. Throughout, there are consultations with private sector economic forecasters. The department updates the 'economic and fiscal outlook,' which, in recent years, has included a five-year forecast of revenues, expenditures, and surplus (or deficit). This becomes the starting point for budget preparation.

Normally, in June, the cabinet convenes a one- or two-day 'retreat' to consider in the broadest of terms the basic elements that could underlie the upcoming budget.[24] This cabinet discussion is usually focused around three streams of information. One stream is fundamentally political. This usually takes the form of a 'political update' with the Prime Minister's Office and political pollsters providing the results of the most recent public opinion surveys of major issues of concern to the electorate and of the government's performance as perceived by the public. The second stream is economic and fiscal with the minister of finance setting out in the broadest of terms the 'economic and fiscal update.' This stream usually stresses the uncertainty and risks that underlie the economic prospects for the country and is focused on the fiscal forecast emphasizing the 'extremely tight' fiscal situation with little or no room for any major expenditure initiatives. Depending upon the severity of the fiscal situation, the president of the Treasury Board or a separate minister assigned the task by the prime minister may be called upon to report on ongoing efforts to review government expenditures and programs.

The third stream is concerned with the government's priorities. If a Speech from the Throne (SFT) is in the offing for a new session of Parliament in the fall, then the focus for discussion will be on which priority areas should receive attention in the SFT. Otherwise, the Privy Council Office provides ministers with an 'update on SFT implementation' to help ministers 'take stock' of government priorities. The chairpersons of the policy cabinet committees (usually one or two focused on 'domestic affairs' and one on 'global affairs') report on priority initiatives that have emerged from discussions of ministers within their committees. The discussion from this cabinet meeting sets out 'the summer workplan' in broad terms to guide officials in central agencies and line departments in their budget preparations. Government MPs and the government caucus will be involved in general discussions on the budget preparations; the extent and shape of those discussions depend on the predispositions of the prime minister.

By October, departments and agencies submit to the Treasury Board their Annual Reference Level Update (ARLU). These are technical submissions containing estimates of expenditures for the upcoming year on the basis of existing authorities and previously approved changes. They are not used as the vehicle to request new funding. Officials of the Treasury Board Secretariat scrutinize these departmental estimates for technical mistakes, and the results form the basis for eventual appropriation legislation supported by information contained in the estimates.

In October, the minister of finance provides his cabinet colleagues with an overview of the 'economic and fiscal update.' This includes information on the achievement of fiscal targets for the fiscal year just completed the previous April, and updates for the current year and future years. The focus is on the fiscal surplus (or deficit), revenues and expenditures, the debt, and inevitable expenditure pressures. Ministers will normally 'put markers on the table' for new expenditure initiatives they would like to see included in the upcoming budget. Again, depending on the prime minister, general discussions on the emerging fiscal stance and on the broad budget themes will be held with MPs in government caucus.

In the fall of each year a formal pre-budget consultation process begins. In late October or early November, the minister of finance appears before the House of Commons Standing Committee on Finance and sets out the current and prospective economic situation, which he relates to the government's broad budget policy objectives. This has become an increasingly important public event, televised nationally and widely reported in the media. During this appearance, the minister of finance presents the 'Economic and Fiscal Update' document, which provides supporting material for his presentation and sets out the broad economic outlook and fiscal parameters for the upcoming budget. The minister of finance and department officials hold a series of consultation meetings with various stakeholders and interest groups outside government, and the committee holds public hearings calling upon various witnesses to testify before it. The focus of these discussions is on both the themes and potential proposals for the budget. Throughout this period, the minister and finance officials are engaged in a series of bilateral meetings inside government with spending ministers and officials putting forward proposals for inclusion in the budget. The committee conducts public hearings with expert witnesses, interest groups, and the general public and publishes a report in December. The report contains several minority opinions along with the committee's majority report. In recent years, the opposition has decided to use one of its 'allotted days' (see below) to debate the general budget policy on the basis of the report and the minority opinions. Parliament has no decision-making role in this pre-budget process and no votes are taken.

Throughout the fall, the president of Treasury Board tables in the House of Commons several documents reporting on the performance of the government. The 'Managing for Results' document provides an overview of government-wide efforts to strengthen results-based management and accountability. 'Departmental Performance Reports' (DPR) for each department and agency, which are part of the estimates, provide information on program results over several years and the extent to which performance targets are being met. The president of the Treasury Board tables summaries of the corporate plans of Crown corporations in Parliament through a document entitled 'Annual Report to Parliament on Crown Corporations and Other Corporate Interests of Canada.' The minister of finance tables the 'Annual Financial Report of the Government of Canada,' which serves as an ex post report on the implementation of the budget plan. The Public Accounts of Canada includes the annual financial statements and record of transactions showing all federal spending, borrowing, and taxation. Throughout the year, the Department of Finance publishes the monthly *Fiscal Monitor*, which reports on the monthly fiscal results, comparing the results for each month and year-to-date for the same period during the previous fiscal year.

Throughout December and January, the minister of finance meets with the prime minister, sometimes including one or two of their closest and most senior political and public service officials to consider the major new expenditure allocations or reductions proposed in the budget. Bilateral meetings between the minister of finance and spending ministers may continue if it is deemed necessary to 'hear out' ministers or to secure agreement on particular initiatives. At a morning meeting of cabinet on the day of the budget in late February, the minister of finance highlights for his colleagues the broad budget themes and priorities and sets out the general strategy he intends to use to gain public support, blunt opposition criticism, and deal with media questions. In the late afternoon the minister unveils his budget in Parliament. There is a 'lock-up' in the morning and afternoon of budget day at which government officials answer questions and brief the media and interest group representatives. The budget is a comprehensive statement of the government's fiscal framework. It implements some but not necessarily all of the government's priorities as outlined in the Speech from the Throne, and it can sometimes contain priorities not included in the Speech from the Throne. The budget sets out the overall level of revenues, expenditures, and surplus (or deficit) and relates them to the macroeconomic outlook; and it contains the new expenditure initiatives (or major expenditure reductions), expenditures to maintain existing programs, tax expenditures, and proposed changes in tax laws. The budget is a major event in the government's calendar and is widely reported in the media, with extensive comment from the opposition parties, interest groups, other levels of government, and columnists, journalists, and editorialists.

Normally, a few days after the budget, the president of the Treasury Board tables in Parliament the estimates which set out the details of the government's spending plans for the upcoming fiscal year.[25] The estimates documentation consists of three parts. Part 1 is the government's expenditure plan outlining total government expenditures by broad category of payment. Part 2, known traditionally as the 'Blue Book,' supports the Appropriation Act and provides a detailed listing of the resources required by individual departments and agencies for the upcoming fiscal year in order to deliver the programs for which they are responsible. This document identifies the spending authorities (votes) and the amounts to be included in subsequent appropriation bills that Parliament will be asked to approve to enable the government to proceed with its spending plans. It also contains, for information purposes only, an estimate of the costs of statutory programs (accounting for 65 per cent of total government expenditure) for which spending authority has previously been granted through existing legislation. Part 3, 'Reports on Plans and Priorities' (RPP), contains the individual expenditure plans for each department and agency, excluding Crown corporations.[26] These documents provide detailed information on a 'business line' basis, including information on objectives, initiatives, and planned results with links to resource requirements over a three-year time horizon. RPPs also provide information on human resource requirements, major capital projects, grants and contributions, and net program costs. The RPPs are tabled by the president of the Treasury Board on behalf of the minister who is responsible for the department or agency.

Under House of Commons rules, the estimates must be presented to Parliament no later than 1 March, one month prior to the start of the fiscal year. Following the tabling of the estimates, the House of Commons begins its deliberations. This is known as the Business of Supply. Because Parliament will not finish its deliberations until just prior to the summer break at the end of June, it grants the government interim supply from the beginning of the fiscal year in April until the end of June.

The estimates are then automatically referred to the standing committees of the House of Commons.[27] For example, the Standing Committee on Human Resources Development and the Status of Persons with Disabilities examines the proposed expenditures and the RPP of the Department of Human Resources and Skills Development. The Committee on Government Operations and Estimates reviews the expenditures and RPP of central agencies, specific expenditure items across all departments, Crown corporations, private foundations that distribute government funds, horizontal government programs, and the use of contingency funds. The standing committees call upon ministers, senior officials, and other interested parties to appear before them. In their reviews of departments, standing committees have available a number of documents: the budget, the government's expenditure plan, the estimates and RPP for the department, and the Departmental Performance Reports tabled in Parliament the previous fall. If by 31 May committees have not reported back to the House of Commons on the estimates that they have been studying, then they are deemed to have reported.

The rules governing the running of the House are contained in the standing orders, which require that a certain number of days are reserved for debate of the government's expenditure proposals in full House session. There are twenty such days, referred to as allotted days, that are reserved for the opposition to use to debate topics of their choice. These days are not used to debate the estimates per se. Rather, the opposition uses them to debate general policy on matters of their choice. On the last of these allotted days in late June (the end of the supply period), House of Commons rules provide for the appropriations legislation to be voted on in a single evening session. The appropriation bill then goes to the Senate where it is approved and finally given royal assent by the governor general.

The president of the Treasury Board tables supplementary estimates in the late fall and spring to obtain the authority of Parliament to adjust the government's expenditure plan, as reflected in the estimates for that fiscal year. Funding for these supplementary estimates is provided in the budget previously tabled in the spring and is, therefore, built into the existing fiscal framework. The supplementary estimates serve two purposes. First, they seek authority for revised spending levels that Parliament will be asked to approve in an Appropriation Act. Second, they provide Parliament with information on changes in the estimated expenditures to be made under the authority of statutes previously passed by Parliament.

The Office of the Auditor General is an agent of Parliament and undertakes independent audits – performance, compliance, and financial – of the programs and expenditures of departments and agencies. Its main relationship with Parliament is with the Standing Committee on Public Accounts, chaired by an opposition member. The work of the Auditor General addresses three questions:

1 Were programs and activities run economically and efficiently and is effectiveness measured and reported?

2 Did the government collect or spend the authorized amount of money for the purposes intended by Parliament?
3 Is the government keeping proper accounts and records, and presenting its financial information accurately?[28]

The Auditor General presents to the House of Commons up to three reports a year, in addition to an annual report. These reports, complete with an advanced media 'lock up,' are major and highly visible events and provide an important focus for opposition criticism of the government, all of which is widely reported on in the media.

This brief description of the budgetary process gives us some idea of how the major events unfold and how the relative roles and responsibilities of the budget office are performed by the Department of Finance and the Treasury Board Secretariat. But we only see the tips of the icebergs floating in the water. Hidden from our view are the grinding and scraping of the giant ice blocks underwater and the vast stretches of still water where nothing is happening at all. This perspective provides a dry and superficial view of the roles and interactions of guardians in the budgetary process and hides the real action and inaction that is taking place below the surface. To understand the guardians, we need to go below the surface.

Different Guardians

By nature, guardians do not naturally reveal themselves. Protecting the public purse, like minding the chicken coop from the ravages of the wolves, is never an easy task even at the best of times. Better to do it quietly and quickly in the darkened hours of night than under full exposure of the midday sun. For guardians, working behind closed doors has been the traditional way in which they have plied their craft, and this continues even in a world of increased transparency and openness in government. When it comes to matters of public money, prudence and probity prevail and no self-respecting guardian ever wants to be seen by his/her colleagues as giving in too early or too much to the seemingly insatiable appetites of spending ministers and scheming officials. It is one thing to be seen as soft by outsiders but quite another to be viewed as a lightweight by colleagues. Acquiring and maintaining a reputation for guardianship among fellow colleagues is what guardians hope to achieve. When it comes to certain expenditure programs they may not know as much of the details as the spenders, but they do know more than anyone else at the centre of government. In fact, in several areas of the budget – most major transfers programs to provinces, territories, and individuals; public debt charges; and tax expenditures – guardians in the Department of Finance know more than anybody else. Knowledge and information, coupled with the lessons of experience about how to act on any specific expenditure issue – sometimes slowly 'in the fullness of time' but never with hesitation – is what builds reputation.

For a time in the immediate post-war period, the Department of Finance and Treasury Board Secretariat guardians were cut from the same cloth. Like the time honoured 'Treasury official' in Britain, there was in Ottawa 'the Finance and Treasury Board officer.' The origins of the cloth were from the Department of Finance. In the early years, senior Finance officials, who would go on to assume some of the most powerful positions in government, often migrated to top positions in the Treasury Board Secretariat, considerably strengthening its role and influence. In reflecting on the promotion of Robert Bryce in 1947 to the position of assistant deputy minister of Finance and secretary of the Treasury Board, an observer noted: 'What the Treasury Board needed was a strong Secretary with an appreciation of the priorities in expenditure which could affect employment, income, prices, interest rates and other fiscal matters.' The result, according to the observer, was that 'the Treasury Board became more deeply involved in departmental activities and responsibilities ... (with) the Secretary ... in effect downgrading the responsibility of the Deputy Ministers of other Departments.'[29] Over the next several decades other senior officials with considerable experience and influence in the Department of Finance would take on the job of secretary to the Treasury Board, including Simon Reisman, Al Johnson, and Gerard Veilleux.[30]

Since the 1970s, Finance and Treasury Board guardians have no longer been cut from the same cloth. A former Treasury Board Secretariat official explains:

> ... in Program Branch we regarded Finance as rather ivory towered. Simon [Reisman, then the deputy minister of the Department of Finance] and company liked to hold forth about how expenditures had to be cut and departments reined in, but we in the Branch were the ones who had to go out and do the butchery. It wasn't as easy to find ways of making cuts – sensible cuts – as Finance seemed to think.[31]

Speaking of the late 1960s and early 1970s, another former Secretariat official observes that 'some of the TBS folks considered that the Finance men were far too ideologically wedded to the "market discipline" mindset and strongly opposed government "intervention," even where TBS analysts could see some public good.'[32]

Differences in Finance and Treasury Board guardians are significant today. The most senior Finance officials, almost to a man (there are still very few women in the senior ranks), have had long and distinguished careers within the department. Every deputy minister (there have been fifteen since Ken Taylor struggled to support Finance Minister Gordon in his controversial 1963 budget after the minister's unsuccessful efforts to persuade Prime Minister Pearson to allow Robert Bryce to leave the position of Clerk of the Privy Council and become his deputy minister) has been a 'Finance man.'[33] Some have stayed closer to the department than others, but all have had brief, high-level experience within and outside the federal public service. Some had short assignments as assistant secretaries in the Privy Council Office, others as assistant deputy ministers or deputy ministers in large policy and program departments such as Employment and Immigration, Energy, or Industry, while still others gained international experience at such organizations as the International Monetary Fund, the OECD, or the World Bank. Others have had experience in the Bank of Canada or Revenue Canada, but very few ever worked in the Treasury Board Secretariat.

The pattern has been similar for assistant and associate deputy ministers in the Department of Finance. The recruitment for most positions at this level is from within the department.[34] By the time the skilled 'Finance man' becomes an associate deputy minister of finance it is not uncommon for him to have held three or even four assistant deputy minister positions within the department, including in fiscal policy, tax policy, intergovernmental affairs, or economic policy. Up and coming junior officials are brought along quickly, sometimes 'farmed out' to a policy oriented department or moved 'up the street' across from Parliament Hill to be 'rounded out' in the Privy Council Office by working for 'Finance North'– the Liaison Secretariat for Macroeconomic Policy – or in one of the policy secretariats. What does it mean to be a 'Finance man'? A long time senior official observes: 'Our career at Finance is a duty. For everyone there is, and has always been, a sense of strong collegiality in the department; we are all pushing in one direction and all on the same wavelength. We have a deep sense of pride and accomplishment, for example, in the way we dealt with deficit. People outside of government tell us that they really appreciate what we have done for the country.'[35]

In contrast, secretaries to the Treasury Board do not spend their careers in the Secretariat. They are not 'Treasury men' (again, there are few women at the most senior ranks); they are 'departmental men.' Since Finance Minister Gordon's 1963 budget there have been twelve secretaries. Only three were 'Finance men' – Simon Reisman (1968–70), Al Johnson (1970–3), and Gerard Veilleux (1986–9). The others pursued their careers and developed their skills in the rough and tumble world of departments – Industry, Foreign Affairs, Health and Welfare, Employment and Immigration, Consumer and Corporate Affairs, Transport, Citizenship and Immigration, Agriculture, Defence, and Fisheries and Oceans. Some had considerable exposure in the Privy Council Office or the Public Service Commission, but all were fundamentally men of departments.

New secretaries to the Treasury Board, who are appointed by the prime minister on the recommendation of the Clerk of the Privy Council, are more on a 'tour of duty' than in pursuit of a life-long ambition in the treasury. 'I was put in the job to stand up to the president and to rebuild the relationship with Finance,' explains one secretary.[36] In taking on the job, they accept congratulations from some of their colleagues, but those offering condolences are more to the point since they understand how difficult the task can be and how much the new appointee's success is dependent on the cooperation of former departmental colleagues. When secretaries leave the Treasury Board, some move to important deputy minister positions in the public service such at the Canadian Centre for Management Development (now the Canada School of Public Service), the Department of Foreign Affairs and International Trade, or the Canadian Security Intelligence Agency. Others, after productive careers, leave the public service entirely and take on new jobs in important national or provincial institutions.

Similarly, most Treasury Board budget officials do not make their careers in the Secretariat.[37] Typically, they come to the Secretariat for a short period of time and once there they are rotated quickly through several positions, because their superiors are afraid that they will become 'too close' to the department whose expenditures they oversee. After a two- or three-year 'tour of duty,' they typically return to a spending department or agency. This pattern is the same for almost all professional budget staff from the newest recruits of junior analysts up to and including the most senior level executives occupying positions of assistant secretaries and deputy secretaries. As a former official explains, this has been a long-standing practice:

When I went to the Program Branch as a Director in 1971 ... Gordon Osbaldeston as deputy secretary had a policy of recruiting people from line departments who brought with them knowledge of the programs they were to be assessing. He also had an explicit policy that analysts and directors should not stay in the branch longer than about three years.[38]

This process of regular horizontal rotation to and from spending departments was supported by a structure of hierarchical layers of personnel within the Treasury Board Secretariat, which provided a permanent backstop for the rotation and an effective redundancy among the organizational levels.

More recently, in the face of restraint, delayering, and streamlining, the rotation of secretariat officials has taken on a new twist. 'The greater concern now,' explains a top official, 'is with retaining good analysts, not rotating them out.'[39] A recently departed official, reflecting on the diminished influence of the Secretariat, notes that, 'in the last five years, there has been a marked shift in the Secretariat and a very high turnover in the staff.'[40]

Guardians Diverging: 'Let the Managers Manage ... Come Hell or High Water'

The differences between the guardians in the Department of Finance and the Treasury Board Secretariat are, however, more fundamental than these traditional differences in staffing. Today, these differences reflect an increasing divergence in the culture of the two organizations as a consequence of two fundamental and distinct forces over the past fifteen years. In a nutshell, one force has been the gradual introduction of various mutations of new public management throughout the public service. It was predicated on the view that there were too many central rules and controls standing in the way of departmental performance and efficient programming. The other was the preoccupation with the deficit, a concern that emerged slowly and sporadically over the late 1980s and early 1990s to become the overriding public and political preoccupation in the mid-1990s.

The first force had enormous impact on the Treasury Board Secretariat and its evolving culture as it attempted for years to fundamentally, but only partially, transform itself into a 'management board.' The first formal step was taken in 1996 in a dramatic and far-reaching decision to eliminate the Program Branch, which had been the influential 'budget office' and the backbone of the Treasury Board Secretariat since its inception. The second step was the formal announcement in 1997 by

Prime Minister Chrétien that the Treasury Board would be constituted as a 'management board.'

The second force played directly into the hands of the Department of Finance. In reinforced the department's traditional function of being the sole and exclusive manager of the fiscal and expenditure framework and sharpened its new-found role as the government's major budget cutter. As the Treasury Board Secretariat continued to grapple with how to deal with the generation-old cry to 'let the managers manage,' the Department of Finance focused exclusively and single-mindedly on eliminating the deficit, 'come hell or high water.'[41]

For several years Finance and Treasury Board guardians continued as they had in the past, to work closely together despite the increasing and diverging forces that threatened to pull them apart. The essence of their working arrangement is best described by two international students of budgeting, Lotte Jensen and John Wanna: 'The Canadian system "works" on a system of shared norms of agreed windows and veto-points within which issues such as policy integrity are considered and the politics fought out.' This uniquely Canadian arrangement of guardians stands in stark contrast to the more traditional, cooperative Australian approach which, as described by these same students, is a '"fortuitously bifurcated" CBA (central budget agency) ... with two actors working in tandem, enabling Treasury to frame aggregate expenditure while the Department of Finance is able to specialize on business advice, expenditure controls (in-year and year-on-year), financial management and previously public sector reform.'[42]

Prior to the early 1990s, before the deficit became the number one public and political priority, Finance and the secretariat operated, as described by Jensen and Wanna, under 'shared norms of agreed windows and veto-points' about who does what in the budget process. Finance would start with determining the overall expenditure framework and setting the expenditure levels for the major statutory programs. It would propose specific target levels for savings in operating and program expenditures and, after some discussion and occasional negotiation with the TBS, an agreed level of savings would be included in the fiscal framework. How the savings were to be achieved – whether, for example, through across-the-board reductions, expenditure freezes, selected expenditure reviews, establishing annual productivity dividends, or some other measure – was left up entirely to the Secretariat to determine. The only concern of Finance was that the expenditure savings would be real, in the sense that they were ongoing and sustainable and would be delivered to 'the bottom line.'

During this period in the 1980s, there was also some expenditure flexibility within the fiscal framework, which provided the Treasury Board with opportunities to make limited expenditure allocations to departments. The Treasury Board also found considerable room for delegating increased responsibilities and authorities to departments and agencies in exchange for achieving program results. Department and agencies, which had suffered under several decades of centrally controlled rules and regulations that were increasingly seen as undermining their attempts to become more efficient and effective, were willing collaborators. Continuous, centrally directed, across-the-board cuts to departmental operating budgets provided the rationale, if not the evidence, to the Treasury Board of the need for increased efficiency in program delivery and yielded sizable and ongoing expenditure savings to the Department of Finance.[43] If the Treasury Board guardians felt the cuts were going too far or if departments could clearly demonstrate risks to health, safety, and security, they had recourse to the Treasury Board controlled operating reserve of ongoing funding, which Finance regularly provided within the fiscal framework.

In the 1970s and the early 1980s, when the fiscal framework was considerably less restrictive and there was significant inflation in the economy, this reserve was substantial and was an important and annual source of funding for spending departments and agencies. As a result, there were regular and continuous negotiations and exchanges between the Treasury Board program analysts and senior staff on the one hand, and between departmental financial and program officials on the other, over the size of the incremental funding that would be provided to departments to maintain existing programs and services. It was not just money, however, that was being transferred between guardians and spenders. There were also important exchanges of information, mutual confidence, and predictability. This up-to-date, detailed information in the hands of secretariat officials gave them a unique perspective and practical insights into the operations and programs of departments. Other organizations at the centre of government – the Department of Finance and the Privy Council Office – did not have this kind of access.

The expenditure and program data that the secretariat had at its fingers tips, coupled with its first-hand organizational knowledge about the array of departments and agencies, meant that information could be readily assembled at the centre of government to effect budgets, change organizations, and influence operations. If, in his budget, the minister of finance wanted to emphasize more integrated and efficient service delivery or rationalize and privatize Crown corporations, agencies, and other government entities, he had a close partner in the guardians of the Treasury Board to provide knowledgeable advice and, most important, to ensure effective and smooth central implementation of budget decisions.

Guardians and Central Reserves

This changing relationship between the Treasury Board Secretariat and the Department of Finance is perhaps best illustrated by examining how guardians handled reserves within the overall expenditure framework. Reserves are 'the repositories of discretion' within the budget process, and the exercise of discretion by guardians speaks to their relative influence with each other, with spenders, and with priority setters. In a nutshell, as fiscal restraint increased under pressures to focus on eliminating the deficit and as departments were given increased flexibility and autonomy under the banner of new public management, central reserves were dramatically reduced and rationalized within the Department of Finance. Joanne Kelly and Evert Lindquist summarize the fundamental principles that have shaped reserves in Canadian budgeting. These principles are intended to:

- establish an aggregate planned expenditure limit,
- deliberately under-allocate that total to departments,
- maintain the discipline that departments manage within their allocated totals in the absence of further policy decisions or severe and unavoidable workload increases,
- hold the difference between the total allocated spending and the total planned spending in a number of reserves, and
- use these reserves as a total to allow policy development throughout the year and to manage the incremental spending pressures that arise.[44]

The division of responsibilities for the management of central reserves between the Treasury Board and Finance rests upon the most enduring feature of the budgetary system in Canada – the distinction between new policy on the one hand and existing programs on the other. It first found practical meaning when the Planning, Programming, and Budgeting System (PPBS) was introduced in 1968, and was soon made operational in budget planning and budget decision-making in the form of 'A,' 'B,' and 'X' budgets. The 'A' budget consists of those expenditures required to finance existing programs at current levels of service with provisions for 'A-base increases' set aside within central operating and program reserves for increases in workload and inflation (called price). The 'B' budget consists of expenditures required for underwriting the costs of new programs or the expansion of existing programs with funds for such purposes held in central policy reserves. The 'X budget' consists of expenditure reductions to existing programs in order to finance the cost of new programs. Under PPBS, these concepts were made operational and formed the basic architecture around which departments and agencies structured and formulated their budget requests and on which requests were reviewed by the Department of Finance and Treasury Board and considered by cabinet and its committees, the minister of finance, and the prime minister. In short, 'B items' were and still are matters of new policy to be determined by some combination of the minister of finance, the prime minister, and sometimes cabinet, while 'A items' were and still are matters of existing programs and services to be decided by the Treasury Board and its Secretariat.

Traditionally, there have been three types of central reserves structured around this fundamental feature of the budget: policy reserves, operating and program reserves, and statutory and quasi-statutory reserves. Policy reserves provide funds for new initiatives, which at various times over the past several decades have been decided by the minister of finance, the prime minister, or cabinet and its committees and, most recently, by the minister of finance and the prime minister on their own. At times the determination of these policy reserves has been more open and visible to spending ministers as was the case in early 1980s with the Policy and Expenditure Management System (PEMS) when they were formally determined by the cabinet Committee on Priorities and Planning on the recommendation of the minister of finance and then assigned to each cabinet committee for the determination of new initiatives. More recently, and at most other times, they have been less open and visible, determined largely by the minister of finance with some consultation with the prime minister, occasionally provided to cabinet committees to manage, but more often held privately within the fiscal framework by the Department of Finance. With each new pairing of prime minister and minister of finance, the process has been slightly adjusted and tailored to suit their operating styles, personalities, and particular circumstances.

Operating reserves have traditionally provided funds to ·departments for increases to the base of existing programs for increases in workload or price. The Treasury Board has controlled this reserve, and during periods of significant expenditure growth in the 1970s and 1980s, the reserve was a major source of annual expenditure increase for spending departments. It provided the Treasury Board Secretariat with a source of funds for a detailed review of the departmental request for increases to the 'A-base' through the 'program forecast' submissions culminating in the annual 'Main Estimates' as well as a ready source of funds to meet urgent 'in-year' requirements that emerged throughout the course of the fiscal year. While the size of the reserve gradually diminished in the 1980s and early 1990s, as departments and agencies made their requests to the Treasury Board through the Annual Reference Level Update (ARLU), it was still sufficiently sizable that most departments found it in their interest to prepare credible submissions for negotiation with the Treasury Board Secretariat and its influential program analysts. This meant that Treasury Board officials continued to play an important and significant role in expenditure allocation and budget negotiations. It also meant that Treasury Board officials had reliable and up-to-date information on departmental programs and budgets. The use of central operating reserves, although of diminished size, continued until the mid-1990s.

The statutory and quasi-statutory reserves have traditionally been used for increases in expenditure for statutory programs such as public debt payments, old age security payments, or fiscal equalization as a consequence of changes in demographic structure and economic indicators and for quasi-statutory expenditures such as payments and services for veterans and leasing costs for Public Works and Government Services. This reserve has been managed by the Department of Finance with considerable influence by the Treasury Board Secretariat on allocations from the quasi-statutory reserve.

Traditionally, who controls the reserves was not contested. However, there have always been underlying tensions between the Treasury Board and the cabinet committees over expenditure allocations. In the 1970s, prior to the introduction of the Policy and Expenditure Management System in 1980, there were growing conflicts between the two. On one side, there was a concern on the part of the Privy Council Office and certain spending ministers that the Treasury Board was operating as 'a star chamber' and was turning down expenditure requests for new initiatives that had previously been approved by cabinet committees. In short, some were seeing Treasury Board encroaching on the determination of new initiatives. On the other side, there was the concern of the Treasury Board, which is best described in the words of a former senior Treasury Board Secretariat official:

> Ministers would routinely send program spending proposals to cabinet committees, which in that constraint-free environment virtually always cheered and gave their approval, after which the decision would be sent to Treasury Board 'to consider the resource implications' – but of course once we had a Cabinet decision in front of us there was not much we could do. When Al Johnson was secretary [of the Treasury Board] he once said to ministers, 'With this system you don't need a Treasury Board, you just need an adding machine.'[45]

The result of these two colliding forces was that cabinet and its important cabinet Committee on Priorities and Planning was increasingly becoming the visible arbitrator of disputes between spending ministers in cabinet committees and guardian ministers in the Treasury Board.

When PEMS was instituted in 1980 there was considerable contestation among central agencies (Privy Council Office, Department of Finance, and the Treasury Board Secretariat) over who would control increases to the 'A-base' and who would control increases in 'B expenditures.' PEMS, which established top down 'expenditure envelopes' for nearly a dozen areas of expenditure, was introduced in order to exert greater discipline on the system and to ensure that expenditures and government priorities could be more closely linked. The key issue was the determination and management of the reserves and, in particular, whether under PEMS the four cabinet committees, which were responsible for managing the 'expenditure envelope' within their assigned sectors would, in addition to managing their policy reserve, also manage the respective operating reserve. After much debate the issue was resolved by the Privy Council Office. It decided to leave the responsibility for the management of operating reserves with the Treasury Board on the grounds that cabinet committees of ministers are more interested in new initiatives than in existing operations and that there was risk that operating reserves could be too easily drained by the committees in order to fund new spending initiatives. Spending ministers could not be expected to operate as guardians, and the long-held distinction of institutionally separating increases in the 'A-base' for existing programs from increases in the 'B-budget' for new programs was maintained.

The twin forces of increased autonomy for departments and increased focus on the deficit were mutually reinforced and fundamentally changed the structure and use of reserves. As departments were given more flexibility and latitude in the management of their operations – including the institution of single operating budgets, elimination of central controls on person-years, the carry forward to the following fiscal year of up to 5 per cent of operating budgets, and increased retention of funds raised from cost recovery – there was less reason for central operating reserves. In short, the rhetoric moved from 'let the managers manage' to 'make the managers manage' and, in the minds of the Secretariat, departments could not be made to manage if they were being continuously 'bailed out' by the Treasury Board.

With ongoing concern about mounting deficits and the need to control expenditures, departments were increasingly expected to fund new initiatives through reallocations from within their own resources. In the words of one battle-worn 'treasury hand,' central reserves became 'sitting ducks for spenders.' Throughout the late 1980s and early 1990s, central policy reserves for increased spending were gradually abandoned under the pressures of fiscal restraint. At first the size of policy reserves was reduced; then multiple reserves were combined and removed from the authority of policy committees and retained in the Department of Finance. Finally, the practice of including an explicit and visible policy reserve in the budget was abandoned formally.

The operating reserve of the Treasury Board was gradually reduced each year and a tiny, short-lived program reserve, intended for minor policy initiatives was eliminated a few years after it was established in the early 1990s. By the time the government announced its 'new' expenditure management system in 1995, the Treasury Board signalled that it had moved from 'funder' to 'banker' and that departments would become 'borrowers' from a small operating reserve that would be used as 'a line of credit ... to bridge finance projects with significant productivity pay-back.'[46] As if to foreshadow the extensive use of 'prudent budgeting' that has characterized the post-1995 period – an important subject I take up in chapter 7 – a 'contingency reserve' was retained and managed by the Department of Finance to cover 'the risk of statutory expenditures exceeding projections, such as unanticipated increases in transfer payments due to changing economic conditions.'[47]

Guardians Apart

It is not surprising that these forces – increasing managerial authority
for departments and significant cuts to expenditures – have affected
the long-standing relationship between guardians in the Department
of Finance and the Treasury Board Secretariat. It is not so much a question of differences over issues or approaches to specific expenditure
matters. Nor is it simply a powerful Department of Finance exploiting
a weakened Secretariat. In one sense it is more fundamental. When it
comes to budget allocations, Treasury Board is not so much exploited
as it is ignored. The relationship of guardians, once based on clearly
defined specialized responsibilities, has been considerably weakened
through the changing roles of each. As the Secretariat has moved more
towards 'a management board,' it has, in the words of one senior
Finance official, 'moved away from expenditure analysis.' As he
explains, 'They are not challenging departments. They no longer have
the knowledge, the information, or the expertise when it comes to
expenditure.'[48] As the Department of Finance focused on cutting
expenditures to eliminate the deficit, it made a number of decisions on
its own that it might otherwise have deferred to the Secretariat. A top
Secretariat official explains, 'In Finance there is a siege mentality; they
do everything themselves; they don't trust and they don't ask for assistance.'[49] It is not so much that there are disagreements between the
guardians; it is more that on matters of public expenditure, the Secretariat is, and feels, ignored by Finance.

There is a telling point about the size of the wedge between the two
guardians. Early efforts to improve the relationship actually seem to
have made it worse. When Finance Minister John Manley spoke in
bold terms of 'reallocation for transformation' and in his 2003 budget
announced that $1 billion would be reallocated from existing expendi-
tures, the Treasury Board Secretariat was called upon to find the
money. But it was unable to do the job. A senior Secretariat official
explains:

We went to Treasury Board ministers with proposals for specific cuts.
Ministers turned us down. They made it clear they did not want directed
cuts. They only wanted cuts that ministers would propose themselves.
Ministers said, 'Why are we cutting when the financial situation has
improved?' As one minister said in an earlier briefing: 'Why am I the minister of cuts when the rest of the ministers are the ministers of spending?'

In the Secretariat we took the view that a simple across-the-board cut would be a failure. We did not want to do it that way. In the end, the reallocation was a lot of smoke and mirrors with reductions to amounts set aside in the fiscal framework and no real cuts to programs or operations.[50]

One Finance official offered this perspective on the issue: 'When the departments found out (that the Secretariat had been turned back by its own ministers), the Secretariat lost all its credibility. They lost their ability to challenge departments.' The result, according to the official: 'When Prime Minister Martin subsequently set up the new expenditure review committee of cabinet, the Secretariat was not asked to support it because they did not deliver on the last reallocation exercise.'[51]

As the Treasury Board Secretariat became increasingly sidelined in matters of budgeting, it was not content to sit on the bench. It looked for new ways to play. A senior Secretariat official recalls:

We made a claim for $1 billion to fund the eroding stock of infrastructure in the public service, but [he quietly whispers] the real reason was to make the Secretariat relevant with Finance and with departments. We were able to get PCO support; we got the money for two years, but we could not sustain it. Finance would put no further money into the framework. It was one of our biggest mistakes, a two-year wonder, and a major tactical error. Why? It widened the gulf between the Secretariat and Finance.[52]

The search for relevance by the Secretariat is understandable when one appreciates the weight of the responsibility that Finance officials have come to believe that they must shoulder. 'You have to understand Finance,' explains an overworked but satisfied senior Finance official. 'If someone looks hesitant or looks slow, then Finance takes over. It has to be that way because it is our budget and we are responsible for it.'[53]

Experienced guardians instinctively know the importance of a good relationship between Finance and the Treasury Board Secretariat. One Finance official explained it this way: 'The relationship right now is at an all time low – the previous deputies didn't speak. There is a critical need and opportunity to improve it and I stressed that in my first briefing with the new deputy. When the relationship at the top is not working, my relationship becomes all the more important.'[54] A top Secretariat official puts it more bluntly: 'As a budget office we have lost our credibility. We need to get back to being a budget player, to rebuild our capacity to analyze the A-base and to function as the budget office on the "small p" programs of government. The deputy minister of Finance is prepared to work with us on this.'[55]

The traditional and specialized partnership where Finance and the Secretariat officials would stand side by side has evaporated considerably. An associate deputy minister of finance reflects:

> The Secretariat needs to be strengthened to focus on the small program items, the discretionary items of expenditure. I remember fifteen years ago, TBS was on top of the programs and had lots of knowledge about how they worked and how effective or ineffective they were. When I dealt with Agriculture expenditure issues I had a senior TBS official at my side with an intimate understanding of the department and how it operated. He knew the ins and outs of the programs and the department. He could advise me on how much the program had lapsed in expenditures the previous year, the quality of the management of the program, duplication and overlap with other programs, and how effective and efficient it was. We don't have access to that kind of detailed program and expenditure information today.[56]

Another Finance official explains that 'we [he names a senior Treasury Board Secretariat and PCO official] met on a weekly basis and went over the expenditure items and planned approaches for dealing with them. But when we had to deal with the key matters on the budget, we excluded the Secretariat.'[57] Rarely, if ever, do the differences spill out from behind closed doors into the open corridors of the departmental spenders. Instead, the two guardians just simply stand apart.

As Treasury Board officials have become significantly less influential in shaping budget allocations they have lost their capacity to secure program and budget information from spending departments. With less information they have done less expenditure analysis and have less advice to offer on matters of program expenditures, all of which has weakened their position with the Department of Finance, with Privy Council Office priority setters, the spending departments, and the financial watchdogs. Although Finance has temporarily taken on some of this detailed expenditure work itself, it knows that the key to longer-term success rests on working with the Treasury Board Secretariat to rebuild its expenditure analysis and advisory capacity. However, as the increasingly separate guardians of Finance and the Secretariat begin to address this internal challenge in search of new and more effective ways to work together, they continue to face the ongoing external challenge of dealing with the continuous demands and increasing aspirations of spending departments and spending ministers.

3 Why Spenders Keep Spending

Success in Ottawa is measured by, 'Can you get money?'

Deputy minister

Deputy ministers are not necessarily spenders, and most worth their salt will have ideas about how to get more bang from the existing bucks, or even shrunken bucks. Central agency airheads infrequently listen.

Former deputy minister

The key question for a spender is, Do you deal with Finance or do you deal with PCO and a cabinet process? You want to be as opportunistic as you can. If you think you can get a deal with Finance, you take it.

Spending deputy minister

On budget items the minister of finance wants as little cabinet process as possible. Many ministers will choose to try to make a deal with the prime minister or the minister of finance. Chrétien made as few deals as possible.

Deputy minister

The Department of Finance is the biggest spender in government.

Senior Finance official

Spenders are everywhere in government. The Canadian government consists of a great number of spending ministers and spending departments, agencies, and Crown corporations. In a large thirty-nine-person cabinet, there are thirty-seven spending ministers with responsibilities for various departments, agencies, Crown corporations, and other organizational entities. Only two ministers – the minister of finance and the president of the Treasury Board – are guardians. In a smaller twenty-seven-person cabinet, there are only two guardians. In 2004, Prime Minister Martin added twenty-eight parliamentary secretaries to this constellation, each with assigned responsibilities and all with access to cabinet documents and decisions. All but one, the parliamentary secretary to the minister of finance, were spenders.

There is great diversity in the organizational structure of government, and spenders in every different organization argue that through their expenditure programs they fulfill a unique and important public requirement.[1] The total number of organizational entities of all types and sizes is 414. The mainstay of the organizational structure are the twenty-five departments and central agencies that shape laws, policies and programs, provide services to Canadians, and manage their own budgets. They include entities such as Health Canada, Agriculture and Agri-Food Canada, Canadian Heritage, Industry Canada, the Department of National Defence, and Fisheries and Oceans Canada. In addition, there are numerous service agencies – including major ones such as the Canadian Food Inspection Agency, the Canada Revenue Agency, the Border Services Agency, and the Parks Canada Agency – and seventeen Special Operating Agencies that include the Passport Office, Indian Oil and Gas Canada, and Consulting and Audit Canada.

There are twenty-seven independent tribunals and quasi-judicial bodies such as the Canadian International Trade Tribunal and the Public Service Staffing Tribunal that make decisions or hear appeals to give effect to government policies at arm's length from the government. There are eighty-seven Crown corporations and other Canadian government corporate interests ranging from the Canada Mortgage and Housing Corporation, the Post Office, the Bank of Canada, to the Canadian Broadcasting Corporation and small entities like foundations, port authorities, and land corporations. These entities provide businesslike services within agreed policy and legislative frameworks, and are overseen by ministers. There are 205 entities classified as miscellaneous organizations that are very small, of lesser budgetary importance, and generally advisory in nature, including the Arctic Waters Advisory Committee, the Canadian Centre for Occupational Health and Safety, and the Great Lakes Fishery Commission.

Spenders are not just organizations; they are also people. For ministers and deputy ministers, spending has been the common measuring stick by which they are assessed by their peers. Surprisingly, despite all the talk about the importance of policy innovation and skilful management by ministers and their deputies, spending still remains an important ingredient for building reputation. A skilled minister, in combination with a smart deputy, who can get his way with the minister of finance on a difficult file, is considered 'on his way up.' Weaker ministers who cannot be expected to get the resources necessary to implement a key government priority are assigned by the prime minister to less important and less visible portfolios. Ask any retired minister to reflect on what he/she accomplished and almost to a person the immediate response has to do with putting in place some major economic, social, or international spending initiative. It may have been extending employment insurance to provide a year's maternity leave, establishing an innovative child tax benefit, connecting the country to the Internet and the information highway, 'fixing medicare,' upgrading critical municipal infrastructure, equipping the Armed Forces for peacemaking in addition to peacekeeping, or re-establishing the nation's international presence abroad. While prime ministers may secure a major international trade agreement, keep the country out of an unwanted war, or strengthen national unity by clarifying in legislation the terms for possible secession, it is spending ministers and their spending officials who secure their lasting reputations for their ability to mobilize public money to achieve public purposes.

Standing outside the spenders in Ottawa are the spending premiers, mayors, and First Nation chiefs and other Aboriginal leaders. A federal–provincial fiscal system in which constitutional responsibility for areas of large and rapidly growing public expenditure (e.g., health, education, and welfare) is in the hands of provincial governments and that embraces the tradition (enshrined in the constitution) of inter-regional fiscal equalization has meant that large sums of public money in the form of direct expenditures and tax points are transferred from the federal to the provincial and territorial governments. Premiers see the federation in terms of its alleged fiscal imbalance – a federal government with perpetual and automatic surpluses and provincial governments with increasingly costly expenditure obligations.[2] Provincial premiers and territorial leaders see federal expenditures not only as a means for dealing with pressing policy problems but also in terms of what expenditure increases can mean for them politically and for the autonomy of the governments that they represent. Provincial premiers and territorial leaders are spenders, and they view the federal government as the guardians of a growing federal public purse.

When it comes to mayors and municipal leaders, the spender-guardian dichotomy is just as pronounced if not more so. This increasingly influential coalition of spenders is prepared to push its case hard. As 'creatures of the provinces,' they lack independent constitutional authority and, perhaps more importantly, their fiscal capacity to raise significant revenue on their own pales in comparison to the demands of their citizens for urban services. Traditionally dependent on diminished fiscal transfers from deficit-ridden provincial governments, these urban spenders are increasingly and more successfully making their case directly to the federal government.

Rounding out the constellation of spending claimants are the approximately 600 First Nations bands, their chiefs, and leaders. The constitutional responsibility of the federal government for Aboriginal affairs and its fiduciary responsibility to Aboriginal peoples makes the federal government the prime, and in many instances, the exclusive target for these spenders. The fiscal capacity of Aboriginal governments is sharply limited and their social and economic needs are extraordinarily great, with the consequences reflected in major unsolved problems, a continuation of significant differences in life outcomes between Aboriginal and non-Aboriginal Canadians, and a steady stream of dramatic and widely reported media stories about social and community neglect and personal and individual tragedy and destruction.

Most spending ministers and spending public servants are never content with the same level of budget from one year to the next. Indeed, they see a large part of their jobs as developing and advocating new policies, programs, and projects, all of which require additional budget resources. During periods of budgetary expansion, they want to ensure that they are getting at least their 'fair share' of the available new money. During periods of budgetary restraint and reduction, they want to ensure that they maintain their budgets, or at a minimum, take no more than their 'fair share' of the budget cuts. This chapter focuses on how spenders get money, how they keep it, and how they spend it.

For spenders, it is one thing to get new money or to protect it from cuts and reductions imposed by central guardians and it is another to actually spend the money that is available. In part, spenders are judged by guardians on whether and how well they spend. Spenders that lapse money at year-end soon develop a bad reputation with guardians. 'We know that a very large amount of any new money that is given to the Department of Foreign Affairs lapses and therefore we tell them, 'Don't ask for new money,' explains a Treasury Board assistant secretary. Similarly, spenders that simply get new money based on their promises but do not spend it become an ongoing target for cuts and reductions by guardians.

Spenders know that in order 'to get' they have 'to give' and that means providing information to guardians in exchange for expenditure increases or for protection from budget cuts. The reciprocity of information and budget exchanges between spenders and guardians serves their mutual interests. Information about performance is costly to compile and complicated to understand for both spenders and guardians. Information about priorities is simple and more easily obtainable. This chapter also explores the reciprocity of expenditure increases and expenditure information exchanges between spenders and guardians.

Getting Money

Talk to any minister or deputy minister in Ottawa about how the town works and one is immediately struck by how much they view the world from the perspective of the allocation of public money and how much of their time and effort is devoted to trying to get new money for new policy initiatives. A chance encounter on Sparks Street Mall with a busy minister scurrying to his departmental office elicits the unsolicited self-satisfaction of having just 'gotten an item through cabinet committee' and onto the priority list for funding in the next budget. Barely into a 'how's it going' conversation with a deputy minister and one hears, with pride, about their latest accomplishment in 'locking in a budget item with Finance' so that their minister can then come forward and 'cut the final deal.' For ministers' political staff, the preoccupation is the same. They enjoy a deep sense of satisfaction when they have had a 'good meeting' with the PMO and their intimate counterparts in the finance minister's office over a spending proposal that their minister has long been pushing. Officers in spending departments, who have laboured over the preparation of the briefing material for their deputy to use in putting forward the department's best case to Finance, feel a personal sense of achievement when they are 'debriefed' by their deputy within hours of a 'positive meeting' with the Finance deputy and his colleagues in his twentieth-floor boardroom. Even those more distant departmental officials, operating on the front lines of service delivery, feel a belated sense of pride and confidence when they eventually come to learn that last month's budget provided some new money for spending in their region.

When it comes to getting money, not all departments are created equal. Some, through years of practise, are skillful and hence successful, whereas others are rarely, if ever, in the running. A retired senior official reflects on his experience in the mid-1980s and early 1990s:

> Industry Canada starts to prepare for the next budget the day after the last budget. They have a process in place to develop upcoming budget themes, strategies for linking to budget themes, priorities for various proposals, expenditure initiatives, the necessary memoranda to cabinet, one-pagers, and pre-budget discussions with Finance. They were very successful in getting money in the budget. Health Canada based their case on crises or shortages or other problems. They were less organized, less sophisticated, less analytical, and less successful. Veteran Affairs never got any new money in a budget because they could never make their case and were never able to develop proposals that they could link to the priorities of government.[3]

Whether spenders go to Finance or the Prime Minister's Office to get new money for a new initiative depends upon a number of factors. For one skilled departmental spender there was no doubt:

> You go to PMO. For a number of years at HRDC [Human Resources Development Canada] we had been undertaking and evaluating a series of self-sufficiency pilot projects which paid income supplements to welfare recipients if they got off welfare and took a job. Early on we took an initiative to PMO to establish the program on a more permanent basis. After some discussion and providing them with information, PMO included it in the government's 'Red Book' for the upcoming election in 2000. They liked it and, once it got into the 'Red Book,' it became an item in the Speech from the Throne, and Finance included funding for it in the budget without any cabinet consideration.[4]

Ask any number of experienced deputy ministers about how spenders get new money and it invariably comes down to three things: link the proposal to the priorities of government, do your homework, and have a constituency. All three are necessary and all are used by spenders in varying degrees, depending on the circumstances. One highly successful and respected spending deputy carefully measured his words and put it this way:

> You have to have a goal. You have to be an activist and the role of the public service is to be activist. The public service still has a huge role to play. You have to work very hard. You need to do the policy work – to follow Ivan

Fellegi's seven steps to policy.[5] They are all important. You need to be smart: You need an evidence-based approach. You need to have better analysis than the Department of Finance and you need to know the file much better than they do. There are lots of routes to success. You need to be able to compromise on the instruments, but you need to save the goals. You need to have allies and friends and you have to know that you will make enemies if you are doing your job. You have to have knowledge of the decision-making system and know how to make it work. You have to know how to play for the endgame. You have to know how to deal with success. When you have success you have to be able to demonstrate to the minister of finance and to the prime minister that you have solved the problem and that there is appropriate recognition for the government of this. You need to have third-party allies. If you are dealing with an education issue you need to have the Association of Universities and Colleges of Canada in your pocket. And you need the support of PCO and PMO, or at least have them willing to talk to you. You need to be able the keep the discussion going inside the central agencies with the PMO and the PCO, not just with Finance.[6]

'For us to get money,' instructs another spending deputy minister, 'we have to do the policy work to show that infrastructure supports the priorities of the government. No matter what the program, you need to show how it helps to achieve the government's priorities. We linked infrastructure to Kyoto, to the environment, and to trade. Now we are going for the third round and we need to link it to this [Paul Martin's] government's priorities.'[7] And how is that done? The skilled deputy walks to his desk and picks up and reads the 'speaking points' from a two-page briefing note he used the previous day in a meeting with officials in the Department of Finance:

- Strategic infrastructure is about supporting trade, it's about bridges and transportation that improve trade.
- Resources from the north: it's about access to the mines and deposits in the north.
- Water management: it's about ensuring the management of water, ensuring water quality.
- The new economy: it's about electronic infrastructure and high speed connections.
- It's for regional development, for example, a pan-Atlantic tourism initiative to diversify the economy, or improved railway infrastructure in the west.[8]

There is little doubt that government priorities drive public money. Some priorities, however, can be so divisive of ministers that unless they become the personal priority of the prime minister they are not likely to move ahead. 'You have to get the prime minister on side when there is a real potential for a split in cabinet,' instructs a deputy minister. 'It is then a leadership issue and it takes the prime minister. You need to demonstrate to the Prime Minister's Office that this is an issue that the prime minister has to take on his shoulders.' 'On Kyoto,' he explains, '_____ [names a top policy adviser to a prime minister] was against it. He hated me in the end, arguing that it would do great damage to the government in western Canada.'[9]

How does a prime minister become convinced? The deputy minister recalls an instance where a sophisticated argument was used to crystallize the priority of Kyoto in the mind of one particular prime minister:

> The PM was not a man of vision, and yet this was a vision issue in the sense that it had a long term time frame – fifty to 100 years. It was the last year of his mandate. Could we take a step now consistent with the way this issue was likely to evolve over the longer term? The Canadian public supports it, but nobody knows what it really is. The oil patch was against it. Big business was against it and believed it would not happen. President Clinton viewed Canada as the number one partner and felt we could provide leadership. We reminded the PM that he was committed to meeting the Kyoto targets and that Canada had gotten what it wanted from the agreement: recognition of carbon sinks and tradeable emissions. Yes, the developing countries were not part of it but they took fifty years to join the WTO [World Trade Organization] and besides they were generally not responsible for creating the problem. Yes, the U.S. would not do it under President Bush, but for reasons that were transparently corrupt from a public policy point of view. It was a matter of doing the right thing when the Americans were doing the wrong thing.

He goes on to further explain that, 'with the prime minister, you play the angle – you say, "either you want it or you don't. This is not a cabinet issue. It is your issue. Your ministers will rag the puck until you take it."'[10] The result was that, in the 2003 budget, the minister of finance announced $2 billion in new funding over five years to help implement the Climate Change Plan and, in the 2005 budget, the minister of finance added another $3 billion in new funding over five years for climate change and sustainable development. All totalled, when extended for a further five years, it came to $10 billion over ten years, a sizable total in its own right, although, another spending deputy 'argued it was not that much since farmers were getting $6 billion for not growing certain crops.'[11]

Getting a spending initiative to be seen as a priority is necessary, but it is not sufficient. 'You have to do your homework in order to be taken seriously by Finance,' explains another spending deputy minister, 'and when there has been little policy work done, it is a tougher job. There's been lots of policy work done on health and labour markets but not much on infrastructure. We had to understand what was infrastructure policy, why was it important, what did it link to, and how do you do it.' Linking the analysis to the concerns of the Department of Finance is the next step. 'With Finance you have to show them how you are a solution to some of their problems. Public infrastructure can be explained in terms of prosperity and productivity, a major concern of Finance. For us, we needed analysis and research that linked infrastructure investment to GDP growth. While there can be lots of debate on this, Finance takes that type of analysis seriously.'[12]

How far should spenders push the analysis? The short answer is as far as a guardian will take it.

> While we need to be on the same wavelength as Finance, we do not want to exaggerate the importance of our proposal because Finance, gets told by everybody that their proposals are 'investments' that will help the economy. Most of the time this is bull____ and Finance is not favourably disposed to bull____. For example, the Federation of Canadian Municipalities needs to stop talking about the 'infrastructure deficit'. This language is not helpful with Finance. On health care, nobody talks about a deficit and they got money. With deficit talk there is no sense of trade-offs and choices. The demand for everything – highways, transit, rail, etc. – is just aggregated and there is no differentiation across sectors. It's simply a wish list, driven by the various sector interests. The sector projections are developed only on the basis of population growth and there is no accounting for technological change.[13]

For skilled spenders, getting money from guardians requires that they think like guardians.

Building on priorities and doing your homework are necessary, but so too is having a clientele and a constituency for the proposal. For infrastructure, the key to lining up support is knowing that 'every

infrastructure has a location.' 'It must be somewhere,' notes a this deputy minister, 'and that means we can connect it to real places and real
people. When we go to cabinet with our multi-year plan, everything
will be linked to real places – flood control on the Fraser River in British Columbia and on the Miramichi in New Brunswick, and in the
North, bridges to deal with melting ice roads and infrastructure to support a new natural gas pipeline.'[14]

Spenders look for support from outside and inside government. 'On
infrastructure,' he/she explains,

> outside players were important, most notably the Federation of Canadian
> Municipalities, who had a close relationship with the prime minister. The
> Liberals found they could work with mayors as a counterweight to the
> provinces. The Federation was a major source of pressure on the govern-
> ment and they got the priority established. Inside government you need
> the support of regional ministers. The influence of regional ministers is
> unbelievable. I never really paid that much attention to them in all my
> years in government until the last year or so. I am sure the prime minister
> told his ministers that he wanted regional ministers to be important,
> because they are acting like major players. The regional influence from
> regional ministers has doubled in its importance. And with this, we are
> spending more.[15]

The support of key sector ministers is also important for spenders,
and spenders have learned how to handle this support with care. The
deputy minister explains: 'The Ministry of Transport doesn't like it when
we talk to regional ministers about infrastructure because he wants the
money to come directly to his department so he can fund the individual
projects himself. On the other hand, when Transport has the support of
strong regional ministers and wins on a spending issue like the Pacific
Gateway project, it is treated as a separate, one-off pro–British Columbia
decision and that way the project can be done without distorting the
infrastructure program.'[16]

Spenders get support for their spending programs by providing
assurance that the benefits of spending will be distributed fairly and
equitably. 'In renewing the infrastructure program,' explains the deputy minister, 'the minister thought about it and quickly concluded that
it must be "roughly fair." That meant we worked out a formula of
equal per capita shares by province, with the exception of Prince
Edward Island and the Territorial governments which got a bit more

because their populations were so small and with per capita shares they would not get enough money to do a project. Because we established "rough fairness" across the country, we were able to put in place a minimum threshold of $75 million for projects in large jurisdictions, which allowed us to have fewer projects and avoid spreading the money over many smaller, less effective ones.'[17] Another deputy minister explains how fairness is critical in getting support from ministers: 'On Kyoto we had the deputy prime minister from Alberta and the minister of energy from Saskatchewan. We had to ensure a fair distribution of the pain on a regional basis. Also, we could not create competitive problems for industrial sectors by concentrating the pain on one or two; everybody had to share a bit.'[18]

Spenders know they are in competition with other spenders for limited resources, especially those spenders who have responsibilities in the same policy area. Therefore, spenders work with guardians to show them that they have their interests in mind. 'The minister and I,' explains a senior official, 'went to Finance and we agreed to hold hands with them. Finance thinks it is a better investment to put money into a strategic infrastructure program with alternative categories for eligibility, such as "public transportation" and "trade corridors" than simply putting it into Ministry of Transport highways. Finance loves our approach because it forces choice. We can help Finance with their problem of getting choices and trade-offs made and ensure that there is some competition for the scarce resources.'[19]

Keeping Money

During periods of significant and prolonged expenditure restraint, spenders refocus their attention from getting new money to maintaining their existing base of money. During these times, skillful spenders can actually become part guardians, at least when it comes to the question of total government spending. As spenders attempt to keep money, they take gradual steps as part guardians. A former deputy minister explains: 'During all my eight years as a deputy minister and indeed before that as a central agency guardian, the pre-eminent public policy issue was not the constitution, daycare, and defence. It was the huge and yawning deficit and debt that the government faced and the very real prospects of becoming an impoverished nation. Like most other deputies of the day, I was convinced that, if we didn't get that under control, there was no point in carrying on with ordinary business.'[20]

It takes, however, considerable time and a significantly deep and prolonged period of restraint before spenders become as convinced as this
deputy. At the outset, spenders naturally look for ways and means of
avoiding any cuts or real reductions and compressions in their budgets.
If there is no escaping the cuts, they will sometimes offer up to guardians
'musical ride'[21] proposals for which there is no political appetite or political will to cut, or they will propose 'cash management' reductions such
as project delays and deferrals. A former distinguished deputy minister
who served as both a spender and guardian recalls: 'I remember the four-
teen expenditure cutting exercises that took place in the Mulroney years.
Before them were the many "X budgets" that the Liberals ran, including
a number that I managed for them during my TBS days. What virtually
all of these exercises had in common was an emphasis on avoiding political controversy, so the cuts made were those that would be least visible:
cut the capital budget, defer maintenance, temporarily freeze hiring, and
so on.'[22] For some time spenders are prepared to accept these across-
the-board cuts and reductions in their operating budgets. However, after
continuous rounds of such reductions, they become vulnerable to 'death
by a thousand cuts' as they no longer have the capacity to maintain and
protect their essential and most important programs, and they find that
their department's physical and human capital has eroded and is at risk
of decay.

At that stage, and sometimes before, spenders are actively considering ways to protect their key programs by eliminating or restructuring
programs which may no longer be needed. But they are not always
successful. A former deputy minister explains his experience in the
early 1990s:

> With my detailed experience of the Indian Affairs and Northern Develop-
> ment budget – and if you brought to that, as I did, the developmental,
> capacity-building objective – there were some programs that ought to have
> been cut back severely, notably those that created intolerable pressures for
> people to keep living on Indian reserves. This fiscal apartheid was holding
> back too many people, sapping enterprise and creativity, and creating
> dependences that made what we have done to Newfoundland look like a
> doodle. At the same time we had programs that were really starting to
> work for Aboriginal people – post-secondary education chief among them
> – which needed structural reform more than new money. I wanted to
> change post-secondary education: providing money for accomplishment
> rather than mere attendance and more money for critical technical degrees

and less for teachers, social workers, and bloody lawyers. I also wanted money to match our constitutional and Charter obligations – welfare rates and educational spending that matched the provinces' per capita amounts, as well as money to settle legal claims obligations. This was hard but not impossible. Unfortunately, the only response from the central guardians was 'freeze spending.' I lost a minister over that. We got 4,000 letters from white Canada, one of which supported Finance.[23]

However, as fiscal restraint continues, the political feasibility of reducing or terminating programs increases. 'The 1995 "Program Review" budget was the exception that proves the rule,' explains a former deputy minister. 'It was prepared in an atmosphere of impending financial crisis, which made politically possible the elimination of expenditures that had previously been regarded as too sensitive.'[24] In this environment, spenders may get some of the smaller reallocations from guardians that they want but they may also lose out to the guardians on their desires to phase out, rather than completely eliminate, the large, important expenditure programs. A former senior official reflects on his difficult and unsuccessful experience in the mid-1990s:

> The overwhelming sentiment of the best of the senior officers in the department was that we had to get out of regional and sectoral subsidy programs. We worked hard to bring the regional agencies under some kind of control, and succeeded to the degree that we brought them into the portfolio. We stole their budgets for serious or inescapable programs, like the TRIUMF reactor at the University of British Columbia. We wanted to wind down DIPP [the Defence Investment Productivity Program] and other programs, but we wanted to do it carefully and over a period of years. The finance minister, in the 1995 budget and in a move unique among Quebec ministers, 'zeroed out' the spending for the program, a program that, more than any other, supported the crown jewels of Quebec manufacturing. I was personally abused for warning of the consequences. The program was cancelled. The howl was forceful and straight into the Prime Minister's Office. The finance minister then commanded that DIPP be reinvented, under a new name – Technology Partnerships Canada.[25]

Spending Money

Getting money (or even keeping it) is one thing, spending it is quite another. Whether and how a department has spent its money in the past is an important influence on future spending decisions. Spenders, guardians, priority setters, and financial watchdogs all have a different perspective on past spending. For spenders, it is the confidence and assurance that comes from having in place the program delivery systems to ensure that the money is spent within the time constraints of the fiscal year and the requirements of the programs. For guardians, how well a department spent its resources in the past is the clue to how tough to be on them in the future. Departments and agencies with reputations for ineffective spending, for putting existing programs at risk by deliberately underfunding them, or for bending the financial rules, all come in for extra scrutiny by the Treasury Board. For priority setters, departments that have done their spending provides evidence that the government has focused on what it says needs to be done and that it has lived up to its publicly expressed spending commitments. For the financial watchdog, spending provides the opportunity to audit departments and agencies on their compliance with the government financial policies and to assess the performance of their programs and their management.

In Ottawa, all spenders know that in order to spend they need two things – money and authority. Almost all existing money is already contained in the approved budgets of the department or agency. The relatively smaller amount of additional new money comes through the approval of the minister of finance and the prime minister as part of the budget. 'The system focuses on the last $10 billion of expenditure,' explains a somewhat frustrated senior Treasury Board Secretariat official, 'and the $190 billion of existing expenditure goes to the same place that it did the previous year.'[26] In terms of authority, for much spending, it already resides within the department or has been granted to the department on an annual or ongoing basis by the Treasury Board and by Parliament as part of the annual estimates or statutory approvals. For any specific new spending program, as well as for existing programs where authorities that have not been specifically assigned by legislation or delegated to departments, spending departments require specific authority from the Treasury Board to spend.

At first blush one might think that guardians would insist on a close linkage between the allocation of funding to departments and the granting of authorities to permit the spending of the funds. For example, the threat of turning down a requested budget increase might be useful in securing agreement to an authority. Or, upon closer examination of the design of a program and the authorities necessary for its implementation, guardians might conclude that a smaller amount of funding is required than what had been set aside earlier as part of the government's budget. It is often erroneously assumed, and even stated, that Treasury Board allocates the expenditure budget and approves the program in order that departments and agencies (subject to the approval of Parliament) can spend. In practise, this is not the case. A veteran senior Treasury Board official sets the record straight: 'Treasury Board does not approve the funding and, for that matter, it does not actually approve the program. It only approves the authorities – the terms and conditions – necessary to deliver the program. Its "push back" is formal, but from an expenditure point of view, it is not effective. We accommodate ourselves to the expenditures.'[27] A spending deputy minister confirms this: 'I live and die by Treasury Board submissions. But, I don't go there for money, only for authority.'[28]

Do spending departments ever receive less money from the Treasury Board for a new program than had been previously been set aside in the fiscal framework or included in the budget? 'Almost never,' is the quick reply of an experienced Secretariat official. 'TBS program analysts have no incentive for recommending fewer resources even if it could be argued on the basis of more detailed inspection and analysis that less money is required. There is no alternative claimant for the resources because, if any trade-offs were made, they were done much earlier at the time that the money for the initiative was locked into the fiscal framework.'[29] 'Money can be frozen or fenced by the Treasury Board, pending a departmental report to the Secretariat,' explains a Treasury Board program analyst, 'but their budgets aren't reduced.'[30] He goes on to explain:

> Allocations to programs that are made in the finance minister's budget almost never get changed. If, in the rare instance they are to be changed, the burden of proof rests with the Treasury Board. I can only remember one case and it was a real fight. It was an airport security initiative where the initial budget allocation, based on a very rough estimate, was $30 million. Subsequently, the department got $18 million when their submission came forward to the cabinet committee and eventually only $15 million when it came to the Treasury Board. This happened because it was very clear to everyone that there were many fewer airports requiring security than initially estimated.[31]

Even if, subsequent to an initial expenditure approval in the budget, an infrequent expenditure adjustment is made, it can sometimes work to the benefit of spenders and not guardians. A senior Treasury Board Secretariat official explains:

> When a Parks Canada submission for authority to complete the parks system came to the Treasury Board, we were concerned that an awful lot of new money was being used to create new parks while the current parks were collapsing and falling apart. There was inadequate funding for capital and for ongoing maintenance and repair, and a huge overhang of expenditure just to support the existing infrastructure. It takes twenty years to set up and get a new park up and running, from the initial surveys, the archaeological and cultural work, and the design and consultation work up to the actual opening of the park. When the item came forward to the Board we approved the new funding but only on the condition that the minister would go back to cabinet and outline all the program integrity problems associated with maintaining and sustaining the current inventory of national parks. We got cabinet support for this increase in maintenance and operating money and the amount was built into the fiscal framework. This was clearly only a second-best solution, if it was even that. The proper decision should have been taken earlier and that would have been to curtail the plans for new parks in order to increase the operating and capital funds required to maintain the existing parks.[32]

In short, new expenditures do not regularly compete with existing expenditures.

There are some important reasons why the government does not like to reduce funding levels for new initiatives that have already been included in the finance minister's budget. 'All hell would break loose,' declares a spending deputy minister, 'if we got less money from Treasury Board than had been set aside in the budget and the fiscal framework. In fact,' the deputy goes on,

> we have found that we have to make public announcements on our projects before we get approval from the Treasury Board. Doing the due diligence to get the terms and conditions and all the authorities approved takes a lot of time. We are making deals with the provinces and municipalities who are putting their own money into the projects as well. If, before we could announce a project, we had to wait until we completed our full due diligence and received approval from Treasury Board, we would be constantly scooped by the provinces. A cabinet committee of ministers reviewed this whole matter and explained it to Treasury Board, and while Treasury Board ministers didn't like what they heard, they knew it had to be done this way.[33]

The Reciprocity of Expenditure Information
and Expenditure Increases

Spenders don't naturally give information to guardians and guardians don't naturally give expenditure increases to spenders. No spender wants a guardian to use the information later to turn down a request or, worse yet, to cut a program. Spenders will, however, provide information to guardians when it is in their interest to do so and when it strengthens their case for their spending proposal. For spenders, this has increasingly become a matter of providing information about how the new spending proposal contributes to and furthers the government's priorities. Less emphasis is placed on providing information about how the proposed new program or program expansion will actually perform. This is particularly the case for information exchanges among officials at the more senior levels. For the guardians, the information provided by spenders about the linkage of the proposal to government priorities is rarely useful for determining whether one proposal should be funded and not another, or whether the department should absorb the costs from within its existing A-base of expenditures. The information that guardians need for expenditure analysis and expenditure management and planning – a detailed and fine-grain costing of the A-base of expenditure programs that can be easily aggregated and disaggregated in relation to proposals for new spending and for reallocations – is not readily available. It must be created; therefore, there must be an incentive to do it. It must also be relevant to the decisions at hand, and it must be up-to-date.

To get this information, guardians face a fundamental conundrum. In short, they need what spenders have – detailed and timely information – and spenders have little or no incentive to provide it to them freely. This detailed information largely resides with spenders, and experienced guardians have come to learn that they cannot create this information without the support and cooperation of spenders. They have learned that the information they receive from spenders is often distorted, incomplete, discontinuous, and inaccurate. Central directives and requests from guardians to spending departments for expenditure and program information yield only generalized information and not the information that guardians need to do effective program and budget analyses.

As a result, securing reliable and relevant information from spenders requires that guardians be able to give them something in return. The fate of guardians to acquire this critical information rests on their ability to grant expenditure increases, to provide increased certainty through the commitment of multi-year expenditures, and to allow for financial and management flexibility. When guardians are unable to grant these concessions to departments, the budget information they receive from departments dries up. This is the reciprocity of budgets and information. It is implicitly understood by guardians and spenders at all levels and it affects information flows at all levels. An experienced assistant secretary of the Treasury Board Secretariat explains it this way: 'It is much easier to get information from a department if you deal with budgeting and affect their allocations. It is the dollars that matter, that is how you become relevant.'[34] A program analyst observes that 'an internal study on streamlining the work of Treasury Board concluded that Treasury Board submissions, even the routine ones, were important to program analysts in getting useful information about the department and its programs. For example, in analysing a submission about the RCMP forensic lab, I got information that was very useful in dealing with another submission on their automated processing which showed they had extra capacity to reallocate to other things.'[35]

Spenders and guardians point to different causes for this lack of program and expenditure information in the Treasury Board Secretariat. One former senior Secretariat official explains that, 'in the 1990s, we devolved a lot of authority and decision-making to departments and allowed them to realign their priorities. This significantly reduced the information flow from departments. The deterioration in the information was significant. While we had some pockets of information it was no way near what we had in terms of quality and quantity in the mid-1980s. For example, in the Department of National Defence, the expenditure categories and classifications are now so broad that you could drive a tank through them.'[36]

Another Treasury Board Secretariat official concludes that 'the lack of new resources that can be provided to departments means that the Treasury Board has become less engaged with departments. As a consequence, we get much less information. The MYOP [Multi-year Operational Plans] briefings used to provide an annual focus where we could review all the programs of the entire government in one place and at one time and provide some funding for key issues of health and safety, risks to security, etc. That is no longer done; it is simply a technical exercise in which the departmental reference levels are mechanically updated and TBS program analysts are no longer involved.'[37]

Whatever the causes, the lack of reliable expenditure information in the Secretariat about individual departmental programs is a serious problem for guardians of both the Secretariat and Finance. 'TBS does not have good information on the A-base of expenditure and nobody is looking at the A-base,' laments a senior Secretariat official. 'The departments themselves don't even have the information because the (1995) "Program Review" cut many of their resources and since that time the Treasury Board has never asked for the information.'[38] When it comes to horizontal, cross-departmental expenditure issues – like spending on Aboriginal initiatives, climate change, immigration, and the North – the situation is more serious and more challenging. 'It took _____ [names an assistant deputy minister] and his team more than seven months just to determine the amount of spending on Aboriginal programs and to find that we were spending $8 billion annually on 360 programs, across thirty-six departments and agencies.'[39] 'We need a new Treasury Board Secretariat that is on top of this program information,' declares an associate deputy minister of finance. 'This detailed information is not the forte of the Department of Finance, but it should and must be the forte of the Secretariat.'[40]

Priorities and Allocations, Not Performance and Allocations

When spenders come to learn that they can no longer secure expenditure increases from the Treasury Board Secretariat, they stop providing them with reliable and accurate budget information. Instead, they shift their attention to what gives them the greatest chances of spending success. At one time when the Treasury Board Secretariat had considerable influence on the allocation of new money, whether in the form of increases for new initiatives, additional money to expand current programs, or 'price and workload' increases to keep up with inflation and population growth, spenders made their case in terms of what they expected the program to achieve. Determinations about the number of clients served, the cost per client served, and the benefits received were important factors in determining whether or not a new expenditure allocation would be made. In short, the analysis of the program and its budget, usually but not always in comparison to others, were important in determining the decision. In part, this was because allocations of new money were being made to many programs and the basis for differentiating between programs was a relative assessment of how well they were performing or expected to perform.

More recently, as governments have sharply focused their new expenditure increases on a limited set of declared priorities, spenders have come to learn that having documentation to demonstrate they have a well-performing program may meet their obligations for reporting on results but it does not necessarily secure a budget increase. Only if the spending initiative is a major priority of the government does it have a real chance for new money. For spenders, the key to securing new money is to link the proposal to the government's limited set of priorities rather than to the performance of the program. As a result, top-level spenders in departments put more time and effort into strategizing, designing, and marketing new spending proposals and interpreting and linking them to government priorities than they do on reporting on the results of their existing programs. Spenders have increasingly learned that the best pay-off is to spend their time on priorities and not on performance as they have seen budget allocations for new money increasingly decided by the fiscal guardians in Finance, with the support of the priority setters in the PMO and the PCO, rather than by the program budget guardians in the Treasury Board.

As the Treasury Board Secretariat guardians were losing their influence over direct expenditure allocations to the priority setters and Finance guardians, it was a natural step, in the context of the newly reconstituted Treasury Board (the 'Management Board'), to attempt to re-establish the balance by launching a set of government-wide initiatives aimed at improving program performance and securing program results. Other OECD countries, many of whom had embraced the reforms of new public management, were doing the same. The Treasury Board performance initiative, launched in 2000 after considerable effort, was unveiled with significant profile under the banner of 'Results for Canadians.'[41] This performance initiative was not, however, linked to budgeting and to expenditure allocation. 'The information that we had from the performance review, the accountability framework, managing for results, and the program review activity structure, was simply "too aggregated" to be of use in budgeting,' explains a senior Treasury Board official. 'It didn't provide an effective window into the departments.'[42]

A further attempt has been made through an initiative known as the 'Management Resources and Results Structure' to link programs (called the program activity architecture) and their results to expenditures budgets. A senior Treasury Board official explains the problems: 'Our TBS colleagues who were focused on performance, results, and outcomes were doing their work totally unlinked to budgeting and the budgets of departments and agencies. You know, it is not "results at any price." The question is, How much does it cost and is it worth doing? Without that information we cannot decide trade-offs and without trade-offs we cannot make good budget decisions.'[43]

The journey continues, but the frustration remains. Another veteran Secretariat official candidly explains:

> We are struggling to develop a framework – Management Resources and Results Structure – that can link budgeting to results, but it is at a preliminary state. It has thirteen areas of government expenditure and priority at the highest level. What we need is a unit of budget analysis that can be linked to the A-base of departments so that it can be aggregated across departments to provide analysis on horizontal programs, and so it can be linked vertically within a department to its A-base of expenditures, to its objectives, and to the results that are expected to be achieved. How you get the information for this is very difficult. Frankly, the framework is at some risk as the little bit that has been done has resulted in a lot of kicking and screaming by departments. The expenditure management information system is having serious problems and has yet to get us any systematic, regular, and reliable budget and program information. Departments believe that any information they provide to TBS in this manner might be used to affect (reduce) their budgets; they do not see how it might help them in their requests.[44]

Spending departments confirm their own worries. A former chief financial officer of a large spending department explains: 'When TBS began to put in place the new Management Resources and Results Structure I was very worried, and I called _____ [names an assistant secretary] because I was concerned that they might reduce an area of our budget if we indicated in the report that we did not spend all the funds for one activity but allocated it to something else.'[45]

Canada is far from alone in its inability to link directly performance information to budget decision-making. In a recent comparative study of five leading countries (the United States, the United Kingdom, Australia, New Zealand, and the Netherlands), it was found that what governments have been able to achieve by way of developing systematic and reliable program performance information and linking that information to budget decision-making has fallen considerably short of what they have actually promised.[46] At one level this should not be surprising. There is more to budgeting than performance. Indeed, experience and research have indicated that budget decisions are influenced by a large number of factors in addition to the performance of specific programs (e.g., priorities, budget levels, previous budget base, regional and stakeholder interests, politics, personalities). Even securing reliable, timely, and relevant performance information in New Zealand, where its use has been an important part of its public sector reforms since the 1980s, has proved to be a challenge that requires discipline, clarity of purpose and concept, and ongoing adjustment and commitment of resources.

Having a concise and readily understandable set of intentions based upon some clear concepts (e.g., the New Zealand distinction between 'outputs' and 'outcomes,' which most other countries have adopted) or a simple and seemingly reliable set of tools (e.g., the Program Assessment Rating Tool in the United States), does not automatically translate into their utilization and their effectiveness. Clear concepts and solid tools are important, but so too is support and encouragement for those who are defining the performance measures, assembling the information, and linking it to budget allocations and reallocations. In this regard the more decentralized and somewhat more flexible approach that Australia has taken to the development and implementation of performance information, providing a relatively large role for agency heads in shaping the measures and the information to the unique needs or their own agency, offers some promise of greater utilization of the information at least by top-level agency decision-makers.

While Treasury Board guardians struggle to put in place a government-wide system that can provide even a semblance of linkage between expenditure and performance information, spenders continue to focus much of their high-level attention on developing expenditure proposals and linking them to government priorities rather than to program performance. Priorities are increasingly important in the budgetary process and in determining its outcomes, as is the role of priority setters.

4 The Priority Setters at the Centre

Where do you go when you want new money for a major policy initiative – the PMO or Finance? Oh, you go to PMO.

Former spending assistant deputy minister

It's who do you know in the PMO … We must move to address this democratic deficit.

Paul Martin[1]

The Speech from the Throne is the prime minister's and the budget is the minister of finance's.

Former assistant deputy minister for policy

The relationship between PMO and PCO depends upon the personalities. The finance minister and the clerk didn't get along and I didn't get along with the clerk.

Former adviser to a prime minister

Public money goes to the heart of any government. The budgeting and management of public money is central to its credibility. 'The centre' of Canadian government – the Prime Minister's Office and the Privy Council Office – is not prepared to leave budget allocations to be determined simply through the bilateral interplay of spenders and guardians. Individual spenders have their own priorities and they are not necessarily those of the government and may not fit with those of the prime minister. Guardians can say 'yes' to this, 'no' to that, and 'maybe' to something else, but there is no natural dynamic to ensure they will attach the right words to the right priorities, or to the non-priorities. Budgeting is about 'how much money' gets spent or is saved. It is also about 'what' it is spent on, 'where' it is spent, 'where' the money is taken from, and, by extension, 'who' benefits and 'who' loses. The outcomes of budgeting are the visible and universal measuring rods for recording the weight and influence of people inside Ottawa – ministers, prime ministers, ministers of finance and officials, and outside Ottawa – premiers, business and labour leaders, and social reformers. Budgets speak to their reputations, stature, and influence and to what they hold to be important. Government priorities shape budgeting, and budgeting shapes government priorities.

'The tradition with budgets,' explains a former adviser to a prime minister, 'had been that the minister of finance was concerned with taxes and tariffs and setting the fiscal framework, and the Treasury Board dealt with allocations. If the prime minister did not support the minister of finance on a budget item, then the finance minister had to leave.'[2] Prime ministers knew they had to support their finance ministers because there were always more spenders than guardians. They also knew that the budget was a matter of confidence for the government in the House of Commons. They also knew that budgets were limited in scope and if the prime minister wanted a major expenditure initiative, such as a new federal–provincial social program, to proceed, it could be announced by the prime minister outside the finance minister's budget. This meant that on most matters of expenditure, most prime ministers were prepared to leave questions of allocation to the minister of finance and the Treasury Board with expenditure priorities being sorted out in the normal bargaining process between spenders and guardians.

Over the last thirty years this has changed. 'Gradually, with [Finance Ministers] Lalonde, Wilson, Martin, Manley, and now Goodale,' explains the former adviser, 'the budget has become the single most important policy event for the government.'[3] It is the event where the minister of finance, not the prime minister, unveils the government's major new initiatives and defines their relative importance in terms of how much or how little new money is to be spent. In short, the minister of finance, not individual spending ministers, announces in one place and at one time the new initiatives to be undertaken in every area of government activity; from defence to health, education, culture, and social development; from foreign affairs to agriculture, fisheries, and mining; and from transportation to industrial development, municipal infrastructure, and Aboriginal programs. While the finance minister is speaking on behalf of the government and on behalf of all ministers, it is his budget. As the importance of the budget has increased, so too has the importance of the minister. As the adviser explains:

> I sat in the gallery [of the House of Commons] with _____ [names a former finance minister from the 1960s] as we listened to the current minister of finance present his budget and announce one new spending initiative after another, all of which were the responsibility of other ministers. After a while the former finance minister turned to me and, with his wry sense of humour, quietly inquired, 'What minister do you suppose the minister of finance will be next?'[4]

The Centre

In budgeting, the minister of finance is important, but in Ottawa, the prime minister is 'the centre.'[5] In the budgeting and management of public money, as in all matters of governance, the prime minister can link issues together or he can separate them out. He can pull things towards himself or he can push things away on to others. He can use the established expenditure management machinery of government such as the Treasury Board or he can create new machinery in the form of special committees of cabinet or the assignment of specific ministerial duties and responsibilities. Some newly created machinery can be used to telegraph a lack of confidence in existing people and existing institutions. It can be used to counterbalance an increasingly influential minister of finance. It can be used to signal an ongoing change or reform in the way things are to be done. New temporary machinery can indicate the urgency required to tackle a pressing problem of the moment and the assignment of an important responsibility to an 'up and coming' minister. The prime minister can focus on the broad objectives and leave the details to his ministers and other officials or he can get immersed in the details himself. He can consult broadly with his cabinet, caucus, and others; he can rely upon his tight circle of trusted advisers; or listen to no one and trust his own instincts. He can draw upon his existing cadre of cabinet ministers or he can bring in and promote new ministers, while at the same time demoting and firing others. He can bring emerging items before caucus for discussion and debate or he can bring fixed decisions to them for information and public announcement.

Prime ministers either instinctively know or soon come to learn that the annual budget provides the opportunities whereas the day-to-day management of public money contains the problems. It is through the budget that prime ministers implement many, but not all, of their priorities. Some prime ministers, however, believe that at times they can become too dependent on their finance ministers and their budgets for the announcement of new spending initiatives. For example, five months in advance of the 24 February 1998 'education budget,' after several years of significant expenditure reductions, Prime Minister Chrétien foreshadowed the $3-billion Canadian Millennium Scholarship Fund in the Speech from the Throne on 23 September 1997, and elaborated on its details the next day in the 'leaders debate' in the House of Commons.

All prime ministers come to the job with priorities, or upon taking office they soon develop them. They may have been in politics for a number of years, serving as important ministers and handling the most difficult files, or they may be newly elected to office with extensive experience in the political party and its organization. They will not know exactly which priorities to push on their first day on the job, but they soon learn that without a limited set of priorities there is little focus in government and without focus, few accomplishments. They also come to learn, sometimes the hard way, that only a few things can be 'very, very important' and therefore priorities must be sharply limited and narrowly focused.[6] They also know that without public money, priorities are only unkept promises, and that it is through the allocation of resources in and around the budget that promises become realities.

Some prime ministers come to the job declaring that they have a clear and limited set of priorities, as was the case with Prime Minister Harper in his minority government of January 2006. But this is the exception. 'His five priorities,' as explained by a former top PCO official, 'showed discipline. They were doable and they were modest, and they stood in sharp contrast to the many priorities of Mr Martin. But they are really only tasks and none of them requires the prime minister in order to accomplish them. In fact he is focused on Quebec and its demands for more autonomy, on fiscal imbalance, and on Afghanistan and our military. There is, however, power in the message of the prime minister saying that there are five priorities.'[7]

While less ambitious priorities may become crystallized on the campaign trail before coming to office, the larger ones often require some time in office and consideration of the opportunities as they unfold. An experienced deputy minister recalls a meeting with Prime Minister Mulroney:

I remember free trade. Mulroney was against it and everybody that was advising him was against it. Big business said they hated it. Macdonald's royal commission recommended we do it, but as they said, it was 'a leap of faith.' Simon Reisman and I went to visit the prime minister and Simon took him through the arguments for free trade, describing all the advantages. The PM said, 'Simon, you are losing me,' and got up from his boardroom and went into his office and came back with a copy of the royal commission report. He put it down on the table and said, 'You see this. It is supported by Macdonald, a Liberal, and it is opposed by Turner, the Liberal leader of the opposition. We're going to do it.'[78]

Prime ministers also come to learn that buried in the day-to-day management of public money are the real problems of government – problems, which if unearthed and placed into a particular context, have the potential to overturn a government. Nothing resonates more with the public and the media than the alleged mismanagement of public money. A serious matter of corruption or a simple matter of mismanagement that can be transformed into a public money scandal can provide the opportunity for the opposition to 'unmake the government.' It is a made-for-media event, with journalists shaping and influencing the story through their well-established reporting techniques of simplification, dramatization, personalization, and pre-formed storylines.[9] A prime minister that places a premium on ethical behaviour within the ministry, a well functioning set of internal controls, and a strong and able Treasury Board might be able to reduce the threat of public money scandals or perhaps detect and correct such problems before they become major public issues. But no system is fail-safe and, in the end, every prime minister will invariably be faced with allegations of mismanagement of public money on his/her watch.

The Most Important of All Relationships

When it comes to new money for new priorities or major expenditure reductions to deal with a ballooning deficit or to reallocate to new initiatives, there are two important players at the centre. As an associate deputy minister in the Department of Finance puts it, 'The key decisions for new important expenditure initiatives are made by the minister of Finance and the prime minister.'[10] Together or apart they stand above all others. The prime minister cannot do it without the minister of finance and the minister of finance cannot do it without the prime minister. There is no relationship that is more critical to the functioning of government and to the determinants of the budget.

Every prime minister and every minister of finance develop their own relationship and way of operating with each other. There have been more than twenty such relationships since 1948 when Louis St Laurent became prime minister and asked Douglas Abbott, who had been the minister of finance under Prime Minister Mackenzie King, to remain in the job. All these relationships are different, depending on personalities, background, aspirations, and circumstances. Some relationships, like those between Prime Minister Pearson and Finance Minister Gordon, can be close and candid, based upon many years of joint experience and friendship. Others, like those between Prime Minister Trudeau and Finance Minister Turner, can be more formal, somewhat awkward and even difficult, based upon different styles, personalities, priorities, and aspirations. Still others, like those between Prime Minister Mulroney and Finance Minister Wilson, can be professional and businesslike while respecting their significantly different personalities, styles, and ambitions. Yet others, like those between Prime Minister Chrétien and Finance Minister Martin, can be uneasy, tense, and highly competitive, requiring strong, ongoing contacts between and among one or two of the most senior political and public service staff in order to make the relationship work.

No matter what the personalities, the backgrounds, the aspirations, or the circumstances, when it comes to the budget certain characteristics largely define the relationship. Donald Savoie writes that in discussing the budget process with his close advisers, Prime Minister Chrétien once observed that 'he could not afford any light to show between his minister of Finance and himself.'[11] Chrétien was referring both to public disagreements and to disagreements between the two in front of cabinet colleagues and deputy ministers. A former adviser to a prime minister, in describing the relationship between the prime minister and the minister of finance, recalls that he never forgot the lesson when the prime minister announced that he would be cutting government expenditures and did not inform his minister of finance. Not only does the finance minister need to be informed, he must also be supported visibly by the prime minister both inside and outside government. The adviser explains:

My job was a bridge between the prime minister and the minister of finance. I established a good working relationship with [names a deputy minister of finance and a key adviser in the minister of finance's office]. We established a team and the prime minister provided strong support for his minister of finance. We did things together. I would support the minister of finance in any discussions outside this group. For example, when a minister or deputy minister would call me, I would always say that I supported the minister of finance. If we had to fight it out, we would do that in private, between the minister of finance and myself. I would get pushed by deputies and ministers but I always knew I did not want to show any difference between us and the finance minister. I would not make the case for them. I would just say, 'You go ahead and make your pitch to the minister of finance.'[12]

The importance of the relationship between the prime minister and the minister of finance, particularly at budget time, should never be underestimated. A former top aide to Prime Minister Chrétien writes: 'No matter how much he might have wanted to help Tobin [a strong spending minister with a close personal relationship to the Prime Minister], the institutional relationship between a prime minister and a finance minister at budget time was far more important to Chrétien than internal Liberal Party politics.'[13]

'Showing no light' does not simply mean that prime ministers and finance ministers agree on budget matters; rather, and perhaps more difficult, it means that they must make every effort to conceal their differences. Some differences stem from different personalities and different political aspirations, while others are a function of their different roles and status within government and their political party. Prime ministers and ministers of finance have different perspectives and interests in the budget. 'In general, the finance minister pushes for tax cuts,' explains an associate deputy minister of finance, 'and the prime minister pushes for expenditure increases.'[14] A former senior economic adviser in the Privy Council Office in the mid-1990s put it this way: 'The core difference in my time between PCO and Finance was that PCO tended to have more of a social agenda than did Finance, which was focused on economic performance and fiscal policy.'[15]

On all matters, but especially on budget matters, the relationship between the prime minister and his minister of finance is a subtle one; differences are more likely to be handled through the skillful art of anticipation than through overt confrontation. A former senior adviser describes the extent of the nuance underpinning the relationship:

The minister of finance came to a pre-budget meeting with the prime minister and set out a series of proposed budget items. The finance minister said he had strong views on the first ten items, while on the eleventh he did not have a strong view. In fact, he could go along with either option A or option B. The prime minister considered the items and agreed to all ten items as proposed by the minister of finance, and then the prime minister said on the eleventh he wanted B. After the meeting, the finance minister told me that he was devastated. I retorted, 'But, you got everything you wanted; how could you possibly be unhappy?' 'Because,' he explained unhesitatingly, 'the PM should have known that on the eleventh item the decision should have been A and not B.'[16]

'There are normally two types of budget disagreements between a prime minister and his minister of finance,' explains a former senior adviser. 'The one is really quite silly and it relates to items that the prime minister might want included in the budget at the very end of the process, after $149.999 billion of a $150 billion budget have been decided. It was small stuff in the overall scheme of things – a few million – but it was something the prime minister wanted for a member of Parliament or for caucus. The prime minister was always concerned with balance; whereas the finance minister would try to argue that such initiatives would break the fiscal framework.'[17]

'The other disagreements are the bigger ones,' explains an adviser:

The prime minister and the minister of finance had a big disagreement in the _____ budget, as the prime minister was very concerned that proposed cuts to seniors' benefits would destabilize the situation in Quebec and this would contribute to uncertainty in Quebec in the face of the referendum. To the contrary, the minister of finance argued that the fiscal markets demanded expenditure cuts and, that significant and real expenditure cuts were needed in order to ensure economic and political stability. The prime minister did not agree and he said he would not do it.[18]

Just days before the unveiling of the budget, the initiative was removed.

Whatever the differences, making the relationship work between the prime minister and the minister of finance is their responsibility and that of their closest advisers. For the prime minister, it is knowing when and how to come to the support of his minister of finance in front of spending ministers. For the minister of finance, it is knowing how many – sometimes very few – face-to-face budget meetings can take place with the prime minister. 'I certainly met with the prime minister,' explains one minister of finance, 'but essentially the responsibility to prepare a

budget is the minister of finance's, so that I would have sper
with _____ and _____ [names two senior advisers in the Prime
Minister's Office] than I would with the prime minister.'[19] For the most
senior advisers it is 'working hard with Finance to get agreement ahead
of time to ensure they had a good meeting, whether it was at the Hill
Office or at 24 Sussex, because the relationship could not stand a bad
meeting.'

When disagreements can no longer be contained, there is a parting
of the ways. The decision on 2 June 2002 by Prime Minister Chrétien to
'fire' Finance Minister Martin and/or the decision by Mr Martin to
'quit' the Finance portfolio signalled that one or perhaps both men
concluded that the time had come when their disagreements, which
were increasingly being exposed to the light of day inside and outside
government, could no longer be tolerated. That differences and disagreements exist is part of the relationship. It is also part of what
makes the relationship effective. What is important for sustaining the
relationship, however, is that these differences and disagreements be
internally contained and quietly managed.

Priorities, Big and Small

When it comes to government priorities, most Canadian prime ministers are most concerned about national unity – depending on the
times and circumstances, some more than others. Although threats to
national unity wax and wane for each prime minister, no one prime
minister wants to preside over the break-up of the country and all
want to be able to argue convincingly upon leaving office that the
country is more unified than when they first arrived. The national
unity priority can be linked to many files, often files that have expenditure implications. Public expenditures, large and small, are justified
in the name of national unity. Sometimes it is particular initiatives that
are specific to a region such as a 'fisheries package' for Atlantic Canada, an income stabilization program for western wheat farmers,
industrial contracts for Ontario and Quebec firms, or special programs for forestry product workers and owners to offset the harmful
effects primarily in British Columbia of the U.S. challenges to the
Canadian export of softwood lumber. At other times it involves
national initiatives that touch all provinces and territories, such as the
adjustments to the equalization formula and associated energy agreements, the signing of a national health accord, or adjustments to the

funding and benefits of employment insurance. It can involve a seemingly endless series of smaller, but no less contentious, expenditure programs that range from funding the sponsorship of community events with the use of the Canada word-mark and Canadian flags (usually seen on government ads), to the awarding of construction and maintenance contracts, to support for conference and cultural centres, hockey arenas, and art galleries.

How do prime ministers get what they want from the minister of finance's budget? This may seem like an odd way of asking the question since after all the prime minister stands at the top with his hands on the levers of power. But remember, the prime minister stands alone and he must continuously ensure that the levers in his hands are connected to real processes that can compel men and women to produce real outcomes. As a former senior adviser to a prime minister explains, 'Sometimes the minister of finance needs to be told he is not the prime minister and he needs to be reminded that he does not decide all the budget priorities.'[20] 'To be sure,' explains a former top PCO official, 'the prime minister must support his minister of finance, but it is not blind support. In the end the prime minister holds the axe and if he wants to marginally adjust the fiscal framework, it will be adjusted. But it is a question of judgment.'[21] To get what he wants, the prime minister must therefore influence the minister of finance through a skillful combination of directions, promises, threats, and counterthreats. In doing so he focuses on two areas – orchestrating the priorities that shape the budget and advocating specific measures for inclusion in the budget.

Prime ministers know that it is too late to await the annual budget process if they are to shape the contents of the budget. They also know that determining priorities through strategic planning in government is all too often a daunting and unproductive task, usually producing more paper than actual decisions. Over the past forty years there has been much written on the various and often failed attempts by prime ministers at strategic planning.[22] Evert Lindquist provides a summary of the rise and fall of planning in Ottawa since its formal beginnings in the late 1960s.[23] If there is one trend, however, that is now well established, it is the tighter linkage by the prime minister, his office and the Privy Council Office of campaign platforms, transition planning, the Speech from the Throne, and the budget. The political groundwork begins with the preparation of the election campaign platform by political parties which can take the form of a single overall document or a series of individual announcements strung out over the course of the campaign.[24] The public service groundwork begins with the transition planning in preparation for a new government and a new prime minister. This work is undertaken at the centre of government by the Privy Council Office as well as in each department when an incumbent government nears the end of its mandate.

The formal planning and priority processes of the government and cabinet provide a general framework for government direction. For the Privy Council Office, the campaign commitments and the Speech from the Throne provide the 'starting point' for the budget. 'For budget planning,' instructs a senior PCO official, 'I start with the campaign promises and the priorities in the Speech from the Throne. We elaborate the proposals a bit and then we cost them ... We and the Prime Minister's Office spend a great deal of time on the Speech from the Throne, and the key is to understand what the prime minister actually said and to ensure that it is reflected in the speech. But,' he cautions, 'getting the right themes for the budget requires a lot of interpretation about the items that are in the Speech from the Throne.'[25]

'We need to deal with PMO when they are doing the priority setting business,' explains a deputy minister. 'For example, if you want to get a spending proposal in the Speech from the Throne, go to the PMO, not PCO, unless it's to the clerk.'[26]

In practice, the formal cabinet planning process for determining government priorities has limited impact in the determination of budget priorities. When it comes to setting priorities for the budget, the key players – priority setters, spenders, and guardians – all know that the priorities of government that emerge from the cabinet planning process never provide the clarity and precision that is required for budget allocations. A top aide to a prime minister recalls his years of experience in the 1990s:

Discussions in cabinet on government priorities were never useful in helping to clarify the precise priorities for budget planning. We would simply hear from ministers that health or national defence was a priority, but ministers never came to a joint view on what specifically should be done. After a day of cabinet discussion on priorities things were no more focussed in terms of specifics than they were the day before. The priorities that emerged were pretty much the same generalities that we went into the meeting with. The cabinet discussion had no impact in making the priorities either clearer or more specific. We never had good discussions of priorities in cabinet when it came to matters of money and the budget. Ministers may have had strong views on certain items but they did not want to fight each other. In fact, the best policy and priorities discussions invariably were on non-financial matters such as the war in Iraq or same-sex marriage.[27]

It has not been for want of trying that ministers have had difficulty in determining budget priorities. 'We have tried everything with cabinet ministers,' explained one senior PMO official, 'overviews, planning sessions, even voting, but it has never worked.'[28] For sure, every cabinet finds it difficult if not impossible to set specific priorities for budgets. The collective agreement on any single, specific budget priority means that the spending ambitions of one, or at best, a few ministers are met, but those of most other ministers are precluded. Individual ministers, if forced to choose, soon learn to prefer that budget priorities remain vague and general so that as many of their own priorities can be justified under the broad, overall general heading. The end result is that, at best, priorities determined by cabinet remain multiple, conflicting, and vague. Indeed, this has been the underlying explanation in the literature for the lack of cabinet-determined specific budget priorities over most of the last century.[29]

In the 1970s and early 1980s, when budgets were expanding, ministers attempted to participate and often did participate in the collective determination of priorities because, in the end, there were many priorities and there was more new money for everyone or nearly everyone. Priorities were, without a doubt, numerous, soft, and flexible and so, too, were expenditure decisions, but there was an opportunity for spending ministers to secure items in the budget by participating in cabinet committee discussions. As the fiscal situation dramatically hardened, so did budget priorities and expenditure trade-offs. As long as everyone was forced to participate in the cuts and reductions, individual ministers were prepared to go along with the narrowly focused budget priorities as decided by the prime minister and the minister of finance. 'With the government's commitment (in the mid-1990s) to eliminate the deficit,' instructs a former top PCO official, 'the budget became "the everything," and the decision-making process for nearly everything. Everything was approved in the context of the budget with the decisions being taken by the prime minister and the minister of finance, using as little cabinet committee process as possible.'[30]

In this environment, ministers have little incentive and interest in a collective discussion with their cabinet colleagues of real budget priorities around specific spending proposals. A seasoned Treasury Board official explains:

When a minister comes forward with a spending proposal to cab
mittee there is no incentive for any minister to challenge any other minister because they all know that the decision on whether the item goes
ahead will eventually be made by the prime minister and the minister of
finance. Cabinet committees then simply provide approval in principle
for nearly all items that come before them. They say yes to everything.
There is no competition for funds at the cabinet table. In the past, cabinet
committees tried to rank order priorities and they even tried to vote on
the items, but nothing has worked because no action by any minister
affects the actions of any other. Why would a minister want to frustrate
his or her colleague in cabinet committee?[31]

In short, ministers know that the prime minister and the minister of
finance will decide on the specific new expenditure initiatives, independent of whatever general priorities may emerge from a cabinet or
cabinet committee priority setting meeting. On the rare occasion when
ministers collectively come to agreement in cabinet committees on a
clear and specific expenditure priority, they do not provide guidance
for the initiatives that are under consideration by the prime minister
and the minister of finance. Instead, ministers act strategically, in their
own individual interests, ignoring all the proposals assumed to be on
the list of the prime minister and the minister of finance and strategically put forward one or two consensus spending proposals not on the
list. In short, these cabinet committee priority discussions on expenditures serve to increase the scope for spending; they do not help with
the determination of priorities for trade-offs.

As ministers began to ignore the items on the priority list of the prime
minister and the minister of finance, the prime minister and minister of
finance began to ignore the cabinet committees even when there was
opportunity for additional spending. A newly appointed senior Treasury
Board official observes that 'in some budgets, the minister of finance and
the prime minister are not even picking the small items from the priority
list of proposals put forward by cabinet committees.'[32]

A frustrated senior Finance official, one in a long list of officials commenting on this perverse behaviour, laments his experience:

In 1998, the cabinet committees were restless and they wanted to have
funds to pursue initiatives. Finance Minister Martin agreed they would
get some funding and they had to set out priorities for their funding, from
one to ten. They did a pretty good job, but they put on the cabinet committee list those items that they knew Martin and Chrétien wanted at the

bottom of their priority list. For their efforts, ministers were provided with $300 million, but it didn't stop there as lots of ministers tried to get back-door deals with the minister of finance. In fact, we spent double the $300 million on back-door, side deals. All 'the Martinites' [the finance minister's supporters] got funded and there was some real concerns raised by lots of ministers. It was a sickening process.[33]

The Prime Minister's Arms

In budget making, as in central processes of government, the reach and grasp of the prime minister extend from his two arms – the Prime Minister's Office (PMO) and the Privy Council Office (PCO). Gordon Robertson, a former and highly respected Clerk of the Privy Council and secretary to the cabinet, has provided the most fundamental and the most enduring distinction between these two important offices. 'The Prime Minister's Office is partisan, politically oriented, yet operationally sensitive. The Privy Council Office is non-partisan, operationally oriented, yet politically sensitive.' He goes on to observe that 'it has been established practice between the principal secretary to the prime minister and his senior staff on the one hand, and the clerk of the Privy Council and his senior staff on the other, that they share the same fact base but keep out of each other's affairs. What is known in each office is provided freely and openly to the other if it is relevant or needed for its work, but each acts from a perspective and in a role quite different from the other.'[34]

Gordon Robertson's first dictum, 'sharing the same fact base,' often leads to sharing the same list of priorities for government. To be sure the PMO will want to focus on one or two big priorities and those expenditure programs of personal interest to the prime minister. The PCO will worry about due process and due diligence to ensure that there has been adequate and required interdepartmental consultation among officials prior to expenditure proposals being considered by cabinet. The PCO also worries about maintaining cabinet solidarity and avoiding, or carefully managing, ministerial discussions around expenditure proposals that might split the cabinet. The PCO, but particularly the PMO, understand the need for some small expenditure allocations to the non-priorities to ensure all ministers are on side with the few, large priorities. A former PMO adviser explains: 'Every minister has got a lot of stakeholders to deal with and some must be satisfied, and that requires spending some public money. On defence, the defence contractors are an important

and powerful lobby. And then there is the caucus and i⸱
budget you need two or three things in order to satisfy t⸱⸱
the caucus. When the minister of finance provided funding for the volu⸱⸱
teer firefighters, he got a standing ovation at national caucus.' But there is
a limit to how much can be spent on non-priorities. 'What I wanted to
avoid most,' he continues, 'was making spending decisions on proposals
that were non-priorities. This meant that funds were dispersed too
broadly and key priorities were underfunded or not funded at all.'[35]

In general, it is thought that finance ministers are less inclined to
want to have a large number of small items in their budgets. Certainly
this is the case 'in any cabinet discussion,' explains the former PMO
official, 'where the minister of finance would emphasize how tight the
fiscal framework was and that he could not afford very much, if anything, by way of new expenditures. What the minister of finance
wanted to avoid most was a shopping list of initiatives.'[36] It is, however, not just prime ministers who are concerned about balancing budgets by providing some small expenditure items that can benefit
particular political constituencies. Some ministers of finance are as
well, especially those with aspirations for the prime minister's job and
who wish to raise their stature with certain Members of Parliament.
But, in the eyes of the prime minister and the PMO, finance ministers
want to be seen as protecting the integrity of their budget from political incursions, and therefore they make their case for including 'non-
priority initiatives' in their budgets on the high ground of priorities
rather than on the low ground of politics, even if the credibility of their
argument might seem like a stretch. The former PMO aide recalls:

> One time the minister of finance included a very small expenditure item –
> some $35 million over several years – on the priority list to be announced in
> the budget. I asked him what the item was and why it was on the list. It sure
> didn't look like a priority to me. He explained it was to deal with single-
> industry communities in remote and rural locations, which he explained in
> his view was going to become the biggest, most fundamental and most
> important issue in the twenty-first century.[37]

The priority setters in the PCO and the PMO work closely together in
the determination of budget priorities. While they have taken over some
of the budget priority setting space that traditionally was occupied by
the Department of Finance, they do not work on their own. The Department of Finance has a strong interest in ensuring that priorities for each

budget are established and that they reflect the concerns of their minister and the ongoing preoccupations of the department with Canada's economic and fiscal performance. As a key economic adviser in the PCO observes, 'There is always room for misinterpretation [of the priorities] by the Department of Finance. They have their own agenda – both fiscal and policy.'[38]

Relative to the Department of Finance, priority setters in the PMO and PCO have more influence in determining what programs will receive new spending than in determining what specific programs will be cut. When it comes to the nasty job of expenditure cuts, central priority setters prefer to leave the task to the guardians. In the 'Guns of August' cuts in the summer of 1978, when Prime Minister Trudeau announced a $2.5-billion reduction in government expenditures, he left the actual decisions about what and where to cut largely in the hands of the president of the Treasury Board and its then influential Secretariat. More recently, the minister and the Department of Finance were largely left to their own devices in deciding how much the expenditures of each department would be reduced in the 1995 'Program Review' budget. The former minister of finance put it clearly: ' ... essentially what happened is that _____ [the deputy minister of finance] and _____ [the associate deputy minister] and I sat down one day in my office and we went through government spending line by line, department by department, and we arrived at a set of targets, a cut in every single government department but one. We said that is what they had to do if we were going to hit our 3 per cent (of GDP deficit reduction) target in 1998.'[39]

Sometimes the Department of Finance appears to play a larger role in shaping the budget priorities and the Privy Council Office a smaller role. This can happen when a general understanding has emerged between the prime minister and the minister of finance about a single overall and dominant theme and priority for the budget. While it may appear that the Department of Finance is determining priorities, this is not the case. They are, however, determining the budget proposals with the support and input of spending departments to the exclusion of the priority setters in the Privy Council Office. This happened in the 1998 'Education Budget' when the minister of finance and his department worked exclusively with only one spending minister and department – the minister and Department of Human Resources Development Canada (HRDC) – and quietly fashioned a set of budget initiatives.

Priority setters in the PMO and the PCO cannot act independently of the minister and the Department of Finance in determining budget priorities. Nor can the minister of finance and his department act independently of the prime minister and the PMO and PCO priority setters. The more it is a question of what should be the overall priority for the budget, the more the influence from the prime minister and the priority setters. The more it is a matter of what should be the initiative to effect the agreed priority, the more the influence from the Finance guardians. A senior adviser to a prime minister put it this way, 'The prime minister decides the budget priorities on what he thinks are important. He had kids, the knowledge economy, and health care. He then left it to the finance minister to develop the proposals and to recommend the levels.'[40]

It is very rare that there is a fundamental and visible disagreement over what the overall priorities should be, largely because these themes have already been reflected in the government's campaign commitments, in its Speech from the Throne, and in various speeches by the prime minister and the minister of finance. More often it is a question over the timing and sequencing of expenditure initiatives and the amount of new funding that can be provided for a specific priority initiative at that time. But when it comes down to the crunch, the PMO is the ultimate priority setter, prepared to declare and articulate the two or three big priorities that should shape the budget. At the level of priorities, the authority of the prime minister's closest advisers to speak politically and personally on his behalf is accepted and is uncontested by all.

While there may be agreement on the priorities, PCO is not prepared to simply let the expenditure proposals of either the guardians in Finance or the spenders in departments go unchallenged. This has become increasingly the case as more and more major budget decisions are being taken by the minister of finance and the prime minister without the benefit of full and complete review of proposals by ministers in cabinet committees and by officials in interdepartmental committees. A former top PCO official explains it this way:

> The PCO job is a policy challenge role and it is most important when the proposals don't go through the cabinet committee process. We need some proof that the proposal will work, that it is needed, that it is costed, and that it will produce desired results. We need a rigorous analysis, an evidence-based approach. When only two people – the minister of finance and the prime minister – are making the decisions and there is a growing disquiet with bilateral deal-making, the clerk needs to ensure there is a rigorous review. There is a need for counter-balance in the system.[41]

Priority setters in the PCO are more prepared than their counterparts in the PMO to get down into the details of spending proposals. This can and does lead to differences over what priority initiatives should receive funding. A former assistant deputy minister recalls his experience:

> On the 'learning agenda' there were meetings with PMO, PCO, Industry Canada, and HRDC. The PM [prime minister] agreed to attend a high pro-file skills summit and the PMO was looking for a major 'announceable' for him. We [Industry Canada and Human Resources Development Canada] were considering the establishment of a national learning institute along the lines of the independent foundations like the Canada Foundation for Inno-vation in order to make use of year-end money. PMO was pushing hard for it and PCO was opposed to it on the grounds there was no new money available for this. We discussed things right up to the day before the summit without a clear indication of what if anything would be announced. The day of the announcement I was on the morning plane to Toronto and _____ [names an adviser to the prime minister] told me that the prime minister would be announcing $100 million for the creation of the new institute.[42]

Some might think that officials in the Prime Minister's Office prefer a Privy Council Office that focuses more on the process of priority setting and budget making than on the actual proposals themselves. This tends not to be the case. Top PMO officials do not depend upon the PCO to caution the prime minister that balancing many small budget initiatives can all too easily lead to too many priorities and too little focus. In most circumstances, the minister of finance and his department are all too ready to do that. But experienced, top PMO officials do understand that a Clerk of the Privy Council who is prepared to immerse him or herself into the substance of budget proposals, to challenge proposals and to put forward specific views can serve as a useful ally and effective foil in dealing with the minister and the Department of Finance, both of whom have a considerable monopoly on the assumptions and information that underlie each initiative. A former senior PMO official lamented a clerk who was not a 'full-budget player' and applauded another who was, because it meant that the prime minister could exert more influence with the minister of finance in getting more of his priorities into the budget, at higher levels of funding. From the PCO perspective, a rigorous PCO challenge function increases the likelihood of weeding out risky propos-als and dealing with unwelcome problems, especially when the final budget decisions were being taken by only two people – the minister of

finance and the prime minister – without the benefit of cabinet committee consideration.

The experienced clerk, however, instinctively knows that getting too
close with the PMO and having to become too assertive with Finance
and spending deputies and ministers on specific budget proposals can
put him/her on slippery ground. Sometimes it is better for the clerk to
let the top political priority setters and the top fiscal guardians fight it
out, knowing that, as the most senior public servant, maintaining cabinet solidarity and government unity must in the end be the top priority for government and ultimately, indeed, for the prime minister.

Gordon Robertson's other dictum that the Privy Council Office and
the Prime Minister's Office 'keep(ing) out of each others affairs' provides the clue for understanding how skillful spenders deal differently
with these two offices. A spending deputy minister explains:

> PCO wants to know that you have done your due diligence and that your
> individual problem – your department's or minister's problem – is not
> going to cause a collective problem for the system. PCO hates when there is
> a major problem at the cabinet table. They do not want a split in cabinet – a
> split along left and right, or between Quebec and the rest of Canada. When
> there is a real potential for a split then you have to get the prime minister on
> side. It is then a leadership issue and it takes the prime minister. You then
> need to demonstrate to the Prime Minister's Office that this is an issue that
> the prime minister has to take on own his shoulders.[43]

As a former clerk of the Privy Council Office explains, the advice
from PCO may be subtle but it does carry weight: 'These interventions
by PCO staff will generally take the shape of subtly formulated suggestions to the authors of cabinet memoranda and will have the effect
of directly influencing policy formulation.'[44] However, even if the
advice of PCO is more soft and impressionistic than hard and factual, it
is especially critical for, and often sought after by, departments with
aspirations for new spending. 'We need PCO so that we can understand what is going on,' explains a big spending deputy minister.

> Last week we met with _____ [names a top PCO official] and got an
> overview of the government's priorities in the short and long term. He
> made it sound very clear, but in reality it is complete chaos – I know, I've
> been there. But, clarity or not, we do need PCO for 'a reading' on where we
> are in the cycle and a sophisticated assessment of where ministers are: are

they nervous? are they anxious? are they in a crisis mode? are they receptive? We need to understand how important federal visibility is for ministers. For example, with Quebec we need to figure out whether the government wants to make deals with the province right now or should we 'hang tough' for future negotiations. We can never get a clear answer but we do need some sort of reading so we don't screw up.[45]

For the ambitious and sophisticated spending departments, the Privy Council Office's 'take' on priorities is never enough. Getting the views of the Prime Minister's Office is 'especially important,' continues the spending deputy minister,

because we and the minister need to be able to tell others – departments, Finance, and even the PCO – that what we are proposing matters politically. When the PMO is not strong on Quebec, you need to let others know the proposal is supported by _____ [names a strong Quebec regional minister]. In other PMOs, the chief of staff could speak for Quebec. We need PMO to push both Finance and PCO when issues are urgent and need to be done quickly. The decision-making process takes time, and it may be necessary to set up an accelerated process. For example, the timing on a project in Ontario was critical and we used our minister's chief of staff, working with PMO, to get PCO to accelerate the decision-making.[46]

On matters of priorities and expenditures, clerks of the Privy Council have different styles. A former assistant deputy minister who worked closely with several explains how one was a facilitator and the other a director:

_____ [names a former clerk] in chairing meetings of ministers would start by making it clear that he expected that ministers would focus on the following issues and provide some clarity or direction with respect to A, B, or C. He indicated that it was up to them to decide, but these are the areas or issues where decisions are needed. He indicated that it was the role of officials to facilitate the discussion. In contrast, _____ [names another former clerk] is very skilled at dealing bilaterally with the ministers that he has to in order to bring them onside. In negotiations on the _____ [names a major file of the prime minister], he knew he needed a particular minister's support and he stayed very close to him and his office, deliberately targeting all his efforts to get it and making accommodations only where absolutely necessary.[47]

Whatever the style of the clerk, perhaps his most important responsibility in the making of any budget is to keep ministers on side and avoid a major split between a spending minister and the minister of finance or a split within the cabinet. This essential responsibility is also shared by the chief of staff to the prime minister. 'What to avoid most,' explains a top adviser to a prime minister, 'is a clash between the finance minister and the prime minister that could lead to a split in the government.'[48]

Top officials in the PMO and the PCO are expected to be proactive and to anticipate bitter and irreconcilable clashes between spenders and guardians and to implement counter-strategies to avoid unwanted ministerial resignations. Sometimes, when there is a real and imminent threat of a fundamental difference on a budget item between a powerful spending minister and the minister of finance, the concerted and coordinated efforts of PMO and PCO are not successful. A former top PMO adviser recalls:

_____ [names an influential minister] decided he would use his relationship with the prime minister to beat the minister of finance and he chose a significant expenditure increase for _____ [names a major new spending initiative] to do it. He had a list of a half dozen budget items and got everything from the minister of finance, but one. Any other minister would have been happy with that. These were agonizing sessions. The deputy minister of finance called me to say that this major spending proposal was not included in the budget and that if it was to be included he was not sure that his minister would stay in the job. The clerk and I got on the phone to the prime minister who asked, 'What does the departmental deputy minister think of the proposal?' We told him that he was not pushing it as hard as the minister. The prime minister asked us to draft up some budget language along the lines of a vague possibility for the proposal sometime in the distant future. The next day we called the prime minister and he asked us to call the departmental deputy minister and read him the proposed language. I asked, 'Should we call the minister?' The prime minister said, 'No.' We then called the deputy minister and read him the language. The minister claimed he never saw the budget language until it was in the budget. He had a fit and said that he was betrayed by the minister of finance.[49]

Traditionally, the PCO has shaped government priorities in its role as 'the gatekeeper' to the cabinet decision-making process. Acting on behalf of the prime minister and in the interest of collective ministerial decision-making, the PCO has traditionally shaped and determined what, when, and under what circumstances various spending proposals get onto the agenda of cabinet and its committees. PCO has the power to decide whether and when a spending proposal is ready for consideration by a cabinet committee by ensuring, through consultations with the Treasury Board Secretariat and the Department of Finance, that the spending department has undertaken the necessary homework – detailing and costing the proposal, conducting the necessary interdepartmental consultation, engaging and consulting stakeholders as needed, and linking the proposal to the government's priorities.[50]

In the past this gatekeeping role was particularly important and effective when the minister of finance, the Treasury Board, and, in some instances, cabinet committees were making individual expenditure allocation decisions throughout the course of the fiscal year and outside the regular, annual budget preparation process of the minister of finance. However, since 1994, with the introduction of what was dubbed as the 'new expenditure management system,' the gatekeeping role has changed significantly. In an effort to restrain spending, the government required that 'decisions on new initiatives and any spending reallocations required to finance those initiatives will generally occur during the budget planning process.'[51] While this has had not stopped the flow of spending proposals coming to cabinet from outside of the regular budget planning process, it has contributed significantly in changing the way in which ministers consider spending proposals that come before cabinet committees. In short, because any and all proposals for new spending are now considered and automatically approved in principle by cabinet committees to be later decided by the prime minister and the minister of finance, the importance of the PCO as a gatekeeper to cabinet decision-making has diminished.

What is now important is not the gatekeeper to the cabinet committee where little or nothing is determined by way of expenditure decisions because everything is simply approved in principle, but the gatekeeper to the prime minister and the minister of finance where some expenditure proposals are turned down or ignored, and others get funding and approval to proceed. The consequences, some of them unintended, of this seemingly progressive change in the expenditure management system have been significant and far-reaching. A veteran Treasury Board official reflects on the frustration shared by many:

Cabinet committees are engorged with memoranda to cabinet (MCs). One department – Indian Affairs and Northern Development – has over fifty individual cabinet submissions under way. With fifty submissions for one department rattling around in the system, there is no sense of priority and it is absorbing a lot of unproductive time and taking away from other things. We are analysing all these MCs and when they go forward we spend most of our time preparing briefing notes for the president of the Treasury Board, which are never used at cabinet committee because there is no interest or incentive for any minister – including our own – to criticize or take on the proposals of another minister.[52]

To make matters worse, explains the disheartened official, 'when departments go to cabinet committees with spending proposals the costing is dreadful and there is an absence of information and knowledge about what is in the A-base of existing spending and no requirement to link the new proposal to the A-base.'[53] If the committee 'decisions' are of little consequence for spending – approval in principle for everything – there is little incentive to do good analysis on any of the proposals.

Fifteen stories higher, in the East Tower of L'Esplande Laurier, an associate deputy minister of finance shares the same frustration:

On the smaller budget items, cabinet committees actually do operate like focus groups, every spending proposal gets approved in principle and no minister challenges the proposals of his or her colleagues because they all know that in the end it is the finance minister and the prime minister who decide. Sometimes the small budget proposals have approval in principle from cabinet committees, but at other times they have not yet been approved by cabinet committee and are considered after the budget when the spending levels and program have already been announced.[54]

Priority Setters and Shift Points

Priority setters have become powerful and influential actors in the budgetary process. A considerable degree of their influence stems from the continuing need for restraint in government expenditures and the widespread political and public commitment to a balanced budget or better. The collective will of spenders and guardians, operating together, sometimes in conflict and sometimes in cooperation, has turned out to be insufficient to determine the budget priorities with the precision and specificity that is now required for focused and tight budgets. Priority setters who can stand apart and above the day-to-day scrimmages between the spenders and guardians can have considerable influence in not only shaping the shifts in fiscal directions but also in determining the priorities to be included within the budget.

While priority setters may stand above the fray, they do not work strictly on their own in accordance with their own script. Working from the political and policy centre of government, they have fashioned a planning and communication process that translates the political commitments contained in party platforms and campaign messages into a governing agenda as set out in the Speech from the Throne. This document, no longer a general statement of wishes and general intentions that can sometimes be quietly forgotten, directly shapes and influences the contents of the budget. It is the PMO and PCO priority setters who make the important interpretations as to what the general words of the speech actually mean as they craft the thematic statements and directions to shape the proposals in the budget. Priority setters work with and through both spenders and guardians. If a specific policy priority is to be pushed, priority setters do not hesitate to engage with a spending department, agency or minister in influencing the minister and Department of Finance. To priority setters this is not spending but investing. If restraint is called for, they are ready to say no to spending departments and ministers in order to protect a narrow and predetermined set of prime ministerial priorities. To priority setters this is not restraint but priority spending. For them, priorities are not only about planning and trade-offs but also about communicating and convincing.

Individual spending ministers have found it difficult to reach consensus on a set of specific, operational budget priorities, preferring instead to find protection under the umbrella of general government directions and broad objectives with the hope that they can justify their projects under the 'catch-all' priority. As spending ministers collectively have failed to crystallize budget priorities, priority setters have more than ever resorted to making the priority determinations themselves. While Finance guardians would prefer the flexibility and influence that comes from determining the precise budget priorities themselves, in the face of the need for clear priorities to either reduce spending or strictly limit increases to what is important, they are increasingly engaged in discussions on these matters with the Prime Minister's Office and the Privy Council Office. With increasingly focused and defined budget priorities, political conflict among ministers and departments increases because so

many are left out, and so too does the importance of ef
management on the part of central priority setters and gu
    Every serious spender, minister or deputy minister, i
nificant new money, 'checks with' the Prime Minister's Omce aru ...
Privy Council Office to ensure that their proposal 'gets on' and, with
any luck, it's placed near the top of the priority list. Similarly, major
spending interests outside government do not simply make their case
to the spending department and the guardians but also seek out the
support of the central priority setters. Not only are priority setters
influential in bringing forward particular expenditure proposals but
they are important in shaping the 'shift points' that occasionally occur
in the normal incremental process of budgeting when the expenditures
of one department or area of government increase dramatically or
when it is determined that the overall expenditures must be reduced
significantly.

    Priority setters focus exclusively on the front end of the budgetary
process. They are concerned with where the new money goes, who it
goes to, and how much. They are prepared to argue strongly and
sometimes vehemently against specific expenditure proposals for fear
that they will take funds away from what they consider to be the real
priorities. In general, they worry little, sometimes not at all, about how
the money is to be spent or what program results will eventually be
achieved, although, on occasion, a Clerk of the Privy Council may
come to see the need for a vigorous PCO challenge role as specific budget allocation decisions are increasingly being taken exclusively by the
prime minister and the minister of finance. It is not because program
results are unimportant, but rather because they are busy getting the
priorities determined that priority setters are prepared to leave these
matters of budget implementation to be shaped by the interaction
among spenders, guardians, and financial watchdogs. If priority setters focus on the priorities for public money, then the financial watchdogs are preoccupied with the performance of public money.

5 The Financial Watchdog: A Bark with a Bite

In God we trust; everything else we audit.

Anonymous

An audit is the difference between what is and what should be.

Assistant Auditor General

Canada's Auditor General Act ... lists the duties of the auditor general as auditing, reporting, and expressing opinion, bringing to attention and advising both Parliament and officials of government. The underlying reason – the purpose of the auditor general's work – is, however, not made explicit.

Otto Brodtrick, 'How Does an Auditor General's Office See Itself?'[1]

Accounting ... is a useful device for taking the debatable – like goals, strategies, the division of labor, and the locus of coordination and control – out of the realm of the political and therefore beyond the realm of debate.

Mark A. Covaleski and Mark W. Dirsmith, 'The Budgetary Process of Power Politics'[2]

We are not the watchdog, Parliament is the watchdog; they watch over the public purse. We provide information, assessment, and assurance so parliamentarians can do their job.

Assistant Auditor General

External audit has become a vicious beast. The more you use it, the more you have to feed it.

Former top Privy Council Office official

In 1963, when Walter Gordon was the minister of finance, Auditor General Maxwell Henderson and his office were not players in the budgetary process. Their responsibilities, as set out in the Financial Administration Act under which the office had functioned since 1951, were to report on revenues as they came in, and on expenditures after they went out. However, this was about to change. For the next thirteen years, this 'embattled crusader for taxpayers' interests'[3] issued reports on 'non-productive payments.' In doing so, he set the stage for his successor, Jim Macdonnell, to spearhead the most fundamental changes to the Auditor General Act. Macdonnell's rhetorical claim[4] in his 1976 Auditor General's report that 'Parliament – and indeed the Government – has lost, or is close to losing, effective control of the public purse'[5] was widely accepted by the media, the opposition, and the public as an accurate description of the current situation. To deal with the political fall out, the Liberal government of the day agreed to dramatically expand the mandate of the Office of the Auditor General (OAG).[6]

With this new act, the focus of the OAG shifted dramatically and fundamentally from financial audit to 'value for money' audit (now called performance audit), displacing much of the burden of financial audit to internal auditors in departments and agencies.[7] With this major legislative change, the Auditor General acquired significant, new influence in shaping how the expenditure of 'public money' in the form of budgets would be assessed in terms of the 'value' or performance of government programs. In short, the Auditor General and his or her office – the financial watchdog – had become important players, all be it indirect players, in the budgetary process.

The road that transformed the role of the financial watchdog into a budget player was paved by a significant and important guardian – the Treasury Board Secretariat. Up to the 1960s, when budgeting was done by line-item, there was no need to link expenditures to programs. No one needed what they could not use. Money was allocated to buy things – planes, pencils, and paper clips – and to pay public servants to undertake assigned tasks. Financial audits – to determine if the financial transactions conformed to the laws and regulations – were sufficient for guardians, parliamentarians, and the public to judge probity and compliance in the use of the public money. However, as Sharon Sutherland notes, when the Treasury Board Secretariat established on a government-wide basis the requirement to link expenditures and programs by introducing the Planning, Programming, and Budgeting System (PPBS), it 'opened the door [for] the OAG to become a future program auditor who would undertake validation of departments' reported program results.'[8] If the government was to have a program budget, then the government's auditor should 'audit' the spending departments' evaluative and performance work on their programs. Today, the Auditor General is not just 'a' program auditor; he/she is 'the' program auditor, and as such has become an important player, passing independent judgment on the linkage between the expenditures provided by guardians and the results achieved by spenders.

Since the mid-1960s, the program budget has established the essential logic that not only determines how budgeting is to be done – by program expenditures – but also how achievement is to be measured – by program results. Ironically, the introduction of the program budget has created a major and insurmountable problem; that is, the need to establish on a government-wide basis program results that are true and verifiable and can be linked to program expenditures. As explored in chapter 3, decreeing that this will be done is one thing; making it happen has proved to be quite another. Since 1971 none of the expenditure and performance management reforms and procedures have come close to solving this problem of objectively linking budget expenditures with program performance. The reforms and procedures have been continuous and there have been many. To name only a few, there was the Operational Performance Measurement System (OPMS) and Management by Objectives (MBO) in the 1970s; the Policy and Expenditure Management System (PEMS) in the early 1980s; the Increased Ministerial Authority and Accountability (IMAA) in the mid-1980s; the Expenditure Management System, Business Planning, and Program Review in the mid-1990s; Reform of the Estimates and Results for Canadians, and Performance Reporting in the early 2000s. In fact, the Auditor General has developed a 'model'[9] for rating departmental performance reports and has consistently reported on the 'the painfully slow progress of departments toward managing for results'[10] and the 'disappointing progress.'[11] As long as this problem cannot be solved – and there is much experience and theory to suggest that it will not be – there is every reason to believe that the watchdog will continue to exercise important judgments on what governments have and have not achieved through public expenditures.[12]

To be sure, when it comes to specific budget issues facing government – how much public money to spend, where to spend, and how to manage – financial watchdogs do not have direct and immediate influence, as is the case with spenders, guardians, and priority setters. Their vantage point is from outside the budget and, indeed, from outside the government of the day. They are not insiders who shape and influence specific budget decisions as they get made in the budgetary process; rather, with their continuous and regular public reporting, they focus on government spending 'after-the-fact.' At best, their influence in and on the budgetary process is indirect, long term, and subtle.

Understanding the role of financial watchdogs in the budget process begins with understanding the OAG. In the words of the Auditor General, the office 'audits federal government operations and provides Parliament with independent information, advice and assurance to help hold the government to account for its stewardship of public funds.'[13] The most significant 'audit' is the performance audit (previously called value for money audits) with about thirty conducted each year and absorbing nearly 60 per cent of the OAG budget. These so-called audits – more accurately, 'management studies' – focus on the following questions: Are programs being run with due regard for economy, efficiency, and environmental impact? Does the government have the means in place to measure their effectiveness? In the face of criticisms by many about the difficulty in drawing clear lines between policy and administration or between directions and management, the Auditor General takes the position that these 'audits do not question the merits of government policies. Rather, they examine the government's management practices, controls, and reporting systems based on its own public administration policies and on best practices.'[14]

Building Credibility on Professionalism and Independence

Financial watchdogs focus beyond the budgetary process – reporting on what has happened or not happened with the public money that has been spent by departments and agencies. It is, however, through their public reports and their high level of credibility with the opposition, the media, and the public, that financial watchdogs exercise considerable indirect influence throughout the budgetary process. By focusing on one of the most fundamental questions of budgeting and indeed of governance – Is the taxpayer getting 'value for money' from government expenditures? – these watchdogs rise above the preoccupations of spenders, guardians, and priority setters heavily involved in the transactions of budgeting. If the other players focus on the 'doing' of budgeting, then the financial watchdogs associate themselves with the 'so what' of budgeting. To be sure, watchdogs address questions after the fact – after the priorities have been determined, after the guardians have made the allocations, and after the spenders have done their spending. In this regard, their influence over budgeting will never be more than indirect. They are not influencing directly a budget as it is made; rather, through their published findings about previous budgets and how the public money was spent, they have indirect influence on future budgets and on the public's and media's perceptions of budgets and public money. They have significant influence with Parliament, the media, and the public about how governments are perceived in terms of the size, allocation, and management of the public budget. What, then, is the nature of their indirect and subtle influence on budgeting, how is it exercised, and to what effect?

Financial watchdogs derive their influence from their perceived credibility, which is anchored in their developing a reputation for professionalism and their independence, both of which they carefully control. 'Credibility is our most important asset,' explains a top ranking OAG official, 'and our credibility is a function of objectivity and independence. Credibility is critical because we make recommendations and if people were to attack the fundamentals of our work that would weaken our recommendations and they would not be supported.'[15] 'Credibility is key,' insists a former Auditor General. 'You must not lose your credibility. Part of your effectiveness is due to the importance and prestige of the office. You can not do shoddy work. There is a very high degree of credibility with the work of the office. It does quality and professional work and it defends the basic principles of good accounting.'[16]

But the exercise of their professionalism and independence depends on an important paradox that all experienced auditors have come to understand and that the most skilled incorporate into their day-to-day practice. The paradox is that the inherent conflict and disagreement, which almost always exists between the overseers of public money on the one hand and the managers of public money on the other, must be overt and visible for watchdogs to have significant influence.[17] Within government, this conflict can be between departmental spenders and central guardians, or between spending ministers and Treasury Board ministers, or spending departments and the OAG. Within a weak parliamentary and strong cabinet system of government, most conflicts will remain invisible to the public. However, those conflicts that become most visible and overt are those concerned with disagreements between the government of the day and the opposition parties who are trying to 'unmake' the government. The independence of an Auditor General acquires special meaning when there are visible disagreements between political parties, and the work of the Auditor General invariably produces audits and reports that make these disagreements visible. Governments need external watchdogs to maintain their legitimacy with the public to govern, and opposition parties need watchdogs to assist them in holding governments to account and to establish publicly some of the reasons why they should take over the governing. Lest anyone be under the mistaken impression that an Auditor General's report cannot contribute, at least in part, to the downfall of a government, they should look no further than the report of the Auditor General into the sponsorship program deposited in the House of Commons on 10 February 2004, the results of the Gomery Commission of Inquiry, and the election of Prime Minister Stephen Harper's Conservative minority government on 23 January 2006.[18]

When conflicts over matters of program performance remain internal to a department or even internal to a government, they are usually absorbed and managed. In some cases, the conflict might simply be ignored; in most other cases, departments and governments quietly make adjustments to their practices and procedures or to their programs and budgets without the distracting fanfare of the media spotlight, parliamentary question period, or sometimes rancorous political debate. When the conflicts, however, are external and visible – between government and opposition parties – they are considerably more difficult to ignore, harder to absorb, and require considerable adjustment and visible change. These adjustments and changes are almost always made within the caldron of parliamentary partisan debate and under the glare of the media.

When two parties (spenders and guardians or government and opposition) find that they have little by way of disagreement on the administration and performance of an expenditure program, then financial watchdogs find that they have little to do. An Auditor General whose annual reports simply affirm that programs are difficult to manage but the government and officials are doing about as well as anyone could expect is not likely to raise conflict between government and the opposition, although it might prod the opposition to question the competence and professionalism of the auditor. Only when there is disagreement – usually centred around, whether and the extent to which a program and/or the expenditure of public money is uneconomical, inefficient, and ineffective – can financial watchdogs make a visible contribution. Financial watchdogs will argue that, by presenting 'the facts' as objective and independent, their audits bring a level of professional judgment to

what is otherwise simply a political debate. But they will also acknowledge that conflict is an inherent and necessary ingredient in their work.
Like the overnight watchdog, the success of the auditor is rarely judged
by the number of robberies that are invisibly prevented, but by the number of robberies that are visibly detected and the number of robbers that
are caught.[19]

In Canada's parliamentary system, the legislature is responsible for
overseeing the government and its actions and for holding the government accountable for its handling of public money. As described by the
Auditor General, the office is responsible for 'legislative auditing,' which
'plays a central role in holding governments to account.'[20] According to
a former Auditor General, the office 'provides objective information,
advice, and assurance that parliamentarians can draw on in their scrutiny of government spending and performance. Elected representatives
need this independent reporting so they can effectively question or challenge the government on its actions.' On interviewing auditors, one is
immediately struck by the extent and depth to which this common language and basic logic is ingrained in the professionals of the audit community and in the practise of their craft.

The influence of the financial watchdog rests on the premise that publishing information that is perceived to be independent and credible
about the government's errors, mismanagement, and poor performance
is a powerful tool in the hands of the opposition, the media, and the
public. The reason why much public knowledge and information is not
normally powerful is because it is disputed, contested, and often conflicting. As a consequence, the public does not come to view most
knowledge and information as independent and authoritative. It is simply another study, another report, or another analysis, and it is seen to
carry with it the organizational biases, prejudices, and distortions of the
particular institution, profession, or discipline that prepared it. In capi-
talizing on the inherent conflict between governments and opposition
parties and in carefully nurturing with the public their own independence and professional reputations, Auditors General around the world,
and especially in Canada, have been particularly successful in maintaining and enhancing the credibility and independence of their public
knowledge and, in so doing, making it powerful and convincing.

When it comes to matters of public money and program performance,
auditors explain in their own words how they develop and maintain a
reputation for credible and professional work. In short, it comes down to
being able to convince the public that the auditors are right:

Doing credible work and professional work is extremely tough. For example, on the issue of the taxation of income trusts we had a different view than the Department of Finance. The professional legal community, because they had clients benefiting from the existing income trusts arrangements supported the Department of Finance, although in private they told me that we were right. I needed to be absolutely sure that what my auditors were telling me was right. You need to be right and this is very complex.[21]

For auditors, professionalism is about not making mistakes. 'We never want to make a mistake because that will erode our credibility. We constantly check and recheck everything, and then recheck again,' explains a senior assistant auditor.[22] 'What you want to avoid,' explains a former Auditor General, 'is any mistake or any failure. Failure means a loss of credibility and as a result you will suffer in the eyes of Parliament and in the eyes of the public.'[23] A senior OAG official elaborates:

You have got to be right, and most important, avoid being wrong. Being wrong means making a factual and material error, for example, assigning a responsibility to an organization that it does not have, getting the numbers wrong (saying the cost was $10 million when in fact it was only $3 million), or saying that something was done in a department when it was not. We cannot be wrong because it puts our credibility into question and our credibility is most important. When we tell something to Parliament or the public, we have to be right because they have come to believe that what we tell them is right. They believe it and then they believe in us.[24]

'Being right,' instructs a former top OAG official, 'requires quality work and, to ensure that, our modus operandi is to go outside and get the best possible professional advice we can.'[25] 'We peer review nearly everything,' notes another senior auditor, 'and we work to agreed standards on performance audits. On financial audits, we use the same standards as the most reputable private sector accounting firms, like for instance, Ernst and Young.'[26] If one determinant of credibility is the perception of professionalism, then the perception of independence is the other. 'Independence is absolutely key to our credibility,' asserts a former Auditor General:

The AG has got to be seen as not being part of the system; someone who gets no benefit from it. In Canada, unlike in Australia – and in Europe it is worse – the AG does not come from the public service and does not return to it. Once your term is up, you're gone and you're done. The AG has a ten year term, operates with the hiring flexibility of a separate employer, and has funding for external professional contracts. In the public sector, the AG is seen to be more independent than in the private sector, because he doesn't need to provide special professional services for part of his funding. However, having to get agreement from the Treasury Board on the AG's budget undercuts the independence of the AG. The appointment process for the AGs is ok. It is non-partisan. In British Columbia, the need for the formal approval of parties in the House puts aside any suggestion of a political appointment, although at the federal level there is an informal discussion with party leaders. We need to make sure that the independence is preserved, because independence means there is no reason to dilute the message.[27]

When independent external sources confirm contentious auditor findings, the Auditor General reminds Parliament and the public. This helps to build credibility for the office, explains a senior official:

Immediately after the release of the first Gomery report into the sponsorship program and its advertising activities, the auditor general put out a press release indicating that Justice Gomery had confirmed her audit findings. It was important to do this because there were a number of experienced, high-profile witnesses who had sharply challenged the AG's findings and said that she was wrong. It was necessary to confirm and reinforce the fact that we were right.[28]

The credibility of Auditors General is a function of how they are perceived by Parliament, the public, and the media. Sometimes they might be perceived as less relevant to the affairs of the nation, at which point a newly appointed Auditor General might search for new ways to enhance the relevance and reputation of the office. One former top auditor explains how, during his term, it was necessary 'to have a vision of the OAG that went beyond the strict letter of the mandate':

We viewed our mandate as 'making a difference' and we called it that. It required an imaginative work plan and a real good appreciation for the management challenges facing the public service. It allowed the OAG to focus on major and important issues facing the government like human resources, governance, Crown corporations, Revenue Canada, and the deficit. There is, however, a fine line that divides your mandate from matters of policy and you need to be careful that you do not cross it. It is not a sharp line, but a virtual line. From time to time you are challenged, but if you are never accused of crossing the line, then you are not exercising your mandate enough. The minister of CIDA [Canadian International Development Agency] said it was none of our business to comment on whether the international aid budget was spread too thin across too many countries and too many projects. We knew it wasn't our mandate, but we also knew there was a need to get the limited and declining budget more focused on key priorities. On the government's fiscal deficit issue, we were concerned with the consequences. I did not want it to be said later, 'Where were the auditors?' We needed to find an angle – a legitimate perspective – for the AG. We focused on information and the quality of the economic and fiscal forecasts by the Department of Finance ... How often do you cross the line? Not often, three or four times in ten years. But, when you have credibility, you don't have to stick just to the sure issues.[29]

Auditors General are closely attuned to how they are perceived by the public and the media. At times, Auditors General can become worried that increased public attention might lead to a 'misunderstanding' of the role of their office, particularly in terms of its relationship to Parliament and to parliamentarians. As explained by one auditor, a skillful Auditor General takes great care in his/her public communications about the role of the office:

The AG no longer uses the term 'watchdog' in her speeches. There has been a lot of confusion in the press, thinking that we are the watchdog. In Washington, the GAO [General Accounting Office] views themselves as watchdogs and they even have tee shirts with a watchdog on the front. This can lead to problems and confusion: the notion that the AG is a personality in her own right when, in fact, she is an agent of Parliament. The term 'watchdog' underplayed the role of Parliament and the role of parliamentarians.[30]

Maintaining credibility requires knowing how to handle success. For the Auditor General the appearance of too much success can, in fact, be dangerous to one's credibility. The sponsorship scandal and the widely reported public inquiry by Justice Gomery into the program has given the Auditor General a public and media profile that, over time, could diminish her credibility with parliamentarians. She is careful in her communications to adjust this perception. A senior auditor explains why:

Under Sheila we have focused on better communication – writing and communicating in simple and plain language. In part this was because of the sponsorship scandal and because of the extensive publicity about the office. Radio talk shows were lauding her. She was receiving dozens of roses from taxpayers. *Saturday Night* magazine had a full page picture of her on the front cover under the title 'watchdog' and *Reader's Digest* referred to her as 'the taxpayers' friend.' There were even calls for Sheila Fraser for prime minister and for Governor General. This was a misunderstanding of the role of the Auditor General because, at the end of the day, all we can do is advise Parliament and it is up to them ... [this is] the result of too much success, perhaps. If the AG is perceived too much like this we might be vulnerable to partisan political attacks and that would damage our credibility and destroy our independence.[31]

Professionalism and independence are the cornerstones for credibility.

The Performance Audit: The Audit for All Reasons

The performance audit is an effective and influential tool in the hands of a skilled external auditor. The performance audit, while appearing to ask simple, technical, and seemingly objective questions, actually focuses on the most political and subjective of all questions – How well is government doing? Auditors insist that they are simply asking the question – Does government have the information and the systems in place to know how well their programs and expenditures are doing? 'Performance audits are no longer called value for money audits because,' as a senior auditor explains, 'value for money determinations are really the responsibility of Parliament.'[32]

Most auditors through their training and experience have come to believe that performance audits are more akin to objective 'audits' than to the more subjective 'management studies,' which in fact they are. Even when pressed, auditors remain firmly convinced of their own professional position. 'What makes a performance audit an audit and not a management study,' insists a senior auditor, 'is that it uses criteria that are clear and explicit, and these are well established criteria. These standards are widely recognized by the professional associations like the CICA [Canadian Institute of Chartered Accountants] and the CSA [Canadian Standards Association]. We audit against the expectations that have been set out explicitly by Treasury Board in their policies and procedures.'[33] Another senior auditor puts it this way, 'Performance audit is called an audit and not a study because it is required to be done that way as part of the professional standards established by the CICA.'[34]

Whatever the questions – policy or otherwise – posed by performance audits, the answers are conveyed as factual 'audit findings' and not as opinions, points of view, or observations. While parliamentarians, the media, and the public would be hard pressed to distinguish between 'performance audits,' 'financial audits,' 'special examinations,' and 'studies' (the terms of the Auditor General), they do appear to accept without question the legitimacy of an audit as an important, perhaps the most important, determinant on whether or not there is value for money in the government's expenditures and programs. This is because most people, in situations of doubt, conflict, mistrust, and danger, will check up on one another. For example, it is in these situations that we check the video replay to see if the puck went over the line, check out a second medical opinion, or check up to see if our children did their homework. Experience has indicated that when it comes to matters of public money, citizens make considerable demands for checking up on it and, hence, they are prepared to readily accept the need for and the findings of an independent performance audit.

The use of the performance audit has increased significantly in the past fifteen years. Just over forty years ago, when Walter Gordon was minister of finance in 1965, there were no performance audits. By 1981, when Allan MacEachen was the minister of finance and Kenneth Dye was just beginning his ten-year term, only a small portion of the OAG budget went to performance audits. Today, performance audits take up 60 per cent of the budget, with thirty such audits being undertaken each year. The performance audit has become the audit for all reasons. Most important, it is called an audit and not a study or an examination. Because it is called an audit, it has come to be seen by many in the public as objective; it is seen to be about public money, usually considered mismanaged, wasteful or lost; and it is seen to be about identifying errors, errors of omission as well as errors of commission. This allows the performance audit to focus on nearly all aspects of the management and mismanagement of public money – from misuse of public funds, to breaking government rules, uneconomical expenditures, duplication of expenditure, inefficiency and waste in government, ineffective programs, lack of results, misappropriation of expenditures, bribery and corruption, failure by politicians and public servants to take action, and so on.

The Auditor General Act gives the OAG 'considerable discretion' to determine what areas of government to examine when doing its performance audits. How does the OAG decide what performance audits to undertake? In its own words, it

- focuses on the areas in which federal government organizations face the highest risk,
- consider(s) a topic area significant if it has the potential for improving government results,
- take(s) into account such practical issues as the availability of its financial and human resources, and
- identifies the areas that are most significant and relevant to Parliament.[35]

One study suggests that the Office of the Auditor General 'moves with public and political opinion.'[36] When asked by a member of the Public Accounts Committee how the Office of the Auditor General chooses the areas for 'value for money' audits, one Auditor General replied:

We have our antenna up and we are scanning the environment all the time. We try to be abreast of all issues of interest to Parliament. I am made particularly aware of all the political issues that face the House, just to know what the to-ing and fro-ing is in political issues. Where they impact on audit issues, they are discussed immediately and considered in our plans.[37]

While the auditors 'pay particular attention to requests for audits from parliamentary committees,' they are quick to note that 'the ultimate decision about what to audit rests with the Auditor General.'[38] A former top official explains: 'The office has a disciplined approach to its work plan, a multi-year, three- to five-year plan, with the first year being pretty certain and years two and three having some flexibility in case something unexpected happens. We seek input from the Public Accounts Committee and other committees of Parliament, but parliamentarians are usually content to simply concur in what we propose and to ask questions.'[39]

Mutual Expectations

Despite their independence, financial watchdogs have considerable dealings with other players in the budgetary process. They need these interactions to ensure that their work is accurate and relevant, and, perhaps most important, to avoid charges that they have made mistakes. To preserve and maintain their independence, a set of mutual expectations about their role has developed among various public money players. Everyone – spenders, guardians, and priority setters – accept that the job of the financial watchdog is to keep its eyes on things and, when things start to go wrong, to bark loudly. Indeed, between the financial watchdog and each of these three players, there is a set of mutual expectations that govern behaviour. No one expects the financial watchdog to view a glass of water as half full; it is invariably half empty (some say 'always broken'), because the job is to detect what could or has gone wrong and to compel spenders, guardians, and priority setters to take corrective action. Auditors are pessimistic because all others are expected to be optimistic. Auditors are sceptical because others will be credulous. Auditors are watchers and reporters, and spenders, guardians, and priority setters are planners and doers. Auditors audit for mistakes knowing that when publicly exposed, spenders, guardians, and priority setters will be forced to correct them. Spenders, guardians, and priority setters look for opportunities knowing that they must abide by the constraints of prudent, economical, and efficient public management if they are to avoid negative audit reports. In their dealings with one another, each player expects the other to do his/her job.

'I dealt with the Clerk of the Privy Council, the secretary and president of the Treasury Board, and the deputy minister and minister of finance,' noted a former Auditor General, 'and with deputy ministers, although much of the work and relationship with departments was undertaken by the OAG staff under the responsibility of the assistant auditors general assigned to various portfolios.' But the relationship is more than this. A former Auditor General insists that being an agent of Parliament 'does not preclude our relationship with government. A purist might say we should have no relationship with government but that would be counterproductive. We are independent from the executive, but they seek our advice on issues of management and accountability. We are not interfering with the governing role. Having the relationship with the government helps you to produce an audit report that is useful.'[40]

The financial watchdog, however, as an agent of Parliament, stands apart from the spenders, guardians, and priority setters who are an integral part of the government of the day. As it should be, the independence of the watchdog clearly limits the direct influence that the auditor general has over the budget process while at the same time it strengthens his/her indirect influence. As a result, not every disagreement can be temporarily resolved between financial watchdogs and spenders, guardians, and priority setters. There are and will be fundamental areas of disagreement between them, usually based on deeply held financial and accounting principles. Unlike spenders, guardians, and priority setters, financial watchdogs do not need to reach agreements through compromises and adjustments in order for budget decisions to be made. Budgets will be and are made with and without financial watchdogs. Instead, financial watchdogs work from what they can encourage others to perceive as generally accepted accounting principles in order to maintain their independence and credibility. This means that sometimes there will be mutual adjustments and compromise. As one Auditor General noted: 'I had a relationship with the executive of government that was productive. Deputies sought out our views and I went to them as individuals. The relationship does not need to be adversarial.' But it also means that at other times there will be stalemates and stand-offs and 'agreements to disagree.'[41]

Watching Both Spenders and Guardians

When it comes to the relationship between the watchdog and spenders, the initial assumption may that they get along with each other, but more important is the respect for their fundamental differences. It is not a matter of trust without verification; nor is it, trust first and verification later. For the auditor, it is verification first, and possibly trust later. A seasoned senior OAG official explains:

> There is a mythology about how deputy ministers deal with the AG. When a new AG arrives all the deputies say: 'We are here, we are your friends, and if you understand our environment we will get along.' That is how _____ [names a former AG] was received. Things, however, quickly changed, and the attitude of _____ [names a former AG] changed when a couple of deputies became economical with the truth.[42]

For at least one senior audit official, the relationship of the OAG to departments and agencies is still one that is 'cordial, but not cozy ... It's a professional relationship. We want to ensure that our risk assessment is valid from the perspective of the department and so we share it with them and meet to discuss it. For any of our audits, it is critical to go over the objectives, terms of reference, and criteria with the department. When an audit is confrontational, it does not serve anybody.'[43] Good relationships with departments are important because the OAG

wants to ensure that departments and agencies follow-up and implement the audit findings. 'In general, we are doing a pretty good job,'
explains the senior AOG official. 'For many years our post-audit surveys have indicated that after four years about 45 per cent of our audit
recommendations are being implemented.'[44]

At first blush, one is tempted to think that the financial watchdog
has the greatest differences with spending departments. To be sure, the
OAG keeps a watchful eye on spending departments and regularly –
four times a year – produces large public reports critical of departmental spending practices and their financial management. These audit
reports provide an opportunity for departments to respond to the findings of the Auditor General, with a surprisingly large portion of the
responses not so much disagreeing with the AG's findings but, rather,
indicating that improvement and corrective action have already been
underway for some time. Experienced spending ministers and deputy
ministers instinctively know that picking a public, visible fight with
the Auditor General is almost never a winning strategy.

In fact, however, while rarely seen, the most fundamental and most
deeply divisive issues are usually between the financial watchdog and
the guardians – the Treasury Board Secretariat and the Department of
Finance. 'With the Treasury Board Secretariat there was the most friction and the most discussion,' explains a former top audit official. 'The
Auditor General and the secretary or a deputy secretary of Treasury
Board are in front of parliamentary committees all the time.'[45] Part of
the friction arises from the unique nature of the relationship between
the Auditor General and the Treasury Board. The Auditor General
'audits' how well or how poorly the government performs both in its
general management and financial management functions. The AG
also believes that she/he has a responsibility to occasionally advise the
Treasury Board and the government on what the standards should be
for proper management in general and effective financial management
in particular. In short, not only does the Auditor General audit performance against government standards but it also has a hand in determining what those standards will be. A senior OAG official explains:

> The AG does play a role in shaping the government-wide policies and
> standards that we in turn use when we audit government operations, pro-
> grams, and expenditures. In the mid-1990s, we pushed the TBS to estab-
> lish a clear set of standards for the monitoring and auditing of financial
> management. At the time, TBS had a document, more than an inch thick,

described as 'one hundred thousand good things for financial management.' It included everything imaginable, did not set clear priorities, was
a 'one-size-fits-all' model, and viewed departmental senior financial officers as simple bookkeepers. We developed a joint process with TBS to
review and modernize the standards, and we developed a joint model
called the 'financial management capability model.' There was some
reluctance on the part of TBS to implement it because of the NIH [not
invented here] phenomena. But eventually, with modification, discussion,
and the increasing need for change, it was finally accepted by the Treasury Board as the financial management standard.[46]

But the senior official offers a caution:

There are real limits on how far we can push the government, because
what is most important is that in the end we maintain our independence
and our credibility so that we can audit the performance of the government
against the standards set out in the policy. When it comes to accounting
and financial management, there are professional claims, and we in the
OAG are entitled to have a professional view and to share that view with
the TBS and the government. A lot depends upon the nature of the relationship between the OAG and the deputy ministers. Sometimes it is closer
and sometimes it is more distant, but the OAG is always independent. For
example, right now when the government is making a great many proposals for significant administrative change, we are not and do not want to be
that close. Why not? Because we do not want to be perceived as pushing
the government's administrative reform agenda when we will subsequently be responsible for auditing its performance against it.[47]

How far, then, does the AG go into setting the financial and managerial
policy standards against which it will audit the government? Quite some
distance. 'But you want to avoid getting dragged into a discussion on
proposed legislation,' instructs a former top official.[48] However, according to one OAG official, 'when the professional reputation and interests
of the office are at stake we believe we have a right and duty to have a
view on a policy issue. For example, the introduction of accrual accounting into the government was something that we needed to have a view
on and we had a duty to express our views on it.'[49] Since 1986, the OAG
has been promoting both accrual accounting and accrual-based budgeting. Both were introduced in the 1990s in Australia and New Zealand,
and there is little doubt among budget analysts that it 'introduces biases

toward capital spending which is amortized over the life of the asset, and away from non-capital spending.'[50]

With the minister and the Department of Finance, the Auditor General also has significant disagreements – disagreements that go to the most fundamental principles of public sector accounting. 'With Finance,' explains a former Auditor General, 'there were very distinct issues: reporting around the surplus and the deficit, and the handling, from an accounting point of view, of certain policy decisions such as the establishment of arm's-length foundations. We simply agreed to disagree.' He goes on to explain how angry a finance minister can be with inflexible accounting principles: 'One night I got pulled out of meeting for an urgent call from the minister of finance. He was just getting onto "the *Challenger*" [airplane] at the airport and he had three items he was ready to put in his budget. From an accounting point of view, they were all non-starters and I said, "No way." If I were to give in I might just as well pack my bags and be gone. The minister's reaction the next day: _____ [names a senior Finance official] called to say that minister's plane "took off" without having to start the engines.'[51]

'Auditors,' explains one, 'are not prepared to let politics stand in the way of good accounting,' even if it means that 'a rift can develop between the minister of finance and the Auditor General around such issues as the accounting of foundations, also on the payments for the equalization deals with Nova Scotia and Newfoundland.'[52]

More recently the Auditor General has gone considerably beyond simply proposing standards for financial management and accounting. In 2006 the Auditor General assessed the government's entire expenditure management system, which extends from the centre of government to departments and agencies. In her own words, this system 'is at the heart of the operation of government … (and) touches everything that the government does.' In undertaking this so-called audit, she concluded that

- the system 'has become less effective since the budget went into surplus,'
- the Treasury Board Secretariat's annual update of funding for existing programs is done 'without a systematic review,'
- 'the secretariat lacks the necessary financial and performance information to perform its expenditure oversight,'
- 'opportunities for trade-offs between new and ongoing spending may be missed,' and
- 'central agencies can not always properly assess new proposals.'[53]

Clearly, the Auditor General is significantly extending her reach and influence from 'audits' of government practices and procedures to broad ranging studies of the most central political and administrative decision-making processes of government. Surprisingly, with the exception of denying the Auditor General access to cabinet confidences, there has been little 'push back' from the government – the various central agencies (Treasury Board Secretariat, Department of Finance, and the Privy Council Office) have simply responded by generally accepting her numerous recommendations.

The Watchdog and Internal Departmental Auditors

The internal auditors in departments and agencies are the distant cousins of the auditors in the Office of the Auditor General. One might be tempted to think that they stem from the same blood lines, but they do not. They are more like the out-of-town in-laws who are occasionally seen, but more often forgotten. While auditors in the internal audit bureaus in the departments and agencies are also financial watchdogs, they are not outposts of the OAG. Where the role of the Auditor General is clear and in some sense simple – to provide information to Parliament in order for parliamentarians to hold the government to account for its stewardship of public money – the job of the internal auditors is not. Their role is complex and ambiguous because they must serve several masters. Their job is to provide information and opinions, 'independent from line management,'[54] to the minister, the deputy minister, and the Comptroller General on departmental and government-wide management concerning 'the adequacy of the controls, processes and measures to mitigate risks.'[55]

The internal auditors, formally called the chief audit executives, serve three different masters, each with different interests. First, they must provide the deputy minister with 'annual holistic opinions ... on the effectiveness and adequacy of risk management, control, and governance processes in their departments, as well as reporting on individual risk-based audits.' Second, they must 'support' the comptroller general who 'report(s) annually to Treasury Board on the state of risk management, control and governance processes across government, addressing fundamental controls, including basic reporting controls for financial statements, thematic or sectoral controls, and the results of risk-based internal audit work carried out within departments.'[56]

Third, they must advise the departmental audit committee in preparation for the annual in camera meetings with the minister on significant items arising from their work.

On the one hand, internal auditors are part of the department, 'reporting to the deputy minister,' while on the other, they are expected to ensure their 'organizational independence.' They also report to the independent departmental audit committee, which under the 'preferred model' has its entire membership from outside government and, at a minimum, at least more than half. This important committee is responsible for the 'active oversight of core areas of departmental control and accountability in an integrated and systematic way.'[57] In addition, 'after discussion with the deputy head,' they are expected to 'inform the comptroller general without delay of any issue of risk, control or management practice that may be of significance to the government and/or require the Treasury Board Secretariat's involvement.'[58]

It is not just deputy ministers who worry about this dramatic increase in the independence of internal audit and the risk that audit committees independent of government will be uninformed about the nature of the department's business. A former senior official in the OAG explains that 'internal audit is done for management, for senior management in the department. They are working for the deputy minister. I am concerned that the new proposals of the government [in the Federal Accountability Act] are trying to make internal audit too independent and that it will be another external audit. Internal audit is for management. It is and must be a tool for the deputy minister. The key issue is not independence. It is access [to the deputy minister].'[59] The auditor also worries that the working papers of departmental internal auditors, unlike those of the Auditor General, are accessible under ATI (Access to Information) legislation. As a result, 'they are less than fully effective. They cannot call a spade a spade because even before they complete their audits, partial and incomplete results will be publicly available under ATI.'[60]

The Watchdog and Parliamentarians

The financial watchdog, as an agent of Parliament, is very sensitive to its concerns and needs, to its committees, and to individual parliamentarians. Like the skilful spender, auditors have learned the importance of cultivating a clientele and a constituency. 'Our relationship with

Parliament is the most dynamic of any institution in government, at both the federal and provincial levels,' boasts a former top auditor. 'We meet fifty to sixty times a year with parliamentary committees, and no other institution in government comes even close to that. This is unique in Canada and around the world. It is a great accomplishment.'[61] At least one member of Parliament, however, feels that Parliament has become too dependent on the Auditor General: 'The auditor has gone to a status where we agree with everything she says ... the auditor is a little too powerful in the eyes of the [Public Accounts] Committee [and] we shouldn't become too raptured.'[62]

Auditors focus their efforts on parliamentary committees and not on individual MPs. Meeting with parliamentary committees to either secure their concurrence to the Auditor General's work plan or to explain their audit findings is one thing, responding to a request from an individual member of Parliament is another. 'What you do not want to do,' explains a former Auditor General, 'is to get dragged into the political agenda of an individual member of Parliament who, for example, might have a bee in his bonnet about a military base closure or a grant to a particular organization. When a Bloc MP wanted the AG to audit a contribution from Heritage Canada to the Canadian Council on National Unity, we simply did a brief report and concluded that we had no jurisdiction with respect to accessing the records of the council. It is, however, easier to turn down a request from a single MP than from an entire committee.'[63]

Indirect Influence, but Influence

Years ago, in a simpler world of budgeting, the Auditor General and his/her office were viewed as an offspring of the guardians, an independent voice that advocated restraint in government and the prudent and economical management of public spending. But, in recent years, the OAG – through a dramatic expansion in the use of its legislative tool, the performance audit; its increased credibility with Parliament, the media, and the public; a careful nurturing of an image of professionalism and independence; and the publicly accepted myth of the objectivity of audit – has become a full-grown budget player. At one time, the strength of the watchdog was found in its bark; the ability to 'blow the whistle' on waste and misuse of government expenditure. Today, the reports by the financial watchdog have increasingly more bite as the credibility of the Auditor General in the eye of the public has significantly increased and its public trust of governments, politicians, public servants, and public institutions has significantly decreased.

While the influence of the AG on the management of public money is direct and considerable, her/his influence on the actual budget is only indirect and subtle. Focusing on the mismanagement of public money after it has been spent, the Office of the Auditor General, through the use of its powerful performance audit, indirectly shapes the public's attitudes and views about how much, where, and through what means public money should be spent in future budgets. 'I am very concerned with the increasing influence of the Auditor General,' notes a former top Privy Council Office official. 'At one time, the Auditor General provided global assurance for government, but with value for money and performance auditing, the AG has become the pet of the opposition. This external watchdog has had an unbelievable impact on the government's agenda.'[64]

The increase in the Auditor General's influence found much of its origins in the establishment of program budgeting. When budgeting became structured around programs and what they purported to accomplish and actually did or didn't accomplish, rather than around line-item inputs and how many were used, there opened up a whole new world of activities and linkages that needed to be watched and reported on. The Auditor General needed to ensure that independent reports were being produced on whether programs had clearly defined objectives; outputs, results, and outcomes were specified; costs and expenditures were identified; and all of these could be related in order to assess probity, efficiency, and the possibility of assessing effectiveness of public expenditures. Increasing concerns about how well public money was being managed and how it was being spent began to indirectly influence public perceptions about how big the budget should be, where allocations should be made, and how well public money was managed.

Financial watchdogs have been especially successful in creating a public image of professionalism and independence, both of which have substantially contributed to their credibility in the eyes of the public. Many citizens see them as agents of the taxpayer rather than as agents of Parliament, operating with independence and autonomy to produce seemingly unassailable public information and analysis to hold the government to account. Much less visible has been their increasing ability to 'work below the radar' in the development of important relationships with guardians (Finance and the Treasury Board Secretariat), spenders, and priority setters (the Privy Council Office). Not only are they directly reporting on what the government does with its public money and how well or how poorly it does it, but with their powerful performance audits and high level of public credibility, they are also indirectly influencing and even shaping the government's policies, standards, and systems by which these judgments are made.

As their names suggest, the four principal public money players – spenders, guardians, priority setters, and financial watchdogs – have separate, distinct, and competing interests in the public money process. To be sure, these roles can and do creep together and can even overlap as the various players test their independence and autonomy over others. For example, at times, the Department of Finance guardians have become spenders and the financial watchdogs have pushed beyond the limits of their audit mandate and attempted to influence departmental spenders or central guardians. However, over the long term, no one role can sustain itself by doing the job of others. Indeed, each expects the others will do their own jobs. Over time, the interaction across these four players creates a stable pattern of mutual expectations, which guide and condition their behaviour. As the influence of one player changes – becoming too strong or too weak – the behaviour of the others slowly adjusts. This pattern of expectations and behaviour across the players can be explored by focusing on the three major decisions in the public money process: determining fiscal aggregates, allocating expenditures, and securing efficiency in program delivery and prudence in financial management. The next chapter examines how these decisions get made through the interactions of the players.

PART THREE

The Public Money Processes

6 Fiscal Aggregates: Controlling Totals

Thank goodness for a strong government commitment to a balanced budget or better. Right now it's the only way we can maintain some discipline.

Finance assistant deputy minister

The budget plan ... provides the aggregate planned program spending number, the aggregate public debt charge number, the aggregate revenues, and out of that comes the planned budgetary balance.

Former deputy minister of finance[1]

... the fiscal framework ... what that means is that, essentially, the minister of finance will do a status quo projection of his revenues, his existing expenditure commitments, and on the basis of that set of projections, what he will say is, 'Do I have extra money?' If he comes to the conclusion that he has extra money, then he has got to decide where it is going to go. Is it going to go to spending? Is it going to go to tax cuts? What is he going to do with it?

Former finance minister Paul Martin[2]

What they've [the IMF] said is the forecasters tend to be conservative in making their projections. And then the government is conservative in assessing those projections. And what that actually means is that we make very sure this country is not going to run a deficit again.

Former finance minister Ralph Goodale[3]

We believe the deficit has been the only effective restraint on congressional spending ... Relying on the deficit to check spending is admittedly a second-best solution – but it is better than nothing.

Milton Friedman, 'Why the Twin Deficits Are a Blessing'[4]

How does the government decide how much it should spend, how much it should raise in revenue, and how large the fiscal surplus or deficit should be? In other words, how does the government set its fiscal framework – its overall level of expenditures, revenues, and the fiscal balance? Getting answers to these seemingly straightforward questions is not as simple as it might first seem. To be sure, no government starts from a blank sheet of paper with full and complete discretion to shape and then determine these three levels at will. Nor do governments simply accept the inevitability of economic and fiscal trends with the levels for expenditures, revenues, and fiscal balances simply emerging as if untouched by human hands. When it comes to public money, the government has choices, however limited they may appear to be at times. Citizens and taxpayers expect the government to create choices and to exercise its discretion in making them, and all governments inherently understand that it is in their interest to do so.

As complex as these choices may seem to outsiders, the government, more specifically the minister of finance and his department, in consultation with the prime minister has a well-developed approach for making these decisions. In short, decisions about the fiscal framework are taken with an eye to past problems, current challenges, and future prospects. The fiscal framework itself is a record of the past. It is the cumulative result of the fiscal impact of past decisions. It records at the most macro and fundamental level the size of the public sector relative to the private economy. It is a record of who won and who lost in the critical battles over whether and how much should be spent on public programs and how much should remain in private pockets through the limitation or reduction of taxes. It tells a nation and its people about how indebted it is to itself and to those investors outside its borders who are holding some of the debt paper and formulating impressions about how much more debt they are prepared to underwrite and at what rates of interest. It records the rate of growth in the fiscal aggregates and establishes a benchmark of perceptions about whether certain aggregates are growing too fast or too slow. It provides information on the record of a government's economic accomplishments and failures that various domestic and international fiscal and expenditure watchdogs use to compare to previous commitments. When compared over time to the fiscal frameworks of provincial and municipal governments, the fiscal framework of the federal government is used to create impressions and provide information around contentious matters of fiscal imbalance or balance within the federation.

The fiscal framework is a stocktaking of the current situation. At any point in time, the state of the government's fiscal framework indicates what the government is currently doing or about to do. The fiscal framework is the reservoir of financial resources, from which flows much government action. It is a comprehensive financial account that highlights the costs of carrying on with the existing expenditure commitments of government. It is a summary ledger that includes the potential source of funds for new spending initiatives that are fully developed and ready to go, for others that are still in an embryonic state, and even for some not yet on the drawing board. The fiscal framework is a document that disciplines the ambitions of the government and its spending ministers and departments and sets out the fiscal anchors for the budget.

The fiscal framework is a signal for the future. It is a document of intentions and promises. It forecasts the fiscal parameters within which the government will operate over the near term. It provides a future expenditure framework within which spenders are expected to formulate their plans and around which priority setters and spenders can shape their aspirations. It signals to private sector investors and consumers the government's fiscal intentions and, when combined with the government's (the Bank of Canada's) monetary policy, it is the essence of the government's overall macroeconomic management strategy. The framework carries weight. It provides commitment to the public. It provides a government-wide, financial framework within which the financial watchdog can undertake his/her work. It sets out the fiscal targets, usually in the form of the fiscal balance, to which the government will be held to account by the opposition, the taxpayer, and the investor.

Credibility and Uncertainty

In establishing the fiscal framework, the minister of finance, with the support of the prime minister, seeks to establish a level of control and predictability in the government's expenditures, revenues, and fiscal balance. Without sufficient control there will be chaos – ballooning and undisciplined expenditures, unstable and volatile revenues, unwanted fiscal imbalances, and escalating public debt which, in turn, will significantly reduce the government's discretion and make control ever more difficult. But as much as finance ministers and prime ministers might try, they instinctively know, or come to learn, that control is an illusive concept. In an uncertain and impressionistic world, it is never possible to get the control over the fiscal framework that may be required in the circumstances. In fact, when it comes to the fiscal framework, they don't think or speak in terms of control – it is too difficult to achieve. Instead, they think and act in terms of establishing credibility and dealing with uncertainty.

Establishing and maintaining fiscal credibility in a world of uncertainty is the major and constant challenge for the finance department and minister. A senior official reflects back on a decade (mid-1980s to mid-1990s) of limited success and significant underachievement characterized by new problems and changing circumstances:

> By 1984 we had had a deficit for some time but there was not a lot of major concern about it. Up to that point, it was viewed as a cyclical and not a structural problem – things would improve as the economy improved. We had general support from economists and academics. By 1985, however, and with a new minister, we realized we had to make some structural changes in order to deal with the deficit and move toward balancing the budget. But our plans were quickly derailed in 1985 by our proposed modifications to OAS [Old Age Security] when the elderly lobby in the person of 'Charlie Brown' chastised the prime minister for undermining 'the sacred trust.' After that we lost all interest in deficit reduction. Exercises were attempted but nothing happened in 1986. In 1987, we made structural changes on the tax side believing they would be important for the economy and the fiscal framework. We wanted to focus on PIT [personal income tax], CIT [corporate income tax], and sales tax all in one, but the United States went ahead on business tax and therefore we had to focus on PIT and CIT, with GST [goods and services tax] going later. We had to make the structural changes revenue-neutral, which of course had a fiscal cost in the short run.
>
> In 1987 there was the stock market crash and 'black October.' The Bank of Canada acted quickly and increased the money supply, and, as it turned out, things turned around fairly quickly, in fact, faster and better than expected. With an election coming up in 1988, ministers decided to spend. By 1989 we were into recession, which was exacerbated with rising interest rates in 1990–1. We didn't get any rebound after the recession. NAFTA [North American Free Trade Agreement] cost us in the short run with lower growth and less revenue. We had some troubles with the economic and fiscal forecasts, but we tended to be closer than the other forecasters. We were well within the reasonable errors. The minister [Michael

Wilson, minister of finance 1984–91] tried to cut expenditures but no one listened to him. By the time Maz [Don Mazankowski, minister of finance 1991–3] got there it was pre-election. We misread the economic signals and with a pending election we misread the public opinion, not recognizing that there was, at that time, a public appetite for expenditure reduction. By the time the Chrétien government came into power in 1993, Finance had been totally discredited.

They came in with a commitment to reduce the deficit to a level of 3 per cent of GDP in three years. In the first budget in the spring of '94, we did some expenditure reduction, wage freezes, and grants and contributions reductions. But the mood was pessimistic. The day after budget I got on a plane to Toronto with the budget watchers – private sector people the minister had invited to come to Ottawa to help sell the budget – and it was just doom and gloom. They said the government 'didn't get it.' That was a real shock to the government. We had had in the budget a commitment to do a program review and said the savings would be reallocated to other priorities. By the summer of '94 we did a complete shift with all those savings now to go reduce the deficit. We had failing grades on the first budget. There was a widening gap in Canada/U.S. interest rates, our credit ratings were falling, the *Wall Street Journal* referred to us as a 'third world country,' there were concerns about us 'hitting the wall,' and a threat that IMF [International Monetary Fund] might come in and take over. As a result, program review savings became fiscal savings.[5]

In matters of the fiscal framework, establishing and maintaining credibility and dealing with the uncertainty go hand in hand. This is because the fiscal framework is a prediction of future commitments and a visible record of past accomplishments. If current accomplishments do not live up to past predictions, then future predictions have little credibility. In short, the markets, investors, consumers, taxpayers, the opposition, and the media do not believe the fiscal framework and fiscal projections and targets it contains. As one former minister of finance put it, 'Canadians want to know if you are delivering on whatever you said you would do. They want to know ... "Did you cut my taxes?" And if you didn't, why you didn't.'[6] In an uncertain world, and there is much uncertainty surrounding the economic and fiscal outlook, it is an increasing challenge to establish and maintain a 'credible track record'– to ensure that past promises and commitments are realized in the future. One way to increase the likelihood of future achievement is to lower the current promises and commitments. But, at the

extreme, this becomes a government with no promises and no expectations – a 'do nothing government' which can not garner and sustain
the support of the public or the markets. Because fiscal frameworks are
filled with promises and commitments, the achievement of which is
uncertain, ministers of finance, their department, and the prime minister know that dealing with uncertainty is the key to building and maintaining credibility.

Ministers of finance constantly worry about the credibility of their
fiscal framework, especially when they face large and growing deficits
and debts. 'I was absolutely amazed,' explained one, 'at the total lack
of credibility that the Canadian minister of finance had when I put
these financial projections in front of them [financial institutions] and
said, "We are going to deal with our deficit."'[7] When his first budget in
1994 was not well received, Paul Martin described how he felt as a
minister of finance lacking credibility:

I went to Japan, to Tokyo, and they said, 'You are going to meet with the
minister of the post.' And I said, 'What am I meeting with the minister of
the post office for? We owe the Japanese a lot of money. Why am I meeting with this minister?' And they said, 'Because, in fact all of the foreign
debt held by the Japanese government is held in and is run by the post
office.' So I walked into the room. I sat down. There was a rather high
desk. I sat on one side and the Japanese minister on the other, who didn't
speak English, and they simply said 'The Canadian minister of finance' ...
[then] he took out a big book ... and I could see him going through Came-
roon, Chad, and then he came to Canada. The other countries had about
this much [holds up his right hand and reveals a very small vertical space
between his thumb and index finger]; Canada was about this thick [holds
up his right hand and reveals a large vertical three-inch space between his
thumb and index finger]. This is the debt book. It was about this thick
[holds up both hands and reveals a vertical space of about eight inches
between the top of his left hand and the bottom of his right hand]. And I
made my case and all he did is, he looked at me and said to me in Japanese – it was translated – 'I have been the minister of the post office for
quite some time. When I first started here, the Canada book was this
thick. It seems to get bigger every year. When is it going to get smaller?'
And he said it in a way that didn't make me feel very good.[8]

An earlier minister of finance, who hurriedly put together his 1993
budget in the midst of a Conservative Party leadership race that

spring, experienced the cold reality of hard-headed investors and sceptical media who did not believe the numbers in his fiscal framework.
Finance Minister Mazankowski's budget included five-year fiscal projections that were a simple extension to years three through five of the
across-the-board expenditure reductions that had been included a few
months earlier in his two-year financial statement of 2 December 1992.
Within the first hour of the budget lock-up, held in the early afternoon
just prior to the minister of finance unveiling the budget in the House
of Commons, it became apparent to the media that there was little
credibility in the numbers in the fiscal framework. A budget and a fiscal framework, presented in the final stages of the Mulroney government against the backdrop of many years of both Conservative and
Liberal five-year fiscal forecasts that regularly had not been achieved,
was not seen as credible.

Finance ministers know that if they can establish credibility, they will
be given the benefit of the doubt. A former minister of finance explains
how he needed concrete expenditure cuts to establish his credibility:

> Previous times when governments had said that they were going to cut
> spending to achieve a deficit target, they didn't make the decisions. They
> just simply said 'Our spending is here; we are going to get it to here. We
> give you that guarantee and that is it.' And then the decisions are to be
> made during the time the budget projections are playing out. In our par-
> ticular case, we said, 'That is not going to be good enough. We will not
> have any credibility when we go to the markets unless the decisions have
> been taken. They may play out a little bit later, but the decisions have to
> be taken so that we can say there is no doubt that we are going to bring
> "X" spending from "A" to "B."' The only way we could do that was to
> have an extensive discussion throughout the town, throughout Ottawa,
> with all of the public servants of the bureaucracy and the ministers. There
> had to be complete buy-in to what we were doing.[9]

Both the minister of finance and Department of Finance officials know
that their economic and fiscal forecasts are fraught with uncertainty.
Commodity-exporting countries like Canada, Australia, and New
Zealand can experience larger and more frequent exogenous shocks than
countries with more closed economies. In the face of continuous insecuri-
ties about how the economy will unfold and what the levels of expenditures, revenues, and fiscal balance will be, guardians have developed
elaborate and time-tested methods for hedging against uncertainty.[10]

The greater the political commitment that is given to meeting a particular fiscal target – a balanced budget or a specified deficit level – the more guardians take precautions. This is because the minister of finance and his officials must achieve the target and it would be politically unacceptable to fall short of it. The smaller the deficit or surplus target and the closer it is to a balanced budget, guardians will once again hedge against uncertainty. This is because when the fiscal balance is close to zero, even small swings in expenditures or revenues can change the positive perception that accompanies a surplus into the negative one that goes with a deficit. The government literally changes its colours, moving from being in 'the black' to being in 'the red.' 'We cannot go into the red even a bit,' instructs a top Finance official 'because once we cross that line there is no difference between $1 billion and $5 billion.'[11] As a senior Finance official observed, 'We tried to be prudent before 1994, but it really didn't make much difference when the deficit was predicted to be $28 billion and it turned out to be $28.5 billion.'[12] If the fiscal target is firm (e.g., the entire fiscal dividend is to go to reducing the deficit, as became the case with the program review savings in 1995), guardians again will hedge against uncertainty. This is because there is little room for interpretation or reinterpretation of the target after the fact, when, a year later, updated forecasts and the actual fiscal numbers are published. The further out into the future that a fiscal target is, the greater the uncertainty and, hence, the more that guardians will hedge. This is simply because with the passage of time, 'there are more things that can go wrong' and there is less margin for error.

The political requirement for a balanced budget or better – even as an implicit, rather than a formal, rule – has significant effect on the extent to which the Department of Finance hedges against uncertainty in its economic and fiscal forecasts. A finance assistant deputy minister explains that 'life was actually easier until we balanced the books, after which people didn't believe our fiscal forecasts. To ensure balanced budgets or better we had to build a lot of prudence and contingency into our budget forecasts by erring on the more conservative side. To ensure we do not go into the red, we need to build in $6 billion to $10 billion annually.'[13]

This is confirmed by an independent comprehensive examination of economic and fiscal forecasting that concluded that 'to guarantee the government does not incur a deficit requires a cushion in the order of $7 billion to $9 billion in the fiscal forecast.' This explains, in part, why the author of this independent report recommended that the government 'shift from the no-deficit target to a fiscal rule of achieving a surplus, on average, over the economic cycle.' However, even under this rule of achieving a surplus over the economic cycle, which allows for the possibility of deficits, the report notes that the government 'would want to hedge its bets to improve the likelihood of achieving its targets. A cushion in the range of 1% of revenue flows (almost $2 billion at current levels) would be a low-end-of-the-range provision.'[14]

Guardians attempt to instil credibility and hedge against uncertainty by building prudence into every stage in the budgetary process and into every component of the budget, including the economic outlook, the fiscal forecasts of expenditure and revenues, the fiscal framework and fiscal targets that it contains, the fiscal dividend and how it is to be used, and the costing of direct expenditure and tax expenditure initiatives that compete for new funding. As a result, according to a recent independent analysis, Canada has 'larger and more conservative fiscal forecasts errors than most other countries.'[15] The study goes on to explain that 'the aggregate forecast error is composed of small but consistently one-sided errors in fiscal subcomponents, which appears characteristic of a conservative forecasting approach.' To describe these prudent forecasts, however, as 'forecast errors' is to be mistaken. They are not errors. Rather, they are a rational way by which officials, ministers, and governments attempt to hedge against the inevitable uncertainty they face and to avoid the 'mistake' that actual deficits turn out to be larger than predicted or balanced budgets turn into deficit budgets. A long-time senior Finance official explains: 'The biggest mistake to avoid was to turn out a larger deficit than predicted. The minister read the riot act to the department and made it clear that we do not spend money we do not have and there is only one direction for error and that is on the side of prudence.'[16]

A number of commentators have described budget forecasting as a mysterious process. 'Economic sleuths at the International Monetary Fund (IMF) took a crack this week at solving one of the great Canadian mysteries of the past decade: Why does Ottawa routinely get its budget forecasts wrong? ... When conservative forecasts from the private sector are fed into a Finance Department that also had a conservative bias, the result has been a string of budget surpluses that exceed all expectations.'[17] Far from being a mystery, there are rational reasons and processes that underlie these outcomes. To explain what is actually done to achieve these outcomes, we need to examine how the Department of Finance prepares the economic and fiscal outlook, sets the fiscal framework, and establishes the fiscal dividend.

The Prudent Economic and Fiscal Outlook

Budget planning begins with the economic and fiscal outlook.[18] It is undertaken by the Department of Finance in four steps. The first step is determining the economic assumptions. Finance surveys about twenty private sector economic forecasters on a quarterly basis after the National Income and Expenditure Accounts data are released by Statistics Canada. Each fall, Finance conducts consultations with an economic advisory group, which includes the chief economists of the major chartered banks and leading economic forecasting organizations as well as representatives from different regions across the country. The range – and it is a substantial range – of the annual private sector forecasts of real GDP growth, inflation, unemployment, and interest and exchange rates forms the basis for the government's macroeconomic assumptions. Through meetings and discussions with the external forecasters, Finance refines these assumptions to ensure model consistency. From the 1994 budget to the 1998 budget, prudence was explicitly incorporated into the economic outlook and the fiscal projections by adopting economic assumptions that were more pessimistic than the average of the private sector economic forecasts, including higher interest rates and weaker economic growth.[19]

The second step is the development of the status quo fiscal projections for the fall Economic and Fiscal Update, which is presented by the minister to the House of Commons Standing Committee on Finance. Officials in the Fiscal Policy Division of the Department of Finance produce the detailed fiscal forecast of revenues and expenditures. They analyse the range of the private sector economic assumptions and feed them into a macroeconomic model (the Canadian Economic and Fiscal Model) in order to develop aggregate revenue and expenditure projections for the balance of the current year and for the next five years. The officials also draw upon the fiscal projections undertaken by four private sector economic forecasting organizations, based on tax and spending policies in place at the time of the last budget.[20] Prudence is built into the revenue and expenditure forecasts through a set of deeply entrenched standard operating procedures. For example, if, because of uncertainty, junior analysts set out a range for the forecast of a particular revenue source with high and low limits, senior forecasters will pick the lower limit. Revenue numbers are always rounded down and expenditure numbers rounded up.[21]

Fiscal forecasting is never easy and it can become more difficult when the government's accounting standards change. 'With accrual accounting, forecasting revenues is much more difficult,' notes a senior Finance official, 'because when we close one year we need to decide how much accrues from the previous year. When the high-tech stock bubble burst we had to pay out $5 billion in income tax refunds because of huge capital losses and this meant a very large reduction in revenues that we had to accrue to one fiscal year.'[22]

'How you build in prudence,' explains a senior Finance official,

> is by having a very good understanding of both the drivers and risks of revenues and expenditures. On the revenue side you have to understand that each of the sources – personal income, corporate income, sales tax, and non-tax revenue – is very different. For example, PIT [personal income tax] data comes in on a monthly basis and it is updated accordingly. Before we moved to accrual accounting, we had adjustments at year-end. With the numbers not coming in until July, we could be out by as much as $1 billion to $2 billion on the fiscal year that had just closed [the end of April]. You had to compare this to where we were the last time, a few years before that, and then be very cautious. On CIT [corporate income tax], 40 per cent of the revenue comes in December and it is not until February or March that we have a clear picture. We had problems with the GST collected by Quebec and one year we were $30 million short, so next year we upped the forecast and built in a 5 per cent forecast growth factor.'[23]

The Department of Finance will pull together all the individual expenditure forecasts by program, building prudence into each forecast at every step. The key is to isolate the areas of expenditure that are the largest and the most uncertain. A Finance official provides an overview explanation:

> On expenditures, one key is employment insurance and sometimes we miss it. It's driven by the number of people unemployed, the number receiving benefits, and the level of inflation. We looked at historical relationships between the number of unemployed and the number receiving benefits but it tended to stay constant when we thought it might be going down. The big expenditures, the CHST [Canada Health and Social Transfer] and equalization are now easy to predict. With the previous programs of CAP [Canada Assistance Plan] and EPF [Established Programs

Financing], it was difficult because the one was a cost-shared program with the provinces and the other was an entitlement, with the amount of cash being a residual amount after the value of the tax points transferred to the provinces were calculated. We had problems with big jumps but not any more, since we have gotten off cost-sharing and entitlements. Now it works on a formula. Similarly with equalization, before the most recent changes, when the Ontario economy did well, we found that we were remitting huge sums of money to the provinces. Under the new arrangement, we simply guarantee a flow that increases at 3 per cent annually. This makes forecasting a lot easier. For defence spending forecasts, we use the Annual Reference Level Update (ARLU) and any supplementary estimates.[24]

The restructuring of certain fiscal transfer programs to formula funding has made it easier to predict expenditures. But even then considerable uncertainty still exists. 'The challenge,' explains the official, 'still remains and that is to estimate the lapse in overall government expenditure. We thought that with squeezed departmental budgets and increased departmental flexibility the size of the lapse would reduce. This has not been the case. We continue to have about a $3-billion lapse each year on about $50 billion in non-statutory expenditures. That is high.'[25]

It is not just the big items that Finance worries about; it also builds contingency into small expenditure and revenue items. 'We need to estimate the impact on expenditures of pending court cases, aboriginal land claims, pension liabilities, and loan guarantees, and therefore we talk to the Department of Justice, Indian Affairs, and the Treasury Board Secretariat, and we get information from the Offices of the Comptroller General and the Auditor General. We set aside money for natural disasters ... there has been at least one major disaster a year that the Disaster Financial Assistance Program can't handle. When we estimate, we err on the side of prudence.'[26]

The third step is to update the status quo projections contained in the fall Economic and Fiscal Update for the upcoming budget. Finance updates the fiscal projections on the basis of the most recent survey of private sector economic forecasters and the most recent financial results. Once again, the forecasters select more pessimistic economic assumptions and ensure their updated expenditure and revenue forecasts are conservative.[27]

The fourth step is to adjust the fiscal projections for prudence to derive the fiscal surplus for budget planning purposes. This involves two explicit determinations, which are central to the fiscal framework. One is the establishment of an explicit annual contingency reserve to guard against unforeseen circumstances and the other is to build into the framework an explicit amount for economic prudence. Both these decisions provide further protection against achieving a smaller surplus than projected or, worse yet, falling into deficit. The annual contingency reserve is large and is normally set at $3 billion per year and, in the absence of the passage of Bill C-67 (an act respecting the allocation of unanticipated surpluses), if it was not needed, it was applied at year-end to reduce the federal debt. The economic prudence is generally set at $1 billion in the first year of the five-year fiscal framework, rising to $4 billion in year five. If this amount is not needed, it becomes available to fund new expenditure or tax reduction priorities.

The Prudent Fiscal Framework: Achieving Achievable Targets

Not only do the finance department and minister build contingency and prudence into the economic outlook and fiscal projections, they also build prudence in to their fiscal targets. When it comes to the fiscal framework, the challenge in recent years for every minister of finance has been the same – first, how to establish both credible and achievable targets and, second, how to ensure that these targets are achieved and not underachieved. Former minister of finance Paul Martin explains the reform that he put in place to increase his chances of establishing achievable targets and then achieving them: '... governments had always budgeted on a five-year basis and we felt that on a five-year basis it simply gave you too much slack. You ended up with the judicial hockey stick, which is what most government projections look like. So we said that we would set out five-year numbers, but we would budget on a two-year basis, on a rolling two-year set of targets that we could hit.'[28] This was a significant and fundamental innovation in the mid-1990s when the deficit stood at a record level of $42 billion. Instead of projecting that the deficit would be eliminated in four or five years, the minister only promised in his 1994 budget that the deficit would be reduced to a level of 3 per cent of GDP by 1996 (i.e., to $25 billion), a target that had been set out as a Liberal Party campaign commitment in its 1993 'Red Book.'[29] He provided no economic and fiscal forecasts beyond two years.

The advantages of having a modest short-term target as opposed to an ambitious long-term target became even clearer to Mr Martin as he reflected a decade later on the unforeseen events that arose as he pre-pared his 1995 budget. He explains:

> ... the international financial situation ... continuously threatened to throw Canada off course. The Mexican peso crisis was the first. They all had the same source. Essentially, Mexico's currency, the peso, was pegged to the U.S. dollar. They had a certain level of U.S. reserves to basically support that peg. The international financial markets at one point deter-mined that those reserves were insufficient and subsequently it came to the point that the Mexican financial statements were not sufficiently transparent. As a result of that, they started to pull money out of Mexico. U.S. reserves started to go down and then the great hedge funds and the speculators ... who got phenomenal power – almost impossible for any government to fight them off – suddenly realized that the Mexican peso was a one-way bet down. So what they started to do was to sell the peso today for delivery in 90 or 120 days (sold it short). This put phenomenal pressure on the Mexican peso. The peso plummeted. As it plummeted, this caused huge consternation and uncertainty in financial markets around the world, and what happens is that financial markets look for the next vulnerable country and that next vulnerable country was Canada, because we had not yet brought down the budget to deal with the deficit. We were still regarded as a third world, a banana republic, and our inter-est rates skyrocketed, just went right through roof. They spiked.
>
> ... I had just finished dealing with all of these government depart-ments, telling all of these ministers, 'That is it. You have given [expendi-ture cuts] at work. We are not going to ask you to give anymore. We have got our budget.' All of a sudden, I found my debt service line just having gone completely bonkers, way, way up. This goes back to the two-year targets ... If I had been in a five-year set of projections, what I probably would have done is to say, 'Look, this ... is a blip. This will work itself out and in five years I will be okay.' But because I had committed to two-year targets ... I didn't have that grace. I had to hit my one-year target and my two-year target. So I went back to the drawing board and we went back to every one of those departments and I said, 'I am sorry; you gave at work; now you have to give at home.' You can understand that I didn't get any Christmas presents from any of my colleagues.[30]

While some countries, some state governments in the United States, and a few provinces in Canada have found it is in their interest to estab-lish fiscal targets in the form of legislated rules, federal ministers of finance and the department have not. One exception was between 1991 and 1994 when the 'Fiscal Control Act' imposed legislative limits on the federal government's ability to spend. The essence of the limitation was that any spending in excess of the legislated target could be offset by cutting spending below the target over the following two years. In addition, expenditures related to emergencies and to strongly cyclical programs such as employment insurance were exempt. According to a former associate deputy minister of finance, 'The Mulroney government's experience taught at least one useful lesson: in the end, the legislation was so complex that it failed to pass the communications test. Actual expenditures were quickly driven well below the initial targets. Rather than revising the targets down, the incoming Liberals simply allowed the legislation to lapse. Few Canadians noticed.'[31]

Recent ministers of finance have not used formal legislative rules to enforce their targets; instead they have come to rely upon political will. 'Former finance minister Paul Martin's bold declaration that the Liberal Party's fiscal targets would be hit "come hell or high water" was,' in the words of a former senior official, 'probably more powerful a commitment than specific fiscal rules would have been.'[32] A current official concurs: 'We don't need legislation when there is political commitment. Besides, legislation has lots of holes and it's too complicated.'[33]

Whether a non-legislative rule is effective or not depends upon the extent of public and political commitment to it. An embattled senior Finance official explains:

> Having the fiscal anchor of a balanced budget or better is extremely useful. It is a dogmatic rule that is deeply embedded into the mindset of the minister and the government. When Tim O'Neill proposed loosening the rule in order to improve fiscal forecasting, it didn't take the minister any time to publicly express the necessity of the balanced budget. It is a deeply engrained commitment, a rule that neither the prime minister nor the minister of finance will break. When the U.S. went into deficit we thought it might be hard to sustain, but the PM argued that it differentiated ourselves from the U.S. and we could use our surplus as a basis for building a competitive advantage.[34]

Perhaps it is not an exaggeration to say that when and if a federal government puts in place legislated expenditure limits or balanced budget legislation, it is a clear sign that there is a lack of political commitment within that government. Former finance minister Michael Wilson

(1984–91), who put in place the spending control legislation, reflects back on his difficult experience with spending colleagues and spending attitudes: 'If I had to do it all over again, I'd have attacked Lalonde's [Liberal minister of finance, 1982–4] deficit from the start. I could never get the support I needed in cabinet to get it under control, and I'm sorry for it.'[35]

Instead of formal, legislated fiscal rules, the government has over the past ten years elected to announce a fiscal target of a 'balanced budget or better.' This policy target, announced and reinforced by the minister of finance and the prime minister on an ongoing basis – 'we will not go back into deficit' – and sustained through budget surpluses or balanced budgets in every year since 1997–8, enjoys broad public support. While the 'balanced budget target' allows for flexibility in that it can be achieved by actions on either or both revenues and expenditures and sustained by a growing economy, some rules, such as those relating to debt levels, are more uncertain for governments and thereby place finance ministers at greater risk.

In the aftermath of achieving a balanced budget, there was some pressure on the Martin government to establish a target level of debt to GDP. The rationale centres around important arguments that matters of public debt are intergenerational in nature and the fiscal framework only extends out five years, that interest payments on the public debt consume 20 per cent of total public expenditure, and that expenditure pressures will increase in the future as demographic change takes place. There are, however, 'tricky issues,' as one former Finance official explains, 'with targeting a variable, such as the ratio of debt to GDP, which the government cannot control directly. For instance, small errors in projecting the path of nominal GDP could require profound fiscal corrections. As well, GDP can be revised substantially, again requiring large fiscal corrections, which may not be appropriate for current economic circumstances.'[36] However, as these seemingly large uncertainties and risks were reduced through increasingly positive economic and fiscal results, Finance Minister Ralph Goodale, in his 23 February 2005 budget, reaffirmed the government's objective set out in the 2004 budget to reduce the federal debt-to-GDP ratio to 25 per cent by 2014–15.[37] In his first budget of 2 May 2006, Finance Minister Jim Flaherty confirmed that the new Conservative government would achieve a debt to GDP target of 25 per cent by 2013–14, one year earlier than previously projected.

The Elastic Fiscal Dividend

One of the most important decisions the minister of finance and prime minister make for upcoming budgets is if there will be a 'fiscal dividend,' how big it should be, and how it should be used. Technically, the 'fiscal dividend' is the amount by which revenues exceed expenditures without any change in tax policy or in expenditure programs. This establishes the margin of manoeuvrability for the government. It is the amount of discretion that the government has. It is what the minister of finance and the prime minister focus on.

The question of what should be the size of the fiscal dividend is not straightforward nor is it a mechanical residual that simply emerges from a Department of Finance computer. While its general magnitude is determined by what results from the conservative assessment of the economic outlook and the prudent massaging of the forecasts of expenditure and revenues, its more specific size is shaped by taking into account a set of inevitable and unavoidable expenditure pressures that need to be dealt with and by considering the prospects for achieving suggested expenditure savings for reallocation. In the end, however, its precise size might be fine tuned and refined through an intimate chat between the minister of finance and the prime minister over one or two specific new expenditure increases from the PM that will need to be done and around suggestions for expenditure reductions from the minister that might not be done at that time or in the manner proposed. In short, how big the fiscal dividend actually is depends not just on the economic situation, fiscal projections, and unavoidable pressures but also on how it might be achieved and for what it might be used.

'The prime minister,' explains a former senior adviser, 'was always concerned that the fiscal dividend was being underestimated and that the minister of finance was holding back money for when he might become prime minister. As a result, the prime minister had his own formula in mind about how big the surplus should be. He would say with 300,000 new jobs created, revenues should go up by so much, and it was always more than what Finance estimated.'[38]

Determining what portion of the fiscal dividend will be used to increase expenditures, reduce taxes, or pay down the debt is an important political and policy decision for any government. To be sure, it reflects the political ideology of the governing party with Conservatives generally more prone to reducing taxes and paying down the debt, the New Democratic Party (NDP) favouring spending over other uses, and the Liberals inclined towards a balanced approach but with a distinct emphasis on spending. Within the broad parameters of the governing party's political ideology, finance ministers and prime ministers have generally preferred to have the discretion to decide on an annual basis what the appropriate mix should be. This allows them the flexibility to shape fiscal policy in light of fluctuations in the business cycle, the requirements for macroeconomic policy, the time remaining in the government's mandate, and the needs of the government to differentiate itself from the opposition parties.

Since 1997, when fiscal surpluses first emerged after years of deficits, the prime minister instinctively understood that it was in his interest to establish more specific rules around how the fiscal dividend would be spent. Prior to that time when dramatic cuts and reductions were being made to government spending – in effect, a negative fiscal dividend – the prime minister was content to provide the essential behind the scenes support to his minister of finance, allowing his minister, supported by a 'Program Review' Cabinet Committee, to make specific decisions on what to cut. Once the government had a positive fiscal dividend extending over several years, a broader set of choices opened up and the prime minister, along with his priority setters in his office, were no longer prepared to defer as much decision-making to the minister of finance and his guardians.

The personal predispositions of finance ministers and prime ministers undoubtedly shape their fiscal choices. For example, a review of the eight budgets presented by Mr Martin, whether in deep deficit or significant surplus, indicate his preferences for assisting persons with disabilities, often by way of tax expenditures.[39] Finance ministers, when they have the flexibility of a fiscal dividend, often focus on tax reductions. With a small fiscal dividend, they are prone to emphasize various tax expenditures that can be targeted to particular groups, industries, or sectors without some of the administration and risk of mismanagement associated with direct expenditures and without the need for time-consuming and difficult consultation with provincial and territorial governments as required by the Social Union Framework Agreement and other intergovernmental protocols. As the fiscal dividend increases, finance ministers see opportunities and sometimes a requirement for reductions in personal and corporate income tax. They worry about keeping the Canadian tax system competitive with the United States, its largest trading partner. They also worry about the size of the debt, especially since its carrying costs absorb one-fifth of total expenditures and are highly sensitive to increases in interest rates. All this leads ministers of finance and their department to generally favour tax reductions and deficit reduction over increases in spending.

Prime ministers, on the other hand, are more inclined to spending, in large part because they know that their finance ministers, whatever their personal predispositions, are functioning as guardians and in that role are propelled by strong incentives and interests to curtail spending and maintain a competitive tax system and a manageable debt load. Prime ministers worry that the tax reduction aspirations of their finance ministers might crowd out spending priorities. Prime ministers want to ensure that sufficient resources are available for the key spending priorities of the government, be it children, health care, cities, Aboriginal initiatives, fiscal transfers to provinces, education, or the military. Prime ministers, and those who aspire to the job, also know that a little spending here and there can be helpful in maintaining ministerial loyalty, cabinet solidarity, and caucus support. All this leads busy prime ministers, who lack the time and sometimes the fiscal experience to probe their finance ministers, to consider the imposition of parameters or rules for what is to be done with the fiscal dividend.

In a speech in 1977, Prime Minister Chrétien first set out the government's commitment to the '50/50 principle' for the allocation of the fiscal dividend (half for new spending and half for debt reduction and tax cuts). This was a firm commitment but a loose target. It provided general direction but, unlike the explicit deficit target, did not lock the government into quantifiable achievements each and every year; rather, it extended over the course of several years. This allowed the government to undertake large spending in the early and middle part of its mandate, balanced against significant tax cuts in the last year of its mandate. The government was able to interpret and reinterpret the target over time while still creating the general public perception that it was taking a firm and balanced approach in managing the fiscal affairs of the nation. There was little or no accounting of how well it was achieved. As Finance Minister Ralph Goodale admitted, the target 'hasn't been rigidly adhered to.'[40]

It is not surprising that the 50/50 principle came from the prime minister and not from the department and the minister of finance. It gave the prime minister the certainty that tax cuts would not overshadow new spending, while providing a simple, and seemingly balanced, message that could be readily communicated to the public.

Because it was only a principle and not a hard target, it provided the finance minister with the flexibility to fine-tune the fiscal mix of his budget initiatives. To be sure, it reduced the discretion of the finance minister and his department who are normally accustomed to a freer hand in shaping these major fiscal choices. 'At first,' explains a former senior adviser to the prime minister, 'the finance minister didn't mind it too much and didn't push back real hard, but as the surplus grew, he came to feel that too much was going to spending and not enough to tax cuts and deficit reduction.'[41]

Prudence and Its Consequences

Effectively hedging against uncertainty through conservative economic and fiscal forecasting and prudent budgeting helps the finance minister, the department, and the government to build and maintain fiscal credibility. But experience indicates that it does not take much time before too much hedging, and the building in of too much contingency, can erode credibility and destroy reputation. A seasoned Finance official explains: 'We had a credibility problem with our forecasts, but now we have a new kind of credibility problem. When we had a deficit and we forecasted $24 billion and it turned out to be $9 billion nobody said boo. Once we moved to a balanced budget we were accused of deliberately underestimating the surplus. It was viewed as deficit reduction by stealth.'[42]

There has been increasing and widespread criticism that surpluses have been systematically and deliberately underestimated. Not only is it a matter of significant discussion among economists and academics but also it is widely reported and discussed in the media, debated by parliamentarians, and raised as a major credibility issue in election campaigns. One 'think tank' analyst concludes that 'the 2005 budget continues to underestimate likely actual federal revenues by about 3 per cent (or $6 billion per year) over the next two fiscal years. This is smaller than the average revenue errors which marked recent budgets (which underestimated revenues by an average of 5 per cent since 1996), but still creates a substantial and artificial cushion underlying the federal budget.'[43] At the political level, the issue is cast as one of 'deception' when the opposition Finance critic accuses 'the Liberals of once again having been caught hiding behind false numbers and are not telling Canadians the truth about how much surplus money is available to fund priorities.'[44] Even a newly appointed Liberal minister of finance expressed his concerns about his cabinet colleagues and their criticisms. He once observed publicly that '[my] critics [tell me], "You always cry wolf. You say the situation is very tight every year, with no room to manoeuvre, and then when the books are finally closed – surprise, surprise – there are several extra billions of dollars that we didn't expect that just automatically go against the debt." I understand that frustration. Indeed, I have expressed it myself in my previous roles around the cabinet table.'[45]

The real rub is not that deficits have been consistently overestimated and the surpluses consistently underestimated. Perhaps, ironically, as the newly minted finance minister has implied, it is more fundamental. It is about who controls what. Through the use of conservative forecasting and prudent budgeting, the determination of how a significant portion of the fiscal dividend is to be spent comes to rest in the hands of the minister of finance and his department. The allocation of this money is seen as being beyond the reach of the prime minister, other ministers, the cabinet, the Parliamentary Committee on Finance, and those engaged in the pre-budget consultations. The new monies emerge as surpluses at year-end and, through the application of generally accepted accounting principles carefully monitored by the financial watchdog, these additional surpluses are automatically used to reduce the outstanding debt. Since surpluses were first achieved in 1997, the government has been able to reduce its debt by $63 billion to a level of $500 billion in 2005, representing 38.7 per cent of the GDP.

As the larger-than-forecast surpluses increased in size and continued each year, not everyone was content with letting them just 'slip to the bottom line' to reduce the debt. The prime minister saw his budget discretion being reduced and unnecessarily curtailed. Spending ministers saw their proposals being turned down in the fall only to see 'unexpected' surplus money available in the spring. Parliamentarians, both government and opposition, saw missed opportunities to reduce taxes or undertake new spending. The minister of finance, too, saw that other opportunities were being missed under the banner of conservative forecasting and prudent budgeting. But most significant of all, particularly for the minister of finance, he found that the great strengths of prudence were undermining his credibility.

Finance knew that it had to somehow deal with these concerns in order to rebuild its credibility. Experienced officials, however, implicitly understood that as long as the government wished to maintain a policy of a balanced budget or better there would continue to be unanticipated budget surpluses at year-end. This meant that there was only so much that improvements in economic and fiscal forecasting could offer. The requirement that year-end, unanticipated surpluses could only be used to reduce the debt created the further perception that the Finance guardians were using public money in support of their own guardian interests at the expense of spenders who saw their important needs go unmet, priority setters who had to put national projects on hold, and taxpayers who were clamouring for tax reductions.

Finance began first by searching for ways in which a part of the significant unanticipated year-end surpluses could be used for spending. Through years of experience both spenders and guardians have come to learn the severe limitations of year-end, one-time money. If the year-end money goes to departments and agencies, it must be spent in that year and it cannot be used to underwrite the annual costs of ongoing programs. If it is spent in that year, it will be late in the year and, in the absence of plans, it may not be spent wisely thereby increasing the likelihood of criticism from the financial watchdog. Furthermore, spenders are reluctant to accept one-time, single-year allocations from guardians because the price of acceptance may well be that spenders will be forced in the future to find money from within their own internal budgets to meet the necessary ongoing costs. Guardians are reluctant to provide one-time, single-year allocations to spenders for fear that they only see the 'nose of the camel' with skillful spenders marshalling the political arguments and support to come back later for additional allocations.

For the Department of Finance the key in trying to figure out what to do with the one-time, year-end surplus was to find compatibility in its seemingly contradictory roles – one of guardian and the other of spender. As a spender, Finance needed the certainty of ongoing spending, and as guardian, it needed the certainty of knowing that the ongoing spending had limits.

Enter the independent foundations. Under the general rubric of increasing the use of alternative service delivery arrangements, the Department of Finance searched for new and innovative ways by which one-time, year-end money could be converted into ongoing expenditures. It found a method through the establishment of independent foundations, operating beyond government and governed by a board of directors with majority representation from outside government. 'To transfer the money to the foundation and to book the expenditure in that year, we needed to introduce the legislation and to have signed the funding agreement with the foundation,'[46] explained a senior Finance official. Spenders and priority setters liked this arrangement because it allowed the government to flow large amounts of year-end funding into major government priorities. Financial watchdogs did not because it pressed up hard against important accounting principles. The Auditor General kept a watchful eye on the arrangement and was unprepared to sanction it. According to the Auditor General, 'We cannot state unequivocally that the government's method of accounting for foundations contravenes the accounting standards established by the Public Sector Accounting Board (PSAB) of the Canadian Institute of Chartered Accountants. We have therefore continued to issue unqualified opinions on the government's summary financial statements ...'[47]

From 1996–7 to 2003–4, the government created eleven independent foundations, including the Canada Foundation for Innovation and the Canada Millennium Scholarship Foundation.[48] Over this time period, the government transferred more than $9 billion to the eleven foundations. These upfront payments are made many years in advance of need. In March 2004, nearly $7.7 billion of these funds were still in the foundations' bank accounts and investments, earning interest. With transfers of this magnitude, concerns about the accountability of foundations have grown, most notably concerns expressed by the Auditor General and accountability experts that the foundations are not answerable to Parliament through a minister and, therefore, are not under the direction of a minister.[49]

This year-end spending was not only used to fund independent foundations. Finance found new ways to transfer it to provincial and territorial governments to help underwrite part of the cost of increasingly larger expenditure commitments of the federal government in the area of health care. 'Just before the 2005 First Ministers' Conference on health care,' explains a senior Finance official, 'we revised our forecast. We took the minister through the revised forecast with its increased surpluses. He immediately saw the good news and phoned the PM. The minister did a great service to the team but he took the heat and flack for the revision in the forecast. But we could not keep doing this; we had to do something different.'[50]

The trigger for doing 'something different' came in 2005, during what a senior official in the Fiscal Policy Branch of Finance described as 'the most difficult time for me when our projected budget surplus of $1.9 billion turned out to be $9.1 billion.'[51] The opposition ridiculed the minister of finance for being 'dyslexic.' By that time it had become increasingly clear to Finance that the development of various mechanisms for the spending of large year-end surpluses was not the answer. In an effort to rebuild its credibility, the Department of Finance developed and the government introduced Bill C-67, an Act Respecting the Allocation of Unanticipated Surpluses. Although the bill was never passed by Parliament, it required that any unanticipated surplus above $3 billion (the amount set aside in the fiscal framework for contingency) be divided one-third to tax relief, one-third to spending priorities, and one-third to reducing the accumulated deficit. 'Ministers were frustrated,' explains a senior Finance official, 'because they had no say in how the unanticipated surplus was spent and they felt they were not being rewarded for having behaved properly. Parliament had no say in the allocation. There was a bias against tax reductions because the costs were ongoing and a bias in favour of one-time spending on independent foundations.'[52]

The problem was not just that Finance's credibility for accurate fiscal forecasting was at risk. Just as important, explains a Finance guardian, 'spending ministers and departments viewed this year-end money as free. It's too late to cut taxes and with only $3 billion to $6 billion there is little sense in just paying down the debt. In expenditure terms, however, this is significant money and it's free. Our problem was we could create no sense of trade-off or choice. There were not enough options about how the money might be used.' In addition, this 'free money' had further distorting effects among spenders. 'When we funded Agriculture Canada's commitments for BSE [Bovine Spongiform Encephalopathy] from the unanticipated year-end surpluses,' explains the official, 'other departments argued that this was unfair. They said BSE was, that year, a predictable expenditure and it should be funded out of the budget thereby leaving the unanticipated surplus available for other claimants.'[53]

Finance guardians never like to put in place budgetary incentives to encourage spending, let alone legislation, that 'creates expectations for spenders.' There is already incentive enough for spenders; they do not need further encouragement. However, Finance guardians fundamentally recognized that with a political and public commitment to a 'balanced budget or better,' and with the inherent uncertainties surrounding economic and fiscal forecasting, there will, and there must be, unanticipated year-end surpluses. For a time Finance was prepared to direct these surpluses to its own spending priorities and those of the government, in effect, becoming spenders themselves. But over time, as their credibility as both honest forecaster and objective fiscal guardian was eroded they came to recognize the need for more visible and certain change. 'With the legislation,' explains the senior Finance official, 'there is now some discipline in government and the requirement for the development of spending plans in order that we can get some choice and trade-offs.'[54]

If the negative consequences of prudent economic and fiscal forecasts produced one kind of change initiated by the Finance guardians internal to government, it was to provoke a fundamentally different kind of change by parliamentarians external to the government. Within days of convening Parliament in April 2006, the new Harper Conservative government announced the establishment of a new parliamentary watchdog, the parliamentary budget officer (PBO) as part of its Federal Accountability Act. This new officer is intended to support Members of Parliament and parliamentary committees with independent analysis of economic and fiscal issues and to improve transparency and credibility of the government's fiscal forecasting and budget planning. It is too early to assess the implications that this new budget watchdog will have; nonetheless, I consider it in more detail in chapter 10, 'Budget Reforms.'

Containing Aggregates by Making Allocations

For more than a decade ministers of finance have doggedly pursued 'a balanced budget or better.' While the balanced budget is not a legislatively based fiscal rule, it has become deeply ingrained in the minds of both the public and political parties as seemingly sensible economic and fiscal policy. Like the lessons learned the hard way by those who experienced first hand the devastation of the Depression in the 1930s, so too, many citizens and politicians remember the problems associated with increasing deficits and ballooning debts in the late 1980s and early 1990s. It seems that no one wants to 'go back into deficit,' even if some day the short-term requirements of the business cycle might suggest that this is effective fiscal policy. Finance ministers, however, have learned that continuously being assured of achieving balanced budgets comes at a cost. That cost is the reduced public confidence that comes from the necessity to build large contingencies into economic and fiscal forecasts and the criticism that Finance guardians are allocating these 'unanticipated surpluses' in a seemingly unplanned and unaccountable manner at year-end. The record over the last decade indicates that no finance minister is prepared to substantially increase the risk of going into deficit by reducing substantially the prudence that gets built into the forecasts and the budgets.

Through the use of external, independent reviews of economic forecasting and the greater transparency and information contained in the budget papers, the minister and the department have taken some steps to improve their credibility. These actions have helped, but only in a small way. As the minister and the department have locked themselves into prudence, they have been forced to develop new budget techniques for dealing with the consequences that have emerged. The determination of the guardians to increase their certainty in establishing and achieving their fiscal targets has created new and different problems in terms of how they would make budget allocations at year-end.

The first step was the creation of a large number of independent foundations, with the legislative basis to operate outside of government, thereby permitting large amounts of one-time budget allocations to be transferred to them at the end of the fiscal year. While this raised new and increasingly major issues for financial watchdogs in the form of a lack of accountability of these foundations to ministers and in turn to Parliament, it did provide opportunities for priority setters to secure major new spending directed at government priorities, rather than seeing the year-end surpluses simply 'slip to the bottom' of debt reduction. The second step was the attempt to deal with the increasing criticism of spenders and some guardians who rightfully claimed that all the decisions on the allocation of the so-called unanticipated surplus were being made exclusively by the minister and the Department of Finance without reference to other competing interests. By proposing fixed allocation rules in legislation, which provide for more certainty and balance in the allocations, the Finance guardians were prepared to reduce significantly their own discretion in making these budget-allocation decisions.

Determining and achieving the fiscal aggregates – expenditure, revenue, and fiscal balance – is a critical part of any budget. It is never an easy task. Deciding what the fiscal balance should be is one thing and achieving it is another. In fact, to be successful, fiscal guardians undertake these two activities together. Figuring out what fiscal target to announce depends on knowing how to achieve it. Achieving the target and the way it is done shapes promises about future targets. In addition, how the determination and achievement of the fiscal targets is actually done is impacted by, and impacts on, other key elements of the budgetary process, especially the important activity of budget allocations.

7 Budget Allocations

The budget is an allocation document, not a framing document.
Former top Privy Council Office official

The system focuses on the last $10 billion of expenditure and the $190 billion of existing expenditure goes to the same place that it did the previous year.
Treasury Board Secretariat assistant secretary

... for an initiative to move forward to actually have spending authority you have to get a source of funds or a planned source of funds, and that is the crucial part of budget development.
Former deputy minister of finance[1]

I don't like the budget process since we changed it in the 1990s where all new expenditures have to be considered in the budget in the context of the fiscal framework. This ties everything to the annual budget cycle. We need to be able to make side deals with the minister of finance, like ministers made with Lalonde in 1983.
Spending deputy minister

You need to keep the issue alive within the system while the prime minister makes up his mind.
Spending deputy minister

When it comes to allocations of public money, the key question is always the same: How does the government decide how much it will spend on defence and how much it will spend on health; how much will go to Agriculture and Agri-Food Canada and how much will go to the Department of Foreign Affairs and International Trade? In fact, governments do not make decisions on these specific questions; at least not directly and explicitly. These decisions are not only too difficult for governments to decide, they are also impossible for governments to make. They are too difficult because they require that each year the budgets of all departments and agencies be reduced to zero and then decisions on their budgets for that year start from a zero base. This requires that the government's entire budget be remade each year. Zero-based budgeting is not politically feasible because it ignores history, requiring the government to reopen all the political wounds of previous budget battles that have healed over with the passage of time.

To my knowledge, governments do not practise zero-based budgeting, because it is not in their political interest and capacity to do so. These decisions are impossible for governments to make because it requires them to have a comprehensive rationality about a multiplicity of uncertain and often conflicting objectives, programs, and consequences that are beyond the capacity of government decision-makers to calculate. It also requires them to have the ability each year to make explicit value choices across an infinite array of competing and contentious decisions, all of which are fraught with deep-seated and oftentimes divisive conflicts. The value conflicts that are inherent in these choices are simply too difficult to reopen and resolve year after year. Even if sufficient conflict could be managed, public servants and politicians do not have the cognitive capacity to consider all the options and all the consequences and then to select the single and best option to achieve a set of objectives. Try as they might, public servants and politicians cannot contain and manage the conflict and acrimony that underlie each of these difficult choices and everywhere threaten to spillover and undermine the trust and confidence which underpins their collective decision-making processes.

Spenders, guardians, and priority setters do not concern themselves with the base of ongoing spending each year. Nor do they undertake a comprehensive analysis of expenditure increments by comparing each new expenditure proposal against all others that are under consideration in that year or that have been made in previous years. Instead, they undertake a fragmented and partial analysis of particular increments – the specific proposals for expenditure increases (and occasionally decreases). In short, budgeting is incremental and fragmented. By focusing only on the specific proposals for change and making comparisons to only a few alternatives and by ignoring the base of ongoing expenditure, spenders, guardians, and priority setters are able each year to reach agreement on the contents of the budget. It is the gradual accumulation of these annual incremental decisions on expenditure increases, periodically sprinkled with the occasional expenditure reviews and decisions on reductions, that determines how much gets spent on defence and how much on health.

In reality most of the budget does not actually get allocated. It simply rolls over from one year to the next. Finance ministers focus on demands for new spending, not on the base of existing ongoing spending. One former minister of finance explains it this way, in response to a question of why he did not focus on a reserve that had been previously set aside in the fiscal framework: 'There was no demand for new money. This is often the case when you get into multi-year funding. It simply is built into the framework and when it is an item below a certain level, it is simply grouped with a whole bunch of other items under one – the descriptive line such as "other spending" – and, therefore, would never come to anyone's attention. It would not come to anybody's attention except somebody who, deep in the bowels of the Department of Finance (is) doing reconciliations.'[2]

Allocations Types

There is no simple answer to how budget allocations are made in those few areas of the budget where new spending it to be undertaken, but one thing is certain: without a source of funds in the budget there is little or no prospect for an allocation of new money however worthy the cause or intense the political pressure. 'A source of funds in the fiscal plan,' instructs a former deputy minister of Finance, 'is an indication that monies have been put aside potentially for a use ... If there isn't a planned source of funds, then their initiative can't go forward.'[3] For departments and agencies, securing expenditure allocations are all about getting a commitment to putting a source of funds into the budget and then getting the money out of the budget. There are many ways into the budget, but they are all through the minister of finance, except for what a convincing prime minister might want or need. A former minister of finance explains in his appearance before an inquiry:

> Mr. Finkelstein: I am the minister. I have come to you as Finance Minister. I have said, 'I would like to do this program.' What happens if you say no?

The Rt. Hon. Paul Martin: Well, it is pretty well over unless – I mean, the Finance Minister can be overruled by the Prime Minister, but essentially, if the Finance Minister says 'no' then you are going to have a long year ahead of you.

Mr. Finkelstein: Now let's say the Finance Minister says 'yes'; then what does the Minister do?

The Rt. Hon. Paul Martin: The Minister may well have been to Cabinet committee prior to coming to see the Minister of Finance and he will have made his proposal to his colleagues and they, the minister's colleagues, will give it an approval in principle or they will say 'No, we don't like it.' Nine times out of ten it gets an approval in principle because all Ministers want to get approval in principle and there is a reasonable degree of cooperation among them.[4]

Once past the general principle that there must be a source of funds, the answer from all participants – spenders, guardians, and priority setters – about how allocations are made is invariably the same: 'it depends.' It depends on the skill and determination of the spending minister and his/her department, particularly the deputy minister. It depends upon the ability of the spenders to form a tight alliance with the priority setters in the Prime Minister's Office and in the Privy Council Office. It depends upon the priorities of the government and the specific themes that the prime minister and the minister of finance wish to push in the budget. It depends upon the fiscal and economic situation and the extent to which the guardians can turn back the spenders on the basis that there is no new money available. It depends upon where the government is in its mandate, with a greater likelihood of new expenditures and tax reductions in a pre-election period and the greater likelihood of expenditure cuts in the earlier part of the mandate.[5] It depends somewhat on luck and on timing. Sometimes, after years of not receiving any 'new money,' a small department like Veterans' Affairs can find that it is now 'their turn.'

Through years of experience with budget negotiations, public servants and politicians have come to see a number of distinct types of budget allocations. Each type is distinguishable from the others and each allocation contains different incentives and dynamics for the participants and, hence, produces different alliances and arrangements among them. To be sure the same allocations are sometimes called different names by different players. For example, what is viewed as an important new initiative for a spending department might well be viewed as a minor item by an overworked guardian in the Department of Finance who sees the initiative as a discretionary expenditure unrelated to the overall theme of the budget. Nonetheless, budget allocations can be grouped into the following categories:

- the big fixes
- the big-ticket items
- the must dos
- the small items
- tax expenditures
- reductions, and
- reallocations

Budget allocations for 'the big fixes' and 'the big-ticket items' are usually decided without determining their detailed program design, which is considered after the money has been set aside in the fiscal framework. These allocations are often priority-driven with priority setters wanting the assurance that major allocations are being made to the pressing priorities of government; guardians wanting the certainty that within the context of the overall fiscal framework strict expenditure limits have been placed on these yet-to-be-developed and designed programs; and spenders content with the flexibility that comes from knowing that they can subsequently flesh out the program design to meet the funding that invariably will be made available to them. Allocations for the 'must dos' are sometimes based on detailed program design when, for example, it is fully known that a specific payment must be made to settle a legal claim for compensation for government wrongdoing. When, on most other occasions, it not clear 'just what natural disaster will hit but the probability of something happening is high,' then an expenditure allocation is often set aside 'notionally' in the fiscal framework in the absence of detailed program design.[6]

Allocations for tax initiatives in the form of tax expenditures and for small items such as operational adjustments are almost always made on the basis of detailed designs and the costing of the initiative. On tax expenditures, the Finance tax guardians are in complete control. There is little or no consultation with priority setters or spenders. Because tax expenditures erode government revenues and because there is always great political pressure for reducing taxes for particular groups and causes, Finance tax guardians want the locked-in assurance of both fixed-cost ceilings and detailed design. On the small items, such as operational adjustments and contingencies, central guardians have traditionally made general provisions in the form of central operating and other reserves within the fiscal framework to deal with, for example, 'the rust-out of capital' or salary increases that will emerge from collective bargaining with the public service unions. However, Treasury Board guardians do not release these funds, or more specifically a part of these funds, to spending departments and agencies until they are satisfied with the proposed detailed operational plans and designs from spending departments. Despite 'the drag' that is placed on the flow of funds from the management reserve, a few Treasury Board Secretariat officials boast about the rigour with which they review these smaller proposals. 'We are using a business-case template, drawing upon the old cost-benefit guide to review proposals for the management reserve. We are more rigorous on these proposals than Finance is on proposals for new money. In fact, it is easier to get a proposal as an item in the budget than it is to get access to the management reserve.'[7]

Expenditure reductions are unique in the sense that they are not incremental increases to the budgets of departments and agencies, but actual decrease in their 'A-base' budgets. With expenditure reductions, time-honoured incremental budgeting becomes a new and difficult form of budgeting – decremental budgeting. Depending on the circumstances, such decreases are based simply on a target level for expenditure reduction in the absence of details about how the program or activity will be adjusted, or they can be based on a clearer and more planned design about how the program or activity is to be changed in order to yield expenditure savings.

The Big Fixes

We start with 'the big fixes,' not because they occur on a regular basis – in fact, they have been quite rare – but because they involve big priorities, big money, and hence big politics. However, in recent years, like increasing expenditures, 'big fixes' have been on the rise. These big fixes require large allocations from parts of the budget that fall under the general responsibility of the minister of finance, for example, major transfer payments to provincial and territorial governments. A recent big fix was the $41-billion health-care agreement with the provincial and territorial governments negotiated by Prime Minister Martin in 2005.

Not surprisingly, 'big fixes' require the leadership and weight of the prime minister. It is only the prime minister who can command the authority and muscle to move such large blocks of money. In the abstract, if finance ministers could get their way for such massive fiscal allocations they would generally prefer major tax reductions over huge increases in spending in one single area. 'Big fix' allocations reflect the victory of priority setters over guardians. These allocations stem from the premise that occasionally, and perhaps more often recently, there are single, almost dominating priorities on which the government feels compelled to focus its attention and to which it directs the bulk of its new funding. Even most spending ministers and their officials would have been prepared, in the absence of a dominant government and prime ministerial priority, to have asked for a smaller amount and to have settled for less. These 'big fix' decisions are not taken 'in' the budget in the sense of being initiated by the minister of finance and announced by him on budget day. Instead, they are determined in some other place at some other time, invariably through the leadership of the prime minister, for example, in the context of a series of federal–provincial negotiations in and around a First Minister's Meeting.[8] When it comes to 'big fixes' if, in the federal–provincial context premiers and territorial leaders are spenders and the prime minister a guardian, then within the federal government the minister of finance is the guardian and the prime minister the spender.

Finance guardians get deeply concerned when they see a government and a prime minister preparing to announce publicly their determination to 'fix' a public policy problem. One reason is that experience indicates that public policy problems are never 'fixed,' but invariably, and at best, only temporarily handled, to re-emerge at a later date accompanied by an increasing demand for public money. The other reason is that many of the policy problems that are cast as 'in need of a fix' tend to be intergovernmental issues, requiring more than one level of government to deal with them. It is one thing to try to fix a policy problem where the financial ambitions of other governments are not at play, and quite another to fix a problem which has come to be defined as an 'intergovernmental fiscal problem,' thereby putting the fiscal appetites and aspirations of provincial and territorial (and increasingly municipal) governments on the line. In this latter case, the focus of the 'fix' becomes less a matter of the program and the results – was access to quality health care strengthened and were patient waiting times reduced – and more a question of budget and money – who got how much money and who won and who lost. This is why most prime ministers prefer to have these 'financial deals' worked out quietly in advance before they convene a high-profile and highly visible federal–provincial meeting.

Particularly troublesome for Finance guardians is a major federal–provincial fiscal transfer program, like equalization, involving influential provincial premiers where the outcome and potential fix will often be measured in terms of how much more money is transferred. 'What I have learned and have seen first hand at first ministers meetings,' explains a veteran Finance official, 'is that when provinces and territories get together, everyone will press its demands. They will keep asking and asking for changes to the equalization formula in order to get more money even though they do not expect to get it. But they need to keep asking.'[9] In short, what drives public expenditure on equalization is not simply the complexity of the formula and its many revenue sources that few understand, but the easily understandable provincial interests and personalities that stand behind the changes to the formula.

Trying to fix a smaller problem for only one province – for example, Newfoundland's long-standing complaint about the treatment of offshore oil and gas revenues in the equalization formula – can easily lead to bigger problems for Finance guardians. 'With a multilateral negotiation,' explains a senior Finance official,

> most provinces, after they have pressed their case with us would say, 'You have from heard us, now you decide what the formula should be.' They understand the need for a fine balance to make it work. However, with a bilateral deal with any one province, the dynamics are much different. Each individual province views it simply as a federal government divide-and-conquer strategy. Each province, therefore, is unprepared to back off; it pushes much, much harder and has more influence on the allocation formula.[10]

When a big spending priority, like health care, involving billions of dollars, comes to dominate all other spending priorities, Finance guardians get especially nervous. They, and to a lesser extent other spenders, worry that health care is 'eating up' all the new money and leaving none for other important priorities such as post-secondary education.[11] In the aftermath of the Romanow Report, Finance guardians conducted considerable analysis to determine if large increases for health care threatened to crowd out other spending.[12] Wisely, guardians do not buy the assertions of priority setters that because health is dominant all new money should and will go there and nowhere else.

From experience they know that while a dominant priority will be attended to first, the secondary priorities will not go away. They also know that big fixes are not real fixes, only temporary splints – sufficient to stabilize the breakage for a time but inadequate to complete the entire mending. Within weeks of the signing of the $41 billion national health accord in the fall of 2005, some provincial premiers and the head of the Canadian Medical Association were signalling that they would be looking for more health-care funding in the immediate future despite the prime minister's rhetorical claim that health care had been 'fixed for a generation.'

The Big-Ticket Items

Every budget contains a limited number of 'big-ticket items.' Finance Minister Martin's budget on 10 December 2001, in the aftermath of the terrorist attacks of 11 September, included expenditure initiatives for greater security for Canadians in the areas of air travel safety, intelligence and policing, and emergency preparedness, along with a complementary set of initiatives for more open and effective borders. Finance Minister Goodale's 2004 budget, in the immediate aftermath of the release of the Auditor General's devastating report on the sponsorship scandal, contained almost no big-ticket items.[13] In contrast, his next 2005 'minority government budget' contained ten costly budget items, including large expenditure increases for the health-care agreement that the prime minister had negotiated with provincial governments, a new equalization formula, a major commitment to early learning and child care, increased pensions for low-income elderly, measures to strengthen heritage, initiatives to begin to address climate change, the sharing of gas tax revenues with municipalities, increases in international assistance, measures to improve training and operational readiness of the defence department, and tax reductions for individuals and corporations. Even though implementation of many of the initiatives will not start until the final years of the fiscal plan (2008–9 and 2010–11), the gross expenditures over six years amounted to $83 billion. To avoid defeat of their budget in the House of Commons, the Liberal government secured the support of the New Democratic Party by agreeing to increase expenditures in the areas of housing, environment, tuition, and foreign aid. It also cemented a deal with the Government of Ontario on immigration services, training, and tuition.[14] In total, this added another $19.5 billion to multi-year spending.

Skilful ministers of finance have come to learn that each budget needs a single theme in order to curtail and reinforce those few big-ticket items. Budget themes provide the pretext for the minister and his department to shape and, in some cases, determine the budget priorities and to pre-empt or turn back suggestions of the priority setters. Tightly constructed budget themes are also useful to guardians in fending off the otherwise meritorious budget proposals of would-be spenders because, in addition to the reality of 'limited resources,' guardians can also appeal to 'limited priorities.' When, on the rare occasion, the budget deals with a single big fix, the budget theme is self-evident. More often, however, a budget contains several big-ticket items and more consideration is given to the formulation of a budget theme around which these initiatives can be wrapped.

Some finance ministers are better than others at developing themes for their budgets.[15] Finance Minister Martin, in his eight budgets and one major economic statement from 1994 to 2001, always crafted and communicated his major budget items around a single dominant theme. There was the 'fiscal reality budget' of 1994; the 'program review budget' of 1995; the 'program review two budget' of 1996; the 'staying the course budget' of 1997; the 'education budget' of 1998; the 'health care and health transfer budget' of 1999; the 'children's budget' and the 'tax reduction pre-election economic statement' of 2000; and the 'personal and economic security budget' of 2001. Prime Minister Harper, upon assuming government in 2006, continuously reiterated his focus on five limited priorities, all of which were included as promises in the Speech from the Throne and as initiatives in the 2 May budget around the reinforcing theme of 'focusing on priorities.'[16]

As finance ministers increasingly focus their budgets around single, dominant themes, perhaps only slightly constrained by prime ministers who often want a somewhat more balanced approach, it raises important questions about the future of budgeting. One budget scholar speculates on the consequences of what he calls 'class-based budgets':

Class-based budgets will be prepared in the future covering major fissures in society; men versus women, rich versus poor, young versus old, one ethnic or racial group versus others, one region against another and so on. What will be new about them in the future is that rather than being issued by outsiders, they will be published under the imprimatur of the government, first as supplementary schedules to the regular budget documents, but over time as authoritative statements. Once this occurs, class-based budgets will become decisional classifications; in the course of producing its budget, government will decide how much to spend on the rich or poor, men or women, young and old, etc.[17]

These single themes not only influence the budget but also the budgetary process. They shape, if not determine, who gets ignored and who gets taken into account in the budget process. For example, in the 1998 'education budget,' the minister of finance and his department worked exclusively with only one spending minister and department – the minister and Department of Human Resources Development Canada (HRDC) – and quietly fashioned a set of budget initiatives. Once the priority was agreed to, priority setters in the Privy Council Office and the Prime Minister's Office stood largely on the sidelines. Other spending ministers and departments were excluded. Mr Martin was determined, after delivering four expenditure-reduction budgets, that in achieving the first surplus in more than a generation, major budget items would be focused around investments in education, skills, and innovation. He naturally included in the budget the proposal for the Canada Millennium Scholarship Foundation, which Prime Minister Chrétien had first sketched out as his own initiative in the Speech from the Throne five months earlier. The central pieces of the budget (improvements to student loans, study grants, the Canada Education Savings Grant, an employment insurance premium holiday for youth employment, youth at risk programs, and tax relief for students) were all the responsibility or the interest of HRDC.[18]

By focusing the budget around a single spending department rather than many, the minister of finance and his department were able to present a budget containing the detailed program designs for a complex set of budget proposals. There was no need to make a block expenditure allocation to a general 'learning fund' because of insufficient time to reach agreement with a host of competing departments or other levels of government on the precise design of the programs. In short, a single spender – HRDC – got both the money and the programs through the budget without the costs and uncertainty associated with the normal cabinet approval process. The Finance guardians got a focused and achievable budget that addressed the single most important priority of their minister – education – and were provided with the assured certainty of implementation through the specific agreements they had reached with HRDC on the detailed design of the programs.

At the other extreme, sometimes the program details for a big-ticket item are not known at the time the expenditure allocation is made in the budget. This can often be the case when the initiative involves a large number of competing spending departments and there is considerable need for horizontal coordination and collaboration across government. In short, guardians make allocations to priorities, leaving spenders to decide subsequently how the money will be spent. A former deputy minister of finance explains:

There may not necessarily be policy approval for it [the budget item]. There may not yet be decisions on what the specific nature of it is ... [only] more general agreement that we have to spend monies in a series of areas. An example ... is the Security Contingency Reserve, which was in the 2004 budget. Government had indicated that increased spending for security was a key priority. Over the next five years an amount was set aside of $605 million, but the specific details of how that would be spent had not yet been determined at the time of the budget and there was a cabinet process that would actually make those determinations and decide, and then the monies would move through the various approval processes to actually end up ultimately in the department or agency for spending.'[19]

Sometimes, however, a single thematic budget is rejected because of the need to appeal to a broader set of interests. 'There was Manley's "Christmas tree budget" [18 February 2003],' explains a former top PCO official. 'The chattering class and the elites hate when we don't have a thematic budget. We could have called it "the cities budget," but we didn't want to alienate other people and we wanted to appeal to a broad spectrum of interests.'[20]

The Must Dos

'In any budget,' explains a senior Finance official, 'there are a number of inevitable expenditures – things that we must do.' These 'must dos' are those expenditure items, which through years of experience, Finance officials have come to learn will have to be funded. 'It might be expenditures for public health to deal with a possible pandemic, avian flu, or mad cow disease; or it could be increased expenditures to bolster border security in the aftermath of the 9/11 terrorist attacks,' he says.[21] Not only must these expenditures be made, but because of the priority associated with the initiatives, the legal requirement that they be funded, or simply because they are, an 'unexpected event,' Finance usually finds that it must pay for these expenditures from the fiscal framework rather than having departments fund them from their own resources.

Finance and Treasury Board guardians take great care to determine which items should be included in this category because these items are the first claim to the fiscal dividend. These are bills to be paid, not proposals to be turned down. Few mistakes are worse than initially overlooking a must do because that requires having to find more money for an inevitable expenditure after all of it has been allocated. That is why overall responsibility for dealing with these types of expenditures is assigned to a top Finance official. 'My job in any budget,' cautioned a senior Finance official, 'is to spot the must dos and to ensure that all of them are itemized, costed, and built into the fiscal framework. I know it is a bill that we have to pay and if we have to pay for them, I want to avoid paying for other things.'[22]

Small Budget Items

Every budget, some more than others, contains expenditure increases for 'small budget items' which are not directly related to the theme and priority of the budget. Sometimes they may reflect the particular concerns of the minister of finance or the prime minister to provide funding to a group or a cause which they have come to be associated with or because they believe they need the support of particular caucus members or members of Parliament. For example, Finance Minister Martin in nearly every one of his eight budgets included small tax expenditures (and a few direct expenditures) for persons with disabilities.

At other times budgets include the steady stream of proposals from a broad range of spending ministers and departments. 'My job,' declares a senior Finance official, 'is to protect the "big-ticket items" from the steady stream of small "chicken-_____ items" that have been increasingly creeping into the budget. This has been particularly difficult in the past few years when budgets have become less focused on major priorities and they have looked more like a dumpster of garbage or a Christmas tree of ornaments. Increasingly, in recent budgets, we have had to put in a miscellaneous catch-all expenditure category.'[23] Two recent budgets, both undertaken by the Martin minority Liberal government, illustrate the unfocused budget. The 2005 'Fiscal and Economic Update,' under the general theme of 'creating opportunities for all Canadians,' included twelve separate initiatives ranging from 'immigrant settlement and integration' to the 'child disability benefit' and would cost nearly $10 billion over five years.[24] The 2005 budget included sixty-five separate initiatives ranging from more funding to the National Literacy Secretariat to increased funding for pressing security needs at diplomatic missions aboard, spread across six diverse themes that included accountability, communities, the economy, the environment, international, and social.

These two budgets stand in sharp contrast to focused, single-theme budgets. They represent the victory of the spenders over the guardians and over the priority setters as well. When budgets are unfocused, guardians have considerably less influence and rationale for excluding spending items. Spenders, on seeing an unfocused budget in the making, will press all the more because they know that guardians have less to push back with and that other spenders, like themselves, will also be pushing harder. The focused, single-theme budget provides guardians with the rationale to hold certain important items out of the budget because they do not reinforce the dominant theme. While they might come back for consideration later, 'they do not need to be done now.' This was the case in the February 2000 budget, which was sharply focused on spending initiatives for children. For fear of eroding the budget focus on children, even a $100 million in new expenditure for a related program – the voluntary sector initiative – was not included nor announced in the budget, although priority for the initiative had been set out in the Speech from the Throne and general provision had been made for it within the fiscal framework.[25]

Tax Expenditures

Tax expenditures – tax exemptions, deductions, rebates, deferrals, and credits used to advance a wide range of economic, social, and other public policy objectives – represent a significant amount of public money. As explained in chapter 2, annual tax expenditures in 2003–4 amounted to $154 billion, nearly as large a total as direct expenditures. They have been variously described as 'back-door spending,' the 'dark holes of the budget,' 'the invisible hands,' or 'giving with both hands,' and it is easy to understand why.[26] Tax expenditures generally receive far less attention from ministers, public servants, Members of Parliament, interest groups, and the media than do direct expenditures. They are not subject to the same system of review and scrutiny as other expenditures. Tax expenditures – revenues foregone – are not budgeted in the same way as direct expenditures. In fact, they are not budgeted at all. Since the first tax expenditure account was published in 1979, little has changed with respect to 'the budgeting of tax expenditures.' At the time, this new tax expenditure account was described as 'a device for merely recording outcomes ... rather than [being] a mechanism to structure decisions.'[27] Thirty years later, tax expenditures are still not reported in the budget documents or in the estimates. Instead, tax expenditures are reported separately from the budget, with the items quietly posted each year on the Department of Finance website.

Most tax expenditures are fundamentally different than direct expenditures in the sense that recipients do not receive a payment in the form of a grant or a contribution; rather, they receive a concession or a benefit in the form of a reduction in tax that would otherwise be payable. Those tax expenditures that take the form of *refundable* tax credits are more similar to direct expenditures because low-income recipients of child tax benefits or fuel rebates actually receive a payment – a tax refund – from the Canada Revenue Agency (CRA) when the size of their refundable tax credits is greater than their tax payable. Compared with direct expenditures, tax expenditures, therefore, are generally viewed as less visible and less direct. They are not included in the budgets and estimates of departments; they are not part of the public accounts of the government; they are not reviewed by Parliament or its committees; they do not come to the attention of financial watchdogs; and they are not regularly audited by internal auditors or by the Office of the Auditor General. There has been increased attention on tax expenditures over the past several decades, but the focus has been on modest improvements in their reporting and not on their review and scrutiny.

If direct expenditures emerge through the open interaction and negotiation between departmental spenders and central agency guardians, with priority setters shaping the expenditure agenda and independent financial watchdogs reporting on the shortcomings, then tax expenditures find their origins through the interactions within a closed and tightly knit community of senior public service and political officials within a single department. With tax expenditures, the separate roles of spenders, guardians, priority setters, and financial watchdog are all contained within the Department of Finance. The Fiscal Policy Branch acts as the principal priority setter and 'tax spender' determining the 'fiscal room' that is available for 'tax spending' and shaping the priority areas where tax expenditures will take place. The Tax Policy Branch acts as the guardian of the tax system and through the publication of annual tax expenditure information provides a very limited and incomplete financial watchdog function. The Economic, Social, and International Trade Branches of the Department of Finance are less influential than the Fiscal Policy and Tax Policy Branches. With their ongoing contacts with departments and agencies, these branches act as tax expenditure 'advocates' in the interests of their respective sectors.[28]

While there might be 'push back' from the PMO and PCO priority setters in an effort to ensure sufficient front-door spending relative to back-door spending, the Fiscal Policy Branch, with the minister of finance, have the upper hand in striking the overall balance. Arguments that tax expenditures can be used to circumvent the requirements for formal consultation with, and in some cases concurrence with, provincial and territorial governments under the Social Union Framework Agreement (SUFA) are compelling reasons for 'going through the back door.' So, too, are arguments that the tax expenditure can be efficiently and quietly delivered by CRA through the seemingly 'neutral' tax system, without the political and organizational uncertainty and distortions that can sometimes accompany highly visible departmental grants and contributions programs. The Fiscal Policy Branch is not, however, an unconstrained spender of tax expenditures, undeterred by the costs of foregone revenues. The costs of tax expenditures matter, and if the fiscal room available for new initiatives is tight and the number of proposals is large, then the scrutiny that they give to any one tax expenditure proposal increases.

The Tax Policy Branch is the only true guardian of tax expenditures, but even there its professional diversity of tax lawyers, tax economists, and tax accountants ensures that there are different perspectives within the branch. The Branch is highly protective of maintaining the integrity of the tax system, pushing back on intrusions that would increase tax complexity, reduce tax self-compliance, erode revenue generating capacity, or undermine the legitimacy of the tax system. While they can occasionally say 'no' to a particular tax expenditure proposal and thereby 'carry the decision' over the heads of the 'tax spending' advocates within the Finance department, more often than not they find themselves implicated in the tax expenditure decision through their involvement in the actual design of the measure. Only they have the experience, the capacity, and the expertise to design tax expenditures that can minimize precedents for further incursions into the tax system, control costs, and maintain the integrity of the tax system. As they have become more involved in the actual design of the tax expenditure initiatives, their independence as the guardian of the tax system is reduced. As their capacity to perform the guardian role has diminished, they have sought new but modest ways to improve the public reporting of tax expenditures.

To spending departments on the outside who are anxious to secure a particular tax expenditure, the Economic, Social, and International Trade Branches may appear to be guardians. Inside Finance, however, they normally position themselves as advocates and spenders. Their influence with the Fiscal Policy and Tax Policy Branches is limited and it depends on several factors. The more costly the tax expenditure, the less influence they have with the Fiscal Policy and Tax Policy Branches. They are most influential when the area is generally recognized to be a priority of government and they can argue that a tax expenditure 'is better' than a direct expenditure because of such factors as the ease and cost of delivery, an extension or expansion of an existing tax expenditure, the avoidance of costly intergovernmental negotiations, or the comparative invisibility of the tax expenditure.

Reductions

Most, but not all, budgets are about spending increases. Some budgets, like those in the 1980s to the mid-1990s, were about spending reductions. Expenditure reductions usually begin as they did in the 1980s as across-the-board reductions. The spenders and guardians framework, involving an ongoing struggle between the Department of Finance and the Treasury Board on the one hand and spending departments and agencies on the other, was particularly effective in explaining these across-the-board expenditure reductions. The underlying concept was one of 'equal sacrifice' with each department and agency receiving its share of the 3 per cent or 5 per cent government-wide reduction in its operating budget and other program expenditures. The only part that was negotiated was the determination of the expenditure base to which the percentage cut would be applied and, after a few years of negotiation, the Treasury Board Secretariat had established a generally accepted formula, identifying specific items such as salary and postage increases that would be excluded from the cut.

From the early 1980s to 1994, these simple across-the-board cuts were applied every year, sometimes more than once. The advantage was that the cuts were easy to make and avoided the difficulties and conflict associated with determining priorities for reduction. The disadvantage, as the reductions continued and increased each year, was that their gradual accumulation soon stripped away the inefficient and discretionary expenditures and began to cut indiscriminately into the core of ongoing government expenditures. Only when the regularity of the across-the-board cuts threatened to undermine the core operations of government and the size of future cuts to deal with increasing deficits became too large, did governments find it necessary to determine the priorities for expenditure cuts. In short, the effect of the across-the-board actions by the guardians had so weakened the spenders that it necessitated an invitation to the priority setters.

Most expenditure cuts are measured from the baseline of projected expenditures, that is, what departmental and agency expenditure levels are projected to be in future years on the basis of the economic outlook and without any change in programs. Sometimes, but not often, when governments believe they are compelled to make 'real' expenditure reductions they take a harder approach. A former minister of finance explains:

> ... many governments, when they talk about a cut in government spending, are actually talking about a reduction in the growth of government spending, especially if they can get it below inflation. So that, in fact, they may well say that if, let's say, inflation is at 3 per cent and they reduce the growth of a government department to 2 per cent, they would define that as a cut in government spending, and we said, 'That isn't going to wash. A cut in government spending has to be an absolute cut in government spending. There has to be a reduction from one year over the next in that spending.'[29]

The requirement for Canadian federal and provincial governments to reduce significantly their budgets, while at the same time making no expenditure increases, has been considerably more frequent in the last decade. However, for most governments the period of exclusive and significant cuts, where no new spending takes place and expenditure levels in one year are actually lower than in the previous year, lasts for only one year or, at most, two. The 'Program Review' budget of 1995, along with its much smaller 'Program Review Two' budget of 1996 is the most vivid example in which expenditure were dramatically reduced, with some departments like Transport Canada receiving reductions of 70 per cent, while others ranged from 50 per cent to 15 per cent, and with only the department of Indian Affairs and Northern Development maintaining its level of expenditure.[30] The spenders and guardians framework does not explain explicitly these large, non-incremental expenditure reductions. Instead, they are treated as exogenous 'shift points' in budgeting.[31]

The role of priority setters is important in explaining these shift points in the budgetary process. Most important is the role of the prime minister, not only in actively and visibly supporting his minister of finance but also in putting in place a tailor-made process to contain the ambitions and eliminate the end runs of spending ministers. Former finance minister Martin explains the support he received from his long-time political rival, Prime Minister Chrétien:

> ... you can understand that there was an awful lot of consternation in the town. The ministers and senior public servants and the other departments constantly sought to basically overturn the process, constantly sought to say that look, the cuts we were imposing on them were unreasonable and were going to lead to the end of the world and I was essentially putting out fires all through the place. Let me say that I ended up being the court of last resort. I took a very tough line and I really would like to say here that I would never have been able to do that if I had not had the unqualified support of the prime minister. Without the prime minister, this would not have worked, but the fact is that people kept going behind my back and everybody's back to him and he just kept referring them back to the committee. So that is why it worked.[32]

Two journalists describe how the prime minister ensured that both his spending ministers and his minister of finance would understand clearly what his support would mean:

> Martin (the finance minister) announced his spending freeze at the start of the (cabinet) meeting. Across the table, ministers could see (Prime Minister) Chrétien looking down, seemingly oblivious. It wasn't clear to anyone but Martin that he had even discussed the matter with the prime minister. About ten minutes into the meeting, one of the ministers spoke on a pet project that required some new money. Martin began to interject. But Chrétien cut him off. 'Didn't you hear the minister of finance?' he asked. 'Just ten minutes ago, he said there wouldn't be any more money.' Another ten or fifteen minutes went by and another minister made mention of a new spending initiative.

This time Martin turned beet red. But again the prime minister beat him to the punch. His patience was wearing thin, too, as could always be discerned by the way he fidgeted in his chair and tapped his pencil. 'Didn't you hear me ten minutes ago?' he demanded sharply. 'I said there is no money. Can't you guys understand that? The next one who asks for new spending, I'm going to cut his budget by 20 per cent' … It was at that moment that Martin would later tell his associates, that he knew Jean Chrétien would be there for him.[33]

When it comes to major expenditure reductions, the prime minister and priority setters do not decide the expenditure reduction targets by department and agency, nor even the broad areas for reductions. As explained in chapter 4, these decisions are left to the guardians. Instead, the prime minister ensures that the essential rules of the game are in place and enforced. The former finance minister explains:

Once there was an acceptance of the targets, then a cabinet committee under Marcel Massé (minister responsible for program review) with me very much lurking throughout the piece was created and a number of ministers were on that cabinet committee and their basic job was to meet with their colleagues. So, for instance, you would have these ministers who were there. Another minister would come in. The minister of 'x' would have his or her budget cut substantially and the minister would come in and have the opportunity to argue that the cut they had to bring in was simply unwarranted. The committee had one instruction. They could give this minister more money, provided they were getting the same amount of money away from another minister. There was a zero-sum game.[34]

Major expenditure reductions are undoubtedly painful and generate deep conflict among ministers and departments. That is the primary reason why 'budgeting by subtraction' – major reductions, without any new expenditure increases – can only be sustained for a short period of time. During this one or two year period of cuts, the conflict can be contained and managed provided there are no successful end runs to the prime minister and/or the minister of finance for either expenditure reduction relief or expenditure increases. This is one-time budgeting. It is budgeting by decrements. On the one hand, it represents the past failings of the guardians to discipline the spenders on an ongoing basis. On the other, it represents the persuasive powers of the guardians to secure the unwavering but time-limited support of the priority setters. It represents the combined but temporary victory of the guardians and priority setters over the spenders who have reluctantly agreed to cooperate, or acquiesce, for the moment with the expectation that spending will resume shortly.

Reallocations

Recently, the federal government has attempted to make expenditure reallocation a component of its budgets. A recent OECD paper defines reallocation as 'the readjustment of expenditures in relation to the current budgetary or medium-term estimates.'[35] This technical definition, however, hides more than it reveals about the difficulty of the task. Budgeting by reallocation is fundamentally different than budgeting by addition or budgeting by subtraction. Reallocation combines both addition and subtraction within the same time frame. Conflict increases as there is no longer the 'fair share' in budgeting by addition and the 'equal sacrifice' in budgeting by subtraction to help 'make life tolerable for ministers.' Winners and losers sit side by side around the same table. The wins are big and the losses even bigger. Because so much goes on in one place or close to one place, and because cuts and increases need to be linked, there is little opportunity for the healing effects of distance and time. This is budgeting for the tough and strong, not for the meek and mild. This is budgeting that is 'in your face, up front, and personal.' This is budgeting that is open for all to see. Budget conflict inevitably increases, and its corrosive effects need to be managed with great skill and care.

Spenders, guardians, and priority setters invariably see two distinct and different types of expenditure reallocation. Guardians and priority setters often focus on reallocations that are centrally directed by government and managed by a special committee of cabinet, the Treasury Board, or the minister of finance who is in turn supported by officials in a Privy Council Office Secretariat, the Treasury Board Secretariat, or the Department of Finance. Spenders, on the other hand, are often focused on internal reallocations that are driven by a department or agency and managed by the deputy minister or a trusted senior official, who is sometimes, but not always, the chief financial officer. Sometimes these internal reallocations are done with the full weight and support of the departmental minister and, at other times, there is less explicit and overt support.

These two types of reallocation – one *across* government and the other *within* departments – have their own sets of internal dynamics that shape the relationships among spenders, guardians, and priority setters. But these two different reallocations are also closely related, with the success of each depending on the support of the other. On the one hand, centrally directed reallocation efforts allow for government-wide decisions and, hence, offer guardians and priority setters the promise of a more comprehensive and more optimal allocation of resources by shifting from the lowest priorities and least effective and inefficient programs to the highest priorities and most effective and efficient programs. On the other hand, centrally directed efforts significantly reduce the incentive for department and agency spenders to undertake their own reallocation exercises for fear that the departmental savings they achieve will not be reallocated to meet priorities within the department but be 'scooped by the centre' to meet other priorities of government.

Incentives are complex and perceptions are important. In any internal departmental reallocation, a deputy minister and his/her team face difficult challenges. On the one hand, if the potential for expenditure reallocations within a department looks too painful, too difficult, and too tricky to the minister and his/her department, then they are less likely to happen. On the other hand, if the reallocations are made to look 'too easy' to the Treasury Board and the Department of Finance and appear to be made with regularity and ease, then departmental officials can give the appearance of having too much expenditure flexibility with the result that they get less credit for what they have done and they are turned down or turned away when they come forward for expenditure increases and adjustments.

When it comes to budget preparation, central guardians focus almost exclusively on reallocation across government and generally ignore the effects of their actions on the spender and guardian interactions that take place within departments. When the centre puts 'everything under the microscope,' it takes what it sees and also some of what it imagines. This provides less incentive for departments to cooperate because the expenditure savings are usually centralized first within the Department of Finance and Treasury Board and there is little or no assurance that any of the resources will flow back for spending reallocation to a department or agency. Furthermore, spending departments have lots of ways to avoid the microscope and, in an environment of reallocation, they will develop new ways to maintain a level of expenditure flexibility. Spenders are skillful at concealing smaller expenditures from central guardians and when under pressure can sometimes negotiate a new expenditure increase in exchange for an old expenditure reduction. The only way for the centre to reduce such gamesmanship is to increase its own capacity, to secure better information, and to increase their managerial influence over departments and agencies.

At the same time, guardians at the centre of government develop ways to secure the cooperation of spenders in reallocation exercises. A frequent strategy involves promising a new initiative or program in exchange for commitments to reduce expenditures. Expenditure cuts are paired with expenditure increases.[36] Decreases and increases are made together for each department or agency, or at least for the most influential. In this way losses are not all concentrated and more losers have some prospects of realizing gains.

Some departmental spenders are skillful in using a smaller internal expenditure reallocation as a means for securing a larger new funding allocation from central guardians. In 2003 the Department of National Defence lobbied hard for $1 billion in new money to meet the increasing costs of the military. The minister of national defence, John McCallum, reasoned that reallocating some money within his department's budget from lower priorities to his highest priority could increase the prospects of receiving new additional money from central guardians at a time of intense pressure for limited new resources. 'It was the only way to make the strategy work,' explains a former assistant deputy minister of defence. 'We had to find a legitimate $200 million in cuts from within the Department in order to show to the minister and the Department of Finance that this was a serious exercise. Without that we would not have gotten the $800 million in new money.'[37]

A key question involves the implicit 'exchange rate' between the spending department's 'old money' and the central guardian's 'new money.' For example, in the government-wide reallocation exercise of 2003, Treasury Board reported that $1 billion 'went to the centre' for fiscal reduction, with an estimated $800 million remaining in departments for internal reallocation. A five-to-four ratio may be a good deal for departments in one context and in one set or circumstances, but not so in others. It may apply to large expenditure deals but not to small ones, and it is likely to vary from department to department as well as depend on whether the government is in surplus or in deficit. Experience indicates that the 'exchange rate' for both small and large expenditures is generally left to be decided in the open market of 'argy-bargy' between spenders and guardians.

The question of the exchange rate is more than just about money. Often the significant constraint affecting whether or not some expenditure reallocations are made hinges on handling the impact of a reduction in public service employment, particularly in areas of high unemployment and government dependency, outside the national capital. An overall central dictum, or even an implicit understanding, that reallocations are not to reduce public service jobs in certain regions or locations of the country, places considerable constraint on individual departments in their reallocations. Broadening the reallocation exercise to include several departments and ensuring careful coordination across departments can sometimes be helpful in overcoming barriers that confront individual departments in securing their own internal reallocations.

Despite the promises, the record indicates that the government has had limited success in expenditure reallocation *across* government and has done only slightly better on reallocations *within* departments and agencies. Finance Minister John Manley in the run-up to his 2003 budget spoke boldly about 'reallocation for transformation.' The result, however, was hardly transformative. As reported by Treasury Board President Lucienne Robillard, the government eventually found $1 billion in largely one-time savings through 'a number of initiatives, including reductions in some activities or lower-than-anticipated use of some services, unavoidable delays in the start-up of some others, and other measures to reduce resources that are currently allocated.'[38] Despite the failures, there have been more recent and ever bolder attempts at government-wide expenditure reallocation. These exercises, which are fundamental attempts at major budget reform and which involve a commitment to a 'continuous culture of reallocation,' are examined in chapter 10, 'Budget Reforms.'

When it comes to reallocation *within* departments and agencies the battle lines are often drawn between headquarters and regions, across program areas, between operations and policy, and between service delivery units and support units such as policy and corporate entities. The annual reallocation of savings that allows departments to carry forward up to 5 per cent of their operating budgets from one fiscal year to the next is a case in point. Departmental chief financial officers (CFOs) have long struggled with how best to get managers to accurately identify and declare projected lapses in their operating budgets midway through the fiscal year in order to get as close as possible to the maximum carry forward of 5 per cent. However, managers are only willing to make accurate declarations as long as they receive a payback in the form of all, or nearly all, of the amount they project. If managers find that the money is simply reallocated by the CFO and the deputy minister to meet departmental shortfalls, managers are not prepared to provide accurate information on potential lapses for the next year. In this context, managers can come to view their own departmental CFOs in the same way that departmental officials often view the Treasury Board and the Department of Finance.

Most deputy ministers find it in their minister's and department's interests to establish a departmental reserve for new and emerging pressures. This has become increasingly important and necessary with the reduction and elimination of central operating and policy reserves. Departmental reserves are normally created on an ad hoc and opportunistic basis through several measures, including securing larger expenditure reductions than required by the centre; consolidating the operating budget carry forward; 'skimming resources' from new initiatives; curtailing various expenditures; reducing specific operating expenditures such as travel; deferring capital expenditures; and not filling vacant positions. There has been generally less effort and less success in creating departmental reserves by systematically determining the lowest priorities, and the least effective and most inefficient programs, operations, or projects. This suggests that strong incentives will be necessary for departments and agencies if they are to create reserves for reallocation through the systematic elimination and reduction of inefficient and ineffective programs. Without the strong and visible support of the minister or the 'political cover' of an overall, government-wide reallocation exercise (in which case the savings typically flow to the centre), it is difficult to secure savings that can change programs and important operations. As a consequence, the amount of savings for reallocation is normally very small, generally less than 0.5 per cent of discretionary expenditures.

Allocations are made from the departmental reserve, usually but not always as directed by the deputy minister on the advice of the CFO, and in consultation with the executive committee of the department or agency. The more uncertain the expenditure situation, including potential pressures that will not be covered by the Treasury Board or the Department of Finance, the more likely that allocations will be made close to year-end, thus increasing the difficulty of achieving effective spending.

More recently, a few departments have experimented with new ways of doing internal reallocations. For example, Agriculture and Agri-Food Canada established a matrix management model where assistant deputy ministers, in addition to their line or corporate responsibilities, have important functional responsibilities as members of corporate boards. Reallocations across activities can be initiated and implemented collectively by these boards with overall coordination and direction provided by the corporate board, chaired by the CFO with the strong and visible support of the deputy minister. This approach can foster cooperation and facilitate some reallocation; however, for it to work, a unique set of conditions must be met:

• A determined deputy minister, followed by another equally determined deputy minister, must be committed to the process.
• A matrix organization and decision-making structure must be in place.
• There must be an assurance of collective accountability for decisions through the use of individual performance agreements and/or other mechanisms.
• Senior executives must make large investments of time and maintain high levels of trust.
• Sufficiently accurate and timely expenditure and program information must be available.[39]

While there has been some limited success with certain expenditure reallocations internal to departments, there are sharp limits on how much reallocation can actually be undertaken in this manner. 'It is really silo reallocation,' explains a top PCO official, 'and the amounts that are reallocated are invisible. Nobody on the outside ever sees them. These types of reallocations can only go so far. It is not possible to close offices, to consolidate regional facilities, or do any number of things through internal reallocation. They require strong political will, political support, and "political cover" across government.'[40]

Budget Allocations Are Incremental

Budget allocations – increases, reductions, and reallocations – are inherently incremental. In periods of economic growth and expanding expenditures, most departments and agencies received incremental budget allocations on the basis of the principle of 'fair share.' In those periods, there was little need to make hard choices among the competing departmental and agency claims because, with a readily available annual fiscal dividend, there was sufficient new funding to provide everyone with something. Conflict was contained by 'being fair' and the calculations were made manageable by focusing on simple increments and ignoring the complexity of the budget base. With increasing fiscal restraint, however, fair share diminished and soon evaporated, and yet spending needs and demands continued. 'Priority setting' replaced fair share. It dealt with spending demands by setting priorities. Conflict increased, but it was made more manageable and acceptable because these priorities were not simply determined by guardians but carried the weight of the priority setters, most notably the prime minister. While each budget increment was larger, calculations were made manageable by focusing on a sharply limited number of expenditure priorities. As everyone – spenders, guardians, priority setters, and even financial watchdogs – paid more attention to incremental spending priorities, there was less focus on the ongoing base of public expenditure. As restraint worsened, spending, even on priorities, could no longer be maintained by itself. Spending gave way to expenditure reductions and the principle of 'equal sacrifice' was coupled with priority setting. Across-the-board operating cuts were made to all departments and agencies while a few high-profile priority initiatives proceeded.

Equal sacrifice like fair share did not provoke conflict, at least in its early stages. Only when the limits of equal sacrifice were reached, with the inability of the government to maintain its core functions and responsibilities, and when the requirement for expenditure restraint became so great that there was no fiscal room for any new priorities was incrementalism abandoned. This represented a shift point in the budgetary process, resulting in fundamental reviews of programs and expenditures and significant and deep cuts into the expenditure base. Budgeting was no longer incremental as spenders were forced to review the base of expenditure. Conflict increased, but it was made manageable through a combination of reductions for everyone (although some much greater than others), the complete abandonment of any expenditure increases, and the promise that the period of 'deep cuts and reductions' would be temporary and that spending would resume. When spending did resume, so too did incremental budgeting in the form of attempts to undertake 'expenditure reallocation' – simultaneous incremental increases and incremental reductions. Because reallocation engendered deep and divisive conflict, the actual reductions tended to be small and non-contentious, focusing on the less visible operating expenditures rather than on the more visible program expenditures. Also to reduce conflict, priorities became more numerous and less focused so that the reallocated expenditure increases could be spread more broadly under the principle of fair share.

Spenders, guardians, and priority setters all deal with a broad array of distinct budget allocations, ranging from the big fixes and the big-ticket items, to the must dos and the small items. In each of these cases the focus is on the real opportunities for increments and not on the base of ongoing expenditures and programs. Budget calculations are simplified by focusing on small changes to the base and conflicts are managed by not reopening past budget battles, which, with the passage of time, have healed and become embedded into the base of ongoing expenditure. Even the infrequent big fixes invariably involve additional incremental resources to a major and dominant priority without a significant reallocation or readjustment to existing spending. Big-ticket items are linked to and justified by government priorities, thereby reducing the need for further analysis and information about program performance and program management. The essential must dos are included in the budget with the knowledge that they must be done and, most important, that all of them have been done. The small items compete with one another and are more likely to occur when there is a requirement 'to balance' the range of initiatives in the budget. Each year budgeting continues to be by addition. In unique fiscal and economic circumstances, it becomes budgeting by subtraction, but only for one or two years. Rarely is budgeting ever by both addition and subtraction. While there may be a need in Ottawa for ongoing budget reallocation, it is an ideal whose time is yet to come.

Allocation is about deciding *where* public money is to be spent. It is inherently incremental, and it is only one part of the budget decision-making process. The next part of the process, as we shall see in the next chapter, is deciding *how* public money is to be spent.

8 Budget Implementation: Financial Management and Efficiency

All the heavy lifting is done by the time that Treasury Board gets to play. It is less a question of guardianship than how it is spent. We focus on the third part of Schick's budget functions.

Treasury Board Secretariat program analyst

Treasury Board will have an overall supervisory function to make sure that government – individual departments – are doing what they said they would do with the monies that have been allocated to them. The main responsibility is the minister's. Supervisory responsibility is given to the Treasury Board. The finance minister is off doing something else.

Paul Martin[1]

We operate primarily on a basis of trust. We believe that departments want to use the guideline and want to apply it in a way that is appropriate. We don't approach this on an assumption that there are departments out there who somehow wish to do something different from the guideline that is given.

Treasury Board Secretariat assistant secretary[2]

The job is not just to say 'no'; it's also to help colleagues achieve their goals.

Chief financial officer

The financial community may be in danger of being overwhelmed. It is faced with conflicting roles, ill-equipped to take on new roles, and vulnerable due to inadequate renewal of the community.

Association of Professional Executives
of the Public Service of Canada[3]

This chapter focuses on budget implementation – what happens after budget allocations are made and the budget is announced. The story of budget implementation is the story of financial management and efficiency in government; it is the story of more than 400 departments, agencies, commissions, and other entities and their relationships with external organizations through various partnerships and alternative service delivery arrangements. It is a story of many unseen successes and a few, highly visible failings.

One is immediately struck with the diversity in the range of government activity and in the size of government organizations. There are large ones like the Department of National Defence with responsibilities for major procurement and the management of billions of dollars of capital assets. There are small independent agents of Parliament like the Office of the Privacy Commissioner. There are regulatory agencies like the Canadian Food Inspection Agency with special administrative and financial authorities enshrined in separate legislation. There are policing services like the Royal Canadian Mounted Police (RCMP) involving both uniformed and civilian personnel. There are client-focused departments like Veterans Affairs and Indian Affairs and Northern Development. There are advisory departments like the Department of Justice with a strong and deeply entrenched professional culture of legal practitioners. There are program development and delivery departments like Agriculture and Agri-Food Canada, which work closely with provincial and territorial governments as they deal with the pressing demands of their clients. At various times some departments, like Citizenship and Immigration or Fisheries and Oceans, seem to be continuously 'in the news' whereas others, like the National Battlefields Commission or the Library and Archives of Canada, are almost never reported on and invariably struggle to increase their public profile. This diversity in purpose, scope, and size means that, when it comes to matters of financial management, 'one size does not fit all.'

On Paper

On paper, financial management and control of public money within government is clear and straightforward.[4] The most basic of all controls is the consolidated revenue fund (CRF) into which all government revenue must flow. All expenditures by the government from the CRF require the approval of Parliament. In Canada, there are almost no exceptions permitting the 'earmarking' of revenues for specific purposes. Those few that do exist require legislative approval. Ministers are responsible and accountable to the prime minister and to Parliament in two fundamental ways. First, they are individually responsible to the prime minister and to cabinet for their own performance in carrying out the responsibilities of the portfolio assigned to them by the prime minister. Second, as members of cabinet, they are collectively responsible to Parliament in supporting the decisions of cabinet and the government.

Parliament confers power on a minister through parliamentary statutes that set out the departmental powers, duties, and functions for which the minister is individually responsible. Many of these powers are normally delegated to deputy ministers and departmental officials, who act on behalf of the minister and are accountable to the minister. Ministers are individually responsible to Parliament and the prime minister for their own actions and those of their departments, including those actions, when they know of them or should have known of them, by all officials under their management and direction.

Under the Financial Administration Act (FAA), the Treasury Board is authorized to establish policies, directives, standards, and guidelines on the management of public money. The policies of the Treasury Board are intended to ensure that expenditures comply with the law, satisfy the needs for parliamentary control and reporting, and ensure the efficient, economic, and prudent use of public resources. Under the FAA, the Treasury Board assigns considerable duties and responsibilities to deputy ministers for the management of public money, with most of the tasks carried out by the chief financial officer (CFO) and his/her staff.[5] The assigned responsibilities include:

- preparing a division of an appropriation or item included in the estimates, at the commencement of each fiscal year, or at such times as the Treasury Board may direct,
- ensuring by an adequate system of internal control and audit that the allotments provided in a division of allotments approved by the Treasury Board are not exceeded,
- establishing procedures and maintaining records respecting the control of financial commitments chargeable to each appropriation or item, and
- providing the required certification to authorize any payment to be made.

Like other OECD countries, there is a continuous structure for reporting expenditures of departments, agencies, and Crown corporations to Parliament. It includes the following key elements:

- expenditures are presented by departments on a program by program basis with a statement of objectives,
- each program is broken down into activities and total costs are displayed in terms of objectives of expenditure,
- non-budgetary items (loans, investments, and advances) are individually displayed by program,
- budget allocations by program are presented for the coming year and are compared to the forecast of expenditures for the fiscal year just ending and to the actual expenditures of the previous year, and
- expenditures are displayed by major categories as capital, grants and contributions, transfer payments, operating, and payments on the public debt.

Behind this seemingly simple framework, designed to ensure the effective financial management of public money, lurks a steady stream of ever-present risks and potential problems for any government. Most often departments and agencies quietly and successfully manage these risks, anticipate the potential problems, and ensure they have in place effective financial controls and proper corrective action. Budgets are quietly implemented as departments and agencies go about their business of signing contracts, putting in place grants and contributions arrangements, providing payments in accordance with legislation and regulations, and paying their bills for the products and services that they have procured.

From time to time, and with seemingly increasing regularity, issues of financial management arise and through the caldron of parliamentary partisan politics and an increasingly probing and attentive media, they take on national attention and prominence. At one extreme was what the media and the opposition erroneously dubbed as the 'HRDC (Human Resources Development Canada) billion dollar boondoggle,' which actually turned out to be an expenditure overpayment of $85,000.[6] At the other extreme was the dramatic and far-reaching Sponsorship Program and Advertising Activities debacle, which resulted in the high-profile Gomery Commission of Inquiry and the conviction and imprisonment of guilty parties, contributed to the defeat of the Liberal government and the victory of the Conservative government in

January 2006, and led both governments to introduce an avalanche of administrative reforms.

The Gomery Commission examined in minute detail (172 witnesses, 136 hearing days, and a 1,000-page first report and a 1,250 second report) one specific area of government activity – the Sponsorship Program and Advertising Activities. This represented public expenditures of $37 million a year, that is twenty-three one thousands of one percentage point (0.023%) of total federal spending.[7] In the management of these specific expenditures, the commission found significant and deeply troubling problems. In layperson's terms, it found three things about this particular area of government activity:

1 There was considerable political input (or interference) in the running of the program.
2 The normal management and administrative controls of government were not in place in this area.
3 Unscrupulous people, inside as well as outside government, took personal advantage of this lapse and failure in basic controls.

In one sense, the responsibility within government for prudent financial management resides with everyone, from the prime minister who sets the tone at the top to various spending and guardian ministers, the countless public servants operating at all levels, parliamentarians and their committees with responsibility to scrutinize public expenditures and hold government to account, the independent auditors and financial watchdogs, and to the citizens and corporations with whom government deals. It is a part of everyone's responsibility, but only a small part. Perhaps surprisingly, there is only a small cadre of officials inside government who can be considered to be 'full timers' when it comes to matters of financial management. They operate on two fronts and form two lines of defence. One is in departments and agencies where the single most senior position is the departmental chief financial officer (CFO). The CFO operates at an assistant deputy minister level, reports to the deputy minister or agency head, and is supported by a cast of 'financial' officials in headquarters and in the major regional offices. The other is the Treasury Board and, more specifically, the Office of the Comptroller General (OCG) of Canada, which is surrounded by a small cadre of 'comptrollers' and supported by other officials in the Treasury Board Secretariat. Standing apart from these financial officers and outside of the government of the day, but ever attentive to its financial actions and inactions, are the financial watchdog – the Auditor General – and the Public Accounts Committee of Parliament.

The First Line of Defence

When it comes to overseeing the government's expenditures and ensuring effective financial management, departmental and agency CFOs are often seen as the first line of defence, and the Treasury Board and the Comptroller General as the second. At first blush, there is a sense of confidence that comes from having two lines of defence and knowing that government is designed, at least on paper, with a capacity to double its efforts, with one line of defenders providing support and protection to the other. The key to understanding how financial management works in government, and on the rare occasion does not, is to examine these two lines of defence – how they work together and how they work apart.

Understanding the role of the first line of defence rests on understanding how it is perceived by the second. The words of a former secretary to the Treasury Board are particularly illuminating, suggesting that much of the responsibility for financial management is handled at the first line – the department – with the second providing assurance and reinforcement:

> ... the oversight function in the federal government is by no means the exclusive domain of the Treasury Board Secretariat, and the system of management within the public sector generally is predicated on the presumption that departments and agencies have in place internal oversight and management systems to allow them to ensure for the due diligence of the expenditure of public funds and the management of issues as well. In fact, many would regard the department functions as the first line of oversight ...[8]

Understanding how this first line actually discharges its financial management function within departments and agencies begins with the departmental CFOs and the diverse ways in which they undertake their duties.[9] Many CFOs are at the assistant deputy minister level, with directors general and directors occupying the positions in smaller organizations. Some CFOs in the largest departments might have responsibility only for financial matters, whereas others also have administrative responsibilities included in their job descriptions. Others, in smaller organizations, might also be responsible for major corporate functions such as information technology or systems. In even smaller organizations, CFOs might have responsibility for the entire corporate suite of functions, including human resources, information technology, administration, and finance. Sometimes a single corporate assistant deputy minister serves more than one department, such as is the case for Finance and the Treasury Board Secretariat and, for a time, was the case for Social Development Canada and Human Resources and Skills Development Canada. At the level of regions, the regional financial officer is usually responsible for all corporate functions, including finance. In a sense, therefore, there cannot be a single perspective on the CFO.

Despite the singular title, CFOs have a multiple role – part guardian, part watchdog, and part spender. They have an abiding interest in ensuring that the spending of public money and the operations of their departments or agencies are conducted efficiently in a government environment where, for all others, efficiency is only one of a number of competing objectives. While their colleagues, their deputy ministers, and their ministers pay lip service to the uncompromising value of efficiency, it is only the CFO who is prepared to laud its continuous virtue in the face of competing and, often times, more important values. As a guardian, it means getting things done for the least cost and best value. Like the watchdog, the CFO is sustained through the currency of information – both financial and performance. The extent to which he/she can keep a watchful eye over the management of expenditures and finances within the department is dependent on the accuracy, reliability, and the timeliness of the information that can be secured. That is why CFOs devote much of their attention to the development of integrated financial management information systems – electronic ways of reliably linking together financial, human resources, and performance information on the programs and activities of the department or agency. As a watchdog, it means securing the integrated information and acting on the results to avoid crises and maintain the reputation of the department as a prudent financial manager. CFOs have close working relationships with their department's internal audit bureau, using their audits and reports as signals of financial risk and weakness so that corrective action can be taken before an issue 'spills into the political arena.'

Probe a bit more and we see that the CFO is also a spender, a fundraiser who is ultimately responsible for maintaining and securing resources for the department. Without a base of ongoing resources the organization would cease to exist, and without periodic increases, however small and incremental, support for the CFO from spending departmental colleagues would evaporate. While CFOs are not responsible for securing the major new program expenditures, they are responsible for ensuring that there is sufficient operational funding to sustain both existing and new programs. As explained in chapter 7, getting Treasury Board Secretariat guardians to agree to such operating funding, which is often seen as simply 'overhead,' can be more difficult than securing from the Finance guardians new program funding, which can readily be expressed in terms of 'benefits and results' and linked to government priorities.

Ask any CFO what the job is and invariably one is confronted with a large and diverse set of responses. The job, like the diversity of the departments and agencies of government, varies considerably. It depends upon a number of factors – the nature of the business of the department, how the function and department are organized, the assignment of other corporate functions (e.g., human resources, information, administration) to the CFO, the issues facing the departments, the dominant 'financial management wisdom' emanating from the Treasury Board Secretariat and the Office of the Comptroller General, the predispositions of the CFO, and, perhaps most important, his/her relationship with the deputy minister and colleagues. All CFOs, however, agree on one thing – 'the job is no longer what it used to be.' 'Where it used to be simply keeping the books,' explains one CFO, 'it is now about developing strategies.' The changing job is seen as 'moving from bookkeeper to financial strategist,' 'integrating financial and performance information to tell a coherent story,' 'moving from transactions to strategies,' 'challenging colleagues,' and 'managing risks.'[10]

Although the job is performed differently by different CFOs, a careful analysis of their responses to questions indicates that all CFOs have two overriding preoccupations. Expressed in the most direct terms, one is 'to get money' for the department and the other is to 'avoid crises' for the department. For example, a CFO in Agriculture and Agri-Food Canada sees his principal role as developing a strategy for financing the department's vast and diverse operations. Given the complexity and multiplicity of funding sources, he needs a strategic approach if he is to tap into a broad range of potential sources to keep the department secure during periods of domestic and international shock such as mad cow disease or trade disputes. Elements of the overall financing strategy for the department include cost recovery, asset sales, revenue generation, TBS funding, internal reallocation, private sector partnerships, borrowing and repayment, and cash management. For the CFO of a large special operating agency, it means 'ensuring there are sufficient funds to run the organization.'[11] The CFO in a policing agency explains the similarity in role to his assumed counterpart in the private sector: 'It's to get the money.'[12] Yet another explained how securing funding means that 'the departmental finance people get invited to the table because your colleagues know they need the support of the CFO.'[13]

It is easy to understand why 'getting money' for the department is a major preoccupation for the CFO. In a nutshell, getting money earns credibility from departmental colleagues. The skillful CFO focuses his/her time and energy on securing ongoing operating funds for the department from the Treasury Board and leaves it to the assistant deputy minister for policy and the deputy minister to go after the Department of Finance for the 'big money.' Getting operating money means building into any major expenditure proposal going forward to cabinet and the Department of Finance all the operational expenditures for personnel, program delivery, management and control, accommodation, systems and information technology, security, audit and monitoring, evaluation, consultation, and anything else. This is often the one and only chance they have to secure operating funds. A veteran Treasury Board Secretariat official notes that those CFOs fortunate enough to reside in certain large and important departments with regular opportunities to secure new expenditures in areas of government priority 'always try to include as much of the operating costs as they can. It may be as much as 18 per cent or more of the total program expenditures.'[14]

It also means being able to capitalize on the infrequent opportunities to put forward a compelling case to the Treasury Board for money to help underwrite the costs of ongoing programs and operations such as information technology or capital infrastructure. 'If a CFO can find a sympathetic assistant secretary at TBS they might come forward for some increased operating expenditures to deal with the rust-out of the fisheries patrol fleet or some other issue of program integrity,' explains a Secretariat official.[15] But for most CFOs, the sympathy is not there and it may require other strategies such as scouring the sources of potential cost-recovery revenue and then 'cutting a deal with the Treasury Board' to retain part or all of those revenues for the department.

'Keeping the department out of financial crises' is the other part of the job. This means not just putting in place a financial control framework but also seeing that it is being used and that it is working. At the most basic level, explains a CFO, 'it's ensuring the department does not overspend its budget,' which is not as simple as it may seem for an organization that is 'chronically underfunded' and 'running too close to the edge.'[16] One CFO in a large capital-intensive department argues that good management controls serve to 'prevent crises and scandals.'[17] Another veteran CFO explains how his job is to 'keep the organization out of any hint of fraud or scandal to ensure that its reputation is protected.' He goes on to explain how an agency with responsibilities for policing can be particularly vulnerable as seemingly small expenditure items like, for example, an employee pension payment can easily get 'blown out of proportion by the media.'[18]

In the current environment, it is easy to understand why CFOs spend so much of their time trying to avoid crises. Better that the CFO and his/her staff unearth looming financial management crises within the department, quietly dealing with them internally, than the Auditor General expose them to a politically charged environment through his/her high-profile public reports. Government waste, inefficiency, misuse of public funds, and corruption are hot topics. When it comes to matters of public money, it is these issues, not questions on the magnitude of public spending or on expenditure allocation, which resonate most with citizens, the opposition, and the media. The scope for missteps is seemingly endless – a controversial project that has overrun its initial budget forecast; a government program that has been inefficient and wasted taxpayers' money; an audit that reveals financial mismanagement and irregularities in government programs and projects; a public servant who has received private benefits in the management of public money; or officials of a political party who peddled their influence in efforts to direct government contracts in exchange for campaign contributions. Whatever the issue, it immediately piques the interests and concerns of citizens and taxpayers; provides a major opportunity for the opposition and a difficult problem for the government; and provides a focus for the media's spotlight. Indeed, such issues are tailor-made for the media and the techniques of journalists. A government that cannot manage public money can become a government with a major scandal, and then it might become a government that cannot govern. Attacks on government's financial mismanagement are fundamentally attacks on the rationality of government and its control systems. At a minimum, they threaten to expose an uneconomical government because they suggest that everything is political and thus undercut the perception of rational management. At the extreme, they threaten to expose a corrupt government.

Victims of Conflicting Norms: The Chief Financial Officer

Scratch the surface and one soon finds that CFOs, like 'the man in the middle,' are victims of conflicting norms. On the one side, they are pushed by the guardians at the centre of government to hold the line on expenditure and to 'challenge' their departmental spenders to get 'value for money.' On the other side, within their own departments, they are prodded and pressed by spending colleagues to find more operating money and by program managers to provide more administrative flexibility to support the efficient delivery of the 'unique' business of the department. If it is not the central guardians who push them, then it is the Comptroller General who expects them to implement centrally developed and directed financial management policies and to alert 'the centre' to potential financial management risks and problems within the departments. All this tempers and constrains the nature of their relationships with their departmental colleagues and their deputy minister, who can sometimes come to see them more as 'central agency spies' than as departmental personnel. 'If you're perceived as the left arm of the Treasury Board Secretariat,' explains a former CFO, 'it is very hard to build trust and credibility in the department.'[19] CFOs are sometimes given short shrift or ignored – some more than others – even by their own deputy ministers. They are often publicly criticized (at least indirectly) by the parliamentary watchdog, the Auditor General, and only rarely are they ever privately praised. The task has never been easy, and in the face of high-profile financial management scandals and crises it has become considerably more difficult.[20]

Over the past decade the job has been made more difficult because of a number of factors. Perhaps the most significant and troublesome has been the increased emphasis placed on various forms of new public management, which press up hard against their traditional responsibilities for prudent control and tight management of financial resources. On the one hand, CFOs have had the long established responsibility to foster prudence and probity in the management of public money and to ensure safeguards are in place to protect against misuse and abuse. This has meant the establishment of rules and regulations over all aspects about how public money is spent. On the other hand, CFOs are increasingly having to work with managers to ensure that public money is managed efficiently and effectively and that program results are achieved. This has meant the granting of increased administrative and managerial flexibility and autonomy to managers and spenders within the department. It has also meant putting in place practical systems that can produce timely and accurate information on the program results achieved while at the same time guarding against the risk that financial management rules are not properly followed.

In the past, as more rules were piled upon more regulations in an effort to ensure tight and secure financial management through a culture of 'command and control,' it became increasingly evident that many of the financial management rules were standing in the way of ensuring economy and efficiency in expenditures and in achieving effectiveness, performance, and results from the programs. In short, CFOs were called upon to lead a government-wide charge to reduce and eliminate unnecessary controls and red tape and to move the culture of the department to one of 'results and performance' while at the same time ensuring that the ever-present problems of financial mismanagement were avoided.[21] This is the inherent conflict and challenge for the modern comptroller or CFO, which was deeply embedded and far from resolved in the 'modern comptrollership' movement with its emphasis on general guidance and policy directions.[22] In short, budgeting and financial management under new public management placed squarely on the shoulders of the CFO a new and different set of responsibilities, which in a 'harder world' of transparency, access to information, and a probing media have become significantly more difficult and tricky to reconcile.

Modern comptrollership became the financial management community's response to new public management. As it was implemented, it placed a new and expanded set of tools in the hands of CFOs and financial managers. As they and their central agency counterparts reduced and eliminated detailed rules, they increased and expanded general frameworks, guidelines, directions, and audit processes. As they relied less on public service rules, they and their colleagues promulgated the use of public service values. As departmental decision-making was increasingly decentralized and staff empowered, less emphasis was placed on 'front-end' rules and greater emphasis on 'back-end' reports and audits in an effort to ensure a measure of control over decentralized operations. As CFOs focused more on program outputs and the achievement of program results, they increased flexibility in the use of program inputs. As their departments did less by way of direct service delivery, and more through alternative service delivery and partnership arrangements with independent non-profit and private sector organizations, CFOs worked with program managers to put in place reporting frameworks and accountability mechanisms.

Many of the new tools – frameworks, guidelines, values, reports, partnerships, and accountability mechanisms – that were being introduced government-wide were soft tools. According to some, these newly developed central agency tools place 'surreal' requirements on departments and managers and the evidence suggests that they are too idealistic for departmental managers to make use of them in the specific environment in which they work.[23] For example, the attribution of specific program outputs, to say nothing of outcomes, to a particular program at best requires a leap in logic and is fraught with uncertainty, conditions, and qualifications. The old regulatory tools, most of which were being de-emphasized and some of which were being abandoned, were hard tools. The rules were there to be followed, not to be discussed. In short, the challenge for the CFOs and their staff became the skillful use of soft tools in an increasingly hard-edged world.

In the face of these changing conditions and conflicting norms of behaviour, there is good reason why CFOs are worriers. One CFO who works in a highly decentralized policy department, with 'lots of senior people and twenty-six of them reporting directly to the deputy minister,' frets over the critical lack of 'financial understanding on the part of managers.' With every regional office having its own business manager, she is 'sometimes reluctant to sign-off financial statements.'[24] Another worries about the need for 'much more accurate and timely financial data through one official system.' Lamenting on his frustrations, he 'refuses to look at data that does not come from the system of record.'[25] Another, operating with what is described as 'seat-of-the-pants' cost estimates, has 'no solid costing capacity' as the agency considers alternative service delivery arrangements for some of its inspection activities.[26] Another laments that his agency's proposals for new expenditures 'are not driven by a strong business case.'[27] Yet another, recently stung by the discovery that an additional $10 million was available beyond the fiscal year at the 'P13' period and could not be used for reallocation, searches for ways to get his spending colleagues to be 'honest and accurate' in forecasting their operating surpluses.[28] All CFOs worry about retaining experienced financial officers, moving new recruits through positions too fast without the opportunity to acquire sufficient experience and understanding, and the general lack of understanding of financial management issues by public servants.

At another level, CFOs worry about getting their colleagues to understand their conflicting role: exercising their 'challenge function' to push back on the spenders in search of more efficient and effective ways of doing things and 'protecting the department' from incursions by the Treasury Board Secretariat and the Comptroller General. An experienced CFO in a large spending department explains: 'The ability to play a challenge role depends on credibility and being seen as a team player in the department. It must be done carefully and colleagues need to feel you are working in their best interests.' His bottom line: 'Speak truth to power, even if it hurts.'[29] But what CFOs worry about most is their relationship with their deputy minister. Even a most skilled CFO, with extensive experience, knows that it is an uphill battle to nurture a close relationship with a deputy minister. 'At the bottom line, everything goes to dollars' and, therefore, 'the CFO must be at the right hand of the deputy. But, this requires a different relationship for most deputies, who are invariably much less interested in management than in policy, with the result that they have less interest in the analysis and the information that we produce than in what is produced by the assistant deputy minister for policy.'[30]

Despite the wishful hopes of all CFOs, most deputy ministers do not view them as their right-hand person. Rather, they are perceived as another member of their management team. The one or two deputy heads that do, invariably head up small departments or special agencies requiring a high level of hands-on management of sensitive operations, and have recruited a skilled and experienced CFO who can act as 'the number two' with the credibility and the stature necessary to challenge spending colleagues. This, however, is the rare exception. When asked whether they see themselves as becoming deputy ministers, most CFOs do not. Their deputy ministers, and the Clerk of the Privy Council, who has ultimate responsibility for making recommendations on these appointments to the prime minister, see it the same way. Furthermore, most deputy ministers are especially cautious about how their CFOs should exercise a challenge role with other colleagues in the department. When pressed, they fear their CFOs lack both the credibility and the information to effectively challenge others on their program spending. This view is also held by the most senior financial comptrollers at the centre of government.[31]

It can be troubling for a CFO when his/her advice is overturned by the deputy minister or the minister because of other considerations. The experienced CFO, like the happy warrior, knows that this can happen only so many times before his/her credibility and that of the staff is severely diminished in the eyes of the departmental spenders. But worse than being overturned is being forgotten, deliberately ignored, or never asked for advice. As one CFO, with extensive experience in the Treasury Board Secretariat, put it: 'The CFO must be able to make the hard recommendation about the proposal, especially when it is not welcome and nobody wants to hear from him.'[32] A sure sign that the CFO is or might be forgotten is reflected in the necessity to issue a government-wide edict that requires all CFOs to provide a formal sign-off on all memoranda to cabinet to certify that the costing and expenditure calculations are sound.

What makes for a good CFO? Professional competence for sure is important, but there is and will continue to be much debate about whether the CFO requires a professional accounting designation (currently less than 40 per cent have one).[33] More than professional accounting degrees, all CFOs agree that what is most important is the 'trust and credibility of their deputy minister and their colleagues.'[34] This is not acquired but earned. In their own words, it is earned by 'knowing the business of the department,' a particularly difficult task for many CFOs who are usually recruited from other departments or increasingly, under the current employment model, from outside government.[35] It is earned by having timely, accurate, and relevant financial and program information that 'everyone uses.'[36] According to one, it will only be acknowledged when 'some deputy ministers are appointed from the corporate services pool of talent.'[37] If effectively exercising the financial management role within departments and agencies has proved to be a major challenge for CFOs, one can take comfort in the fact that they are only 'the first line of defence.'

The Second Line of Defence

To oversee the sensitive and critically important matters concerning financial management, it is not enough to have CFOs located only in departments and agencies. Finances need to be managed and overseen on a government-wide basis and that is why governments have established a 'second line of defence.' In the case of the federal government, this is the Treasury Board Secretariat and the Office of the Comptroller General. A former minister of finance explains:

It isn't that the minister of finance is indifferent to how money is spent. It isn't that the minister of finance isn't concerned with how money is spent, whether the objectives are to be attained. But ... the structure of government is such that it is the responsibility of the minister of finance to set that financial framework, and the responsibility, after the minister of finance has done that, shifts to Treasury Board. The responsibility shifts to another government department. Treasury Board then takes on the responsibility of making sure that everything is well structured, ready for Parliament.[38]

Traditionally, and more often than not, this central government-wide CFO function has been handled by the secretary to the Treasury Board (with assistance from a senior official at the assistant deputy minister level) as part of his/her overall responsibilities. This has, however, proved to be inadequate and, on two occasions, both in times of severe financial management crises, the government has established a separate Comptroller General at the deputy minister level within the Treasury Board Secretariat.

The first crisis was the exaggerated claim by the Auditor General in 1976 that 'Parliament has lost, or is close to losing, effective control of the public purse,'[39] which, in 1977, led directly to the establishment of the first separate Comptroller General and the appointment of a deputy minister level officer recruited from outside government. Sixteen years and three separate Comptrollers General later, the position was abolished in the restructuring and streamlining of government in 1993 as part of an overall reform by the Conservative Campbell government to reduce the size of cabinet, delegate responsibilities, and streamline government decision-making. The second major crisis was the internal audit by Public Works and Government Services Canada (PWGSC) and the subsequent external audit by the Auditor General of the sponsorship program, along with her stinging indictment that 'officials had broken just about every rule in the book,'[40] which led directly to the establishment of the Gomery Commission of Inquiry in 2004. In 2003, Prime Minister Paul Martin had re-established the Comptroller General, and in 2004 a deputy minister level executive officer was again recruited and appointed from outside government.

Comptrollers General may come and go, but even in the best of times the burden of their responsibility remains decidedly heavy, and, in recent times, the burden has been increasing. 'The recreation of the office [of the Comptroller General],' explains the most recent recruit, 'is to put the focus on financial management in government, and also to create a champion for the financial management issues throughout the government of Canada.'[41] But 'focusing' and 'championing' are not easy in government and, when it comes to financial management, it has proved to be especially difficult. A sobering and yet realistic assessment of the task is provided by a respected former Comptroller General. 'It's like selling the unwanted to the unwilling. Deputies invariably have many more pressing and important priorities to deal with than good financial management and improvements to the efficiency in their operations. It is only in a crisis that there is a focus on these issues to a level that sustains the ongoing priority and attention of the deputy.' 'And then,' he adds, 'it's all about assigning blame to people.'[42]

Upon arrival in Ottawa, the skillful Comptrollers General know that in the overall scheme of the upper echelons of the public service and ministers, they are and will be seen as 'lightweights.'[43] They are recruited directly from the private sector and have extensive experience in large, private sector firms. Within government, however, they lack the nuanced perspective and the interpersonal network of trust that are developed and honed through years of public service experience and practice. They also lack an appreciation for the complexity of public sector decision-making, and, more important, they don't know how to cut a practical path through the dense undergrowth of established practice and culture to get overworked deputy ministers and their staff to pay more attention to financial management. While they may be appointed at the deputy minister level, they are not part of the deputy minister community, regularly participating in the weekly 'DM breakfast' with the Clerk of the Privy Council and in other important meetings of the DM community. Even if they remain in the job for several years, they are unlikely to make it into the elite corps of the senior deputy ministers. They are comptrollers apart: part guardian and part watchdog. But unlike the guardians in the Department of Finance, and to a much lesser degree those with responsibility for expenditure management in the Treasury Board Secretariat, they do not have in their hands the persuasive instrument of expenditure allocation. They cannot buy a little more financial management with a little more expenditure. Nor, like the financial watchdog in the Office of the Auditor General, do they have the persuasive power to publish high-profile external audit reports, which, through extensive media coverage and opposition attack, can severely embarrass the government and lead to internal change.

Some Comptrollers General never overcome their lightweight status. They are not so much out-slugged by their opponents as they are ignored. Rarely invited into the centre ring, most of their time is spent shadowboxing in their own corner. A sure sign that the Comptroller General has limited influence is his/her failure to get a 'sign-off' on the job description of a departmental CFO or to be invited by a deputy minister to sit on the hiring board for a new CFO. A few, however, do rise to the middleweight category. A former Comptroller General describes his strategy to 'punch above his weight': 'I sold financial management initiatives to Treasury Board ministers and made recommendations to get political interest. I worked closely with the Auditor General to shape his agenda for his audits and reviews because his work invariably had political prominence. I reached in and engaged, under my direction, a group of senior departmental CFOs in a series of major government-wide financial management issues.'[44]

Victims of the Intractability of Cultural Change:
The Comptroller General

If the departmental CFOs on the first line of defence are victims of conflicting norms, then the Comptroller General and his/her comptrollers on the second line of defence are victims of the intractability of cultural change.

To be sure, Comptrollers General can 'get some traction' by marketing financial management initiatives to the president of the Treasury Board and to Treasury Board ministers. However, this is heavily dependent on the timing and the circumstances faced by the government. Even the inexperienced Comptrollers General know that 'one-off' policies, unveiled and announced in the absence of a specific context, are unlikely to receive the priority and attention of deputies and ministers nor sustain the ongoing support that is necessary for successful implementation.

On matters of improving financial management, getting the announcement is one thing, making it happen is quite another. Indeed the challenge as defined by many, including those most senior in the Office of the Comptroller General (OCG), is especially complicated. Recently, the solutions to financial management problems, like the intractable and complex problems such as the 'democratic deficit' or the 'accountability deficiency,' have all come to be seen by most would-be reformers as dependent on the requirement 'to change the culture' of the organization. Almost to a person, from the most senior officials to the most junior officers in and around the OCG, it is agreed that the approach to improving financial management in government requires 'cultural change.' The answer to the straightforward, child-like question of What is the job of the Office of the Comptroller General? immediately unleashes the apparent intractability and interrelatedness of the complexity of a host of problems:

> The job is to change the culture and the nature of financial management in government. Deputies are being asked to take on impossible jobs in a very complex environment. They must manage very complicated policy issues with major political implications and also manage large and complex operations. This is an impossible job and they can't do both. Therefore, they spend most of their time on policy and not enough on management.
>
> The public service is really a class system when it comes to financial managers and policy people. They're both ghettoized. Financial managers are in a ghetto and they need to get out of it. There is a need for a cultural change.
>
> We need to build pride in the financial community in government. The culture in the financial community is too often focused just on transactions and compliance.
>
> The culture of the 'challenge function' is not well entrenched in the financial community. They do not feel they have the full capacity and authority to challenge. They feel they are not empowered to challenge policy and program people. They feel too shy to offer program advice; they lack self-confidence, feeling that they have not earned the right to challenge programs and policies. They feel they have been unfairly tarnished by the recent financial management scandals. Right now financial managers are being beaten left and right. It will take time to bring about the necessary cultural change.[45]

In an effort to bring about this 'cultural change,' the OCG is attempting to engage departmental financial officers and deputy ministers in a process that is nothing short of a new and ambitious vision for the entire financial community and its relationship to ministers, deputy ministers, and officials within government as well as to Parliament itself. In summary form, the vision contemplates:

- dramatically strengthening the role of departmental CFO and incorporating many of the aspects from the private sector including an accounting certification,
- the CFO playing a role similar to counterparts in the private sector and reporting directly to deputy ministers on matters relating to the planning, allocation, and control of financial resources,

- the CFO being a major participant in discussions of departmental priorities and expenditures, ensuring not only are 'the books balanced' but that there is demonstrable value-for-money associated with expenditures,
- the CFO undertaking a challenge of program effectiveness and expenditures within the department as a normal part of doing business,
- that attitudes and methods will shift from periodic, imposed, across-the-board cuts to a strategic assessment and reallocation, using accepted processes and standards and state-of-the-art financial management tools and information, and
- strengthening significantly the capacity, independence, and relevance of the internal audit function in departments.

Changing culture is necessary and perhaps even possible in the longer term, but the most critical factor in 'getting traction' and beginning the process of change is whether the Comptroller General can effectively engage departmental CFOs, and by extension their deputy ministers, in critical government-wide issues of financial management. This is almost never a major priority of government and, on the rare occasion when it is, such as during the Gomery Inquiry and in the immediate aftermath of its reports, there is no guarantee that deputy and ministerial interest will be sufficiently focused to overcome the underlying obstacles and inherent tensions as they relentlessly struggle to make sense of the avalanche of reform initiatives in the form of new guidelines, frameworks, rules, policies, and audit procedures emanating from the Treasury Board and the Office of the Comptroller General. Furthermore, during times of financial management crisis, the measures taken are almost invariably recognized as an overreaction to the situation with the result that they are less likely to be enthusiastically embraced by spending deputy ministers and their departments.[46] In addition, some deputy ministers are fearful that the Comptroller General and his/her office are attempting to impose a private sector model of financial control on them and their departments.

In large measure, the success of the Office of the Comptroller General turns on its ability to establish a network of skilled and experienced departmental CFOs and, with the support of deputy ministers, to work with and through these CFOs on an agenda of cross-government issues, none of which reside exclusively within the domain and purview of a single department. The perception on the part of some deputy ministers that they are being 'second guessed' by the Comptroller General and that their departmental CFO is operating as 'an agent' of the Comptroller General suggests to some a 'second line of defence' that duplicates and mirrors the first rather than one that reinforces and complements it. However, an experienced deputy minister with a reputable CFO who can work with the Comptroller General to more fully appreciate the 'unique' nature of the departmental business – be it to deliver specialized programs to Aboriginal communities or to employ voluntary sector organizations to deliver community-based programs – can be in a better position to prevent unrealistic and potentially explosive public audits by the Auditor General and to deal effectively with the major financial management issues facing the department. For the Office of the Comptroller General to be seen as a player requires that CFOs become players.

On Becoming Players

On paper, the jobs of the CFOs and the Comptroller General look relatively clear and straight forward, and yet, in practice, they belie a significant number of strong cross-currents and contradictions. Two lines of defence are undoubtedly better than one, especially when it comes to tricky matters of financial management, which, if not handled with great skill can be transformed into a major political crisis affecting the fortunes and the future of a government. Some may find it puzzling as to why it has proved so difficult to strengthen the financial management function, especially when failures in it can and do have dramatic consequences for the reputation of any government. Yet it has proved to be especially difficult to give sustained, high-level priority to financial management and to sort out the roles and responsibilities among and between the central comptrollers, the departmental financial officials, deputy ministers and departmental program officials. When so much of the focus and energy of senior officials and ministers in government is, as it is with budgeting, on pushing through and announcing new initiatives rather than eliminating old programs, there is less time and priority given to financial management.

More than anything CFOs need to become real players in and around the management of public money and, more than anything else, the extent to which this occurs determines the success of the Office of the Comptroller General. Even together, they are, however, only two among many players with responsibility for creating and sustaining the necessary conditions and capacity to ensure the effective management of public money. In this sense, while they are necessary for success, they cannot on their own produce the sufficient conditions. While each department and agency has a unique set of circumstances and ways of doing its particular business, there are several ingredients for strengthening the role of the CFO and its support by the Comptroller General in facilitating more effective financial and expenditure management. These ingredients include the following:

- *Knowing the department's business.* Leading and being an effective player in financial management requires that CFOs have a practical understanding of the department, its programs, its finances, its soft spots, its secrets, and its people. CFOs must be able to work with and through colleagues to accomplish this difficult task. More than one deputy minister has relied upon his/her 'old departmental hand,' steeped in the business of the department to lead on major files of financial management and expenditure management rather than depend on a more recently appointed CFO. To the extent that the CFO has limited experience in government, the deputy minister's inclination is even greater. Quickly learning the essence of departmental business and, in so doing, building confidence with colleagues is a first step for any CFO in developing a more strategic approach to the job.
- *Knowing the inefficient and ineffective programs and operations.* CFOs need to have a first-hand understanding of what appear to be the inefficient operations and ineffective programs in their departments and agencies. This requires the regular and ongoing review, evaluation, and audit of these operations and programs and considered analysis for improvement. It also requires the ability to integrate expenditure and financial information with program and performance information and to combine this with a practical understanding of what can actually be accomplished on the ground in the current circumstances by way of change and improvement.
- *Developing sufficiently accurate, timely and convincing financial, expenditure, and performance data, information, and analysis.* No single system will provide the integrated information for determining where savings can best be achieved and new investments most effectively made. The information will come from many sources internal and external to the department. A key part of the job of the CFO is to ensure that 'the business case has been made' for each reduction,

new expenditure, and reallocation. Doing that requires integrated, thorough, and accurate information and analysis. The CFO is more effective and credible with his/her colleagues in exercising his/her important 'challenge function' when the challenge is based on information and analysis (even though this invariably will be incomplete and partial) rather than on opinion and preference.

- *Establishing a culture of regular expenditure and performance assessment and review by the department's executive committee.* Experience has indicated that the regular, thorough, and systematic review of expenditures and performance by the department's executive committee is not automatic. There are simply too many other pressing priorities taking the scarce time of deputy ministers and their assistant deputy ministers. The CFO has a responsibility to ensure that the deputy minister is leading the executive committee through a regular and ongoing review of departmental expenditures and performance. In short, if the executive committee is not visibly demanding and using expenditure and performance information, then there is less incentive to improve it and there is little incentive for program managers to use it.

- *Anticipating the pressures and the priorities.* Without an understanding of the expenditure pressures and priorities for the department and a realistic assessment of what can be funded or partially funded from the Treasury Board or through the budget, there is little interest and motivation for expenditure reallocation and effective financial management within the department. Managers only see the downside of reductions and none of the upside of reallocations. There are invariably more pressures and priorities than there is money that can be found through reallocation and, hence, there is a critical need for clear analysis and the sorting of pressures and priorities. The CFO needs to be more than just 'the keeper of the pressures and priorities list.' He/she must ensure that the competing demands and pressures are analysed and considered so that priorities can be determined, allocations made, and conflicts managed. Fairness and transparency are important in maintaining integrity in the overall process, and this requires building good lines of information and trust with the program heads in the department.

- *Establishing credibility and trust with departmental colleagues.* All senior departmental officials and every successful CFO emphasize that CFOs must earn and maintain the trust of their colleagues. This is particularly important when it comes to dealing with contentious and tricky expenditure reallocation issues. The CFOs who are trusted have *ability* (competence to meet the expectations of others), *benevolence* (a positive orientation towards others), and *integrity* (commitment to commonly accepted principles). Trust is broken when expectations are violated, and after two violations the damage is usually irreparable.[47] Thus, with the support of the deputy minister, CFOs must clearly and honestly communicate with executive colleagues about how they will exercise their 'challenge and support' functions within the department.

- *Representing the department to the Treasury Board Secretariat and the Office of the Comptroller General to the department.* The CFO is 'the man in the middle,' neither an 'outpost of the Treasury' nor a 'narrow departmental advocate.' He/she needs to work closely with the Treasury Board Secretariat to reach understandings and arrangements that can facilitate effective departmental reallocation. He/she needs to provide operational and policy advice and support to the Comptroller General to ensure effective government-wide financial management and accounting policies that can actually work on the ground. Effective communication across agencies and cultures is an important part of a CFO's job.

The CFO has a pivotal role in ensuring that departments and agencies continuously and effectively monitor the financial status of programs, and in reviewing their performance and effectiveness. CFOs exercise this function as part of the executive team, and their success depends on engaging in regular dialogue with colleagues, anticipating information needs and reporting requirements, and building expertise and systems to respond to the needs in a timely and accurate manner.

This section has focused on the roles of spenders, guardians, priority setters, and financial watchdogs in shaping the three major decisions in the public money process: determining fiscal aggregates, allocating expenditures, and securing efficiency in program delivery and prudence in financial management. It has revealed a significant number of problems and challenges. Whether and how these might be addressed is the subject of the next section, 'New Prospects for Public Money.'

PART FOUR

New Prospects for Public Money

9 Parliament and Public Money

'Where were the Parliamentarians?' It is a fair question, one that identified a
key failure in the management of the Sponsorship Program: the failure of Parliament to fulfill its traditional and historic role as watchdog of spending by
the executive branch of the Government.

Justice H. Gomery, *Restoring Accountability*[1]

If there is a consensus among MPs about the estimates review process, it is
that the documents submitted to Parliament (the Main Estimates, the Supplementary Estimates, the Report on Plans and Priorities and the departmental
Performance Report) raise little, if any, enthusiasm. The size of the documents, their layout and the type of information they contain, their tone and
the style of language they use have been criticized time and time again by
committee members. Despite the fact that progress has been made, this is a
persistent problem ...

MP Reg Alcock, 'Meaningful Scrutiny'[2]

Treasury Board is trying to make parliamentarians into accountants and that is
not their job. They are politicians.

Former House of Commons senior official

When asked whether Parliament is in need of reform, the short and universal
answer from the Parliamentarians with whom we spoke is: yes. In their view,
the institution has, in a sense, lost its way.

MPs Carolyn Bennett and Deborah Grey, and Senator Yves Morin,
The Parliament We Want[3]

Some readers who have come this far will wonder why it has taken so long to bring Parliament into the picture. After all, no public money can be spent without the approval of Parliament. Others might wonder why a full chapter is required. Still others might question why Parliament needs to be considered at all, when, in a Westminster parliamentary system of government, the minister of finance does not propose his/her budget to the legislature for debate and change but instead announces it as a matter of government confidence for approval and passage. To be sure the Canadian Parliament is not just another Westminster system, but instead it has its own features and operates with its own particularities. Compared with others, it has tended to be dominated by single-party majority governments, has a small number of members of Parliament in a House of Commons dominated by a prime minister who is party leader, has an unelected Senate, and has a weak tradition of parliamentary scrutiny of budgetary and administrative matters.[4]

This chapter deals with the roles of Parliament in matters of public money. I use the plural 'roles' because, unlike the traditional perspective that has come to view Parliament in terms of what is supposed to be – a watchdog, whose task it is to hold the government accountable for its stewardship in the spending of public money and to defeat the government if it loses confidence in it – a careful examination of what parliamentarians actually do, or at least attempt to do, indicates that Parliament plays a number of roles.[5] When it comes to the budget, parliamentarians, in addition to being watchdogs, are also part spenders, part guardians, and even part priority setters. To be sure there is much dissatisfaction and even frustration on the part of parliamentarians, students of public administration, and the public about the role that parliament actually plays in matters of public money and in its effectiveness. There is also confusion over the role of Parliament in public money. The key to reducing the frustration and to improvement lies in a better understanding of the accountability watchdog role that theory, tradition, and established practice have called upon parliamentarians to play. But, since things are rarely what they are supposed to be, improvement also depends on understanding the various other roles or partial roles – spenders, guardians, and even priority setters – that Parliament and its parliamentarians have come to take on. We begin first with the fundamentals – the role of Parliament as watchdog in holding the government accountable for its public spending.

Parliament as Watchdog

Ministers and the public service – most of whom are spenders, a few of whom are guardians, and even fewer of whom are priority setters – form the executive branch of government (what I will refer to here as the government). They derive their powers and authority from the Crown and from Parliament, and in turn are accountable to Parliament. The principle of ministerial responsibility identifies cabinet ministers – both spenders and guardians – who are collectively and individually responsible for the exercise of these powers and authority. Inside the executive, public servants are accountable through the chain of command to their deputy minister, who is accountable to the minister, who in turn is accountable to Parliament. Parliament is the body to which the executive is accountable.

The responsibility of the government is to govern – to establish its priorities, to put together a budget with its spending proposals and to present it to Parliament for approval, to put forward legislation, and to manage and administer its programs. In doing so and as described in previous chapters, the government relies upon healthy internal competition and cooperation between its spenders, its guardians, and its priority setters. Parliament does not govern. It approves laws that give the government the powers and the resources to govern. Parliament discusses, criticizes, rarely modifies, and ultimately approves or rejects the legislation and budgets put forward by the government. In holding the government to account, Parliament acts as the watchdog, relying upon a broad set of sources of information, including that provided by its agents of Parliament such as the Auditor General.

As we have seen, it is the government that makes the real decisions on the important matters of the budget and of public spending. As every student of public administration knows, the two great principles of parliamentary control of public money are that the government should have no income that is not granted to it by Parliament and the government can make no expenditures except those approved by Parliament.[6] These principles find expression in the following budgetary practices of government and Parliament:

- There is a budget that brings together all the government's financial needs to provide a clear and unified picture.
- The budget is prepared annually; Parliament does not grant the government permanent rights to spend money, but (with exceptions

for statutory programs for which Parliament has given ongoing legislative approval) requires it to obtain a fresh sanction to spend each
year, and for stated purposes.[7] Money voted for in one year that is
not spent, lapses.
- The preparation of the budget is the job of the government and so,
  too, is the subsequent spending of public money that Parliament
  makes available to it.
- Parliament has the right to debate and criticize the budget.
- The government is responsible for all financial planning and also for
  any changes made to it as a result of parliamentary discussion.
- The government must account fully to Parliament for its management of public money.
- An independent auditor – the Auditor General – reports to the
  House of Commons, audits the accounts, and his/her reports are
  promptly made available to Parliament.
- Parliament monitors the accounts of both revenues and expenditures, in almost any way it chooses, with parliamentary surveillance
  and control being as selective or comprehensive or as loose or rigid
  as Parliament desires.[8]

The application of these practices forms the basis by which Parliament
undertakes its financial watchdog role of the government. This is
indeed what Parliament is supposed to do – or, at least, what our political science and public administration textbooks say that it ought to do.

In this chapter, and within the context set out above, I examine Parliament from the perspective of what it actually does or attempts to do
in terms of the spending of public money. I focus on three areas that are
closely related to the three central functions of budgeting – determining fiscal aggregates, allocating resources, and ensuring efficiency and
sound financial management – as discussed in the previous chapters.
First I ask, to what extent does Parliament, through its parliamentarians and parliamentary committees, attempt to shape government
spending? This is closely related to the budget function concerned
with determining the size of the budget and its priorities. Second, I ask,
how does Parliament actually review and approve public spending
and what influence does Parliament have on government spending?
This is 'the business of supply,' undertaken by a number of parliamentary committees, each with responsibility for a part of the budget. This
task is closely related to the budget allocation function – whether more
money should be spent on defence or more should be spent on social

welfare. Third, I ask, how does Parliament hold the government to account for its spending and the stewardship of the resources granted by Parliament and how well does it do this job? This is closely related to the budget function concerned with efficiency and sound financial management.

Parliamentarians work in these three areas – suggesting budget proposals, approving the estimates, and overseeing spending. However, the actual influence that they can bring to this work is limited. Fundamentally, their influence on the government derives primarily from their membership in the political parties they are elected to represent and not from their status as individual MPs or as members of parliamentary committees. Indeed, because they readily accept party discipline, which is a particularly significant feature of the Canadian parliamentary practice, the influence that they can exert as individual MPs and as members of parliamentary committees on matters of publicly money is sharply limited.

As individual MPs their main deficiency is power; however, they also lack time. The amount of time that parliamentarians can devote to committee work must be balanced against other demands, specifically, the House of Commons, the party caucus, and their constituency. As a consequence, when it comes to matters of public money, parliamentarians have limited time. Over the past several decades, the House of Commons Finance Committee has attempted to influence the level of expenditure and the priorities in the government's budget. The various committees of Parliament have played a role, usually a small and inadequate one, in the review and approval of the estimates through the granting of supply. And the Public Accounts Committee, with the support of the Auditor General, has attempted to maintain an oversight on the actual spending of the government in an effort to hold it to account. In what follows, the role of MPs in the parliamentary committees dealing with these three areas is examined.

Shaping Government Spending: The Commons Finance Committee

Of the approximately fifteen committees of the House of Commons that attempt to deal in various ways with public spending, it is the Finance Committee that gives the appearance of having the most influence. It is the only committee that deals with matters of public expenditure in advance of the minister of finance formulating and presenting his budget to Parliament. All other committees, the nearly dozen that deal with the estimates of departments and agencies as well as the Public Account Committee, reacting to the reports of the Auditor General, deal 'after the fact' with government spending. The House of Commons committees review the estimates after the budget has been unveiled by the minister of finance and after the estimates have been tabled by the president of the Treasury Board. The Public Accounts Committee deals with public spending after the money has been spent and after the Auditor General's report has been tabled.

The Finance Committee also deals with the entire budget itself, or at least with the 'Economic and Fiscal Update,' prepared by the minister and the Department of Finance and presented to the committee each November in advance of a late winter/early spring budget. Members of Parliament enjoy their work on the Finance Committee and unlike some other committees they actively seek out membership on it.[9] Unlike the other committees, the Finance Committee gives MPs the opportunity to 'look forward,' and it gives them the appearance of working on important budget matters facing the country and dealing with critical budget questions that are yet to be decided.

Since the mid-1990s, the Standing Committee on Finance has held pre-budget meetings as a part of the preparations of the budget by the minister of finance. The beginning of these pre-budget consultations in early November is triggered by the high-profile appearance of the minister of finance before the Finance Committee to set out the 'Economic and Fiscal Update' for his upcoming budget. This is normally a five-year economic and fiscal forecast, with the minister of finance indicating that his budget decisions will be taken within the context of a rolling two-year time frame. The minister's appearance before the committee is extensively covered by the media and widely reported. Unlike nearly every other parliamentary committee, this one provides MPs with a unique opportunity for national exposure around important fiscal and budget matters facing the country and their constituents. Perhaps what is most important for the MPs is that this media exposure focuses on fiscal and budget issues that are yet to be determined, and it provides the opportunity for individual MPs to be seen as participants in the actual making of the budget and the various budget decisions. In this sense MPs can be seen as participating in 'setting the fiscal agenda.'

The event is welcomed by the public and the media. It stands out in contrast to the traditional approach to budget preparation, which was done in secrecy by the minister and the Department of Finance without the benefit of public consultation.[10] This more open approach allows the government to publicize in general terms its fiscal intentions in the form of expenditure, revenue, and surplus (or deficit) targets prior to the presentation of the budget. This means that more realistic public expectations can be established about the magnitude of the 'fiscal room' available to the government and for establishing the perception that trade-offs will need to be made across competing demands and interests. Nonetheless, the government usually makes significant revisions in the fiscal and economic forecast between the time that the update is made public and final budget decisions are made. The pre-budget consultations allow the public, interest groups, and parliamentarians the opportunity to put forward publicly their views on what they would like to see included in the upcoming budget. For members of the Finance Committee it provides a unique opportunity to be seen by the public in a national context as individual Members of Parliament who are working to increase the transparency and openness of government around the most important public event of the calendar – the upcoming budget. The committee travels across the country consulting individuals, business, labour, and other groups. As noted by the OECD, with the over-optimism that sometimes accompanies a first and distant look, 'the pre-budget consultations have been an important element in opening up the budget process and creating an atmosphere where the public feels it can have an input.'[11]

For MPs on the committee, it also provides the appearance that they have influence on the budget. At the widely reported committee meeting in which the minister of finance sets out his Economic and Fiscal Update, members can sharply criticize him for regularly under-reporting the size of the surplus; they can propose popular tax cuts or major new expenditure programs; they can reprimand him and the government for excessive spending; or they can propose priority areas for spending in the upcoming budget. As MPs, both government and opposition, they make these recommendations with boldness and determination, fully knowing that they are not responsible for implementing or even deciding on any of them. That is the task of the government, most specifically, the minister of finance.

On the pre-budget consultations, the committee offers the hopes and aspirations for openness and transparency in budget-making by giving everyone a public stage on which they can put forward their budget proposals. On the basis of their hearings and on the individual and collective predispositions of the committee members, the committee publishes a report with recommendations to the minister of finance on what should be included in his/her upcoming budget. With a majority government and the ready acceptance of party discipline, the committee report invariably includes a majority report, reflecting the views of government members, and a series of minority reports from each of the opposition parties. There is no single consensus report from the committee, nor is there any expectation of one, since the issues and recommendations contained in the individual reports are matters of fundamental public policy, reflecting the different and divergent ideological and policy positions of the particular political parties. (When contained in the budget in the form of budget proposals, they become matters of confidence for the government.) The majority and minority reports – sometimes as many as five – that emerge more resemble individual reports prepared by respective party caucuses than those of a single parliamentary committee. The majority report is invariably supportive of the fiscal, economic, and social directions of the government and the minister of finance. The minority reports are sharply critical.

Within the constraints of their party platforms and within the particular fiscal circumstance faced by the government, individual members on the committee come to take on various roles in the budgetary process. When the Mulroney Conservative government was undertaking tax reforms in 1987 to provide tax relief to Canadians and businesses, the Finance Committee, under the colourful and capable chairmanship of Don Blenkarn, provided support as a fiscal guardian.[12] When the Chrétien Liberal government was in deep deficit in the early and mid-1990s, many members, especially those in the government and in the Reform and Progressive Conservative Parties, came to fashion themselves as guardians focusing on the need to reduce spending, eliminate deficits, and achieve a balanced budget. As the government came out of deficits and moved into ongoing surpluses many members, especially those in the governing Liberal Party, took on the role of spenders, pressing for increased expenditures and 'investments' across a broad range of activities. Others stressed guardianship, paying down the debt, reducing taxes, and containing expenditure growth. Still others took on the role of priority setter, using the committee to seek support for what they believed were urgent national priorities such as reducing child poverty, moving forward on the 'cities agenda,' reducing the so-called fiscal imbalance between the federal and provincial governments, ensuring health care was on a stable footing, or giving priority to tax cuts over expenditure increases.

This diversity of budgetary roles played by parliamentarians in the Finance Committee reflects the diversity of the public's views about government budgets and public money. At almost any time there is considerable diversity within the citizenry about the government's fiscal posture, with some arguing to reduce government spending, pay down the public debt, and cut taxes, and others arguing for maintaining and/or increasing government spending to meet pressing national and regional priorities. At other times, broad public opinion can coalesce around a particular fiscal posture such as the need to reduce government spending, increase efficiency in government, and achieve balanced budgets or better. Depending on the circumstances, parliamentarians on the Finance Committee are actually comfortable to play any of these particular budget roles – spender, guardian, or priority setter – because they know that within the broader requirement for party discipline their job is to function as a representative – to represent the views of the citizenry to government. Representing citizen and various interest group views openly in the budgetary process comes naturally to elected MPs and, from the visible purchase of the committee, these views take on the appearance of greater importance to the budget process than they would if they were simply put forward privately by individual Members of Parliament to the government and to the minister of finance.

The Finance Committee and its members can be useful to the minister of finance primarily because they can provide the opportunity for a public forum where individuals and interest groups can present publicly, rather than privately, their ideas on what should be included in the budget. This helps the minister and his officials to better calibrate their own proposals and those put forward by individuals and interest groups when they meet subsequently in the important private meetings. It can also be useful in providing parliamentary support for the finance minister on his budget stance and budget directions, although, this is invariably accompanied by dissenting opposition minority reports.

Insiders and most others understand, however, that the committee has little or no impact on what the minister of finance eventually decides to include in or leave out of his/her budget. But yet the committee provides the appearance for its members that they are, in fact, influencing the shape and the contents of the budget. Those who appear before the committee say so publicly, even though they know that to get their way with the minister and Department of Finance they will need to do much more than simply appear before a parliamentary committee and convince its members. The committee, itself, likes to report on the difficult task its members face and on the hard choices they are shaping. Listen to the exaggerated comments of one witness appearing before the committee as reported in the committee's own report:

> I feel the Finance Committee has one of the toughest responsibilities of any federal committee ... given the events of September 11, what are we going to do right now? We've got all of these requests, and it's like what I went through when I was a chief: 'Manny, what are your priorities going to be? You're a chief so what are your priorities? How are you going to change the world so that your people can live better?' That's the responsibility of each and everyone of you sitting here: How can we continue to have Canada remain strong and how can we have Canada remain a true partner in terms of international issues dealing with the economy or in terms of you name it?[13]

While the public's expectations for the committee are considerable, the actual analytical and professional support it receives through the staff of the Parliamentary Library has been minimal. The new parliamentary budget officer, created by the Conservative Harper government in 2006 as a part of its Federal Accountability Act, is considered in the next chapter on budget reforms. This new agent of Parliament draws its inspiration from the U.S. Congressional Budget Office (CBO), which has played an important analytical role in the support of congressional authorization and appropriation committees in their reviews of the president's budget proposals. The fundamental difference, however, between Canada and the United States is that in the United States the president *proposes* a budget and Congress changes, adjusts, and alters the proposals during the course of its deliberations and approvals. In Canada, with a majority government, the minister of finance *announces* his budget and the House of Commons passes it into law with little or no modification. In the United States, congressmen and -women demand analytical support on matters of fiscal policy, expenditure and revenue projections, and program expenditures because they can and do use this information to influence budget levels and expenditures.

Appearances of influencing the finance minister's budget are important for MPs on the committee. Parliamentarians care deeply about how they are perceived. To say, however, that members of the committee care more about themselves than they do about the country would be inaccurate; to say that they care about how they appear before the country and their constituents would be closer to the truth. If the pre-budget consultations by the Finance Committee are about the exhilaration of important appearances, then the review of the estimates by the approximately fifteen parliamentary committees, to which I now turn, is about the frustrations of trivial undertakings.

Approving Government Spending: The Business of Supply

No part of the budgetary process is as frustrating to parliamentarians as the business of supply – the review and approval of the government's spending plans in the form of the estimates of individual departments and agencies. Indeed, the level of frustration is only matched by the perceived degree of ineffectiveness of the expenditure review process by parliamentarians. Most parliamentarians, expert observers, and other Canadians believe that Parliament is not effective in holding the government accountable for how it spends taxpayers' money. The former clerk of the House of Commons, Robert Marleau, has observed that the Commons has 'almost abandoned its constitutional responsibility of supply.'[14] Parliamentarians themselves, through the publication of three recent reports, have drawn considerable attention to Parliament's frustration and problems with the business of supply.[15] Scholars and practitioners have sounded the alarm bells and raised major concerns,[16] and the Gomery Inquiry's reports and research have focused significantly on the problems of supply and have made some proposals for improvement.[17]

While the problems have become exacerbated in recent years, they are far from new. Indeed, the key to understanding these problems and what might be done about them lies in appreciating the continuous and long-standing erosion of the role of parliamentary legislatures in the review of government spending. In Canada, there is a long history of parliamentarians' frustration with the review and approval of the government's estimates. Shortly after the turn of the nineteenth century, a royal commissioner on the public service observed: 'Supplies are duly voted in the customary course, often at the end of the session in the small hours of the night by jaded members in a tired House ... ' The resulting royal commission report concluded dismally that parliamentary control over the government's proposals for expenditure was 'negligible.'[18] By mid-century, in 1943, it was no better. A Member of Parliament, while fully engaged in debate on supply put the matter rather eloquently:

There is no adequate procedure by which we may put ourselves in a position to deal intelligently with the amounts submitted to us for our approval. Year after year, and this year again, I have heard criticism of the government for having the estimates dealt with so late in the session and in such large amounts. But no matter at what time they are dealt with, the weakness I suggest would still be there. I am going to vote that this item before us be approved by the committee, but I am not in a position to judge whether or not the amount asked for, or an amount somewhat less, might be sufficient to carry on adequately and properly the work of the department.[19]

In 1962, a leading student of Parliament summarized succinctly the criticisms of parliamentarians: 'There is no part of procedure in the Canadian House of Commons which is so universally acknowledged to be inadequate to modern needs as the control of the House over public expenditure.'[20] That same year Norman Ward, in his classic book *The Public Purse*, observed that 'the record of the Canadian House of Commons in the scrutiny of executive expenditures is not good.'[21] In 1968, parliamentarians described the process of supply as 'time consuming, repetitive, and archaic,' with claims that it did not permit effective scrutiny of the estimates, did not provide the House with the means of organizing meaningful debate, and failed to preserve effective parliamentary control over expenditures.[22]

Even with substantial amendments to the supply procedures in 1968 – the first time in over a century – the situation did not improve. In 1993, the pace of criticism and frustration quickened. That year the chairpersons of all standing committees lamented that 'MPs in a majority Parliament have effectively lost the power to reduce government expenditure.' They went on to explain that 'members are therefore making the very rational calculation that there is no point devoting time and effort to an exercise over which they can have no influence.'[23] Two years later in 1995, the situation as reflected by J.R. Mallory was that 'from all sides the view is the same: the review of the Estimates is often meaningless.'[24] Members of Parliament reflected a profound degree of dissatisfaction about the estimates, describing it as 'futile attempts to bring about change,' 'not a particularly useful procedure,' and 'a total waste of time.'[25]

In 1998, parliamentarians lamented that 'the supply process is not taken seriously, is overly politicized, and Members of Parliament do not devote sufficient time and attention to the expenditure of public funds.'[26] By 2003, some parliamentarians openly admitted that 'they are simply overwhelmed' and that 'the traditional notion of "holding government to account" is no longer feasible.' In their words, 'there are too many expenditures, too many reports and too many departmental programs to review.'[27]

This is not a happy state of affairs. It is made more difficult (or perhaps more easy) by the fact that underlying these contemporary criticisms by MPs are deep-seated, historical reasons and traditions to explain why, in all parliamentary systems of government, legislatures have played very limited roles in influencing the budget and the estimates. This, along with a steady stream of failed reforms, suggests the need for a healthy sense of circumspection with respect to the prospects for finding simple and immediate solutions to these enduring and deeply embedded problems.

There are at least three fundamental reasons why parliamentary legislatures have limited influence on the budget and on public expenditure.[28] First, beginning with the Magna Carta in 1215, the King's own income became co-mingled with public tax revenue. To separate the King's money from the public's money and to ensure that it was spent only on authorized purposes, Parliament devised the tactic of voting on appropriations near the end of the session after the King had already spent some of his money. Over time, with appropriations being voted on after the fiscal year was underway, Parliament came to merely endorse spending that had already occurred. This practice has continued to this day, as, under the standing rules of the House, which were amended in 1968, the estimates are deemed to have been reported from committee to the House of Commons by 31 May.

Second, the adoption of a standing order in the British Parliament in 1706 codified a practice that exists to this day and is included in the 1867 Constitutional Act for Canada, namely, 'the House shall not accept any petition for any sum of money ... unless upon recommendation of the Crown.'[29] The purpose of appropriations was to restrain the Crown, and it made no sense for the Commons to vote on money that had not been requested. Parliament was therefore barred by the standing order from initiating expenditure and by the reality of politics from denying requested funds. Its power over the public purse was greatly reduced.

Third, the formalization and institutionalization in eighteenth-century England of what is known today as the budget – a comprehensive statement of revenue and expenditure – served to further reinforce the balance of financial power of the government over legislatures. Ministries of Finance became responsible for developing the government's budget through a reach and a process that extended to all government departments. The result, as we have seen, is that the government knows a great deal about what is in and behind a budget and the legislature knows very little, with the consequence that legislators rarely acquire a deep understanding about how public money is spent or the implications of appropriating more or less.

As a result, most parliamentary committees devote few meetings to reviewing the estimates of individual departments and agencies, have a poor record of attendance, and have a poor record of review. Some committees do not even review the estimates, since under standing orders, even if they are not adopted by the committee, they are deemed to have been reported to the House of Commons. This weakens and can undermine the position of departmental chief financial officers (CFOs) responsible for preparing the departmental estimates. In the eyes of their spending departmental colleagues, the CFOs and the estimates on which they labour are seen as having little consequence. When appearing before committees there is rarely a question on the estimates and the programs and expenditures of the department. Instead, parliamentarians focus on specific projects or issues within their own individual ridings, or, if the responsible minister is before the committee, on partisan policy issues. It also weakens the position of the Treasury Board and its Secretariat responsible for the roll-up and review of the departmental estimates. A former senior official laments that no longer does the Secretariat provide a lock-up for MPs in advance of tabling the estimates since they found that there were even fewer members in attendance than the small cadre of Secretariat support staff.[30] As a consequence, according to one recent study, public officials, be they spenders, guardians, or priority setters, 'have come to regard gaining Parliament's approval as simply a further obstacle to be surmounted.'[31]

There can be little doubt about the need for Parliament to become more effective in its review of the government's public spending. Much of the discussion has focused on the distance between where things are and where they *ought* to be. Furthermore, the two key questions – how effective *ought* it to become and how effective *can* it become – have often been addressed separately. If, however, like the two sides of the same coin, we think of the answers to these questions as one and the same, we might get closer to a reasonable answer that can actually work. As we have seen, the review of government expenditures is an extraordinarily complicated and time-consuming task, whether it be undertaken by the guardians in the Department of

Finance and the Treasury Board Secretariat, or by the financial watchdogs in the Office of the Auditor General and in the internal audit
bureaus of departments and agencies, or by the Office of the Comptroller General and the chief financial officers.

Indeed, as explained throughout the previous chapters, this inevitable complexity leads budget scrutinizers to adopt simple and partial
review techniques. Even ministers of the Treasury Board, who are all
from the same political party and are collectively responsible for the
expenditures of the government, avoid the complexity that is entailed
in a regular in-depth review of the estimates. A highly respected
former deputy minister reflects on his experience:

> When I was deputy secretary of the Program Branch of the Treasury Board,
> the spring review of departmental program forecasts was a huge undertak-
> ing. After staff of the branch had completed their analyses, I would sit down
> with them for weeks of briefings during the course of which we made deci-
> sions about hundreds of millions of dollars – this was a legitimate 'A bud-
> get,' that was not, and so on. At one point I became uncomfortable about
> ministers playing no role in what we were doing, so I organized a presenta-
> tion about how we had handled the submission of a particular department.
> After Treasury Board ministers had listened for perhaps half an hour, the
> president said, 'Well this all sounds pretty sensible. Now let's move to the
> next item on our agenda.' He was quite right; there was other business that
> had to be attended to, and it was out of the question that ministers
> would spend weeks reviewing submissions that we had already reviewed. If
> Treasury Board ministers do not have time to get very far into the expendi-
> ture budget, how much can we expect of parliamentary committees?[32]

There is, nonetheless, no shortage of proposals for reform. Many
have been proposed before and those that have been tried have not
been successful. Others have not been tried, in part, because backbench
and opposition parliamentarians from diverse political parties do not
find the proposals to be in their interests and they do not think they
will work. One of the most recent reform packages included these
three key ideas:

1 Creating a team of specialists in financial planning and performance
reporting to serve the Government Operations and Estimates Committee and other committees of the House of Commons in their
reviews of the estimates.

2 Providing the Government Operations and Estimates Committee with the power accorded the Joint Committee on Statutory Instruments to require, when a committee believes that the government's response to a report is inadequate, that the minister debate the issue raised by the committee in the House of Commons for an hour.

3 Tightening the vote structure of departmental programs, which over the past twenty years has been adjusted to significantly increase the flexibility of the government to organize the financing of its activities.[33]

Over the past half century the most common strategy for strengthening the role of parliamentarians in the review of the estimates has been to provide them with more information that is considered to be more relevant to their needs. Indeed, there has been almost no end to the number of times that this strategy has been used. One attempt was part of the government's initiative in 2000 to get 'Results for Canadians' by more closely linking performance reporting to budgeting.[34] The emphasis was on citizen focused services, public service values, and results reporting. Another, under the banner of 'Reform of the Estimates' and improving reporting to Parliament, required that all departments and agencies table a 'Reports on Plans and Priorities' (RPPs) along with their estimates in the spring. In addition, departments and agencies are required to report to Parliament on the results they have achieved through the tabling of separate 'Departmental Performance Reports' (DPRs).

The key to understanding these documents is to appreciate the fundamental difference between what they are said to be and what they actually are. For example, with respect to performance reports, the introduction to the 'Guidance for Deputy Ministers' states that, 'information on results should be balanced, accurate, and easy to understand.' The Treasury Board Secretariat's 'Preparation Guide: Departmental Performance Reports 2003–04' notes that 'a balanced report implies that your report must treat performance information with fairness. Readiness to acknowledge performance that did not meet expectations shows an ability to learn and adapt. It is an indicator of organizational health and sound management.' In reality, however, after reviewing a number of performance reports, two former deputy ministers conclude that 'it would be hard to call (them) balanced. We could not find a single confession of failure.'[35] While there has been no fully comprehensive and independent study of the extent to which Members of Parliament use information on plans and performance reports in the review of the estimates, all assessments (internal reviews by the Auditor General and external reviews) point to the conclusion that little, if any, use is made of this information by MPs in the review of the estimates.[36] Not only is there little or no demand for this information by MPs but also there is little or no use made of it. It seems that MPs do not demand what they cannot use. It would also seem that parliamentarians do not use departmental expenditure and performance reports because they do not contain information that can be used to embarrass the minister, and officials in spending departments do not prepare such reports for fear that they will embarrass their ministers.

Another way of addressing the issue of improving Parliament's review of the estimates is to ask what incentives parliamentarians need and what disincentives they need to overcome.[37] An analysis of these questions starts from the premise that, without the ability to actually change the expenditure of a department, there is little or no incentive for parliamentarians to systematically demand expenditure and program information. What therefore leads to high quality and relevant program and budget information has less to do with the desire of suppliers to provide it than with the prospect that demanders can actually use it to change an expenditure item. However, as the following analysis sadly illustrates, not only are the current incentives small and disincentives great, but the changes required to be made are not likely feasible for parliamentarians or for the government.

Currently, when standing committees of the House of Commons deal with the estimates, they can reject the estimate, reduce it, or they can simply approve it. In a majority government, the first two options are highly unlikely. Even in a minority government, reductions in proposed expenditures have been rare and minuscule. Committees' ability to influence the estimates is further constrained by constitutional provisions stipulating that only the government can introduce or recommend the appropriation of money out of public revenues.

It can be argued that committees and their members would have greater incentive to focus on the estimates if they could propose modest reallocations, that is, reductions to expenditures in one area coupled with an increase in another. Under this approach, the government could, for example, indicate with the tabling of its estimates that it is prepared to accept, under specific conditions, limited reallocations proposed by committees. To minimize excessive political gamesmanship, specific conditions could be established, for example:

- The committee could have to explain its substantive reasons and provide clear evidence for reducing one area of expenditure and increasing another.

- The size of the proposed reallocations could be limited (for example, 3 per cent of the voted expenditure).
- Committees could be restricted to reallocations within the estimates of the departments under their scrutiny.
- Should the government not wish to follow the recommendations of a committee, it could be required to provide substantive justification that matched the committee's own recommendations and to table a motion in the House restoring the reduction.

In addition, there is the important matter of the confidence convention in parliamentary government – for the government to continue, it must enjoy the support of a majority in the House of Commons. Some observers have emphasized that the lack of interest in the estimates is rooted in the confidence convention which, as currently interpreted, makes any motion to change a vote as a potential test of the House's confidence in the government.[38] There is, of course, good reason to treat the government's budgetary and expenditure policy and the process of supply as matters of confidence. However, it should be possible for some relaxation of the confidence convention as it applies to individual parts of the larger budget and estimates. For example, the government could announce in advance that it would not consider a defeat of a particular vote to constitute a loss of confidence. Alternatively, the government could retain its discretion by identifying those elements of its expenditure proposals it considers to be crucial and therefore requiring confidence.

Some may argue that even with these significant new powers, parliamentary committees would still lack the fundamental expertise to shift money from one program to another. Others would argue that the limited time for committee review of the estimates is insufficient to develop an adequate understanding of the implications of transferring resources within a department's budget. However, information of all sorts be can and is provided to parliamentary committees if the demand for it is there.

Experience also suggests that when it comes to matters of the estimates, the time-worn cliché 'If we build it, they will come' is wrong. Building edifices of more information is not a necessary and sufficient condition for improving parliamentary scrutiny of the government's expenditures. Rather, a more suitable cliché might be 'If they can play, they will come.' The ability to change proposed expenditures, even in a small way, might give parliamentarians greater incentive to more meaningfully scrutinize departmental expenditures. Incentive itself, however, may not be enough. There is a further reason why parliamentarians may not spend much time on the estimates even with the prospects of making some modest changes to expenditure levels. Parliamentary committees, with members from diverse political parties, are likely to find it difficult to reach agreement on substantive reallocations. As a result, they focus on minor, symbolic reallocations that are politically designed to bring attention to an area of particular public concern such as a gun registry or the dealings of a particular Crown corporation.

The recent experience of the Liberal minority government is instructive. The recommendation of the Standing Committee on Government Operations and Estimates and the subsequent decision by the minority Parliament to reduce the budget of the Governor General by 10 per cent in the first quarter of fiscal year 2004–5 indicated that Members of Parliament with divergent political interests could reach agreement. There can be little doubt that the impetus for this $400,000 cut by parliamentarians was politically motivated. It was to send a signal from a group of seemingly beleaguered MPs to the Governor General that she should be more prudent in her public expenditures in the aftermath of extensive publicity about her international tours. Just as important, it indicated to the government that parliamentarians on all sides of the House could come together to change an expenditure level of an important office when they perceived that the groundwork of public support had been sufficiently prepared and the government of the day was unprepared to provide a vigorous defence of the office.[39]

Similarly, there is little doubt that the reduction did have an effect on the programs and operations of the office of the Governor General. The Office of the Secretary of the Governor General announced that it was attempting to 'minimize the impact ... on Canadians' through the cancellation of a program to encourage Canadians to nominate citizens for national honours, the cancellation of research for an educational exhibit, the cancellation of professional training courses for staff, the postponement of plans to modernize office equipment and facilities, and, in an ironic twist, the cancellation of the annual winter celebration for parliamentarians, the diplomatic corps, and the media.[40]

Would-be reformers may not like the answers that they receive when they analyse the incentives and disincentives for parliamentarians to review the estimates. Indeed, this line of thinking suggests that systematic reforms to permit parliamentarians to make modest expenditure reallocations might not be feasible and they might not be as effective as some would wish. All this suggests that the best way to improve Parliament's performance in reviewing expenditures and to reduce the perceived level of their frustration might be to lower the expectations of them. In short, parliamentary committees can never provide a thorough, comprehensive, and complete review of the estimates of departments. Nor should we expect them to. There are, however, several simple strategies for members of the supply committees to consider using: be thoroughly briefed on the department and its expenditures by government officials; decide upon a simple and clear work plan for their investigations; discipline and coordinate their questioning of witnesses; focus consistently on one or two areas of expenditure when the committee believes the department is at risk and when it might resonate with the public and the media; and continue to seek additional analysis and support so the committee can back-up its focused investigations. In short, their reviews at best will be partial, sporadic, political, and reactive. If MPs feel frustrated, and if others perceive them as ineffective in the review of the estimates prior to the spending of public money by government, perhaps there are better prospects for them in their review of public money after it has been spent. This takes us to the Public Accounts Committee.

Holding Government Accountable for Spending: The Public Accounts Committee

On paper, the Public Accounts Committee appears to occupy a central position in holding government accountable for its spending. The objective of the committee is to ensure that the government spends public money only for the purposes approved by Parliament, that waste and inefficiency are minimized, and that the government employs sound financial practices. Since Confederation, there has been a Public Accounts Committee with a mandate to review the public accounts of the government and the reports of the Auditor General. Since 1958, the chair of committee has been drawn from the opposition.

Yet this committee has not had the reputation, prestige or established record for effective, non-partisan work that is enjoyed by its counterpart in Britain. In Britain, the Public Accounts Committee is described as the 'queen of the select committees,'[41] but in Canada, it is the committee on which few Members of Parliament want to sit.[42] Most Members of Parliament do not believe that they can 'get ahead by looking back,' unless they are able to take credit for unearthing information that can be transformed immediately into a major government scandal. For most MPs, there are more effective ways to engage in 'scandal searching behaviour' than by spending the time and effort required as members of the Public Accounts Committee. It is one of twenty committees and it is not considered to be the most desirable for assignment. When asked in the early 1990s to rank the importance of their various duties, both veteran and rookie MPs rated 'acting as a watchdog on government' the lowest of five roles behind 'protecting riding,' 'helping individuals,' 'keeping in touch,' and 'debating in the House of Commons.' In a more recent survey, it was found that the watchdog role was still ranked low, although it was higher than 'debating in the House.'[43]

Most observers note that the weaknesses of the committee are deeply rooted in the context and traditions of the Canadian parliamentary and political system, which are not easily changed. This includes the large turnover of committee membership; the lack of experience in matters of public finance; the lack of interest of MPs in accountability issues; strong party discipline; the difficulty in distinguishing between policy and administrative issues, the latter of which is the purview of the committee; the partisan nature of much of the committee debate; and the unclear status in the minds of many MPs of public servants appearing before the committee. The prescriptions for improvement are seemingly simple, or can be made to appear so. But they have all proved to be elusive and impossible to achieve: more stable and experienced committee membership; a greater interest in accountability issues on the part of MPs; more budget, more analysis, and a permanent staff for the committee; and the adoption of some form of the British accounting officer concept, which would make deputy ministers directly accountable to the committee for certain matters of administration.[44]

One of the difficulties for the committee is that it is often overshadowed by the work and reputation of the Auditor General, who, in much of the public's eye, has come to be seen as 'the watchdog' of government spending. Over 90 per cent of the committee's work is directly concerned with the Auditor General's reports, and the 10 per cent that is not, is usually linked to these reports. The committee is not proactive in proposing what the Auditor General should audit; instead, committee members invariably confirm and acquiesce in what has been set out by the Auditor General in his/her work plan. The Auditor General's reports receive extensive media coverage and commentary at the time they are released, and the committee finds it difficult to add accountability value and publicity value to the Auditor General's high-profile findings. For some

MPs, Parliament appears too weak and the Auditor General too strong. Some MPs have expressed deep concern about their ability and capacity to absorb and deal with the four audit reports that they review each year from the Auditor General.[45] The twelve regular committee members who quietly work away on particular public money issues can sometimes feel outmanoeuvred by high-profile substitute members who readily take the media spotlight when the committee investigates a contentious public issue like the sponsorship scandal.[46]

The Public Accounts Committee suffers from a fundamental conundrum. On the one hand, if it is to find the basis for substantive and in-depth consideration of public money and financial management issues then it must avoid excessive partisanship. This means that it must find small and less important issues, around which a sufficient working consensus across members and across political parties can develop. These minor matters are not the natural pre-occupations of busy members of Parliament anxious to rise within the governing party to a cabinet post or in the opposition party to an important 'shadow cabinet' position. Nor does it provide the opportunity for public visibility since such small issues are never reported by the media. On the other hand, experience indicates that when the committee does deal with major and high-profile issues of financial accountability, like the investigation into the sponsorship scandal, the results are excessive partisanship, lack of diligence, acrimony, and conflict among committee members. If the committee can be considered to be effective at all, it would be more on the very small issues than on the very large ones.

Realism and Reform

The criticisms concerning Parliament's role in the control and management of public money are extensive, broadly based, and ongoing. What is perhaps most noteworthy is the extent to which these criticisms come from parliamentarians themselves. What at one time was a steady drone of concern has, over the last decade, become a fevered pitch of disenchantment. However, it is wrong to conclude that everything about Parliament in its dealings with public money is in need of repair. For example, at the front end of the budgetary process, the Finance Committee has been successful, if only through appearances, in shaping and participating in opening up the pre-budget consultation process, and in providing parliamentarians with opportunities to be associated with the making of the budget. Parliamentarians are content with this committee and anxious to be on it. The new parliamentary budget officer may offer some promise for limited improvement (and is examined in the next chapter on budget reforms).

At the back end of the process, the Public Accounts Committee has enjoyed, and been frustrated with, the support of its strong and influential agent of Parliament, the Auditor General, who provides regular and credible public reports identifying the administrative and managerial shortcomings associated with government spending. Parliamentarians, although less content with this committee than the Finance Committee, do attend and participate in its meetings. Some argue that the committee should and can do more. They argue that 'to achieve its objectives, the Committee must act as a cohesive body, not as a partisan forum,' and its 'appropriate subject should be the areas of administration for which public servants, not Ministers, hold responsibility.'[47] This strategy, however, suffers from two flaws. First, it asks parliamentarians to be something they are not – administrators rather than politicians. Second, it is premised on the ability to clearly and unambiguously separate politics and administration. However, extensive experience has indicated that such artificial separations invariably lead to the slippery slope of unintended consequences where the problems created are larger than the ones solved.

The process that many argue is most crying out for change and reform is the 'Business of Supply' and the cursory review of the estimates by Members of Parliament serving on parliamentary review committees. Many MPs and others have come to believe that these 'supply committees' do not function. Nearly every solution proposed for dealing with the problem has been centred on the notion of providing parliamentarians with better information which they can use to review the estimates. But, because committees have little or no effect on the budgets of departments and agencies, few parliamentarians are demanding what they cannot use.

If the only changes that could be made to improve budgeting and the management of public money were to be found in reforming the legislature, there would be cause for great concern and even some alarm. Those changes to Parliament that might be effective do not appear feasible and those that are feasible do not look effective. When it comes to the management of public money, Parliament is not doing as well as it could, but a closer examination of what it is doing and what it might reasonably be able to do as a democratically elected and representative public institution appealing to higher ideals than just money suggests some tempering of the reformists' expectations. Parliament, after all, does function sufficiently to ensure that budgets are passed on time without the crises and gridlock that can plague other governmental systems. Through their hearings, investigations and reports, parliamentary committees do bring public focus to important and pressing public policy issues – be it health care, strategies for persons with disabilities, or public safety from terrorism – even if these committees do not influence budgetary matters. The nation's expenditures can be brought into line with its revenues, expenditures allocations can permit national priorities to move ahead, and financial mismanagement can be detected, publicly investigated, and corrected. This does not mean that there are not pressing and important changes that need to be made to the budgeting and management of public money, but it does suggest that a productive avenue for 'budget reform' might lie in looking internally to government and in improving the interactions among spenders, guardians, priority setters, and financial watchdogs.

10 Budget Reforms

Prime ministers get the expenditure management system they want and ministers get the one they deserve.

Treasury Board Secretariat assistant secretary

Expenditure Review was successful in part because we had a good secretariat, a very small and effective non-bureaucratic group. Treasury Board Secretariat had failed to get at these items and had lost its credibility.

Former Expenditure Review Committee minister

The Expenditure Review Committee was a failure.

Treasury Board Secretariat director

If, when readers think 'reform,' they also think about changes in 'what kind of government' and 'what kind of people,' they will be on the right track.

Aaron Wildavsky, *The New Politics of the Budgetary Process*[1]

It is sometimes said that each new budget reform is a reaction, occasionally an over-reaction to the failures of the previous reform. Yesterday's reforms become today's practices, and today's practices can become tomorrow's problems. This chapter traces the sequencing of new budget reforms on established budget practices in the Canadian government.

Throughout much of the scholarly and professional literature on budgeting, the words 'budget' and 'reform' have gone hand in hand. It is rare to read about budgeting without also reading about reform. It seems there is near continuous dissatisfaction with the current budget process. Read any scholarly journal or book and you usually find a strong critique about how things are currently being done or not being done. It is the same for reports, interviews, and articles by practitioners. It also seems that there is a near-universal belief that on most matters of budgeting there is a better way. Consequently, much of the literature contains proposals for reform and significant change. Yet the record of budget reforms indicates that the new reforms do not solve the old problems. Reforms almost never turn out to be as good in practice as they first appeared on paper. Perhaps the established ways are not as bad as we might think, or not as bad in the ways that we might think. If budgeting is about anything, it is about underappreciating the present and overpromising the future. Given a choice, however, it is better that budgeting operates more effectively than we think and that we set our aspirations for reforms too high than the other way around. If current budgeting was actually worse than we thought and our sights for reforms too low, then we would run the risk of not only being caught off guard as problems were underestimated but also of seeing little or no prospect for positive change. A healthy sense of scepticism about budget reform may be needed and, while there may not be a single best way, there are undoubtedly improvements to be made.

Budgets and Reforms

It is surprisingly easy to define a series of distinct budget reform periods in Canadian budgeting over the past half century. Most have distinct and clear beginnings, often occasioned by a change in government and political leadership and trumpeted through a series of high-profile public announcements. All the reforms are complex and multifaceted, and yet each is introduced with a name and often comes to be associated with a time-honoured expression or phrase. Most do not have distinct endings but, rather, fade away or slowly lose momentum to be eventually caught up in the sweep and fanfare that accompanies the newest and latest reform. Some reforms attempt to be comprehensive, whereas others are more cursory. With each and every major reform there are a series of mini-reforms and changes that are put in place along the way to accompany and often, but not always, reinforce the original intent. Some reforms have been preceded by extensive research and independent analysis and advice, whereas others have been undertaken in reaction to pressing and immediate crises facing the government.

Over the past forty years, from the Glassco and the Gov‹ ganization Act of 1966 to Gomery and the Federal Accour 2006, there have been six distinct periods of budget reform:

1 'Rational' Reform: The Road to Program Budgeting (pre-1962–78)
2 The Grand Design: Policy and Expenditure Management System (1979–83)
3 Incremental and Continuous Change (1984–93)
4 Program Review and Prudent Budgeting (1994–2003)
5 'A Continuous Culture of Reallocation' (2004–6)
6 Strengthening the Watchdogs: The Federal Accountability Act (2006 and onward)

In varying degrees the reforms have focused on the three competing, yet complementary objectives of budgeting that were introduced in chapter 1 and subsequently developed in chapters 6 to 8: maintaining fiscal aggregates, making budget allocations, and ensuring efficient program delivery and effective financial management. Sometimes the objective of the reform is clear and singular, as it was in the period of fiscal crisis in the mid-1990s with the government's determined focus on eliminating the deficit by cutting expenditures. At other times the objectives have been less clear and more multiple, such as with reforms that attempt to encourage expenditure reallocation and improve financial management. By focusing on the invasion of the new and the succession of the old we can better understand the tensions and difficulties inherent in reconciling these three objectives.

The model of spenders, guardians, priority setters, and financial watchdogs helps us to more fully understand the complexity of the motivations that underlie the various budget reforms, the relative importance of particular roles, and the nature of the interaction across the roles. The purpose of these separate and distinct budget roles arises from the need for a division of labour so that complex budget problems can be broken down into manageable pieces and, through specialization, in-depth consideration can be given to individual parts of the problems. Separate and interdependent roles also constrain the appetites and desires of any one role, forcing each to interact with the others so that budget decisions determining fiscal aggregates, deciding expenditure allocations, or managing financial matters can actually be made. It is through the effective interactions across the budget roles that effective budgeting takes place.

In the broadest and most fundamental sense, the triggers of reform stem from dissatisfaction with either, or both, the outcomes of the budget process or the process itself. Contrary to popular perception, it is not just the guardians who determine when and what is unsatisfactory. At various times over the past half century, financial watchdogs, spenders, and priority setters have all had a hand in squeezing the trigger of budgetary reforms. In 1976, the Auditor General brought public attention to his worries about rapidly rising and uncontrollable expenditures in his annual report. In 1979 and 1980 spenders, concerned about being excluded from important expenditure decisions, complained that the Treasury Board was acting as a 'star chamber' and, at the same time, the priority setters in the Privy Council Office asserted the need for more direct and deliberate links between government priorities and expenditure envelopes. Sometimes, as was the case in the 2006 reform, a single player, such as the financial watchdog, can be perceived as being too weak relative to others. In another sense, the dissatisfaction finds its origins in a perception that one role, usually either spenders or guardians, has become too strong and influential relative to others. This has the consequence of altering the balance within the budgetary process and can literally lead to an unbalanced fiscal situation.

The reforms are triggered ultimately by the prime minister, with the support of the minister of finance and, on occasion and usually of lesser importance, the president of the Treasury Board. Usually, but not always, the reforms come about with a new government and a new prime minister, reflecting changing public attitudes about government spending, taxation, and fiscal matters. There may be a generally shared sense that the economic, social, and political situation faced by the government requires an adjustment in the relative influence of one or more of the principal roles. More specifically, there may be a sense within the Prime Minister's Office and the Privy Council Office that for ministers the current process has become too time-consuming, too complex, and too irrelevant. It may be perceived that one actor has become too strong, but more often the focus is on who has become too weak. Indeed, what is important is the nature and quality of the interactions across the roles and not in the dominance of any one role. The act of actually pulling the reform trigger is usually preceded by a lengthy period of denial, external threat, internal compromise, the pressures of past failure, the promise of future improvement, and other hand-wringing. In that sense, it is never a quick pull but rather a slow squeeze.

'Rational' Reform: The Road to Program Budgeting (pre-1962–78)

When Walter Gordon, the finance minister in the newly elected minority Liberal government, delivered his ill-fated budget on 13 June 1963, the Royal Commission on Government Organization (the Glassco Commission) had just produced a significant and far-reaching report that was to become a turning point in the practice of budgeting and public administration in Canada.[2] It specifically recommended that the government do away with 'line-item' budgeting and adopt a 'program approach' in order to strengthen the 'central direction of government.' It also proposed that greater authority be delegated from central control agencies to departments and agencies to allow them to administer their programs and expenditures. This was best described as 'let the managers manage.'

At that time, and indeed since Confederation, the federal government, like most other governments, was using line-item budgeting. The focus was on costs and controls, with budget requests and allocations to departments being made on the basis of standard objects of expenditure. These objects of expenditure included such tangible items as salaries and wages, postage, telephones, travel expenses, materials and supplies, and repairs and upkeep. There was no need to relate expenditures to the objectives of programs, the services produced, or the results achieved. There was no need for systematic budget planning or forward forecasting. Budgeting was simple and the objects of expenditure were clear and readily understandable to politicians and the public. Responsibility for the overall system rested in the hands of the Office of the Comptroller of the Treasury, which at its peak had close to 5,000 officers scattered in all departments, in all regions of Canada, and abroad.[3] The budget process was sustained by an elaborate system for recording and reporting of expenditures and outstanding commitments. The system included detailed controls and constraints on financial inputs and detailed administrative procedures.

In 1966, when the Treasury Board was formally separated from the Department of Finance, it became a separate department under the Government Reorganization Act with responsibilities for, among other things, managing the government's expenditure budget. This established the institutional foundation for expenditure management and control within the federal government. Two years later, the government announced the formal adoption of Planning, Programming, and Budgeting System (PPBS) and strengthened the role of the Treasury

Board Secretariat, with the Program Branch having responsibilities for budget analysis and advice on departmental expenditure levels and the Planning Branch having responsibilities for program evaluation and performance measurement.[4] Under PPBS, policy and expenditure decisions were separated, with the cabinet committees deciding the programs and policies (what should be done) and Treasury Board deciding the expenditures (how much should be provided). The Treasury Board issued a guide to departments and agencies on how PPBS was to be implemented.[5]

In 1968, newly elected prime minister Trudeau overhauled the cabinet decision-making process. Most notable was the creation of the Cabinet Committee on Priorities and Planning, chaired by the prime minister with overall government-wide responsibilities for determining government priorities, establishing the fiscal framework (on the advice of the minister of finance) and ensuring the implementation of the government's plans and priorities. In 1970, the Treasury Board introduced the concept of 'A-B-X' budgets to support the program review function of PPBS. The 'A' budget consisted of those expenditures required to finance existing programs at their current level of service. The 'B' budget consisted of the financing required for new programs or to expand existing ones. The 'X' budget consisted of expenditure reductions to existing programs to finance any new programs. This concept was made operational and became the overall framework around which departments and agencies formulated their budget requests and the Treasury Board, with the support of the Department of Finance, reviewed them. Major changes, which remain in place today, were implemented to the way the expenditure estimates were presented to Parliament.[6]

In 1974, in response to major difficulties that departments and agencies were having in developing measures of program effectiveness and operational performance as required by PPBS, the Treasury Board put in place the Operational Performance Management System (OPMS). OPMS proposed a comprehensive analytical framework for tracking program outputs in relation to program inputs.[7] The Treasury Board Secretariat promoted Management by Objectives (MBO) in an effort to assess management performance achieved against pre-determined program goals.

The primary concern leading to the Glassco reforms and to the subsequent introduction of PPBS and its associated mini-reforms was a need to create a completely new interaction between spenders and guardians, an interaction that would focus not on the line-item budgets of pencils and paper clips (inputs) but on program budgets for the purposes of surface transportation, fisheries management, military equipment, and employment development (outputs or results). In short, the central idea was that, for government, 'what comes out of a program was more important than what went into it.' Coupled with this was the belief, particularly among spending departments, that under line-item budgeting central guardians had become too strong and too intrusive in focusing on the detailed financial and administrative information, thereby 'micromanaging' the budgets and programs of departments and agencies. For guardians, PPBS offered the prospects for more rational policy and expenditure decisions. For spenders, PPBS, with its emphasis on program budgets and program information – the latter which could only come from spending departments – offered the promise of 'letting the managers manage.'

PPBS emphasized the need for a clear division of labour between spending roles, which were found in the departments and agencies, and central guardian roles, which were reflected in the Treasury Board and its newly instituted and separate Secretariat.[8] The clear division of roles and the requirement to relate expenditures to programs encouraged a great deal of interaction between the program analysts of the Treasury Board Secretariat and the program administrators in the spending departments. The programs and their budgets were analysed and debated by public servants, but because of the enormous volume of individual programs and complexity, ministers became less involved over time, usually deferring to the recommendations of officials concerning the size of program budgets.

The PPBS budgetary process was largely bottom up, focusing primarily on the allocation of expenditures rather than on determining or limiting fiscal aggregates or ensuring prudent financial management. The spender and guardian interactions were around individual programs with the bargaining taking place over budgets and the exchanges over information. Spenders traded program information for program budgets and guardians attempted to control individual program expenditure totals on the assumption these individual actions would control overall government expenditures. It worked out that way for spenders, but not for guardians. Over time, total government expenditure increased significantly, at a rate higher than the growth in the economy.

To make matters worse for guardians, in the pre-election budget of 1974, the government, in a major and far-reaching decision, indexed the personal income tax system to automatically adjust to increases in inflation. Prior to that time, 'the treasury' had been benefiting from the effects of inflation as individuals were automatically bumped into higher tax brackets thereby resulting in an automatic 'fiscal dividend' for the government. This annual 'fiscal dividend' made it easier for the government to find additional revenue for new spending programs or for financing the carrying cost of its increasing public debt. At the same time, the government also indexed to inflation its major social transfer payments to individuals, such as old age security payments to the elderly and child allowances for families, thereby putting additional pressure on its expenditure budget.[9] Over time the statutory programs of the government (i.e., those programs of a continuing nature which did not require an annual vote for funds and which represented over 65 per cent of total federal government spending) would increase significantly and at rate higher than the growth in overall spending.

In 1976, it was the principal financial watchdog, the Auditor General, who brought public attention to the rapid growth in public expenditures through his rhetorical declaration in his annual report that 'Parliament and indeed the government has lost, or is close to losing, effective control of the public purse.'[10] This paved the way in 1977 for significantly strengthening the role of the financial watchdog through far-reaching amendments to the Auditor General's Act, establishing a legislative basis for 'value for money audits.' This ushered in a new era of independent performance reviews of departmental management and programs undertaken by the Auditor General acting as an agent of Parliament. It also led government guardians to establish in 1978 the Office of the Comptroller General within the Treasury Board in an effort to significantly strengthen financial management and program evaluation within government.

At the same time, the guardians in government struggled in their attempts to strengthen the expenditure decision-making process of cabinet in an effort to increase control of overall government spending and to ensure that government expenditures would increase no more rapidly than the growth in the GDP. The government established what came to be called 'the Treasury Board referral system' in an effort to increase guardianship within the system. Prior to that time, new spending initiatives were generally first considered by cabinet committees with little regard to expenditure, and then considered by cabinet and, only after that, referred to Treasury Board for consideration of the resources. The new 'referral system' required that new spending proposals be considered by Treasury

Board prior to consideration by cabinet. It also required that Treasury Board ministers be designated as 'treasury ministers' in their participation in cabinet committee discussions.

Finally, in the summer of 1978, Prime Minister Trudeau launched a surprise government-wide $2.5-billion expenditure reduction exercise, subsequently known as the 'Guns of August,' in an effort to keep the growth in government spending in line with increases in the GDP. The Treasury Board, with the support of the priority setters in the Privy Council Office, centrally managed this budget-cutting exercise. Unlike the traditional bargaining and negotiation between spenders and guardians that was part of the PPBS process, there was no discussion and negotiation with departments and agencies. The Treasury Board guardians focused on the most expeditious way to achieve expenditure savings, recognizing priorities had little to do with the exercise of securing immediate and significant savings. They drew up a list of proposals for departmental expenditure cuts which was endorsed by the cabinet under the watchful eye of the prime minister and subsequently announced by the president of the Treasury Board. The only indication that priority setters were beginning to play more directly on the budget decisions was the announcement of the child tax benefit program, which set the foundation for future direct and tax expenditure decisions in the area of children and family benefits.

Extensive interaction between spenders and guardians around the details of individual program expenditures was not leading to controlled spending but to spending that was increasingly seen by many to be out of control. Controlling the parts did not guarantee control of the total. When it came to budgeting, the whole was indeed more than the sum of its parts. Discipline at the bottom was not translating into discipline at the top. It was time to explore new approaches to expenditure management.

The Grand Design: Policy and Expenditure Management System (1979–83)

As had been done by the government fifteen years earlier, the Trudeau Liberals launched a Royal Commission in November 1976 in the aftermath the Auditor General's scathing report that the government had lost control of the public purse. But unlike the previous Royal Commission, this commission – the Lambert Commission on Financial Management and Accountability – had little impact on the budgeting and financial management reforms that would be implemented by the new Conservative government of Joe Clark.[11] With the release of its report in 1979, the Lambert Commission recommended measures to 'avoid waste in government' and 'strengthen accountability,' including an overhaul of central agencies. It recommended that the government put in place the principal accounting officer concept, similar to that existing in the UK, in order to make deputy ministers personally responsible and accountable to the Public Accounts Committee for financial management.

By the late spring of 1979, the newly elected government of Prime Minister Clark saw the budget problem differently than the Royal Commission. To the new government, it was not that finances were being mismanaged and that expenditures were leaking out from the bottom; rather, it was the need to establish limits at the top. What Clark and his newly appointed ministers saw was a fundamental imbalance between spenders and guardians. In short, spenders were overwhelming guardians who were increasingly finding it difficult to exert limits on overall government spending. The response was to strengthen the hand of guardians through multi-year fiscal planning and overall expenditure limits, not just through the single-handed efforts of the beleaguered guardians but through the visible support of the central priority setters in the Privy Council Office. Immediately upon taking office in May 1979, Clark announced the 'Expenditure Management System,' designed to set government-wide expenditure limits through the publication of a five-year fiscal plan and to establish specific expenditure levels and priorities for policy sectors within which departmental plans and budgets would be considered.[12]

The seriousness of the overall expenditure situation was reflected in the fact that after the defeat of the ill-fated minority Clark government on its December 1979 budget, the significant features of Expenditure Management System reforms were immediately taken up and extended by the new Liberal government in February 1980 under the banner of the Policy and Expenditure Management System (PEMS).[13] While the Trudeau government was concerned about the need for limits at the top, it was more concerned that guardians were operating in isolation from spenders, and both were acting in isolation from the priority setters. For the Liberals the question was not just about limitations on the fiscal aggregates but also about using these limitations to ensure expenditure allocations were linked to government priorities. Limitations became the means for forcing choices among priorities rather than the vehicle for curtailing the size of government. Inserting the word 'policy' into the 'expenditure management system' and calling it PEMS signalled that priorities and expenditures were to be linked, and it ushered in an increased role for priority setters in the budgetary process.

Under PEMS, it was intended that policy and expenditure decisions would be integrated at the macro level by the Cabinet Committee on Priorities and Planning, chaired by the prime minister, and at the more micro level by cabinet policy committees which managed their budgetary envelopes. Budgetary envelopes were to be established by Priorities and Planning, in the context of establishing the fiscal framework on the recommendations of the minister of finance.[14] In total, ten budget envelopes were established with five committees of cabinet responsible for managing two each. In an effort to decentralize priority setting, the Ministry of State for Social Development and the Ministry of State for Economic and Regional Development were established to support the system. Indeed, in the early 1980s, PEMS was viewed by international practitioners as an important and effective innovation in the budgetary process and lauded by academics as a model for others.

Not only did PEMS deal with direct expenditures but it also made a concerted attempt to integrate decisions on tax expenditures within the envelope budget system. More specifically, as part of the 'rules of the game,' tax expenditures and off-budget financing (e.g., loans, loan guarantees, and advances) that were provided to departments and agencies were to be taken into account by the Department of Finance in recommending envelope levels to the Cabinet Committee on Priorities and Planning.[15] For a few years this resulted in a broader analysis and consideration of tax expenditures by the Tax Policy Branch of the Department of Finance as well as the Ministries of State which supported the policy committees of cabinet and by selected spending departments. Decisions about tax expenditures directly competed with decisions about direct expenditures when it came to setting the overall expenditure level for the policy sector or the allocations of new money to departments. The result, according to one observer, was that for 'one brief shining moment,' spenders made fewer demands on Finance for tax expenditures and the minister of finance made fewer unilateral tax expenditure announcements.[16]

To help implement PEMS, departments and agencies prepared Multi-year Operational Plans (MYOPs), setting out the ongoing costs of existing programs for review by Treasury Board. Departments and agencies also prepared strategic overviews setting out the policy rationale and expenditures associated with new initiatives for consideration by cabinet committees. On paper, and as reflected in the 'rules of the game,' the system appeared considerably more integrated than it did in practice.[17] In fact, there were four subsystems operating, all in search of overall coordination. Only in the best of times and for a brief period (1981–2) were these subsystems momentarily linked. These four subsystems and their institutional leaders, which are still very much in evidence today, were macroeconomic management (Finance), major government priorities (Privy Council Office), ongoing expenditure management (Treasury Board), and new expenditure management (at the time, Ministries of State in support of cabinet committees).[18]

The focus of PEMS was on expenditure allocations linked to priorities at the envelope or sector level and at the departmental level. In support of this effort, the newly established Office of the Comptroller General promoted program evaluation and published an ambitious guide, intended to ensure that departments and agencies 'systematically gather(ed) verifiable information on programs and demonstrable evidence on their results and cost-effectiveness,' and 'periodically produce(d) credible, timely, useful and objective findings on programs appropriate for resource allocation, program improvement and accountability.'[19] This proved to have little effect.

Within a few years, by 1983, in the later stages of the Trudeau government, PEMS was showing acute signs of strain. The promises of maintaining limits at the top, of linking sector priorities and budgetary envelopes at the middle, and of ensuring effective program evaluation at the bottom were not being achieved. Cabinet committees were increasingly finding that they were unable to achieve political consensus in order to make real and significant savings to fund new programs. In short, spending ministers were just that – spending ministers and not guardians. When it came to allocations of new money to priority sectors, the minister of finance was increasingly unprepared to make broad allocations of new money by sector and to permit ministers in cabinet committees to then decide on the precise allocations to departments. Instead, the minister of finance increasingly earmarked any new money in the envelopes specifically for particular programs, departments, and ministers. These 'special allocations' or individual 'side deals' between the minister of finance and a spending minister soon came to be 'regular allocations.' This practice effectively undercut the role of cabinet committees to determine allocations within their sector and budgetary envelope, weakened the role and influence of policy committee chairpersons, and reduced the role of the Cabinet Committee on Priorities and Planning in determining overall sector allocations.

This gave the Department of Finance a foothold for subsequently extending over time its reach and grasp to deal directly with the allocation of priority program budgets in various departments, a responsibility which traditionally had been the domain of the Treasury Board Secretariat. There were increasing concerns about the large, expensive, and elaborate organizational structure, in the form of the two Ministries of State (for Social Development and for Economic and Regional Development) and the 'mirror committees of deputy ministers,' which supported 'the system' and two major policy committees of cabinet. Finally, and perhaps most significant, individual ministers were finding that they were spending enormous amounts of time participating in cabinet committee meetings and discussions among their colleagues only to learn that important priority and expenditure decisions were quietly being made elsewhere through some combination of the prime minister, the minister of finance, the priorities and planning committee, or a tight inner-circle of influential ministers.[20]

It is not surprising that PEMS on its own did not provide the means for a spending Liberal government to establish and maintain fixed limits on overall expenditures. Budgeting systems cannot achieve what political will is unprepared to do. During the period 1979–84, real growth in expenditures was outstripping real growth in the economy. Inflationary pressures intensified, interest rates skyrocketed to an unprecedented level of 19.5 per cent, and an increasingly large portion of total expenditures was required to pay the interest on an increasingly larger public debt. Deficits increased each year with the government regularly forecasting a balanced budget in the fifth and last year of the projected fiscal framework but never coming close to achieving it, as each year a significant upward adjustment was made to the expenditure framework.

Guardians were not so much overwhelmed by new spenders as by past spenders whose expenditure programs had become so tightly entrenched through a combination of established legislative and political commitments and future inflationary expectations that they could not be immediately changed and reduced even in the face of a dramatic and worsening economic situation. The promise of regaining expenditure control at the envelope and sector level proved impossible to achieve in the face of what was required – a significant and major reduction of expenditures – to remain within projected overall limits. The limits were not targets to stay within, but rather planned ceilings that could be adjusted upward.

PEMS with its elaborate cabinet machinery and decision-making process did, however, allow Prime Minister Trudeau to push certain issues 'down and out' to be dealt with by others while allowing him and a smaller inner-circle of ministers and advisers to focus on the two dominant priorities of the day – national unity, including the patriation of the constitution and establishment of the Charter of Rights and Freedoms, and the National Energy Program. Pushing things 'down and out' meant that policy committees, armed with the Ministry of State assessment reports which were invariably sharply critical of any increased spending, could scrutinize the spending proposals of their fellow colleagues. To be sure 'a few butterflies were caught, but no elephants were stopped,'[21] and the only major reallocation was an amount of $150 million put forward by a new and inexperienced minister responsible for housing.

From a strict expenditure management point of view, PEMS was premised on fixed expenditure limits at the top in order to force policy committees of cabinet to make choices and trade-offs within expenditure envelopes at the sector level.[22] When the limits at the top became flexible and adjustable, sometimes through significant changes in the macroeconomy and at other times through 'side deals' on expenditure increases between the minister of finance and a spending minister, the incentives to overcome the nasty task of making trade-offs within expenditure envelopes quickly disappeared. PEMS strengthened the role of priority setters in the Privy Council Office and the Prime Minister's Office in the budgetary process and marked the beginning of a formal fiscal and economics unit in the Privy Council Office focused on advising the prime minister on the budget. Just as important, it also signalled the reinstatement and formalization of a major program policy role for the Department of Finance as it made more allocations directly to departments and agencies under the guise of establishing sector-wide envelope levels. This was coupled with the changes that began to reduce the role and influence of the Treasury Board and its Secretariat in the budgetary process as it focused less on new expenditure initiatives and more on adjustments to the A-base of approved departmental spending and in keeping track of the expenditure draws by policy committees, the minister of finance, and the Treasury Board on the policy, program, statutory and operating reserves.

If, for many, the highly formalized structure of PEMS with its supporting cast of institutions and mirror committees was looking too heavy and its actual performance too light, it is easy to understand why. On paper the system looked cumbersome and time consuming, and for most ministers it was.

Incremental and Continuous Change (1984–93)

During his brief tenure in 1984, Liberal prime minister John Turner consulted with then leader of the opposition Brian Mulroney and made a significant change to PEMS. He eliminated the two supporting Ministries of State, deploying the several hundreds of talented analytical staff to policy positions in spending departments and agencies throughout government. For the new prime minister, who had previously been a successful minister of finance (1972–5), the system for managing public expenditures had become 'too elaborate, too complex, too slow, and too expensive.' For the next decade, PEMS was never formally replaced by another system; instead, it just faded away in the course of a series of separate expenditure management and control initiatives introduced by the Mulroney Conservative governments over the course of its two mandates.

In the aftermath of the failure of the 'grand design' of PEMS, the various initiatives undertaken by the newly elected Conservative government were intended to be practical, targeted, and efficient. They would focus on the needs of the economy and on the requirement to cut a 'bloated bureaucracy' and reduce 'excessive overspending through years of Liberal government mismanagement.' The initiatives were variously undertaken by the principal guardians of the system – the deputy prime minister, the minister of finance, and the president of the Treasury Board.

The day after taking office on 17 September 1984, Prime Minister Mulroney announced the establishment of the Nielsen Task Force on Expenditure Review to rationalize government programs and achieve significant expenditure savings. The task force was chaired by then deputy prime minister Erik Nielsen and consisted of two senior guardians – the minister of finance and the president of the Treasury Board – and one major spender, John Crosbie from Newfoundland who was then minister of justice. The task force relied upon significant input from private sector advisers and established nineteen joint working groups represented by private sector leaders and senior public servants to examine both direct expenditures and tax expenditures. As the task force began its important work, a first instalment for expenditure reduction was announced by the president of the Treasury Board in the form of expenditure cuts and cost recovery increases amounting to $3.6 billion. The minister of finance, with the visible and seemingly strong support from the prime minister, announced in his first budget of May 1985 a target of $15 billion in expenditure reductions by 1990–1. But this was not to be. Within days of the budget, on the front lawn of Parliament Hill, the prime minister, under intense pressure from senior citizens in the person of a tenacious, white-haired 'senior' dubbed by the media as 'Charlie Brown,' reversed the minister of finance's budget and declared that his government would not break its 'sacred trust' with seniors by reducing their benefits.[23] This decision came to define expenditure management for the Mulroney government for the rest of that mandate as well as for the next. Fifteen years later a senior Finance official lamented the stark implications that flowed from that critical decision: 'After that we lost all interest in deficit reduction.'[24]

The consequences of attempting to reduce the expenditures of a major and highly popular social program and then publicly reversing the decision had important repercussions for the priority setters. It highlighted, for all, the difficulty in managing the budgetary conflict that invariably results when governments attempt to focus expenditure reductions on only a few ministers, departments, and constituents to the exclusion of all others. Priority setters reluctantly concluded that establishing priority areas for expenditure reduction generated too much conflict. It was one thing for 'General Motors to decide to discontinue the Oldsmobile and quite another for the government to insult the beneficiaries of a program by explicitly declaring it to be a low priority.'[25] It also meant that priority setters, to the extent that they influenced future budgets, would be more prone to work with spenders to assist them in getting approval from guardians for their new initiatives than to work with guardians to bring about structural reforms to major government spending programs.

A year later in 1986, when the Nielsen Task Force completed its work, the chair made recommendations to the cabinet and to the prime minister for expenditure reductions and the elimination of tax expenditures of between $7 billion and $8 billion.[26] There was considerable focus on eliminating subsidies to agriculture, fisheries, transportation, business, and regional development, bolstered by evidence that the government was 'giving with both hands' – direct expenditures as well as tax expenditures. The proposed changes, however, had significant regional implications for a cabinet moulded from strong regional interests. In the end, the government, now acutely tuned into the sensitivities of regional and sectoral interests and not prepared to generate more conflict, did not implement any of the major recommendations.[27]

Over the course of the next several years, the two guardians – the minister of finance and the president of Treasury Board – worked together to propose to the Cabinet Committee on Priorities and Planning and to the prime minister a continuous series of government-wide expenditure cuts in an effort to share the pain and minimize the inevitable conflict. The proposals included packages of cuts to transportation subsidies, transfers to provincial and territorial governments, partial de-indexing of social programs, eliminating 15,000 public service positions, the privatization of Crown corporations, the establishment of a limited number of special operating agencies, across-the-board cuts to departmental operating budgets, and freezes on salaries of public servants, Members of Parliament and Senators. Significant failures and financial crises in Crown corporations led to the introduction of Part X of the Financial Administration Act (FAA), which established a new legislatively based control and accountability framework for Crown corporations.

The Treasury Board implemented Increased Ministerial Authority and Accountability (IMAA), another attempt to 'let the managers manage' by negotiating memoranda of understanding between the Treasury Board and individual departments to increase their authority and flexibility in delivering programs while establishing an accountability framework for measuring performance. There were, however, few takers since the special, tailor-made flexibilities offered were minimal and since some limited flexibilities were already being granted across-the-board to all departments. The government took tentative modest steps and announced the creation of special operating agencies,[28] which were 'discrete operation units within departments that have been given increased managerial autonomy in exchange for greater accountability of results.'[29]

In 1989, in the early stages of a second mandate and in the face of a deteriorating economic and fiscal situation, the prime minister created the Expenditure Review Committee chaired by Deputy Prime Minister Mazankowski in an attempt 'to ensure that the government's expenditures continue to be directed to its highest priorities, and that expenditure control continues to contribute to deficit reduction.' The emphasis

was on the less contentious matters of managing new spending proposals, not on reviewing and reducing existing expenditures. The Cabinet
Operations Committee served as a gatekeeper for new spending proposals, with the actual spending decisions being made by the Cabinet Committee on Priorities and Planning, chaired by the prime minister.

With less success in dealing with fiscal aggregates and expenditure
allocations and reductions, the government slowly began to focus on
areas of financial management and public service reform. In 1990, with
the strong urging of the public service, it launched 'Public Service 2000'
in an effort to reform and modernize the way in which the public service
managed and administered government programs.[30] The primary factor
leading to this reform initiative was a growing frustration that 'managers were being undermined by a culture based on rules.'[31] This accelerated a fundamental change that was already well underway within the
community of guardians. The Treasury Board evolved from an 'expenditure manager' with clear and important interactions with spenders to a
'general manager' with unspecified responsibilities and considerably
less interaction with spenders. From then on, the Treasury Board gradually began to focus more on management and less on expenditure. In
implementing its 'general manager' role, the Treasury Board in 1991
introduced Shared Management Agendas with departments in an effort
to establish a joint agenda between Treasury Board and each department
on specific departmental performance and on the administrative and
managerial flexibilities required by departments.[32]

Over the next few years, the Treasury Board put into place five management tools intended to give departments more flexibility and to
help them increase their expenditure efficiency:

- single operating budgets for departments to increase the flexibility
  between salary and operating budgets,
- the elimination of person-year controls on departments,
- a carry forward to the following year of up to 5 per cent of departments' budgets for operating expenditures,
- increased retention for departments of funds raised from cost recovery, and
- some additional flexibility in the deployment of human resources.[33]

The elimination of person-year controls had significant impact on the
quantity and quality of information available to the Secretariat. 'Information on P-Ys [person-years],' explains a former budget office veteran

in the Secretariat, 'provided the Program Branch with substantial and convenient leverage at the policy table and great insight into the workings of departments.'[34]

During the period 1984 to 1993, a series of continuous and ongoing expenditure reductions were undertaken by the minister of finance and the president of the Treasury Board to projected expenditure levels. These reductions were intended to contain and, in some instances, cut expenditures in order to reduce the growing government deficits and to provide funds for new initiatives. To minimize and contain conflict, these reductions were made to expenditure projections and were 'back-end loaded' with the result that year-over-year expenditure levels were not reduced. Most of the reductions were centrally directed 'across-the-board cuts' to departmental operations and programs. Guardians were able to make these across-the-board reductions with little or no program information from spenders. The cuts were based on the simple and easy-to-implement rule of 'equal sacrifice' for all. In short, guardians found they could make expenditure cuts without dealing directly with spenders. The consequences of this approach to expenditure management were significant and far-reaching. One result was a dramatic reduction in the information exchanges between spenders and guardians, and with that, a significant reduction in the quality of program and expenditure information flowing to the centre and in the capacity of the Treasury Board Secretariat to analyse it.

As the economic outlook became more and more uncertain, the five-year economic forecasts and fiscal projections became less and less credible. Unexpected spikes in interest rates dramatically exacerbated the fiscal situation with the result that increasing amounts of expenditure, well over one-third, were being absorbed to finance the growing public debt. This resulted in increasing dissatisfaction from taxpayers who were seeing less and less of their tax revenues being used to provide them with programs and services.[35]

As expenditures became more difficult to change and to manage, the government shifted its focus from government expenditure to government organization. In 1993, Minister Robert de Cotret, a former president of the Treasury Board, undertook for Prime Minister Mulroney a major review of the organization and machinery of government. The focus was on the ways and means to streamline government operations through the reorganization of government departments and the reduction, rationalization, and elimination of government agencies, boards, and commissions. In June 1993, the new Conservative prime minister Kim Campbell announced a major and far-reaching reorganization of government departments and agencies intended to make government more efficient, more streamlined and responsive, and less cumbersome. This reorganization included:

- a reduction in the number of cabinet ministers from forty to twenty-four,
- the elimination of many small departments and agencies,
- the merging of departments to create large departments such as Human Resources Development Canada and Industry Canada,
- folding the Office of the Comptroller General into the Treasury Board Secretariat, and
- a first step in developing, on a more formal basis, 'ministerial portfolios' that clustered together government departments, agencies, and commissions in order to encourage greater horizontal coordination.

While this reorganization reduced the number of spending ministers and departments that had grown up over the last several decades, it did not strengthen the role of guardians, watchdogs, or priority setters. Confusion in the Treasury Board over its new role continued. The elimination of the Office of the Comptroller General meant that financial management watchdogs in departments and agencies had less influence and status within government. The guardians in the Department of Finance now had to deal with powerful spenders in the enlarged and newly established mega departments of Industry Canada and Human Resources Development Canada (HRDC), and priority setters in the Privy Council Office and the Prime Minister's Office continued to support spenders over guardians. In a nutshell, spenders and their allies had become too strong and guardians and their allies too weak. There was a growing need to strike a new and more fundamental balance.

Program Review and Prudent Budgeting (1994–2003)

With the election of the new Liberal government of Prime Minister Jean Chrétien in 1993, it was not the guardians, however, that struck back first. It was the financial watchdog. The newly appointed Auditor General convinced the new government to permit him to increase his reporting to Parliament from one annual report to three reports a year in addition to the annual report. Furthermore, the minister of finance, in his first budget in 1994, introduced a new section in the budget in which the government would regularly report on its progress in implementing the findings of the Auditor General. While, according to one Finance official, 'it was not widely read,' the new section in the budget did lend credibility to the ongoing role of the financial watchdog.

A few months into its mandate, in October 1993, the new government announced its Program Review which, at the time, was a measured and modest attempt aimed more at 'Getting Government Right' than at reducing government expenditures. As described subsequently by the government, the approach was to 'start by deciding what needs to be done by government and then what can be afforded.'[36] The government announced its intention to reduce the ballooning deficit 'step by step,' beginning first with its election campaign commitment to reduce the deficit to 3 per cent of GDP ($25 billion from a level of $42 billion). In the February 1994 budget, Finance Minister Martin promised to 'review all government spending' and announced that Mr Massé, the minister with responsibilities for the Program Review, would lead the exercise. At the time it was broadly assumed that part of the savings would be used to fund new priorities. Under this approach priority setters were in the lead and guardians were providing support. But by May 1994, when Massé launched the review and wrote to all spending ministers asking that they review all spending within their departments and portfolios, the minister and the Department of Finance already knew, based upon the negative reaction to the February budget, that 'all the expenditure savings would need to go to bottom line' to be assured of meeting the deficit-reduction target.

The priority setters in the Privy Council Office took the lead in structuring the review process and in establishing five tests that departments and agencies were to use in reviewing their programs.[37] But these five were not the only tests that were applied. Reflecting the seriousness of the fiscal situation and the strong need for guardianship, the deputy minister of finance added a sixth, and possibly, in the end, the most important one – the 'affordability test.' This test asked two essential questions: Is the resultant package of programs and activities affordable within the fiscal constraint? If not, what programs or activities should be abandoned? These six tests formed the basis for the Program Reviews by individual departments and agencies. They also formed the basis for the subsequent government-wide review of this work by the Steering Committee of Deputy Ministers, chaired by the Clerk of the Privy Council, and the Coordinating Group of Ministers, chaired by Minister Massé. This review process was unique and, according to one former deputy minister, 'a very substantial factor in the success of Program Review was the special machinery that the clerk established, which brought to bear a disciplined system lacking in most expenditure cutting exercises before and since.'[38]

The guardians insisted, however, over the objections of the priority setters, that expenditure reduction targets be established for each department. The minister of finance and the department established notional targets broadly divided into three categories: very significant reductions over 50 per cent (for example, in Transport Canada); substantial reductions of about 25 per cent for many departments; and smaller reductions of less than 15 per cent. These were then communicated to departments by the deputy minister of finance. With the support of the priority setters, the guardians were now clearly in the lead.

In the fall 1994 Economic and Fiscal Update, the minister of finance committed publicly that 'come hell or high water' the government would achieve its target of reducing the deficit to 3 per cent of the GDP ($25 billion) in the upcoming 1995 budget. Throughout the exercise, the prime minister strongly and visibly supported his minister of finance. Special pleading for adjustments by strong spending ministers to the prime minister were simply turned back to the cabinet committee, which was under strict instructions from the prime minister to ensure that if any relief was provided to any minister then that minister must find an offsetting reduction somewhere else.[39] In addition, and of particular importance, all requests for any new spending were immediately and flatly turned down and turned away. Guardians now had the strong and visible support of the priority setters, and they worked arm in arm against the spenders.[40]

Fears of how the Mexican peso crisis would affect the Canadian economy, with its ballooning deficit and debt, strengthened the resolve of the guardians as well as the priority setters to restructure programs and achieve significant expenditure savings. The crisis, which led to higher interest rates for Canada and in turn higher public debt charges, triggered an upward adjustment in the targets for spending reductions. It also triggered further immediate expenditure savings from Human Resources Development Canada which, up to that point, had been exempt from the Program Review with a 'promise' to yield future downstream saving through its Social Security Review.

In parallel with the public's increasing anxiety about the size of government deficits and the ever-expanding costs of servicing a ballooning debt at the expense of reduced public services, Finance Minister

Martin undertook an extensive process of pre-budget public consultations.[41] These public consultations built upon the earlier efforts in the mid-1980s by Conservative finance minister Wilson to reduce the long-standing practice of budget secrecy and to establish fixed dates for budgets.[42] For Martin, who saw a unique convergence between the needs of the government to reduce expenditures and the growing concerns of the public about increasing deficits, these public consultations provided the opportunity to solidify a fiscal posture of restraint and to get the public to explicitly recognize that hard choices about the continuation of certain programs would be required. By being open and specific with the public about the types of tough expenditure choices required in advance of finalizing the budget and through the unprecedented use of extensive public opinion surveys and focus group discussions, the finance minister was able to shape public expectations, reduce the likelihood that the public would be surprised on budget day, and thereby increase support for his budget and reduce or dull the opposition.

The results of the Program Review were significant and were unveiled by the minister of finance in his budget on 27 February 1995:

- the achievement of a 3 per cent deficit target,
- $29 billion in multi-year expenditure reductions resulting in 1996–7 program spending being reduced to 13.1 per cent of the GDP, the lowest level since 1951,
- elimination of 45,000 public service and military positions with significant incentive programs put in place for early retirement and early departure,
- a significant restructuring of many federal government programs particularly in the areas of transportation, employment insurance and job training, defence and foreign aid, agricultural, industrial and regional subsidies and the elimination of several boards, commissions, and advisory agencies, and
- major reductions in social transfer payments to the provincial and territorial governments through the creation of the Canada Health and Social Transfer, which combined several transfer programs into a block-funded program. This gave provinces considerably less funding with only slightly more flexibility.

Coupled with the 1995 budget the guardians established a new Expenditure Management System,[43] which incorporated a number of features aimed at more rigorous expenditure restraint in an effort to ensure that

- programs continued to be reviewed on an ongoing basis,
- expenditure and deficit targets would be achieved on a step-by-step annual basis, and
- any new expenditures proposals would be considered within the context of the tight fiscal framework and as part of the minister of finance's budget.[44]

Phase two of the Program Review, which was significantly smaller in both scale and scope than phase one, was completed and announced in the March 1996 budget. During this second phase, expenditure reduction targets were not established but savings were achieved through reductions in defence spending and a greater reliance on user fees, cost recovery, alternative service delivery, and contracting out.

The Program Review represented a temporary victory of the guardians, with the support of the priority setters, over the spenders. The exercise was centrally directed and its focus was exclusively top down. The objective was clear and singular – to gradually reduce the deficit to zero through the elimination and reduction of expenditure programs. This was accomplished through a combination of strong political will led by the minister of finance and the prime minister and through the use of prudent fiscal forecasting and prudent budgeting by the Department of Finance. Budgeting became one dimensional. It focused exclusively on reducing the fiscal aggregates. Allocations were temporarily suspended because any allocation of any new money to any spender, no matter how meritorious the cause or how small the amount, would undermine the discipline of restraint and reduction required by all. Even expenditure reallocations were not considered because any flexibility in resources was destined for the government's bottom line.

The Program Review, coupled with prudent economic and fiscal forecasting, restored fiscal balance in 1997 and established the basis for the continuation of a 'balanced budget or better.' It also increasingly consolidated nearly every important aspect of the budget-making process within the Department of Finance. It reinforced and solidified the central locus of decision-making on new expenditure initiatives between the prime minister and the minister of finance, to the exclusion of spending ministers and the president of the Treasury Board. With its top-down emphasis on expenditure restraint, it contributed significantly to the accelerated decline in the capacity and stature of the Treasury Board and its Secretariat in the review of departmental programs and expenditures and in its influence on the budgetary process.

Perhaps most significantly, the two key players – guardians and priority setters – who were instrumental in eliminating the deficit and securing fiscal balance would continue to dominate the budgetary process as increasingly larger surpluses became available for spending. Spending ministers and departments that were anxious to resume their natural interests did not become important players. A tight collaboration of both cooperation and competition between the guardians in Finance and the priority setters in the Prime Minister's Office – even in the face of increasing political and personal tensions between Finance Minister Martin and the Prime Minister Chrétien – ensured that only those who could contribute to the narrow range of priorities in the budget would be allowed to participate. The PMO priority setters ensured that new money would only go to a few priorities (e.g., children, health, and the new economy), and the Finance guardians controlled the design of the initiatives, consulting only with highly selected spending departments like Industry Canada and HRDC when it was necessary to do so.

As fiscal surpluses became larger and as the consequences of prudent budgeting were regularly yielding increasing amounts of 'unexpected' year-end money, the demands from spending ministers and departments significantly increased. The Finance guardians, with the support of the priority setters, found new ways – independent foundations – on which they could expend these year-end surpluses on a focused set of priorities. Pressures from spenders to expand the budget priorities were successfully rebuffed by the priority setters and the guardians, and the few budget initiatives that spread new monies to several ministers and departments, such as the infrastructure program, were carefully controlled and designed at the centre of government.

As prudent fiscal forecasting and prudent budgeting, both necessary to maintain a balanced budget or better, continuously produced year-end surpluses substantially larger than forecasted, the appetite and ambitions of spenders increased. Spenders believed that they had made significant sacrifices and that it was now 'their turn' to benefit from the public purse. Both guardians and priority setters were concerned, however, that the hard-earned benefits of a balanced budget might be squandered across an array of programs and that, in the worst of circumstances, economic or other global shocks could lead the government back towards a deficit situation. The approach therefore became not simply to curtail new spending to new priorities but rather to reallocate expenditures from old priorities to new priorities.

'A Continuous Culture of Reallocation' (2004–6)

In December 2003, when Paul Martin took over as prime minister from Jean Chrétien, he deliberately sought to distance himself and his government from his long-time arch rival. Despite the unsuccessful attempts by the Chrétien government and others before him to make significant expenditure reallocations, within days of taking office, Prime Minister Martin boldly declared that his government would be one of 'the politics of achievement' and he promised a 'continuous culture of reallocation.' As a highly successful former finance minister, he did not want to see the government go back into deficit. As a new prime minister, he recognized that bold, nation-building initiatives like 'fixing medicare for the next generation' and the lengthy list of other priorities he wished to pursue would require large increases in new expenditures. He announced that expenditure management would be a key priority of his new government and that the Treasury Board would be 'remandated to focus on providing rigorous oversight of government expenditures' and 'be responsible for continuous reallocation and realignment of government expenditures.' A new expenditure review committee of cabinet, chaired by the president of the Treasury Board and supported by its Secretariat, was established.[45] What was being called for by the prime minister was not simply the linking of new expenditures to new priorities but also the transformation of old expenditures into new priorities. This required unearthing the base of existing expenditures and breaking the old ground that had significantly hardened and stabilized since the major upheaval of the Program Review nearly a decade before.

One student of budgeting has referred to reallocation as the 'elusive ideal.'[46] In fact, no other Canadian budget reform has promised so much – 'a continuous culture of reallocation' – and yet achieved so little. A recent OECD paper, which compares reallocation experiences across eleven countries, identifies five triggers for reallocation, all of which have motivated reallocation attempts in the Canadian federal government at various times and in various combinations:

1 'Fiscal stress' (revenue shortfall coupled with overspending), which led to a dramatic reduction and restructuring of program spending

through the program review and deficit reduction budgets of 1995 and 1996.

2 'Fiscal abundance' (revenue windfalls which lead to rising expectations for new and urgent expenditure priorities not all of which can normally be financed from the expanding fiscal dividend), which has contributed to various government-wide and internal departmental reallocations since 2001.

3 'Dominant priority,' which motivated reductions in other expenditure areas in order to make large allocations to the priority area of health care in 2005.

4 'New and emerging political priorities' (security, health, safety, defence, and tax reductions), which have motivated ongoing reallocations.

5 'Substitution of inputs' (as a result of changes in the relative price of inputs: operating costs, salaries, and capital), which, along with the need for fiscal restraint and increased efficiency, has motivated smaller and less contentious reallocations.[47]

In theory one might have thought that for Prime Minister Martin, the emergence of one of the most powerful and effective triggers for reallocation – the need to increase funding to the dominant health-care priority – might have provided sufficient political purpose and motivation for ongoing reallocation and strengthened the incentives for both ministers and officials. But this was not to be the case.

In mid-2004, Prime Minister Martin, facing the instability of a minority government and the overriding preoccupation of dealing with the fallout from the Auditor General's report on the 'sponsorship scandal' and from the high-profile public inquiry by Justice Gomery, appointed John McCallum, the minister of national revenue, to chair the Expenditure Review Committee. The support for the committee was removed from the guardians in the Treasury Board Secretariat and given to a small, newly established PCO Secretariat under the watchful eyes of the priority setters. In an effort to identify expenditure savings that could be reallocated to higher priorities, the PCO Secretariat began by assessing existing programs using two sets of criteria: policy tests and implementation tests.[48] The reviews included departmental reviews in the thirty largest departments and agencies, horizontal policy and program reviews, and operational reviews in ten areas of government expenditure.[49]

Departments and agencies, requested to identify the lowest 5 per cent of their operating and program expenditures, were initially sceptical about the reallocation exercise because they feared 'another across-the-board cut.'[50] However, after considerable negotiation with spending departments, the PCO Secretariat was able to put $17 billion (over five years) in proposals to ministers from which they could decide. At the same time, there were also some opportunities for certain departments to benefit from the reallocations as they offered up expenditure reductions in partial exchange for the possibility of securing new money for government priorities through the upcoming budget.

Subsequently, in the 23 February 2005 budget, the minister of finance announced that nearly $11 billion in cumulative savings over the next five years had been found with 89 per cent coming from improved efficiencies in government operations. The net savings were to be achieved through:

- more streamlined government purchasing ($2.5 billion),
- improved property management ($0.9 billion),
- establishment of Service Canada to consolidate the delivery of income security, employment insurance, and other benefits to Canadians ($2.6 billion), and
- departmental savings relating to program and administrative efficiencies, and program reductions and eliminations ($3.9 billion).[51]

The savings were reinvested in other priorities with $2.1 billion in efficiency savings in employment insurance being directed back to the department for either a reduction in premiums or enhanced benefits. The remaining savings, about $8.5 billion, were reallocated through the 2005 budget to other departments to fund new initiatives in defence and security, the environment, support for Aboriginal Canadians, and maintaining the integrity of core government operations.

Some spending departments used the reallocation as a window of opportunity to undertake a major institutional change in their organization and a structural change in their programs and delivery systems. For example, Human Resources and Skills Development Canada successfully convinced Expenditure Review Committee ministers that it could achieve $3 billion in expenditure savings over five years in exchange for establishing Service Canada as a new agency to provide 'a wide range of benefits and services to Canadians – everything from paying EI benefits to issuing passports to accepting tax returns and payments on-line.'[52]

As in any government-wide reallocation there was criticism, particularly from departments and agencies. Some argued that the centre 'scooped' those initiatives that departments and agencies already had underway as ways of reducing costs and improving efficiency, or that the details of the savings identified by the centre had yet to be worked out and the full implications not fully understood. Indeed, Minister McCallum reported on 'the ease' with which the expenditure savings could be identified.[53] When the centre 'takes the low hanging fruit,' it reduces the future opportunities and credit for departments as they confront their own expenditure reallocations. When announced savings are imaginary in some measure, and expenditure targets are firm, this implies another round of negotiations to realize savings from other sources. 'The recent reallocation process was not real and the savings were not real and are not sustainable,' laments a senior Finance official.[54]

If performance to date on expenditure reallocation has fallen far short of it promise, then the future prospects look even less optimistic. Looking into the foreseeable future, it would appear that the important 'reallocation trigger' of fiscal stress will be less important, unless a combination of vastly increased military and security expenditures and significant tax cuts reignites the fiscal imperative. Similarly, the pressure of one dominant priority, such as health care, seems less likely. More likely, impetus for reallocation will not come from a single major pressure but from a combination of several smaller pressures, including a continued political commitment to achieving balanced budgets or better; new and emerging political priorities in response to emergencies and less predictable world events associated with security, health, environment, and poverty; and citizen concerns and demands for increased economy, efficiency, and the elimination of 'waste' in government and for 'value-for-money' in expenditure programs in the aftermath of the Gomery Inquiry.

The Liberal government, in focusing its attention on expenditure reallocation, attempted to change the long-standing and deeply entrenched incentives and disincentives that operate across spenders, guardians, and priority setters. Perhaps not surprisingly, particularly during a period of a minority government, its expenditure reallocation promises outstripped its performance. The new Conservative minority government, against the backdrop of the sponsorship scandal and the Gomery Inquiry, has focused its attention on financial watchdogs in an effort to bring greater discipline and accountability to the management of public money.

Strengthening the Watchdogs:
The Federal Accountability Act (2006 and onward)

Just as royal commissions in the past – Glassco in 1962 and Lambert in 1979 – set the stage for major budgetary reforms, the high-profile

Gomery Commission in 2005 into the Sponsorship Program motivated the new Conservative minority government to undertake a dramatic strengthening of financial watchdogs. Launched by Prime Minister Martin in February 2004, in an effort to distinguish and distance himself from his long-time political rival Jean Chrétien and to make good on his commitment to 'do government business differently,' the commission attracted widespread media coverage and public attention, not just in Quebec where it became as popular for television viewers as a 'soap opera' but throughout much of English Canada as well. Public and media attention was so extensive that just days before Justice Gomery released his first report on 1 November 2005, Reg Alcock, the president of the Treasury Board, unveiled a blizzard of reform proposals designed to show that the Martin minority government was undertaking decisive action prior to the release of the final Gomery report of 1 February 2006. By one count there were 238 initiatives,[55] including a significant increase in new rules and procedures. Perhaps the most significant and potentially far-reaching initiative was the strengthening of the internal audit function within departments and agencies and the commitment to hire 300 additional internal auditors.[56]

The Conservative opposition, with the support of the New Democratic Party and the Bloc Québécois, defeated the minority Liberal government and forced an election in January 2006 prior to the release of the final Gomery report. As part of its overall strategy to set out a detailed election platform, the Conservative Party released its plans for a dramatic strengthening of independent financial and other watchdogs through the introduction of the Federal Accountability Act, which the party had previously drafted when public opinion polls indicated that it would again be the opposition after the 2006 election.[57] At one level, the act reflected an ideological perspective on government, requiring strong countervailing forces to contain the size and role of government in a free society. At another level, it reflected the growing tendency in many countries for increased accountability in what has been described as an 'audit society.'[58] At yet another level, it reflected the particular circumstances faced by a new minority government in the aftermath of a major public money scandal and its determination to distinguish itself from its opposition with the rhetorical commitment 'to clean up Ottawa.'

On 11 April 2006, within days of the opening of the new Parliament, the Conservative Harper government unveiled, as its first legislative priority, the Federal Accountability Act. It was almost a mirror image of what the party had promised in its election platform. The legislation explicitly rejected a significant number of the major proposals put forward by Justice Gomery in an effort to reduce the powers of the prime minister and the Clerk of the Privy Council with respect to the appointment of deputy ministers.[59] The 250-page act, which substantially amended forty-five statues and amended over 100 others, included a broad array of political and administrative reforms from financing political parties to lobbying, appointments, whistle-blowing, auditing, and budgeting. It established five new parliamentary watchdogs, strengthened five existing parliamentary watchdogs, created three new internal but independent watchdogs, strengthened one existing internal watchdog, and codified in law the watchdog-like functions of yet another.[60]

In terms of the management and accountability of public money, the legislation represented a dramatic strengthening of the scope, powers, and responsibilities of financial and budget watchdogs. The measures and the language used to describe them were decidedly reformist in nature and in tone: 'ensure truth in budgeting,' 'strengthen the power of the Auditor General,' 'strengthen auditing and accountability in departments,' 'clean up the procurement of government contracts,' 'provide real protection for whistle-blowers,' and 'designating deputy ministers as accounting officers.'

In all there were six major reforms dealing with the management of public money:

1 The creation of a new budget watchdog, the parliamentary budget officer (PBO), was an effort to improve the transparency and credibility of the government's fiscal forecasting and budget planning. It is intended to provide parliamentarians and parliamentary committees with independent information and advice on economic and fiscal issues.

2 New powers and resources were provided to the Office of the Auditor General to audit any individual and organization that receives public money from the federal government, allowing the Auditor General to 'follow the money' through the growing number of public, private, and voluntary sector partnerships and other multi-party financial arrangements. The requirement, in law, that departments review their grants and contributions programs at least once every five years puts these discretionary program expenditures under increased scrutiny, on a par with, for example, fiscal equalization, which requires legislative review every five years.

3 The independence and influence of internal audit watchdogs were strengthened with the appointment of a chief audit executive within each department and agency, reporting directly to the deputy minister and reporting functionally to the Comptroller General. In addition, the independence of internal departmental audit committees was strengthened by requiring that their membership be drawn largely from outside government.

4 Designating deputy ministers as accounting officers for their departments to make them accountable *before* Parliament to answer questions related to their responsibilities. These included measures to organize resources of the department to deliver programs in compliance with government policies and procedures; maintaining effective systems of internal control; signing departmental accounts; and performing other duties assigned by law or regulation in relation to the administration of the department. In the event a minister and deputy minister were unable to agree on the interpretation or application of a Treasury Board policy, directive, or standard, the deputy minister is to seek guidance from the secretary of the Treasury Board. If the matter remains unresolved, the minister would refer it to the Treasury Board for a decision. A copy of the Treasury Board decision would be provided to the Auditor General as a confidence of the Queen's Privy Council.

5 Procurement was given extra attention by enshrining in law a commitment to fairness, transparency, and openness in the government procurement process, and appointing an independent procurement auditor to provide additional oversight of the procurement process.

6 Finally, every public servant was encouraged to be a watchdog by providing them with whistle-blower protection and incentives. These included significant powers for the new Public Sector Integrity Commissioner; the creation of the Public Servants Disclosure Protection Tribunal to consider cases of reprisal; providing public sector employees with access to legal counsel and continuing to ensure they have adequate access to the courts; and providing a $1,000 reward to public servants who expose wrongdoing in the workplace.[61]

This decision to strengthen financial watchdogs at all levels sprang directly from the perceived failings of the previous system in the aftermath of the sponsorship scandal, even though the Gomery Inquiry dealt with only a small fraction of government expenditures. It also sprang from a declining level of trust in government, which was and remains particularly prevalent in Canada as it is in other OECD countries. For example, a 2006 public opinion survey indicated that politicians were trusted by only 14 per cent of Canadians. They were at the bottom of the occupational list, below car salespeople. At 50 per cent, senior public servants fared better and were in the company of journalists and lawyers, but far below firefighters and nurses at 96 per cent and 95 per cent, respectively.[62] All this has contributed to increased demands from the public for greater accountability in government.

The dramatic strengthening of all forms of internal and external financial watchdogs signalled a change in the traditional dynamic that had operated among spenders, guardians, and priority setters. Less emphasis was being placed on internal reciprocity and adjustment within government and more was being placed on external scrutiny by, and independent reporting to, Parliament and those outside government. There was less focus on a closed process of informal information sharing and mutual adjustment as moderated by the shared internal norms among the spenders, guardians, and priority setters and more on an open and formal process of transparent reports and audits by both internal and external watchdogs. In short, less emphasis was placed on trust within a community of shared interests and competing requirements and more on public reporting, external scrutiny, and independent verification. This change signalled a significant step in the gradual transformation, which had been underway for several decades, from the 'old village' with its closed expenditure community to the 'new town' with its independent and increasingly influential financial watchdogs.

Reforms that strengthened the budget and financial watchdogs affect all three budgetary functions – the determination of fiscal aggregates, the allocation of expenditures, and financial management and program efficiency. With respect to fiscal aggregates, the PBO, as an officer of the Parliamentary Library, has a mandate to provide 'objective analysis' to appropriate Senate and the House of Commons committees on the nation's finances and economy, including economic and fiscal projections. The PBO has a starting annual budget of $2.5 million and fifteen staff, and its mandate requires the cooperation of all departments and agencies, with the Department of Finance providing quarterly updates of its fiscal forecasts.

At this stage, it is too early to determine the precise influence the PBO will have through its analysis of the fiscal aggregates and projections underpinning budgets. It can hardly be compared with the influential U.S. Congressional Budget Office (CBO), which plays an important independent role in the formulation of budget projections. However, future governments wanting to maintain a balanced budget or better through the use of prudent forecasting and prudent budgeting may find that they are under increased public scrutiny by increasingly informed parliamentarians. According to one former Finance official, future governments may find that they are 'embarrassed on occasion,' especially if the PBO can come to 'command the same public credibility and status as the Auditor General.'[63] This will not mean that the House of Commons Standing Committee on Finance will have anything like the amount of influence on overall budget levels that committees like those in the U.S. Congress and Senate enjoy. The Standing Committee on Finance may, however, with the analytical support of a professional and competent PBO and with its televised hearings with the minister of finance, be able to provoke a broader and more informed public debate about the appropriate fiscal stance for an upcoming budget.[64]

As explained in chapter 6, ensuring a 'balanced budget or better' requires that the Department of Finance build considerable contingency into its economic and fiscal forecasts as a hedge against the inevitable uncertainty. Even a competent PBO working closely with an effective Standing Committee on Finance is unlikely to reduce significantly the uncertainty that is inevitable and the contingency that is required. It should, however, be able to force the minister of finance to be more explicit and transparent about the series of cascading prudence factors, contingencies, and internal reserves and set asides that are and must be contained in the fiscal framework on both the expenditure and revenue sides. This would open up the inner workings of the economic and fiscal framework not only to parliamentarians but also to spending ministers and their departments. Going a step further, it is not inconceivable that in exchange for an implicit acceptance of the need for prudence and contingency in economic and fiscal forecasting and, hence the regularity of 'unanticipated surpluses at year-end,' the Standing Committee on Finance might demand some greater influence in shaping principles about how these allocations are used, be it increased expenditures, tax reductions, or deficit reduction.

The potential effect of these watchdog reforms on actual budget allocations is not, however, expected to be considerable. When requested to do so by a committee of the Senate or House of Commons, the PBO has a mandate to provide independent cost analysis of any expenditure or tax proposal under consideration by either House and to undertake research on the departmental estimates before a committee. At best, this may have some indirect effect on departments and agencies to ensure that their initial cost estimates for spending proposals are not underestimated but include the full costs. It is difficult, however, to see how the cost analysts in the PBO will be able to compete with the cost experts in departments and agencies, in the Treasury Board Secretariat, and in the Department of Finance who have direct experience with the actual running of expenditure programs. At times, spenders may find that alliances with the PBO are useful in supporting their demands for additional resources from guardians. At other times, guardians may use the PBO cost estimates to support the reasonableness of their position against would-be spenders. In any event, the cost estimates of a limited number of high-profile and contentious spending initiatives, such as the gun registry, are likely to receive greater public attention and perhaps more informed debate and scrutiny about their proposed expenditures. But, since cost is only one of many factors that are considered when it comes to decisions about expenditure allocations, the impact of the PBO on budget allocations is expected to be limited. Furthermore, the clients for such PBO cost estimates in advance of the passage of the estimates by Parliament are the 'supply committees' of the House of Commons. As explained in the previous chapter, they have almost no influence on budget allocations during times of a majority government and, even in times of a minority government, their influence has been insignificant. If these committees are to play a greater role in budget-making then more needs to be done than simply making cost estimates available to them.

As well, the potential effect of strengthening external as well as internal watchdogs on financial management and program efficiency within government is difficult to assess. At one level these watchdogs are likely to sharpen the public focus and the political attention that is given to matters of financial mismanagement in government. Concern about increased public exposure of financial mismanagement could lead to improved financial management and greater efficiency in the use of public money by government. The manner in which this is undertaken will, however, be critical in determining what actually happens. If guardians and spenders simply put in place more financial rules, guidelines, and frameworks there is real risk that financial management will not be strengthened in the manner in which government operations and programs can become more efficient. In the sponsorship scandal, the Auditor General said that some rules were broken. She did not say that there were not enough rules. Whether the government will be able to meet the prime minister's commitment to public servants that 'this government will not be imposing more regulations ... [but] ... will look to repeal ones that inhibit [their] effectiveness' is far from certain.[65] Experience indicates that this has proved difficult to achieve, particularly when administrative and budget reforms are undertaken in the aftermath of a major crisis.[66]

There is risk that the new chief audit executives with their significantly enlarged staffs, their dramatically increased independence, and their special functional relationship to the Comptroller General could be turned into external auditors where their findings become a ready reservoir of after-the-fact information for the noisy critics of the department rather than a quiet source of information to permit timely improvements and adjustments by internal departmental management and staff. As a former top PCO official succinctly observed, 'Internal audit must be a tool for departmental management, not a tool for Parliament.'[67]

By emphasizing the financial watchdog function, the emphasis is placed on 'following the money' and not on following the results. In short, the focus is on audit, not on program evaluation. Indeed, the resources provided to internal audits in the federal government are increasing dramatically from a level of $5 million in 2005 to a level of $56 million in 2007. In contrast, the resources for program evaluation, which were $6.5 million in 2005, are not planned to be substantially more in 2007.[68] This suggests that when it comes to questions of government performance and its link to budgeting, the upper hand will be decidedly with the auditors who 'audit' programs and their management against a narrow set of financial management and efficiency criteria and not with program evaluators who 'evaluate' program results against a broader set of performance and effectiveness criteria. When it comes to 'the things' of programs and their budgets, this may contribute data and information about whether the government is 'doing the thing right,' but it will not produce information and analysis to be debated and assessed as to whether the government is 'doing the right thing.'

Reflections on Reforms

Over the past half century, the Canadian federal government has undertaken an extensive series of budget reforms.[69] Each of these reforms has been developed to address specific failings or omissions of the previous reforms. PPBS moved budgeting from a preoccupation

with line-item budgets to an analysis of program budgets and purposes, putting in place the basic program and budgeting architecture
for budget decision-making between spenders and guardians. When
program analysis of the individual parts was not well linked to the
overall priorities of the government and there was increasing concern
of maintaining overall expenditure limits, governments put in place
EMS and then PEMS. This form of top-down rationing of expenditures
to achieve both government-wide and sector priorities worked for a
while, but then became discredited through its failure to maintain
overall expenditure limits.

A series of regular expenditure reductions undertaken through both
external task forces and internal expenditure review committees, coupled with an increasing stream of across-the-board operating cuts, not
only failed to ensure overall expenditure limits in the face of economic
downturns but also weakened the capacity of government to deliver
on its ongoing commitments. As the increasingly larger carrying costs
of a ballooning public debt crowded out program spending, Canadians
began to perceive themselves as receiving less in public services while
still paying more in taxes. The efficiency and effectiveness of government spending was under attack and the government launched a government-wide initiative of reporting on program results, although
unlinked to actual budget decision-making. In the face of escalating
deficits and domestic and international pressures and through a combination of prudent budgeting, program review, and political will, program expenditures were dramatically reduced and deficits eliminated.
Prudent economic forecasting and prudent budgeting continued under
a deeply entrenched public and political consensus for a 'balanced
budget or better.' Expenditure reallocation, premised on the need to
meet major pressing expenditure priorities through expenditure cuts
while sustaining fiscal surpluses, has proved difficult to achieve and
has had limited effect. In the face of a major public money scandal – the
sponsorship scandal and the high-profile public inquiry – a new
minority government dramatically strengthened both external and
internal watchdogs in an effort to focus more on accountability and
financial management.

Budget reforms with singular and focused objectives are generally
more successful at achieving their objectives than those with multiple
objectives. However, single objective reforms can ignore other important budget objectives, creating new problems that need to be
addressed later. It seems that budget reform, like budgeting itself can

be nothing but incremental. It is too complicated, too contentious, and too difficult to undertake everything at one time through a comprehensive fully balanced set of budget reforms. In one sense this is not surprising because budgeting is so central to, and so much a part of, government. Budget decision-making is government decision-making. Indeed, would-be reformers of the past came to realize that reforming government was difficult and therefore focused much of their efforts on a seemingly simpler objective of reforming budget-making, only to learn that many of the same dynamics that underpin the way government works also underpin the way budgeting is done.

If we want to understand where budgeting is going, we need to understand where government is going. Like government reform, budget reform is fundamentally political. It is about changing the relative balance of influence among spenders, guardians, priority setters, and financial watchdogs. This suggests that 'doing better with public money' will be as challenging as 'doing better government.'

11 Doing Better with Public Money?

Budget behaviour is learned behaviour and there is a need to change it.

Finance associate deputy minister

Ministers are unhappy with the system, although right now they like the spending.

Treasury Board Secretariat director

In an era of surpluses we need a budget committee of cabinet like the Australians have.

Former Privy Council Office official

A good explanation of the causes of war ought also to be able to explain periods of peace.

Distinguished historian Geoffrey Blainey[1]

It may be an exaggeration to claim that in matters of public money, politicians and public servants, and by extension citizens, get what they pay for. But it does contain an important element of truth. When budgeting was micro and bottom up, guardians used 'the carrots' of budget allocations to get information on program performance and financial management from spenders. Priorities were often the residuals of the process – the unplanned results of what emerged from the market of bilateral bargaining between spenders and guardians. Financial watchdogs stood on the sidelines and attempted to acquire and then apply their new and increasing audit powers to ensure economy, efficiency, and the pursuit of effectiveness in government expenditures. Now that budgeting is macro and top down, guardians have secured limits on overall spending, but because budget allocations are made more to priority areas than to specific programs, central guardians get little guarantee from spenders of program performance or financial management. Priority setters are now into the budget game in a big way as they struggle to ensure that budget allocations are aligned to priorities, with some spenders getting allocations, others cuts, and some nothing at all. Financial watchdogs employ their audit tools within and, sometimes beyond, the scope of their increased mandate and their limited craft. They have nurtured a high level of credibility with the opposition, the media, and the public who have always valued their independence and have now subscribed to their assumed truth. Where previously guardians secured performance and financial management through the carrots of budget allocations, today it is secured, if at all, through the threats of watchdogs carrying the sticks of their published independent reports and audits.

Theory and Practice

The framework I have used to analyse the politics and management of public money is more complicated and more complex than the two-role model of spenders and guardians developed decades ago by Wildavsky, which he successfully applied to describe and explain budgetary outcomes across different levels of government and in different political systems. One of the major advantages of the spenders and guardians framework was its simplicity – a simple model of two stylized roles when combined with a few key variables (a budgetary base and an increment, or the theory of incrementalism) was sufficiently powerful to describe a set of important behavioural dynamics and to explain a broad range of budget outcomes.

Reflecting the 1960s, the spenders and guardians model was a theory of budgeting in the micro that was primarily driven from the bottom up rather than from the top down. That explains why, in part, many would-be budget reformers found it unsatisfying. Not only did it describe a budget phenomenon that to them looked too political and felt too slippery compared with their desires for a more rational and systematic approach, it also suggested a phenomenon that was not easily amendable to planned change, and if there were to be change, it would be more political, fragmented, and reactive than the comprehensive and rational reforms that were 'obviously' required. The concept of the macro, in the sense that priorities might be driven from the top of government and that the desires and bids of spenders might be governed and disciplined by someone or something other than their counterparts (the guardians), was not part of the theory. In the spenders and guardians model, priorities emerged through a process of competition among spenders for scarce resources and bilateral bargaining between spenders and guardians. While the priority setters of the Prime Minister's Office and the Privy Council Office existed and were gradually and increasingly influencing budgets, in the spenders and guardians model, they remained off stage and were not viewed as major budgetary players.

The spenders and guardians model was also a theory that focused primarily on one, all be it important, aspect of budgeting – the question of allocation, Who gets what and how much? It had less to say about matters of setting fiscal aggregates and even less to say about issues of program efficiency and financial management, both of which can and do affect allocations. The theory was developed and came to the fore in the academic literature and was subsequently embraced by practitioners at a time in the 1960s and 1970s when government expenditures were growing rapidly.[2] Each spender was receiving his/her 'fair share' (and more) of what was available. It is perhaps more than ironic that a theory that did not explain well the question of determining fiscal aggregates predated a time when many governments were beginning to spend more than they could afford and there were increasing worries about ballooning government expenditures and skyrocketing public deficits and debts. It seemed that the theories that explained the micro and provided prescriptions for managing it did not guarantee that the macro could be controlled or understood.

Appeals to the theory to help explain the causes of these problems and what might be done about them simply concluded that spenders had become too strong and guardians too weak. The explanation was that the Pogo principle was at work.[3] In short, well-intended spenders were doing it to themselves and, in the process, 'doing in' everyone else. Spenders could only see the good of their own spending and the benefits that they and their clients enjoyed. They saw little or none of the costs of their spending. It was akin to Garrett Hardin's 'tragedy of the commons' with each 'spending herdsman' enjoying the benefits of grazing more expenditure on the common pasture of the public purse while quietly putting the costs onto the taxpayer over the heads of the beleaguered guardians. The end result, in the words of Hardin, was 'ruin ... the destination to which all men rush, each pursuing his own best interest in a society that believes in the freedom of the commons.'[4] In budget terms this ruinous destination took the form of increasing deficits, ballooning debts, the elimination of expenditure flexibility, unsatisfied citizens, and angry and rebellious taxpayers.

On the other objective of budgeting – program efficiency and financial management – the spenders and guardians theory was considerably less relevant. Some will argue that the framework was never intended to embrace this objective of budgeting, although today few would disagree with the increasing importance of it. As governments put in place various initiatives of new public management, centred around the idea that efficiency could be improved by reducing central administrative controls, delegating more responsibility and flexibility to departments and agencies (including the creation of new organizational entities), and then attempting to hold them accountable for the results achieved, the spender and guardian model became even less relevant. As explained in chapter 2, guardians were under intense pressure and were pursuing a dual track of top-down tight fiscal restraint on the one hand, and the delegation of more responsibilities to increasingly differentiated and autonomous spending agencies on the other. The result was that the Department of Finance took on responsibilities for all aspects of budget allocation, while the Treasury Board Secretariat vacated the expenditure field and focused as a 'management board' on matters of service delivery and efficiency under the guise of government-wide performance management.

As the Canadian and other governments began to tilt and, in some cases, transform parts of their budget offices towards issues associated with new public management and its various mutations, the spenders and guardians model became less useful in explaining budget behaviour.[5] To the extent that new public management was given added focus and impetus at a time of severe and continued fiscal restraint, the general conclusion of both academics and practitioners was that the guardians had become considerably more powerful and influential. That certainly was the case in a number of countries, including Canada in the mid to late 1990s, and it was reflected in an increased emphasis on two of the budgetary functions – fiscal aggregates and allocations. In Canada, guardians used prudent forecasting and budgeting, combined with unwavering political commitment, to reduce overall expenditure levels, eliminate individual programs, and dramatically cut departmental budgets. The 'balanced budget or better' became the 'signature policy' of the Liberal governments, was embraced by the

Conservative Harper government, and became deeply embedded in the fiscal psyche of the nation.

The spenders and guardians model explained major expenditure reductions in the same way it handled major expenditure increases. They were viewed as 'shift points' and were treated as exceptions to the regular bilateral bargaining between spenders and guardians, resulting in incremental budget adjustments year after year.[6] Where and how these shift points entered the model was not clearly explained. In that regard, the emergence of priority setters as significant players in the budgetary game is useful in explaining more fully the subtle dynamics that are necessary for governments to undertake such major expenditure changes. It is not just a question of having strong guardians that can overpower weak spenders, but this study suggests that there needs to be effective and influential priority setters who can backstop the guardians and maintain the ongoing support and cooperation of the spenders while managing the increasing budget conflicts that invariably arise among ministers and departments when major expenditure reductions are made. Similarly, at other times, priority setters can help to crystallize events and articulate directions so that large expenditure increases can be focused and concentrated on important government priorities.

The spenders and guardians model has been even less useful in predicting and explaining the problems associated with inefficiencies in program delivery and mismanagement in the expenditure of public monies, and in providing suggestions for dealing with them. Those who were most concerned with these issues – for example, departmental chief financial officers and their officials, Treasury Board Secretariat comptrollers, and the Auditor General – remained off stage and their influence, although only indirect, was never recorded and recognized. Instead, problems of inefficiency and mismanagement of expenditures were ignored or simply explained away as something that was deeply hidden in the untouchable, ongoing base of budgetary expenditures. As spenders increasingly complained that the accumulation of rigid and inflexible central budgetary rules promulgated by guardians were becoming major barriers to the efficient and effective use of departmental expenditures, the spenders and guardians model had little to suggest by way of reform.

As we have seen, the subtle and indirect, but increasing influence of financial watchdogs on budgeting is and can be considerable in shaping the budgetary process and its outcomes. To be sure, the influence of the watchdog is not only about directly shaping a specific upcoming budget decision but also about setting a tone and climate based upon previously published audits that will condition the behaviour of spenders, guardians, and priority setters. For the financial watchdog, influence comes down to credibility, which is a function of the myth of objectivity and the reality of independence. They both go hand in hand. Objectivity is cast as 'being right' and 'never wrong' about the facts and getting others to acknowledge and accept that. Independence strengthens and supports that belief and perception. As a result, political actors who use this audit information do so with the confidence that its factual basis is not contested in a political world where nearly everything else is. It can and therefore is used not just to point out deficiencies in programs and expenditures but also to undermine and reduce the credibility of the government. In short, the public audit information is not just about bringing down budgets with efficient programs and economical expenditures, it can also be about bringing down governments.

The spenders and guardians framework did not help us to predict or understand the increasingly important and influential role that financial watchdogs are now having on the management of public money as they ply their professional craft in what has become 'an audit society.'[7] In the spenders and guardians model, the role of independent financial watchdogs was not explicit and, if it was mentioned at all, it was subsumed under the broader and more visible role of guardian. Waste and mismanagement in government expenditure was hardly a topic of budgetary concern in the model because so much of the focus of budgeting was on the allocation. Clear and rigid administrative rules and detailed budget controls emanating from central guardians were the mechanisms for reducing waste and keeping the potential for mismanagement in check. Whenever problems occurred, the inevitable prescription became more rules and tighter rules.

Matters of inefficiency in programs and expenditures, and concerns about financial management failings, were seen as important to guardians because budgeting was largely micro and bottom up. If the choices faced by guardians in deciding on an expenditure increase were from a set of fully developed programs, then it was easy to choose program A that was efficient and well managed over program B that was inefficient and poorly managed, or over program C that was efficient but poorly managed. The prescribed and detailed rules for securing financial management went hand in hand with budget allocations at the front end of the process. Spenders who were unprepared to meet the prescribed rules were deemed by guardians as unfit to receive allocations. When more of the expenditure allocations became centred not around clearly and fully described programs but among generally defined priority areas, the link between using budget allocations to secure efficiency and sound financial management became less direct. The linkage also became less direct when prescribed front-end rules and micromanagement were reduced and back-end monitoring and auditing was increased. While today spenders who are less efficient and have mismanaged their finances can be severely sanctioned at the back end of the process through the audit reports and findings of watchdogs, there is less opportunity and capacity through micromanagement by guardians to deprive them of spending allocations at the front end of the process.

Some might argue that this is an overstatement of both situations, past as well as present. To be sure, on careful examination, the always assumed 'good old days' are never quite as good as they seemed when compared to emerging problems that go begging for solutions. However, the increasing linkage of the management function in government to the back-end watchdog function and the fragmentation of front-end budget allocation function from the increasingly specialized management function is a cause for significant concern. In the old days, guardians were part-time managers and had in their hands the precision of detailed budget allocations by program and even subprogram to encourage good management and penalize bad. Today, guardians are no longer part-time managers. As the Department of Finance has taken over much of the allocation business, a new specialized cadre of financial managers has emerged in the Treasury Board Secretariat, which is becoming increasingly separate from the guardians. These new specialized managers rely on the reports of auditors to identify management risks and problems and on the threat of public embarrassment to encourage correction.

The spenders and guardians model was bottom up in nature and limited in scope. Like the theory of general relativity (e=mc^2), which explained the relationship of big objects in the universe, it was a reliable and simple predictor of budget allocations in a closed government.[8] The theory of general relativity, however, with its focus on gravity was not successful in explaining small objects – that is, tiny particles. They were explained through quantum mechanics with its focus on electro magnetism. As scientists entered the depths of black holes, regions of enormous gravitational force, the question became which theory to use – general relativity because things were heavy or quantum mechanics because they were tiny?

Enter a new theory called string theory. While highly speculative, it proposes a way to unite and stitch together the theory of the large (general relativity) and the theory of the small (quantum mechanics). It is a theory of the truly massive and the very tiny, combining the smoothness of general relativity with the jitteriness of quantum mechanics. This comprehensive theory, called by some, 'the theory of everything,' comes at a price. The price for comprehensiveness and unity is the increased number of explanatory variables required. String theory requires extra dimensions of space – the 4 dimensions of common experience (that is, 3 spatial and time), plus 6 more, for a total of 10. More recently, 'M' theory, which provides a new perspective on string theory, has added yet another dimension for a total of 11. While one of the objectives of theory is simplicity, it appears that along the bumpy road to building consistent theories there can be a cost of increased complexity.

How does this relate to models for understanding budgeting? The spenders and guardians model is powerful for its simplicity and for its predictions. But it is becoming frayed around the edges, not only in terms of explaining the budget functions of allocations, with an increasing emphasis on reallocation, but especially in terms of the functions of determining fiscal aggregates and program efficiency and financial management. The politics and management of public money provides a broader conceptual model than what has traditionally been the focus of budgeting which, despite Schick's comprehensive framework, has tended to focus primarily on questions of allocations, less on matters of determining fiscal aggregates, and very little on issues of program efficiency and financial management. If we are content to conceive of budgeting as primarily an activity of allocation, and give considerably less emphasis to the determination of fiscal aggregates and place no emphasis on matters of program efficiency and financial management, there is less need for adjusting our conceptual understanding. If, however, we enter the black holes of budgeting in a world of more open and transparent governments associated with explicit priority determination, expenditure restraint and reallocation, new public management, and increasing concerns about accountability, program efficiency, financial mismanagement, then we need to adjust our concepts and our way of thinking. The concept of the politics and management of public money implies a broader framework for budgeting, possibly offering a way of

developing a more unified and consistent way to think about these matters. Compared with the simplicity and intuitive appeal of spenders and
guardians, this new way of thinking adds to the complexity of the
framework. It involves two additional players – priority setters and
financial watchdogs – and considerably more extensive and more varied
interaction among them.

Throughout this book, I have used the framework of the politics and
management of public money as the basis for describing and explaining budgeting in contemporary twenty-first century government. The
framework has provided a more comprehensive approach than would
have been the case with spenders and guardians. It has helped us to
see the uneasy balance among competing budgetary objectives – determining fiscal aggregates, allocating resources, and achieving efficiency
in the management of expenditures. In terms of budget outcomes –
controlling total expenditures, linking expenditures to priorities, and
ensuring efficiency in expenditure and avoiding financial mismanagement – we see that it is rare that the government can achieve simulta-
neously high scores in all three areas. Instead, as government focuses
its limited attention and scarce resources on one, it gives less priority to
another, sometimes with significant and undesirable consequences.

The framework of the politics and management of public money has
helped us to understand that guardians are not monolithic. Treasury
Board Secretariat analysts are not clones of the Department of Finance
who just happen to work on the 'small p' programs of the budget.
Instead, with an increasing emphasis on management issues, their focus
on budgeting has clearly moved from matters of allocation to matters of
management and performance. At the same time, the Department of
Finance has extended its capacity and grasp to deal with practically all
matters of expenditure allocation. Guardians in the Department of
Finance are also spenders, and significant ones at that. In terms of direct
expenditures, Finance develops and designs programs, particularly
those involving 'big money,' that often involve major transfers to provinces and territories and major transfer payments to individuals. The
design of any adjustments to fiscal equalization is closely guarded and
undertaken by Finance under pressure from spenders, in the form of
provincial premiers and their finance ministers, and from priority setters, particularly in the Prime Minister's Office, who view the issue in
terms of national unity and regional considerations. In the hidden area
of tax expenditures, which in dollar terms nearly equals the entire direct
expenditure budget, Finance has exclusive responsibility for designing

the initiatives and determining what goes ahead and what stays on the drawing board. Indeed, the Department of Finance exerts great influence not only because it is a guardian but also because it can act as both guardian and spender and usurp some of the responsibilities of the priority setters in determining budget priorities.

The framework has also helped us to have a more complete understanding of the competitive and cooperative roles inherent in the most important of all relationships in the budgetary process – that between the minister of finance and the prime minister. The priority setter role of a prime minister is important in supporting the finance minister in making the unpopular expenditure cuts required in a period of deep fiscal restraint, but it may be still more important in determining a limited set of focused priorities when the government returns to a surplus position. The experience of a former finance minister cum prime minister indicates that being a good guardian when everyone needs to cut does not guarantee being a good priority setter when some spenders will win and others will not.[9]

The framework sheds light on the front end of the budget process and how governments are increasingly articulating government priorities to determine the aggregate fiscal levels and budget allocations and then using these priorities to explain and sell the budget to the public. Governments have learned that if they do not put their own, readily understandable label on their complex budget, the media will likely do it for them, and it may well be a label they do not like. The Prime Minister's Office and the Privy Council Office, while starting from different vantage points, work in tandem and are major and influential budget players. They are not just 'framers' who work only on the Speech from the Throne, they are also 'deciders' who shape the themes and contents of the budget. Indeed, as described in chapter 4, there is considerable evidence to suggest that prime ministers and their closest advisers are clearly not prepared to leave the determination of budget priorities to the minister of finance and his/her department. The framework sheds new light on our understanding of the critical and important relationship between the prime minister and the minister of finance on matters of the budget. Guardians and priority setters have different interests and they will go to great ends, pushing the relationship, sometimes beyond the breaking point, to get what they want. But, in the face of legions of spenders and aggressive watchdogs, they need each other as much as they need the tight cover of confidentiality in order to manage, without publicity and fanfare, their inherent differences.

The framework, which includes a major role for priority setters inside government, can help us to better understand how and when major shifts to the normal incremental process of budgeting take place. In the spenders and guardians model, such shift points – when expenditures for a particular department or program area increased quickly and significantly beyond the normal incremental and regular adjustment – were treated, as in a regression analysis, like 'error terms,' unexplained by the independent variables of the model: budgetary base, increment, limited calculations, trust, and conflict avoidance. To be sure, the origins of shift points will be exogenous to any model of budgeting constructed from variables largely internal to government. However, by including the role of priority setters within the new model, we might better understand how changes in broader societal preferences, attitudes, and political ideology can be channelled and focused by participants within government and thereby affect the internal workings of the budget process and its outcomes.

The framework has helped to shed more light on the back end of the budget process (some call it budget implementation), a part that is increasingly important but has traditionally been neglected by most budget theory. We have seen how financial watchdogs, through extensive use of their public reports by parliamentarians and the media, have considerable influence on the public perception of the government when it comes to the management (or mismanagement) of public money. Furthermore, recent reforms are not only strengthening existing external and internal financial watchdogs but also creating new ones. When it comes to improving efficiency and financial management in government, we have seen a decrease in the direct influence of Treasury Board guardians through the use of program budget allocations and an increase in the indirect influence of financial watchdogs through published audits and reports.

Reactive, but with Some Resilience

When Canada is compared to other countries using the spenders and guardians framework, the analysis suggests that it has much to learn.[10] While this undoubtedly is the case, especially with respect to the changing role of the budget office, the broader framework of analysis set out and applied in this book suggests there are some important and enduring features of the Canadian system that can adapt and are adapting to meet the new challenges in the management of public money. By Schick's standards – 'a government has the capacity to budget when it can adjust claims and ration to produce desired outcomes' – Canada comes off quite well.[11] The Canadian system finds institutional structure in the central agency network of the Privy Council Office, the Department of Finance, and the Treasury Board Secretariat, the labyrinth of departments, agencies, and Crown corporations, and the influential parliamentary watchdog of the Office of the Auditor General. It is deeply embedded in a parliamentary tradition where the government of the day, in all but a rare minority government situation, has the singular capacity and legitimacy, if it can muster the political will, to act decisively in determining a comprehensive and consistent budget plan for the country and in ensuring its timely implementation. The Parliament, for its part, remains responsible for reviewing overall and departmental budget plans and for holding the government to account on behalf of citizens as voters, taxpayers, and recipients of public services. While Parliament's role in the review of spending needs to be strengthened, it has, with information provided by the independent public auditor, been able to hold governments to account. Through a history of innovation in the design and implementation of federal-provincial and territorial fiscal transfer arrangements and through a tradition of tough intergovernmental bargaining with pragmatic political compromise, the system has accommodated a highly decentralized federation.

In the past, the budgetary system has proved to be adaptable and resilient in the face of changing economic and fiscal pressures on both the global and domestic fronts. The budget reforms of the late 1960s and early 1970s, precipitated by the Glassco Commission, although overly and unrealistically ambitious at the time, put in place the basic budget architecture that continues to this day. The grand reform of the early 1980s, most notably the Policy and Expenditure Management System, was widely applauded by the international budget community and other budget experts. However, it could not attract from a government, distracted by other pressing national issues, the high level of investment in political capital and political support that was required to sustain such a major and elaborate innovation. The decade-long incremental and continuous change (1984–93) brought about a number of important adjustments and adaptations at a time of dramatic and sweeping international pressures and increasing domestic tensions. In the end, however, the system proved to be too fragmented and too limited to deal with the impending fiscal crisis that had been building. By the mid-1990s, focused political will, galvanized by public support, combined with prudent budgeting and adjustments to government machinery in the form of the program review process resulted in a one-time 'shock treatment' that had significant and demonstrable results. When the sponsorship scandal rocked the country and the public trust and confidence in government, a new prime minister, as his first priority, put in place a Federal Accountability Act that strengthened the role of external and internal financial watchdogs. In short, Canadian prime ministers can and do get the expenditure management systems they want, for the times they believe they face.

If the most important characteristic of the system has been its adaptability and resilience in the face of changing external and internal pressures, then the price, which has been high, has been the reactive, ad hoc, and episodic changes that have accompanied this approach. In a nutshell, the budgetary system is 'resiliently reactive.' It is resilient because its critical machinery and underlying decision-making process rest squarely in the hands of the prime minister and, by extension, his minister of finance. Changes can and are made quickly when these two leaders (sometimes fierce political rivals) can come together and see it in their interest to do so. This affords the opportunity to focus the political will of the government, along with adjustments to its decision-making machinery, on the specific identifiable fiscal, budgetary, or financial management problems or crises at hand.

The adjustments to budgetary and expenditure management decision-making machinery are rarely structural and permanent in nature. Instead, ad hoc and temporary arrangements are put in place, such as a time-limited cabinet committee on expenditure review supported by a special secretariat in the Privy Council Office. In a sense, such temporary arrangements are 'work-arounds,' individually decided by the prime minister to get on with the job without the time-consuming and costly requirement to redesign, in whole or in part, the major components of the traditional and permanent decision-making machinery of government. At the same time, they maintain the discretion of the prime minister to reach in and make specific expenditure decisions. When adjustments are made to the permanent machinery, such as the transition of the Treasury Board to a management board, they are just that – transitional. They are gradual, evolutionary, modest in scope, and even partial. They are quietly announced without fanfare and are designed to deal with a particular problem that has emerged, in this case the need for increasing performance in government.

The budgetary system might be resilient, but it comes at the price of being reactive and reactionary. To date, this has been a high price to pay and it may increase sharply in the future. Changes are not made to anticipate future problems that might lie ahead. Instead, they are made – for example, prudent budgeting or program review – to deal with problems that have been plaguing the government for some time. As new problems arise, new solutions slowly emerge. For example, when unanticipated or unplanned year-end surpluses emerged, new spending mechanisms were created in the form of independent foundations to which large amounts of one-time public money could be transferred and then expended over a number of years through an ongoing and continuous program. Actions are generally not taken unless the problem has become, or is beginning to become, a major issue for the government or has developed into a crisis.

The Canadian budgetary system is deeply embedded in the budgetary norms that condition and shape the behaviour of the central budget players – guardians, spenders, priority setters, and financial watchdogs. These players operate with a minimum of formal budget rules and within traditional organizational structures that are sufficiently elastic that they can be readily adapted and bent to suit the required circumstances and their particular personal styles. Through long-standing experience in dealing with the seemingly endless controversies and battles over public money, these central players have developed an innate sense of 'how things are playing (or not playing) in the town.' They have an instinctive feel for when to include and when to ignore the others; when to push ever harder and when to ease off; who to attach to on their way up and who to distance from or provide comfort to on their way down; and when to be satisfied with less for fear of getting nothing at all.

The Uneasy Balance of Competing Budgetary Objectives

There has always been an uneasy balance in Ottawa among the competing objectives of budgeting – determining fiscal aggregates, making budget allocations, and ensuring efficiency and effective financial management. At times there has been an imbalance, sometimes an overreaction as budgeting has swung in one direction at the expense of others. Early attempts in the late 1960s and early 1970s to link budget allocations to priorities through the Planning, Programming, and Budgeting System (PPBS) were unsuccessful. By the late 1970s and early

1980s there was much focus on allocations at the expense of maintaining and controlling budget aggregates. Attempts to control or ration expenditures through the Policy and Expenditure Management System (PEMS) in the early 1980s were not successful over a significant period. Expenditures increased significantly resulting in large deficits and debt by the early 1990s. By the time government gained control of the budget aggregates in the mid and late 1990s, through a combination of prudent budgeting and top-down control, there emerged increasing public and political concerns around financial mismanagement and accountability in the use of public money as reflected in recent financial scandals.[12]

Budgets may sometimes be balanced, but the objectives of budgeting rarely are. Behind the three budget objectives lies a set of fundamental and sometimes competing public purposes. Budgets are suppose to provide control over public money, reflect the values and preferences of the people, and ensure efficiency and effectiveness in expenditure and accountability to public authorities. Yet the experience with budget reforms as described in chapter 10 and elsewhere suggests that the simultaneous achievement of these purposes has proved to be elusive. It seems that when governments focus too much on allocations to a few they are propelled to provide allocations to many, with the eventual result that there is too little control of the overall expenditure totals. If governments are single-mindedly fixated on controlling aggregates at the top they can lose sight of the importance of efficiency and prudent financial management at the bottom. Putting in place restrictive micro controls and rules on programs, expenditures, and processes does not translate into macro control of overall expenditures.

Much of the design of expenditure management systems and reforms has rested in the hands of the guardians in the Department of Finance and the Treasury Board Secretariat with the ongoing support and occasional opposition by the priority setters in the Privy Council Office. To be sure, in the past, this provided for a natural tension and interaction across these two important roles that led to some significant innovations over the years (e.g., PPBS, PEMS, and the expenditure management system, and various attempts at expenditure reallocation) not all of which have been successful. It was, however, largely a singular tension between the Department of Finance concerned with maintaining expenditure totals in the face of the increasing demands for allocations and the Privy Council Office focused on an effective cabinet decision-making process and protecting the prerogatives of the prime minister.

In the future, however, improvements and adjustments must consider a broader set of interactions among the principal public money players as well as a deeper interaction between them. The roles played by financial watchdogs are and will become increasingly important, not only the roles of the Auditor General and new parliamentary budget officer, who operates external to government as the agent of Parliament, but also those of the Comptroller General, the departmental auditors, and the slowly emerging community of departmental chief financial officers, all of whom operate internal to government. The important relationship between the Department of Finance and Treasury Board Secretariat guardians needs to be rebuilt and renewed so they can function effectively from the macro to the micro and from expenditure through programs to performance. The priority setters in the Privy Council Office and the Prime Minister's Office need to find more effective ways by which broad government priorities can be translated into specific and meaningful budget priorities. This will require navigating the treacherous course between the need for top-down budget direction through the interplay of the prime minister and the minister of finance and the requirement for the effective consideration of bottom-up proposals and initiatives emanating from spending ministers. The interaction between spenders and guardians needs to be enriched so that more emphasis is given to matters of performance and results and not simply to priorities and announcements.

Some argue that spenders should be more like guardians, taking into account the broader fiscal and expenditure limits of the government. While this may have some effect during periods of deep fiscal restraint, it is unlikely to be a feasible and winning strategy over the longer term. The analysis in this book suggests that budget players behave for what they are, not for what some might wish them to be. Rather than ask that spenders be guardians, we need to strengthen who they already are and to ensure a more dynamic and fulsome interaction across the principal players – spenders, guardians, priority setters, and financial watchdogs.

Sometimes it might appear that there is momentary balance and appropriate proportion across the three competing, yet complementary objectives of budgeting. But, more often it seems that things are out of balance as one objective overshadows others and sometimes works at the expense of others. Given a choice, some would-be designers of budgetary systems have at times preferred a system that performs well on one or two objectives but fails on others – better that a system overreact than it not react at all. Others have suggested that a budgetary system that scores high on some objectives but fails miserably on others is less preferred to one that has solid but not outstanding grades across all objectives. One conclusion from this study is that when it comes to budgetary systems – the politics and management of public money – there can be no single utopia that can be designed. Budgetary systems work from the ground up, through the self-organizing mix of countless interactions across the competing budgetary roles of spenders, guardians, priority setters, and financial watchdogs. A second conclusion is that a single 'budget system for all seasons' – one that can last through changing conditions – cannot be designed like the infamous all-weather coat to provide protection from wind, rain, snow, and sunshine.[13] Old budgetary systems need to adjust as governments change and react to the new pressures and uncertainties that they must face.

The framework for the politics and management of public money has analysed budget behaviour from the perspective of stylized roles rather than from institutionalized organizations. This framework, with its additional complexity, has helped to understand more clearly the behavioural dynamics that underlie the entire budgetary process. It has been useful in describing and explaining the broad pattern of budgetary outcomes and the trail of budgetary reforms over the last several decades. If this framework accurately describes and explains the budget process as it currently operates in contemporary government, it should also provide some insights into how to define better (there can be no best) the emerging challenges for the budgetary process and general directions for actions that could be taken to address them.

One conclusion from this analysis of public money is that its effective level, allocation, and management depend most on the strength and quality of the interactions among the spenders, guardians, priority setters, and financial watchdogs. Reforms that reduce and discourage these self-organizing interactions are likely to be less effective as are measures that lead to the dominance of one role over the others; those that facilitate a rich and dynamic set of interactions are likely to be more effective. In this regard, three reform initiatives are needed:

- establishing an expenditure review committee of cabinet,
- restoring a Treasury Board Secretariat role in expenditure review and allocation, and
- linking priorities, expenditure programs, and performance.

Establishing an Expenditure Review Committee of Cabinet

Like most other parliamentary jurisdictions, the Canadian federal government has undertaken a number of expenditure management systems and reforms over the years. But, unlike others such as Australia, it has never established an expenditure review committee of cabinet chaired by the prime minister.[14] In Canada, the ad hoc and temporary machinery associated with expenditure review committees chaired by individual ministers has served to deal with particular problems as they arose – the needs for an expenditure gatekeeper in the mid-1980s, for a program review in the mid-1990s, and for expenditure reallocation a decade later. For a short time (1997–9), there was some success with budget priorities and budget allocations being determined almost exclusively by the prime minister and the minister of finance, without the benefit of formal consideration by a committee of ministers and the coordinated and regular review of departmental expenditure plans and proposals by PCO, Finance and Treasury Board Secretariat officials. But as surpluses have grown, along with the new and changing priorities, the requirements for expenditure reallocation, and the necessity of ensuring performance, this bilateral approach has surpassed its limits and there is a need for significant change.

An expenditure review committee of cabinet should be established as a permanent feature of the cabinet decision-making machinery. For this to be both successful and feasible, a number of requirements would need to be met. First, like the Cabinet Committee on Priorities and Planning, it needs to be chaired by the prime minister. No one else can do the job.[15] Second, it should consist of a small group of ministers, including the minister of finance, the president of the Treasury Board, the chairpersons of the two or three policy committees of cabinet, and several senior ministers to ensure regional balance and priority representation.[16] Third, it should be responsible for the annual review of multi-year expenditure plans and proposals of departmental spending ministers. The focus should be on both the 'stock of expenditure' (the existing A-base) and on the 'flow of expenditure' (the new proposals). Fourth, as is the case in Australia, it should function as the 'budget committee of cabinet.' Working within the broad budget themes and priorities as determined by the prime minister, the minister of finance, and the Cabinet Committee on Priorities and Planning, it would be responsible for advising the minister of finance on the expenditure increases and expenditure reductions that should be contained in his/her upcoming budget. This would not be advice that the minister of finance could ignore. Fifth, it would need to be supported by a permanent Secretariat, consisting of senior officials of the Privy Council Office, the Department of Finance, and the Treasury Board Secretariat. Sixth, the president of the Treasury Board should be re-established as a 'budget player,' participating with the minister of finance and the prime minister in their pre-budget meetings and thereby strengthening guardianship within the ministry. Overall, in the words of a former top PCO official, 'the budget would be the result of this process not the cause of it.'[17]

The institutionalization of a permanent support secretariat to this cabinet committee will be especially important for its ongoing success. It will require a nucleus of top-level officials from PCO, Finance, and TBS, along with several senior departmental officials on a rotational basis, all of whom can work together and work effectively with the three central agencies and with the diversity of spending departments and agencies. Coming from a tradition where there has sometimes been excessive competition among central agencies, there will be a need to ensure higher levels of cooperation and collaboration. The secretariat will need to be able to 'reach into and across' these central agencies to ensure timely and coordinated analysis of priorities, expenditure plans, and proposals in the formulation of advice to ministers. Ensuring the cooperation and effective participation of spending departments and agencies will be largely determined by the extent to which the secretariat can secure the cooperation of the three central agencies to ensure that the work of the secretariat in its dealings with departments and agencies is closely coordinated with the regular ongoing work of the three central agencies.

The periodic and ad hoc establishment by prime ministers of special committees of cabinet chaired by various ministers to review departmental expenditures and identify saving for deficit reduction or reallocation had the effect of undermining the legitimacy and effectiveness of the ministers of the Treasury Board and its Secretariat. A committee on expenditure review of cabinet, chaired by the prime minister, would establish a permanent political body for budget decision-making, including major expenditure allocations and reallocations, and provide the basis and context for significantly strengthening the focus and capacity of the Treasury Board and its Secretariat in the area of program and expenditure analysis, efficiency, and government operations.

Restoring a Treasury Board Secretariat Role in Expenditure Review and Allocation

Over the past decade or so, the role of the Treasury Board Secretariat in the budget process, particularly with respect to budget allocations, has been significantly diminished. The focus on the deficit by the Department of Finance, the transformation of the Treasury Board to a 'management board,' the elimination of central policy and operating reserves, and the increasing delegation of authority to departments and agencies coupled with the promulgation of numerous government-wide management frameworks have all contributed to this diminution. As a consequence, the Treasury Board Secretariat has lost its ability and capacity to challenge departmental requests for new funding and to systematically and rigorously review the expenditure base of existing programs. Regular and ongoing interactions between central guardians and departmental spenders over the budgets, allocations, and detail design of programs have greatly diminished. As a result central guardians no longer have on their computers and in their filing cabinets, let alone at their fingertips, detailed program budget information and analysis that are essential to making informed decisions on program budget allocations and reallocations.

TBS appears caught in a seemingly endless bind that has seriously eroded its influence in the system. In budgeting it no longer has a challenge function and, perhaps most important, both the Finance guardians and the spending departments know it. For departments it means that program expenditure approvals by Treasury Board will not reduce the amount of the allocation that has been notionally set aside in the budget. A Treasury Board submission that includes the words 'source of funds: the fiscal framework' provides departments with the protection that the initial funding level for the proposal, previously established by Finance and/or the spending department without regard for the detailed program design, will not be challenged by the Treasury Board. To the satisfaction of some spenders, the Treasury Board may no longer be micromanaging, but on matters of the amount of public money needed to ensure economy, efficiency, and effectiveness of expenditure programs, Treasury Board is not managing enough. In the words of a top TBS official, 'When it comes to expenditure management, the Treasury Board has so much ground to make up that you can't even say we're in the weeds. We're in the roots of the weeds. We need to have knowledge of the A-base of expenditures which we do not have. We have a huge rebuilding process. I say to my people if we do not rebuild we will not have a Treasury Board in three years.'[18]

Current attempts by the Treasury Board Secretariat to put in place a centralized 'Management Resources and Results Structure' is not likely to provide the ongoing interaction between spenders and guardians to yield reliable, accurate, and timely budget and program information. Experience has indicated that spenders give information in exchange· for budget increments and guardians can acquire information from spenders by providing budget increments. There is an important and urgent requirement to rebuild and re-establish the reciprocal exchange between spenders and guardians of budget information and program performance for budget increments if central guardians are to be able to more effectively scrutinize and challenge the budgets of departments and agencies.

Strengthening interactions with spenders, however, will not be enough. The Treasury Board Secretariat also needs to rebuild its relationship with the Department of Finance. The Secretariat needs to become, once again, a budget player in support of the Department of Finance by providing detailed program and expenditure analysis of proposed new spending and the A-base of existing spending. The periodic and in-depth review of one or two specific cross-ministry areas of significant horizontal expenditure such as science, the North, Aboriginals, climate change, or immigration could be undertaken by the Secretariat under the direction of the proposed committee on expenditure review.

Interactions between the Treasury Board Secretariat – in particular, the Office of the Comptroller General – and the internal and external financial watchdogs – departmental internal auditors, chief financial officers, and the Office of the Auditor General – need to be strengthened. A clear and sharp line needs to be drawn between the internal watchdog function, which serves deputy ministers and managers of departments and agencies, and the external watchdog function of the Office of the Auditor General, which serves Parliament. TBS is not an agent of Parliament; it is an agent of government. Unlike the Auditor General, it is one of the governing institutions of government. Unlike the Auditor General, the influence of the Treasury Board does not stem from its independence and its ability to use the opposition and the media to embarrass the government. Treasury Board monitoring and reporting of departmental spending and activities will never carry the same influence as that of the independent Auditor General. If the Treasury Board is to get its way or even a bit of its way on matters of government performance, then it cannot rely solely on its monitoring and reporting role. It needs other avenues of influence in order to get and maintain the attention and commitment of spending departments and agencies. This is where the power of spending allocations comes in.

Restoring the Treasury Board Secretariat's role in expenditure allocation with the ability to challenge departments and scrutinize their budgets will require a concerted effort, including:

- strengthening and clarifying the roles and responsibilities between the Secretariat and the Department of Finance,
- creating ongoing central operating and program reserves which would be allocated by the Treasury Board to meet critical operational priorities of government, particularly those of a horizontal government-wide nature,
- providing Treasury Board ministers with the authority and the information to reduce the allocations for new departmental initiatives previously included in the budget if the Treasury Board review of proposed program design clearly indicated fewer resources are required, and
- mandating Treasury Board ministers to focus on matters of program and operational efficiency to identify expenditure reductions and savings that could be achieved and subsequently reallocated by the proposed expenditure review committee in the budget to higher government priorities.

Linking Priorities, Expenditure Programs, and Performance

Budgeting has become more top down and macro and less bottom up and micro. As central guardians have loosened their grip on the detailed budget and program information that could guide specific program allocations and as priority setters have increased their influence at the front end of the budget process more emphasis has been given to making block allocations to priority areas rather than allocations to clearly developed and designed programs. For example, in the February 2005 budget, large allocations were made in the form of formula financing, particularly in

the area of transfers to provincial, territorial, and municipal governments. The bulk of the $83 billion in new funding for expenditure and tax
saving initiatives provided in that budget was allocated by formula or to
priority areas in advance of the program principles and the detailed
design criteria being established for the individual programs.

At the same time, political parties have found it in their interest to
announce, in election campaigns, detailed spending commitments and
then, as a signal of trust with voters, to deliver on these precise spending initiatives. As a consequence, there tends to be less scrutiny and
analysis within government of these programs and expenditures. For
example, in the January 2006 election campaign, the Conservative
Party set out its expenditure commitments in considerable program
detail in such areas as mandatory sentences for gun offences and other
crimes thereby requiring an expansion of correctional facilities; taxable
payments of up $1,200 annually to families for each child under six
years of age; and tax credits for families of up to $500 per year for fees
for fitness programs for each child under sixteen years of age. Of the
dozens of specific program commitments made by the Conservative
Party during the election campaign, none were substantially rede-
signed or amended through further program and expenditure analysis
as part of the May 2006 budget.

The overall result is that more public money is being allocated to
broad priority areas without the benefit of full program design and
more is being allocated to specific 'promised' initiatives without a reas-
sessment of additional information, evidence, and new circumstances.
More budget allocations are being made, negotiated, and justified on
the basis that they are a government priority or that they are a political
commitment. While priorities and commitments are important drivers
of budgets, there is increasing risk that they are becoming such critical
determinants that they are undermining the importance of and
demand for information and analysis on program performance and
program results. Governments have found that priorities and commitments provide a ready-made rationale for justifying their budgets to
the public. By staking out priorities and commitments through
advance announcements, governments can enhance their credibility
with voters when they deliver the precisely promised programs and
expenditures through the budget. The test of whether or not commitments and priorities have been kept is simple and easy for governments and voters to assess. It is whether certain programs and
expenditures are contained in the budget. It is not whether program

results and performance have been achieved. The problem, of course, with results and performance is that they take time to achieve and are less certain to be achieved and, therefore, both governments and even citizens often make their assessments based on what is announced in the budget today and rather than on what might be achieved by the programs tomorrow.

In Ottawa, the weak link in the program budget chain is not between priorities and program expenditures. Governments can and do get to announce the program expenditures they want through a steady stream of interactions between spenders, guardians, and priority setters. The weak link is between program expenditures and performance. A senior Treasury Board Secretariat official puts it this way: 'We are doing budgeting by announcements. But over time, if the announcements are to prove themselves, they will need to result in real outcomes for real Canadians. That is how governments will be judged. We have lots of ministers for announcements, but no minister for outcomes.'[19]

As explained in chapter 3, there is experience in other OECD countries which have attempted to link more closely (it can never be that close) performance information and budgeting. The experience that underlies the best practices and how they have all evolved through various improvements and adjustments over time suggests the need to have realistic expectations but also clear objectives. In this regard, one conclusion from the U.S. is particularly important for Canada in shaping reasonable expectations: budgeting will, at best, be performance-informed not performance-based. This suggests the need to properly position performance and performance information so that it can help to inform budget decisions. Based on the experience of other countries, the Canadian federal government requires a considerable and sustained investment in performance information as a part of its overall culture and strategic approach to improvement in public sector management and budgeting. The link between performance information and budget decision-making is often subtle and indirect, requiring not only solid and credible performance information that supports regular and periodic program assessment but also a budgetary process that makes some demand for program analysis and performance assessments as a part of regular budget decision-making. Furthermore, an effective budget process will likely be one that uses a broad range of alternative information and analysis (e.g., evaluations, studies, assessments, reports, audits) from a host of sources both inside government (e.g., departments, central agencies, parliamentary reports, internal auditors, Auditors General, royal commissions) and outside government (e.g., policy think tanks, learning networks, universities, private consultants). Finally, in the future, more emphasis needs to be placed on the use of specific performance information and analysis internal to government to inform the interaction of spenders, guardians, and priority setters around individual budget decisions, and less emphasis on providing indigestible quantities of general information to parliamentarians on the overall performance of government departments and programs.

The Politics of Public Money

To be sure, anything as complex and as important as the politics and management of public money can hardly be explained fully through the interaction of four stylized players operating within government and grappling with three difficult areas for decision. Indeed, behind each player lies a myriad of other public and private interests, inside and outside government, and countless numbers of interactions, pressures, attitudes, beliefs, and ideologies within society, all of which have more, and sometime less, influence on questions of public money. In a sense, the interaction of these four players around three decision areas can only stand as simple proxy for the complexity that underlies a multiplicity of specific decisions about public money. Yet these players, through their self-organizing interactions, their mutual expectations, and their simplifying calculations, make some of the most important decisions of government and, perhaps more importantly, they make them stick.

It is sometimes said that if we want to understand where the politics and management of public money are going, then we need to understand where government is going. Budgeting is an important part of government, but it is not all of government. It seems that government's decisions about public money are increasingly being made in an environment where citizens are demanding more from government but they have less confidence it can perform well. In the future, increasing public expectations may put pressure on government to spend more and to improve services, while a lack of confidence in government may make it more difficult to extract revenue from less trusting and more tax-conscious citizens. If these or any other trends in government are to become established, then they will in turn find their way into adjustments and self-adjustments among the roles played by politicians and public servants responsible for the politics and management of public money.

Notes

Introduction

1 Matters of revenue budgeting and taxation, and issues of debt management are outside the primary focus of this book. For an analysis of the former, see David A. Good, *The Politics of Anticipation: Making Canadian Federal Tax Policy* (Ottawa: School of Public Administration, Carleton University, 1980); Douglas G. Hartle, *The Revenue Budget Process of the Government of Canada: Description, Appraisal, and Proposals* (Toronto: Canadian Tax Foundation, 1982); and Geoffrey Hale, *The Politics of Taxation in Canada* (Toronto: Broadview Press, 2002).

2 Some important Canadian studies by academics include Norman Ward, *The Public Purse: A Study of Canadian Democracy* (Toronto: University of Toronto Press, 1962); Allan Maslove, Michael Prince, and G. Bruce Doern, *Federal and Provincial Budgeting* (Toronto: University of Toronto Press, 1986); G. Bruce Doern, Allan M. Maslove, and Michael J. Prince, *Public Budgeting in Canada: Politics, Economics and Management* (Ottawa: Carleton University Press, 1988); Douglas G. Hartle, *The Expenditure Budget Process of the Government of Canada: A Public Choice – Rent-Seeking Perspective* (Toronto: Canadian Tax Foundation, 1988); Donald J. Savoie, *The Politics of Public Spending in Canada* (Toronto: University of Toronto Press, 1990); and Michael J. Prince, 'Budgetary Trilogies: The Phases of Budget Reform in Canada,' in Christopher Dunn, ed., *The Handbook of Canadian Public Administration* (Don Mills, ON: Oxford University Press, 2002). Some important Canadian articles by practitioners include A.W. Johnson, 'The Treasury Board of Canada and the Machinery of Government in the 1970s,' *Canadian Journal of Political Science* 4, no. 3 (1971), 240–59, and 'Planning, Programming and Budgeting in Canada,' *Canadian Public Administration* 33, no. 24 (1973), 23–31; Richard Van Loon, 'Stop the Music: The Current Policy

and Expenditure Management System,' *Canadian Public Administration* 24, no. 2 (1981), 175–99, 'The Policy and Expenditure Management System in the Canadian Federal Government: The First Three Years,' *Canadian Public Administration* 26, no. 2 (1983), 255–85, and 'Ottawa's New Expenditure Process: Four Systems in Search of Co-ordination,' in G.B. Doern, ed., *How Ottawa Spends: The Liberals, the Opposition and Federal Priorities* (Toronto: James Lorimer, 1983), 93–120; and Ian Clark, 'Restraint, Renewal and the Treasury Board Secretariat,' *Canadian Public Administration* 37, no. 2 (Summer 1994), 209–48.

3 Aaron Wildavsky, *The New Politics of the Budgetary Process* (Boston: Scott, Foresman, 1988; New York: Harper Collins, 1992), xxvii.

4 Aaron Wildavsky, *The Politics of the Budgetary Process*, 2nd ed. (Boston: Little, Brown, 1974), xx–xxi.

5 Nicholas d'Ombrain, 'Cabinet Secrecy,' *Canadian Public Administration* 47, no. 3 (Fall 2004), 333.

6 Department of Finance, *Advantage Canada: Building a Stronger Economy for Canada* (Ottawa: Public Works and Government Services Canada, 2006), 34 and 12. Retrieved 23 January 2007 from www.fin.gc.ca/ec2006/plan/plc2e.html. See also Department of Finance, *Budget Plan 2007* (Ottawa: Public Works and Government Services Canada, 2007), 158. Retrieved 7 May 2007 from www.fin.gc.ca/2007/pdf/bp2007e.pdf.

7 Finance, *Advantage Canada*, 35.

8 Discussion with senior Treasury Board Secretariat official, 15 January 2007.

1. Beyond Spenders and Guardians

1 Minister of Finance, *House of Commons Debates for the First Session, Twenty-Sixth Parliament*, 13 June 1963 (Ottawa: Queen's Printer and Controller of Stationery, 1963), 1003.

2 See Peter C. Newman, *The Distemper of Our Times* (Toronto: McClelland and Stewart, 1968); Denis Smith, *The Gentle Patriot: A Political Biography of Walter Gordon* (Edmonton: Hurtig Publishers, 1973); Walter L. Gordon, *A Political Memoir* (Toronto: McClelland and Stewart, 1977); and Stephen Azzi, *Walter Gordon and the Rise of Canadian Nationalism* (Montreal: McGill-Queen's University Press, 1999).

3 For information on the unexplained origins of the tradition of the minister of finance's new shoes see, *The Finance Minister's New Shoes*, available online from www.parl.gc.ca/information/about/process/info/BudgetShoes.asp?lang=E&Hist=N.

4 The expenditure reduction profile was actually over five years and included $1 billion in year one, which had already been achieved, $2 billion in year two, and $3 billion in each of years three, four, and five, for a total of $12 billion.

5 In Ottawa the budget office is divided between the Department of Finance and the Treasury Board Secretariat. The Department of Finance is responsible for management of the macroeconomy and for the fiscal policy framework. The Treasury Board Secretariat is responsible for the operating budgets of programs and the general management of government.

6 See Organisation for Economic Cooperation and Development, ' 24th Annual Meeting of OECD Session Budget officials: Annotation Agenda,' retrieved 14 December 2006 from http://oecd.org/dataoecd/61/21/2633689.doc.

7 Allen Schick, *The Changing Role of the Central Budget Office* (Paris: OECD, 1997), 4. Others express it differently. For an explanation of the complementarities and interdependence of these functions, see Richard R. Allen and Daniel Tommasi, eds., *Managing Public Expenditure: A Reference Book for Transitional Countries* (Paris: OECD, 2001). Because budgeting covers so much, it is not surprising that several different perspectives on budgeting are required. For example, the perspectives of 'politics, economics, and management' and 'macro, micro, and mezzo budgeting' are found in Doern, Maslove, and Prince, *Public Budgeting in Canada*.

8 See, for example, Jeffrey Rubin, 'A Balanced Budget Isn't Always Good Fiscal Sense,' *Globe and Mail*, 2 September 2004, B8.

9 See Wildavsky, *The Politics of the Budgetary Process*. The book was revised in 1974, 1979, and 1984.

10 Ibid., 160.

11 Aaron Wildavsky, *Budgeting: A Comparative Theory of Budgetary Processes* (Boston: Little, Brown, 1975), 7.

12 Charles Lindblom, 'The Science of Muddling Through,' *Public Administration Review* 19 (Spring 1959), 79–88, and 'Decision-Making in Taxation and Expenditure,' in National Bureau of Economic Research, *Public Finances: Needs, Sources, and Utilization* (Princeton, NJ: Princetown University Press, 1961), 295–336; and Charles Lindblom with David Braybrooke, *A Strategy of Decision* (New York: Free Press, 1963). Since the publication of Wildavky's *The Politics of the Budgetary Process* in 1964, the theory of incrementalism has been particularly prevalent in describing the dynamics of the public policy-making process. See, for example, Charles E. Lindblom and Edward J. Woodhouse, *The Policy-Making Process* (Englewood Cliffs, NJ: Prentice-Hall, 1993).

13 Wildavsky, *The Politics of the Budgetary Process*, 131–2.

14 Naomi Caiden and Aaron Wildavsky, *Planning and Budgeting in Poor Countries* (New York: Wiley and Sons, 1974), and Wildavsky, *Budgeting;* Hugh Heclo and Aaron Wildavsky, *The Private Government of Public Money: Community and Policy Inside British Politics* (Berkeley: University of California Press, 1974); and Louis M. Imbeau, 'Guardians and Advocates in Deficit

Elimination: Government Intervention in the Budgetary Process in Three Canadian Provinces,' in Jurgen Kleist and Shawn Huffman, eds., *Canada Observed: Perspectives from Abroad and from Within* (New York: Peter Lang, 2000), 45–56.

15 Savoie, *The Politics of Public Spending in Canada*; Doern, Maslove, and Prince, *Public Budgeting in Canada*; and Hartle, *The Expenditure Budget Process of the Government of Canada.* For a recent review of the spenders and guardians framework, see David I. Dewar and David A. Good, 'Great Books Revisited: Wildavsky on "Rescuing Budgeting from American Administration" and Heclo and Wildavsky on "Village Life in British Budgeting,"' *Canadian Public Administration* 47, no. 1 (Spring 2004), 81–96.

16 For an appreciation of his writings on budgeting, see Naomi Caiden and Joseph White, eds., *Budgeting, Policy, Politics: An Appreciation of Aaron Wildavsky* (New Brunswick, NJ: Transaction, 1995).

17 Aaron Wildavsky, *How to Limit Government Spending* (Berkeley: University of California Press, 1980).

18 Jeffrey L. Pressman and Aaron Wildavsky, *Implementation* (Berkeley: University of California Press, 1973), 143.

19 Wildavsky, *Budgeting.*

20 Aaron Wildavsky, *The New Politics of the Budgetary Process* (Glenview, IL: Scott, Foreman, 1988).

21 Heclo and Wildavsky, *The Private Government of Public Money.*

22 Savoie, *The Politics of Public Spending in Canada.*

23 Sandford Borins and David A. Good, 'Spenders and Guardians: A Budgetary Game of Mutual Adjustment,' Institute of Public Administration of Canada Case Study 1.93 (Toronto: IPAC, 1977).

24 Donald J. Savoie, *Breaking the Bargain: Public Servants, Ministers, and Parliament* (Toronto: University of Toronto Press, 2003).

25 Peter Aucoin and Donald J. Savoie, eds., *Managing Strategic Change* (Ottawa: Canadian Centre for Management Development, 1998).

26 Allen Schick, 'From the Old Politics of Budgeting to the New,' in Naomi Caiden and Joseph White, eds., *Budgeting, Policy, Politics: An Appreciation of Aaron Wildavsky* (New Brunswick, NJ: Transactions 1995).

27 Imbeau, 'Guardians and Advocates in Deficit Elimination.'

28 Joanne Kelly and John Wanna, 'Are Wildavsky's Guardians and Spenders still Relevant? New Public Management and the Politics of Government Budgeting,' in Lawrence Jones, James Guthrie, and Peter Steane, eds., *Learning from International Public Management Reform* (London: Elsevier and Oxford University Press, 2000), 598–614.

29 Tax expenditures are tax measures such as exemptions, deductions, rebates, deferrals, and credits that are used to advance a wide range of economic, social, and other public policy objectives. A discussion of tax expenditures is contained in chapter 2.

30 See Good, *The Politics of Anticipation*, 67.

31 Robert B. Bryce, *Maturing in Hard Times: Canada's Department of Finance through the Great Depression* (Montreal: McGill-Queen's University Press, 1986).

32 Conceptually, the incorporation of spending roles by guardians and guardian roles by spenders is similar to Imbeau's conclusion that under certain circumstances guardians can adopt a 'partial view' of the budget and spenders a 'total view' of the budget. See Imbeau, 'Guardians and Advocates in Deficit Elimination.'

33 Good, *The Politics of Anticipation*, and Hartle, *The Expenditure Budget Process of the Government of Canada*.

34 Donald Savoie, *Governing from the Centre: The Concentration of Power in Canadian Politics* (Toronto: University of Toronto Press, 1999).

35 See, for example, Richard French, *How Ottawa Decides* (Toronto: James Lorimer, 1980); and Colin Campbell S.J. and George J. Szablowski, *The Superbureaucrats: Structure and Behaviour in Central Agencies* (Toronto: Macmillan, 1979).

36 Allen Schick, 'Does Budgeting Have a Future?' *OECD Journal of Budgeting* 2, no. 2 (2002), 25.

37 It should be noted that in 1979 Prime Minister Clark put in place the Expenditure Management System (EMS), which contained many, if not all, of the key features of the Policy and Expenditure Management System (PEMS) that was subsequently instituted in 1980. However, EMS gave more emphasis to setting overall expenditure limits and less to linking expenditures and priorities. See Department of Finance, *The New Expenditure Management System* (Ottawa, December 1979), and Privy Council Office, *The Policy and Expenditure Management System* (Ottawa, March 1981). For a description and assessments of PEMS, see Richard Van Loon, 'Stop the Music: The Current Policy and Expenditure Management System,' *Canadian Public Administration* 24, no. 2 (1981), 175–99; 'The Policy and Expenditure Management System in the Canadian Federal Government: The First Three Years,' *Canadian Public Administration* 26, no. 2 (1983), 255–85; and 'Ottawa's New Expenditure Process: Four Systems in Search of Co-ordination,' in G.B. Doern, ed., *How Ottawa Spends: The Liberals, the Opposition and Federal Priorities* (Toronto: James Lorimer, 1983), 93–120.

38 *The Policy and Expenditure Management System*, 2.
39 Evert A. Lindquist, 'How Ottawa Plans: The Evolution of Strategic Planning,' in Leslie A. Pal, ed., *How Ottawa Spends, 2001–2002: Power in Transition* (Don Mills, ON: Oxford University Press, 2001), 61–93.
40 William A. Niskanen, *Bureaucracy and Representative Government* (Chicago: Aldine Atherton, 1971).
41 See, for example, Andre Blais and Stephane Dion, eds., *The Budget-Maximizing Bureaucrat: Appraisal and Evidence* (Pittsburgh: University of Pittsburgh Press, 1991).
42 See, for example, Francois Simard, 'Great Books Revisited: Self-interest in Public Administration: Niskanen and the Budget-Maximizing Bureaucrat,' *Canadian Public Administration* 47, no. 3 (Fall 2004), 406–11.
43 Once elected, the Thatcher government assigned one of Niskanen's works, *Bureaucracy: Servant or Master? Lessons from America* (London: Institute of Economic Affairs, 1973), to public servants as 'required reading.' See Robert E. Goodin, 'Rational Politicians and Rational Bureaucrats in Washington and Whitehall,' *Public Administration* 60, no. 1 (Spring 1982), 23–42.
44 The core elements of the theory are:

- Bureaucrats are much like officials in other organizations. Their behaviour will differ because of the incentives and constraints they face and not because of different personal characteristics.
- Most bureaus face a monopoly buyer of their service, usually some group of political officials. The effective demand for the output of the bureau is the political sponsor rather than the citizens benefiting from the service.
- Most bureaus are monopoly suppliers of their services.
- This bilateral monopoly relationship between a bureau and its sponsor involves an exchange of a promised output for a budget rather than the sale of its output at a per-unit price.
- As in any bilateral monopoly, there is no unique budget-output equilibrium between that preferred by the sponsor and that preferred by the bureau. The sponsor's primary bargaining advantage is authority to replace the bureau's management team, monitor the bureau, and to approve the bureau's budget. The bureau's primary bargaining advantage is that it has better information about the costs of supplying the service than does the sponsor.
- The sponsors bilateral bargaining over the bureau is weakened because the sponsor has insufficient incentive to monitor the bureau as it shares only a small part of the benefits of more efficient performance by the bureau. Efficiency monitoring is a public good.

- Neither the members of the sponsor group nor the senior bureaucrats have a pecuniary share in any surplus generated by the bureau.

Summarized from William Niskanen, 'A Reflection on *Bureaucracy and Representative Government*,' in Blais and Dion, eds., *The Budget Maximizing Bureaucrat*, 16–17.

45 Ibid., 18. Niskanen attributes the impetus for this change to a critique of the initial model by Jean Luc Migué and Gérard Bélanger. See Migué and Bélanger, 'Towards a General Theory of Managerial Discretion,' *Public Choice* 17, no. 1 (March 1974), 27–47.

46 Ibid., 19.

47 In this sense, the inefficiency should not be called simply 'bureaucratic inefficiency' but rather 'bureaucratic and political inefficiency.' It should also be noted that Blais and Dion observe that, from their perspective, 'it is irrelevant whether it is the total budget or the discretionary budget (that is maximized).' Ibid., 359. I disagree, because as Niskanen explains, the discretionary budget (as he defines it) represents that portion of the budget which is inefficient, relative subportions of which are used by politicians for such things as regional employment and by bureaucrats for such things a hiring more employees than is necessary.

48 Sonja Sinclair, *Cordial but Not Cosy: A History of the Office of the Auditor General* (Toronto: McClelland and Stewart, 1979), 17.

49 Government of Canada, *Federal Accountability Action Plan* (Ottawa: President of the Treasury Board, 2006), 13.

50 Most notable is the 1977 passage of the Auditor General Act that empowered the Auditor General to conduct 'value for money audits.' Ironically, proclamation of this powerful and far-reaching new legislation did not qualify for even passing mention by the news media of the day. See Sinclair, *Cordial but Not Cosy*, 9.

51 Canada, Department of Finance, *Budget Speech*, 23 March 2004 (Ottawa: Public Works and Government Services Canada, 2004), 4.

52 Auditor General of Canada, Opening Statement, November 2003 Report, Press Conference, Ottawa, ON, 10 February 2004.

53 Statement by the Prime Minister at a Press Conference on the Auditor's General Report, Ottawa, ON, 12 February 2004.

54 There are, of course, several other watchdogs/agents of Parliament that, if anything, function like advocates for spending, for example, the Privacy Commissioner, the Information Commissioner, and the Human Rights Commissioner. Paul G. Thomas, 'The Past, Present and Future of Officers of Parliament,' *Canadian Public Administration* 46, no. 3 (Fall 2003), 287–314.

55 This is not to say that there are not occasional meetings between the Auditor General and the Clerk of the Privy Council Office. For example, on the rare occasions when the Clerk needs to 'quietly pass on a message' about a cabinet discussion or when there was a need for a discussion about the implications on the public service after the release of an audit into the sponsorship program.

56 Lindquist, 'How Ottawa Plans,' 61–93.

57 Savoie, *Governing from the Centre*.

58 David A. Good, *The Politics of Public Management: The HRDC Audit of Grants and Contributions* (Toronto: University of Toronto Press, 2003); and Sharon L. Sutherland, 'Biggest Scandal in Canadian History: HRDC Audit Starts Probity War,' *Critical Perspectives in Accounting* 14, nos. 1–2, (2003), 187–224.

2. The Guardians and the Changing Role of the Budget Office

1 Lotte Jensen and John Wanna, 'Conclusions: Better Guardians?' in John Wanna, Lotte Jensen, and Jouke de Vries, eds., *Controlling Public Expenditure: The Changing Role of Central Budget Agencies – Better Guardians?* (Cheltenham, UK: Edward Elgar, 2003), 256.

2 Canada, Department of Finance, *Report on Plans and Priorities, Department of Finance, 2002–3 Estimates* (Ottawa: Public Works and Government Services Canada, 2002). The department also has responsibilities for 'developing regulatory policy for the country's financial sector and representing Canada within international financial institutions.'

3 Ibid.

4 Treasury Board of Canada Secretariat, 'About Us,' retrieved 14 December 2006 from www.tbs-sct.gc.ca/common/us-nous_e.asp.

5 Jim Judd in testimony before the Commission of Inquiry into the Sponsorship Program and Advertising Activities, Ottawa, ON, 20 September 2004. It would appear from his testimony that this Secretary of the Treasury Board does not see expenditure management as the principal role of the Treasury Board:

> Mr. Finkelstein: Let us talk about the expenditure management function. Would it be fair to say that is the principal role that the Treasury Board plays?
> Mr. Judd: It is certainly a principal role. As we said – as we tried to articulate in our document, the Treasury Board plays three interrelated roles and certainly expenditure management oversight is an important and key one of those.

6 Ibid.

7 Treasury Board of Canada Secretariat, 'TBS Organization – Office of the Comptroller General,' retrieved June 2004 from www.tbs-sct.gc.ca/ organisation/com-con_e.asp.

8 For a history of the evolution of the Treasury Board and the creation of the Treasury Board Secretariat, see W.L. White and J.C. Strick, *Policy, Politics, and the Treasury Board in Canadian Government* (Don Mills, ON: Science Research Associates Ltd., 1970).

9 See Table 1: Budgetary Main Estimates by Type of Payment,' in Government of Canada, *2004–2005 Estimates, Part 1: The Government Expenditure Plan* (Ottawa: Minister of Public Works and Government Services Canada, 2005). Interestingly, government documents do not include a breakout of these expenditures.

10 Interview with a senior Treasury Board Secretariat official, Ottawa, ON, 16 August 2004.

11 If the comparison is made between 1963–4 and 2004–5 rather than 2003–4, and if the large ongoing increases in health expenditures resulting from the September 2005 'Health Accord' negotiated by the Martin government are included, then the increase in major transfers to the provinces and territorial government rises dramatically. Instead of increasing from 9.7 per cent of total expenditures in 1963–4 to 16.6 per cent in 2003–4, transfers to provincial and territorial governments increase to 21.3 per cent in 2004–5.

12 See Department of Finance, *Government of Canada Tax Expenditure Account* (Ottawa, December 1979) and Department of Finance, *Government of Canada Tax Expenditures 1995–2004* (Ottawa, 2004), available online from www.fin.gc.ca/purl/taxexp-e.html.

13 Tax expenditures, are not expenditures per se, but rather are estimates of revenues foregone to the government as a consequence of implementing a particular tax measure (e.g., the reduction in a tax deduction). This requires that the estimate of the cost of any tax expenditure be made from a benchmark of the ideal tax system. It also requires consideration of the interaction across many other tax expenditures. Therefore, tax expenditure studies, accounts, and budgets do not produce a total for tax expenditures. Furthermore, the elimination of any one tax expenditure would not necessarily yield the full tax revenues indicated in the tax expenditure account or tax expenditure budget. This is because of such factors as the appropriate benchmark for the measurement of tax expenditures, the interaction of tax measures, behavioural responses, consequential government policy changes, and the impact on economic activity. See Department of Finance, *Tax Expenditures: Notes to the Estimates/ Projections* (Ottawa, 2004), available online from www.fin.gc.ca/taxexp/2004/taxexpnot04_1e.html.

14 Department of Finance, *Tax Expenditures and Evaluations, 2004*, retrieved June 2005 from www.fin.gc.ca/toce/2004/taxexp04_e.html.

15 In the 2 May 2006 budget, the over $9 billion in tax expenditures for the Canada Child Tax Credit was converted to a direct expenditure. This came after several years of urging by the Auditor General who argued that presenting the government's financial statements on a gross basis more properly reflected the nature and size of the government's revenues and expenditures.

16 Total tax expenditures for 1963–4 are an estimate since the earliest available tax expenditure account was not published until 1979 (Department of Finance, *Government of Canada: Tax Expenditure Account, 1979*) and it included tax expenditure estimates for 1976 and 1979 only. Tax expenditures for 1963–4 are derived from an estimated ratio of tax expenditures to total tax revenue of .941 with the actual ratios for 2003–4, 1979–80, and 1976–7 being .985, .968, and .955, respectively. See Department of Finance, *Federal Government Public Accounts*, available online from http://fin.gc.ca/frt/2004/frt04_le.html; and Canadian Tax Foundation, *The National Finances, 1963–64 and 1964–65* (Toronto: Canadian Tax Foundation, 1963 and 1964). For an early and partial estimate of tax expenditures, see Roger S. Smith, *Tax Expenditures: An Examination of Tax Incentives and Tax Preferences in the Canadian Federal Income Tax System* (Toronto: Canadian Tax Foundation, 1979).

17 This is drawn from Jennifer Smith, *Federalism: The Canadian Democratic Audit* (Vancouver: UBC Press, 2004).

18 For a recent review of fiscal equalization, see Expert Panel on Fiscal Equalization and Territorial Formula Financing, *Achieving a National Purpose: Putting Equalization Back on Track* (May 2006), available online from www.eqtff-pfft.ca/english/EQTreasury/index.asp.

19 One reason for the declining relative size of 'small p' programs has been smaller defence expenditures relative to total direct expenditures. In 1964, defence was 18 per cent of total direct expenditure. Today it is only 6.9 per cent.

20 For examples of various descriptions, see David Johnson, *Thinking Government* (Peterborough, ON: Broadview Press, 2002), 354–59; Gregory J. Inwood, *Understanding Canadian Public Administration* (Toronto: Pearson, 2004), 329–331; Kenneth Kernaghan and David Siegel, *Public Administration in Canada*, 2nd ed. (Scarborough, ON: International Thomson Publishing, 1999), 626–33; and Government of Canada, *Federal Budgetary Process*, available online from www.edu.psc-cfp.gc.ca/tdc/learn-apprend/psw/hgw/how-gov4_e.htm#BM4_3.

21 Treasury Board of Canada, *The Expenditure Management System of the Government of Canada* (Ottawa: Minister of Supply and Services Canada, 1995).

22 See, for example, Peter Harder and Evert A. Lindquist, 'Expenditure Management and Reporting in the Government of Canada: Recent Developments and Backgrounds,' in Jacques Bourgault, Maurice Demers, and Cynthia Williams, eds., *Public Administration and Public Management: Experiences in Canada* (Quebec: Les Publications du Québec, 1997), 72–89; Evert A. Lindquist, 'Citizens, Experts and Budgets: Evaluating Ottawa's Emerging Budget Process,' in Susan Phillips, ed., *How Ottawa Spends, 1994–95: Making Change* (Ottawa: Carleton University Press, 1994), 91–128; Evert A. Lindquist, 'Getting Results: Reforming Ottawa's Estimates,' in Leslie A. Pal, ed., *How Ottawa Spends, 1998–99: Balancing Act: The Post-Deficit Mandate* (Don Mills, ON: Oxford University Press, 1998), 153–90; Peter Aucoin and Donald Savoie, eds., *Managing Strategic Change: Learning from Program Review* (Ottawa: Canadian Centre for Management Development, 1998).

23 When Paul Martin was minister of finance (1993–2002), he often claimed that for him budget preparation was a year-round activity.

24 The cabinet is the normal forum for the discussion of budget matters among ministers. However, with the large cabinets of thirty-six under Trudeau, thirty-nine under Mulroney, and thirty-eight under Martin (although only twenty-eight were formally in cabinet), budget discussions were usually first initiated in the Cabinet Committee on Priorities and Planning, which at various times included anywhere from eleven to nineteen ministers.

25 Unlike the budget, there is no longer an estimates lock-up for the media. This practice was cancelled in 2002 when, in the words of one Treasury Board Secretariat official, 'it became evident that there were more officials at the lock-up than members of the media.' Interview, Ottawa, ON, 1 December 2004.

26 Crown corporations are required by law to submit annually a corporate plan to the appropriate minister for approval of the Governor in Council. Each December the president of the Treasury Board tables summaries of the corporate plans in Parliament through a document entitled *Annual Report to Parliament on Crown Corporations and Other Corporate Interests of Canada.*

27 On 4 October 2001, the House of Commons' standing orders were amended to allow the leader of the opposition, in consultation with the leaders of the other opposition parties, to refer the estimates of no more than two departments or agencies to a Committee of the Whole House for review. The chosen estimates are reviewed, one day each, in a five-hour session.

28 Office of the Auditor General of Canada, *Parliamentary Committee Review of the Estimates Documents* (Ottawa: Office of the Auditor General of Canada, March 2003).

29 White and Strick, *Policy, Politics, and the Treasury Board in Canadian Government*, 33–5.

30 When there is migration of personnel from the top of one organization to another, there follows demands for exchange of personnel at all other levels in the organization. This was the case for the Department of Finance and the Treasury Board Secretariat. While these exchanges were important for the Department of Finance, they were critical for the Treasury Board Secretariat, ensuring an effective and common career path for guardians that lasted well into the 1980s. Since the 1990s, exchange flows between the two organizations have slowed to a trickle with only one or two senior Finance officials having moved from the upper floors of L'Esplande Laurier down to the 'street level' of the Treasury Board Secretariat.

31 Correspondence to author, 14 July 2006.

32 Correspondence to author, 24 July 2006.

33 Robert Wright, the most recent Finance man to be appointed (12 June 2006), has had extensive experience in the Privy Council Office and in line departments and agencies, and also worked for a short stint in the Department of Finance.

34 Two recent exceptions were the appointments of Paul Boothe and Mark Carney to the positions of associate deputy minister. The former had spent most of his career at the University of Alberta as a professor of economics, and the latter was an investment banker with Goldman Sachs before joining the Bank of Canada for a brief assignment as deputy governor.

35 Interview with an assistant deputy minister, Department of Finance, Ottawa, ON, 27 October 2005.

36 Interview with a top official, Treasury Board Secretariat, Ottawa, ON, 28 October 2005.

37 To be sure, there have been and still are a few exceptions – the old 'Treasury hands' – who have spent most if not all of their careers in the Secretariat. They are, however, a rapidly dying breed and, with the exception of a handful of officials, there are only a few 'old Treasury officials' remaining.

38 Correspondence to author, 14 July 2006.

39 Correspondence to author, 31 July 2006.

40 Interview with a former senior official, Treasury Board Secretariat, Ottawa, ON, 1 December 2004.

41 From the time it was first coined by Grant Glassco in his seminal Royal Commission report on government organization in 1963, 'let the managers

manage' became the continuous cry of departments and the constant challenge for the Treasury Board Secretariat. In the fall of 1994 when Finance
Minister Martin announced to the Standing Committee on Finance that he
would reduce the deficit 'come hell or high water,' that slogan became the
single target for government achievement that trumped all others.

42 Jensen and Wanna, 'Conclusions: Better Guardians?' 256–7. There is no common terminology in the naming of central guardians. In Australia, the Department of Finance and Administration is similar to the Canadian Treasury Board
Secretariat with responsibilities for the expenditure budget, program spending, and financial review. The Department of Treasury is similar to the Canadian Department of Finance with responsibility for economic and fiscal policy.

43 Ian Clark, 'Restraint, Renewal and the Treasury Board Secretariat,' *Canadian Public Administration* 37, no. 2 (Summer 1994), 209–48.

44 Joanne Kelly and Evert A. Lindquist, 'Metamorphosis in Kafka's Castle:
The Changing Balance of Power Among the Central Budget Agencies in
Canada,' in Wanna, Jensen, and de Vries, *Controlling Public Expenditure*, 91.

45 Correspondence to author, 14 July 2006.

46 Art Eggleton, *The Expenditure Management System of the Government of Canada* (Ottawa: Minister of Supply and Services Canada, 1995), 5. A senior
official of the Treasury Board Secretariat observed that

> not much lending was done and much of the money lent on quasi com-
> mercial terms caused problems as we took both the repayment and
> interest out of department reference levels at the time the loan was made
> – a situation any commercial bank would envy. In a lot of cases depart-
> ments had problems managing within those reduced reference levels
> and the benefits from the 'investment' proved optimistic. Probably the
> most extreme example was the loan to Veteran Affairs for an IT [infor-
> mation technology] investment which required us essentially to 'forgive
> the loan,' and more. (Correspondence to author, 31 July 2006)

47 Interview with a senior official, Department of Finance, Ottawa, ON,
1 December 2004.

48 Ibid.

49 Interview with a senior official, Treasury Board Secretariat, Ottawa, ON,
9 October 2004.

50 Ibid. The president of the Treasury Board officially reported in a media
release in the summer 2003 that the $1 billion, which was largely one-time
savings, was achieved through 'a number of initiatives, including reductions in some activities or lower-than-anticipated use of some services,
unavoidable delays in the start-up of some others, and other measures to

reduce resources that are currently allocated.' A senior official in Finance stated in a 1 December 2004 interview that 'we had to rely on lapses to make up the amount. There was no hard stuff in it. It was fluff.'

51 Interview with a senior official, Department of Finance, Ottawa, ON, 1 December 2004. The cabinet committee was initially chaired by Reg Alcock, the president of the Treasury Board, but later by John McCallum, the minister of national revenue.

52 Interview with a senior official, Treasury Board Secretariat, Ottawa, ON, 9 October 2004.

53 Interview with a senior official, Department of Finance, Ottawa, ON, 1 December 2004.

54 Ibid.

55 Interview with a top official, Treasury Board Secretariat, Ottawa, ON, 28 October 2005.

56 Interview with an associate deputy minister, Department of Finance, Ottawa, ON, 18 November 2005.

57 Interview with a senior official, Department of Finance, Ottawa, ON, 1 December 2004.

3. Why Spenders Keep Spending

1 A comprehensive and up-to-date overview of the organization and structure of the Government of Canada is provided in the *Population Affiliation Report*, available online from www.hrma-agrh.gc.ca/hr-rh/hrtr-or/hr_tools/Intro_e.asp.

2 The perceived fiscal imbalance that lasted for a decade or two after the 1963 budget of Walter Gordon was in terms of the inadequacy of federal funds to meet growing needs. See Rod Dobell, 'There is No Vertical Fiscal Imbalance: Breau's Sophistry,' *Optimum Online* 35, no. 2 (July 2005), www.optimumonline.ca/archives.phtml?volume=35&.

3 Interview with a former senior public servant, Ottawa, ON, 8 October 2004.

4 Interview with a former assistant deputy minister, Victoria, BC, 29 January 2005.

5 The seven steps in the Felligi report are theoretical research; statistics, applied research and modelling; environmental scanning, trend analysis, and forecasting; policy analysis and advice; consultation and managing relations; communications; and program design, implementation, monitoring, and evaluation. *Strengthening Our Policy Capacity* (December 1996), available online from www.myschool-monecole.gc.ca/Research/publications/pdfs/policye.pdf.

6 Interview with a deputy minister, Ottawa, ON, 28 October 2005.

7 Interview with a deputy minister, Ottawa, ON, 27 October 2005.

8 Ibid.

9 Interview with a deputy minister, Ottawa, ON, 28 October 2005.

10 Ibid.

11 Ibid.

12 Interview with a deputy minister, Ottawa, ON, 27 October 2005.

13 Ibid.

14 Ibid.

15 Ibid.

16 Ibid.

17 Ibid.

18 Interview with a deputy minister, Ottawa, ON, 28 October 2005.

19 Interview with a deputy minister, Ottawa, ON, 27 October 2005.

20 Email correspondence to author from a former deputy minister, 25 February 2005.

21 This refers to expenditure cuts that are 'non-starters.' For instance, the termination of the Royal Canadian Mounted Police 'musical ride,' a program which is highly visible and strongly supported by the public and which no government would be prepared to eliminate.

22 Email correspondence to author from a former deputy minister, 16 November 2004.

23 Email correspondence to author from a former deputy minister, 20 February 2005.

24 Email correspondence to author from a former deputy minister, 16 November 2004.

25 Email correspondence to author from a former deputy minister, 20 February 2005.

26 Interview with an assistant secretary, Treasury Board Secretariat, Ottawa, ON, 17 October 2005.

27 Interview with a senior official, Treasury Board Secretariat, Ottawa, ON, 17 November 2005.

28 Interview with a deputy minister, Ottawa, ON, 27 October 2005.

29 Interview with a senior official, Treasury Board Secretariat, Ottawa, ON, 17 November 2005.

30 Interview with a program analyst, Treasury Board Secretariat, Ottawa, ON, 8 October 2004.

31 Ibid.

32 Interview with a senior official, Treasury Board Secretariat, Ottawa, ON, 17 November 2005.

33 Interview with a deputy minister, Ottawa, ON, 27 October 2005.

34 Interview with an assistant secretary, Treasury Board Secretariat, Ottawa, ON, 9 October 2004.

35 Interview with a program analyst, Treasury Board Secretariat, Ottawa, ON, 8 October 2004.

36 Interview with a former director, Treasury Board Secretariat, Ottawa, ON, 1 December 2004 and 25 January 2005.

37 Interview with a former senior official, Treasury Board Secretariat, Ottawa, ON, 1 December 2004.

38 Interview with an assistant secretary, Treasury Board Secretariat, Ottawa, ON, 9 October 2004.

39 Ibid.

40 Interview with an associate deputy minister, Department of Finance, Ottawa, ON, 18 November 2005.

41 Treasury Board Secretariat, *Results for Canadians: A Management Framework for the Government of Canada* (Ottawa: President of the Treasury Board, 2000). At the time, the key features of the framework were building a 'citizen focus' into the management of government activities and services; highlighting the importance of sound public service values; focusing on the achievement of results for Canadians; and promoting discipline, due diligence, and value for money in the use of public funds.

42 Interview with a former director, Treasury Board Secretariat, Ottawa, ON, 1 December 2004 and 25 January 2005.

43 Ibid.

44 Interview with a director, Treasury Board Secretariat, Ottawa, ON, 17 November 2005.

45 Interview with a former chief financial officer, 4 and 12 January 2005.

46 David Good, Evert Lindquist, Jim McDavid, Angus Carnie, Irene Huse, Jessica Ling, John Montgomery, Erin Scraba, and Justin Young, 'A Comparative Study of the Use of Performance Information for Decision-making in Selected OECD Countries' (Victoria, BC: School of Public Administration, University of Victoria, April 2006).

4. The Priority Setters at the Centre

1 Paul Martin, 'Proposals for Reform of the House of Commons' (speech delivered at Osgoode Hall, York University, 21 October 2002).

2 Interview with a former senior adviser to a prime minister, Ottawa, ON, 18 November 2005.

3 Ibid.

4 Ibid.

5 Savoie, *Governing from the Centre.*
6 Jeffrey Simpson, 'Why Mr Red has the Blues,' *Globe and Mail,* 21 January 2006, F1.
7 Interview with a former top official, Privy Council Office, Ottawa, ON, 11 April 2006.
8 Interview with a deputy minister, Ottawa, ON, 28 October 2005.
9 Good, *The Politics of Pubic Management,* 63. See also David Good, 'A Distorted Mirror,' *Vancouver Sun,* 25 July 2005, A7.
10 Interview with an associate deputy minister, Department of Finance, Ottawa, ON, 18 November 2005.
11 Savoie, *Governing from the Centre,* 156.
12 Interview with a former senior adviser to a prime minister, Ottawa, ON, 18 November 2005.
13 Eddie Goldenberg, *The Way It Works: Inside Ottawa* (Toronto: McClelland and Stewart, 2006), 153.
14 Interview with an associate deputy minister, Department of Finance, Ottawa, ON, 18 November 2005.
15 Interview with a former senior economic adviser, Privy Council Office, Ottawa, ON, 26 October 2005.
16 Interview with a former senior adviser to a prime minister, Ottawa, ON, 18 November 2005.
17 Ibid.
18 Ibid.
19 Paul Martin, testimony before the Commission of Inquiry into the Sponsorship Program and Advertising Activities, Ottawa, ON, 10 February 2005.
20 Ibid.
21 Interview with a former top official, Privy Council Office, Ottawa, ON, 11 April 2006.
22 See, for example, Richard D. French, *How Ottawa Decides: Planning and Industrial Policy Making 1968–84,* 2nd ed. (Toronto: James Lorimer, 1984); G. Bruce Doern, 'The Development of Policy Organizations in the Executive Arena,' in G. Bruce Doern and Peter Aucoin, eds., *The Structures of Policy-Making in Canada* (Toronto: Macmillan, 1971), 39–78; and Ian D. Clark, 'Recent Changes in the Cabinet Decision-Making System in Ottawa,' *Canadian Public Administration* 28, no. 2 (1985), 185–201.
23 Lindquist, 'How Ottawa Plans,' 61–93.
24 Since the 1990s the written campaign documentation prepared by political parties is both extensive and detailed. Notable examples include the 'Red Book' of the Liberal Party in the 1993 election, the 'Common Sense Revolution' used by the provincial Conservative Party in the 1995 Ontario provincial election, and the 'New Era Document' used by the provincial Liberal Party in the 2001 British Columbia provincial election. In the 2004 federal

election, all four major parties provided extensive documents, including the identification of specific priorities and the costing of proposed expenditures. The documents, totalling close to 175 pages, carried the following titles: 'Moving Canada Ahead: The Paul Martin Plan for Getting Things Done'; 'Demanding Better: Conservative Party of Canada Platform'; 'Jack Layton, NDP: New Energy, A Positive Choice'; and 'Un Parti Propre au Québec.' In the 2006 general election campaign, Stephen Harper and the Conservative Party put forward a series of many individual announcements each day over the course of the campaign. These were subsequently rolled into a single document, 'Stand Up for Canada,' in the latter stages of the campaign.

25 Interview with a former senior economic adviser, Privy Council Office, Ottawa, ON, 26 October 2005.

26 Interview with a deputy minister, Ottawa, ON, 27 October 2005.

27 Interview with a former senior adviser to a prime minister, Ottawa, ON, 18 November 2005.

28 Ibid.

29 Schick, 'Does Budgeting Have a Future?'

30 Interview with a former top official, Privy Council Office, Ottawa, ON, 11 April 2006.

31 Interview with a senior official, Treasury Board, Ottawa, ON, 17 November 2005.

32 Interview with an assistant secretary, Treasury Board Secretariat, Ottawa, ON, 17 November 2005.

33 Interview with a senior official, Department of Finance, Ottawa, ON, 1 December 2004.

34 Gordon Robertson, 'The Changing Role of the Privy Council Office,' *Canadian Public Administration* 14, no. 4 (1971), 506.

35 Interview with a former senior adviser to a prime minister, Ottawa, ON, 18 November 2005.

36 Ibid.

37 Ibid.

38 Interview with a former senior economic adviser, Privy Council Office, Ottawa, ON, 26 October 2005.

39 Paul Martin, testimony before the Commission of Inquiry into the Sponsorship Program and Advertising Activities. The one exceptional department was the Department of Indian Affairs and Northern Development which was allowed a slight budget increase in the face of rapid growth in the Aboriginal population and their deteriorating social and economic living conditions.

40 Interview with a former senior adviser to a prime minister, Ottawa, ON, 18 November 2005.

41 Interview with a former top official, Privy Council Office, Ottawa, ON, 11 April 2006.

42 Interview with a former assistant deputy minister, Victoria, BC, 19 January 2005.

43 Interview with a deputy minister, Ottawa, ON, 28 October 2005.

44 (Translation) Paul Tellier, 'L'Evolution du Bureau Conseil Prive: Commentaire,' *Canadian Public Administration* 15, no. 2 (1972), 378.

45 Interview with a deputy minister, Ottawa, ON, 27 October 2005.

46 Ibid.

47 Interview with a former assistant deputy minister, Victoria, BC, 19 January 2005.

48 Interview with a former senior adviser to a prime minister, Ottawa, ON, 18 November 2005.

49 Ibid.

50 An elaborate guide to the preparation of Memorandum to Cabinet is available on the Privy Council Office website, www.pco-bcp.gc.ca/default.asp?Language=E&Page=Publications&doc=mc/mc_e.htm.

51 Treasury Board of Canada, *The Expenditure Management System of the Government of Canada* (Ottawa: Treasury Board Distribution Centre, 1995).

52 Interview with a senior official, Treasury Board, Ottawa, ON, 17 November 2005.

53 Ibid.

54 Interview with an associate deputy minister, Department of Finance, Ottawa, ON, 18 November 2005.

5. The Financial Watchdog

1 Otto Brodtrick, 'How Does an Auditor General's Office See Itself?' *Canadian Public Administration* 47, no. 2 (Summer 2004), 226.

2 Mark A. Covaleski and Mark W. Dirsmith, 'The Budgetary Process of Power Politics,' *Accounting, Organizations and Society* 11, no. 3 (1986), 197.

3 Sinclair, *Cordial but Not Cosy,* 68.

4 Sharon S. Sutherland, 'The Politics of Audit,' *Canadian Public Administration* 23, no. 1 (Spring 1986), 118–48.

5 Auditor General of Canada, *Report of the Auditor General of Canada to the House of Commons for the Fiscal Year Ending March 31* (Ottawa: Minister of Supply and Services, 1976), 9.

6 Peter Aucoin, *Auditing for Accountability: The Role of the Auditor General* (Ottawa: Institute on Governance, 1998), 9.

7 Performance auditing is not a uniquely Canadian phenomenon as most OECD countries do performance auditing of some sort.

8 Sharon Sutherland, 'The Office of the Auditor General of Canada: Government in Exile?' working paper 31, Queen's University, School of Policy Studies, Kingston, ON, September 2002, 7.

9 Auditor General of Canada, 'A Model for Rating Departmental Performance Reports,' in *Report of the Auditor General of Canada* (Ottawa: Public Works and Government Services Canada, 2002), chap. 6.

10 Auditor General of Canada, *Report of the Auditor General of Canada: Reflections on a Decade of Serving Parliament* (Ottawa: Public Works and Government Services Canada, 2001), 26.

11 Auditor General of Canada, *Report of the Auditor General of Canada: Rating Selected Departmental Performance Reports* (Ottawa: Public Works and Government Services Canada, 2005), chap. 5.

12 One of the earliest articles, if not the most widely cited, on the inability to determine an objective basis on which to link budget allocations to program outcomes is V.O. Key, Jr., 'The Lack of a Budgetary Theory,' *American Political Science Review* (December 1940), 1137–44. A more recent book on program evaluation describes and explains the extensive professional judgment that is inherent in determining causality in the area of program evaluation. See chapter 12, 'The Nature and Practice of Professional Judgment in Program Evaluation,' in James C. McDavid and Laura R.L. Hawthorn, *Program Evaluation and Performance Measurement: An Introduction to Practice* (Thousand Oaks, CA: Sage, 2006), 401–33.

13 Office of the Auditor General of Canada, 'Office of the Auditor General of Canada,' retrieved 14 December 2006 from www.oag-bvg.gc.ca/domino/oag-bvg.nsf/html/menue.html.

14 Office of the Auditor General of Canada, 'What Is Legislative Auditing?' retrieved 14 December 2006 from www.oag-bvg.gc.ca/domino/other.nsf/html/auqdn_lavg_e.html#33.

15 Interview with an assistant deputy auditor general, Office of the Auditor General, Ottawa, ON, 28 October 2005.

16 Interview with a former auditor general of Canada, Ottawa, ON, 26 October 2005.

17 Mark H. Moore and Margaret Jane Gates, *Inspectors-General: Junkyard Dogs or Man's Best Friend?* (New York: Russell Sage Foundation, 1986), 82; and Brodtrick, 'How Does an Auditor General's Office See Itself?' 233–4.

18 Office of the Auditor General of Canada, *Report of the Auditor General to the House of Commons: Government-Wide Audit of Sponsorship, Advertising, and Public Opinion Research* (Ottawa: Minister of Public Works and Government Services Canada, 2003).

19 For an appreciation of why audit offices find it difficult to see themselves as 'helpers' and 'monitors' as opposed to 'detectors,' see Brodtrick, 'How Does an Auditor General's Office See Itself?'

20 Office of the Auditor General of Canada, 'What is Legislative Auditing?'
21 Interview with a former auditor general of Canada, Ottawa, ON, 26 October 2005.
22 Interview with an assistant auditor general, Ottawa, ON, 28 October 2005.
23 Interview with a former auditor general of Canada, Ottawa, ON, 26 October 2005.
24 Interview with an assistant auditor general, Ottawa, ON, 17 November 2005.
25 Interview with a former auditor general of Canada, Ottawa, ON, 26 October 2005.
26 Interview with an assistant auditor general, Ottawa, ON, 28 October 2005. For a description of the close professional relationship between the Office of the Auditor General and major private sector accounting and management consulting firms, see Denis Saint-Martin, 'Managerialist Advocate or "Control Freak"? The Janus-Faced Office of the Auditor General,' *Canadian Public Administration* 47, no. 2 (Summer 2004), 121–40.
27 Interview with a former auditor general of Canada, Ottawa, ON, 26 October 2005. Under the Federal Accountability Act (2006), and as a means to ensure 'adequate resources to fulfill its mandate,' the budget and new funding requests of the Office of the Auditor General will be considered by an all-party Parliamentary Advisory Panel prior to final decision by the Treasury Board.
28 Interview with an assistant auditor general, Ottawa, ON, 17 November 2005.
29 Interview with a former auditor general of Canada, Ottawa, ON, 26 October 2005.
30 Interview with an assistant auditor general, Ottawa, ON, 28 October 2005.
31 Ibid.
32 Ibid. It should be noted that the Office of the Auditor General became increasingly concerned about the use of the term 'value for money' audits in 2004 when Stephen Harper, as leader of the opposition, promised, if elected as prime minister, to have the Auditor General do more 'value for money' audits so that he could 'follow the conclusions.'
33 Ibid.
34 Interview with an assistant auditor general, Ottawa, ON, 17 November 2005.
35 Office of the Auditor General of Canada, 'What is Legislative Auditing?'
36 Sharon L. Sutherland, 'The Evolution of Program Budget Ideas in Canada: Does Parliament Benefit from Estimates Reform?' *Canadian Public Administration* 33, no. 2 (1990), 133–64.
37 The PAC Minutes, Issue No. 6, 30 May 1989, 6:12, and quoted in Sutherland, 'The Evolution of Program Budget Ideas in Canada,' 154.

38 Ibid.
39 Interview with a former auditor general, Ottawa, ON, 26 October 2005.
40 Ibid.
41 Ibid.
42 Interview with an assistant auditor general, Ottawa, ON, 28 October 2005.
43 Ibid. See also Sinclair, *Cordial But Not Cosy.*
44 Interview with an assistant auditor general, Ottawa, ON,
    28 October 2005.
45 Interview with a former auditor general of Canada, Ottawa, ON,
    26 October 2005.
46 Interview with an assistant auditor general, Ottawa, ON, 17 November 2005.
47 Ibid.
48 Interview with a former auditor general of Canada, Ottawa, ON,
    26 October 2005.
49 Interview with an assistant auditor general, Ottawa, ON, 17 November 2005.
    In 2003 the government introduced accrual accounting.
50 Correspondence to author from a former senior budget analyst,
    24 July 2006.
51 Interview with a former auditor general of Canada, Ottawa, ON,
    26 October 2005.
52 Ibid.
53 Office of the Auditor General of Canada, *An Overview of the Federal Govern-
    ment's Expenditure Management System, Expenditure Management System at
    the Government Centre,* and *Expenditure Management System in Departments,*
    retrieved 11 December 2006 from www.oag-bvg.gc.ca/domino/
    reports.nsf/html/20061100ce.html.
54 Treasury Board Secretariat of Canada, *Policy on Internal Audit* (2005),
    retrieved December 2005 from www.tbs-sct.gc.ca/pubs_pol/dcgpubs/
    ia-vi/ia-vi_e.asp.
55 Treasury Board Secretariat of Canada, *Backgrounder to Press Release: Govern-
    ment Reinforces Integrity of Audit and Oversight* (21 October 2005), retrieved
    2 December 2005 from www.tbs-sct.gc.ca/media/nr-cp/2005/
    1021_e.asp#BG.
56 Treasury Board Secretariat of Canada, *Policy on Internal Audit.*
57 Treasury Board Secretariat of Canada, *Directive on Departmental Audit
    Committees* (2005), retrieved December 2005 from www.tbs-sct.gc.ca/
    pubs_pol/dcgpubs/ia-vi/dac-cmv_e.asp.
58 Treasury Board Secretariat of Canada, *Guidelines on the Responsibilities of
    Chief Audit Executive* (2005) retrieved December 2005 from www.tbs-
    sct.gc.ca/pubs_pol/dcgpubs/ia-vi/rcae-rdv_e.asp.
59 Interview with a former auditor general, Ottawa, ON, 26 October 2005.

60 Ibid. The new Federal Accountability Act allows heads of government institutions to refuse to disclose draft reports of audits and related working papers.
61 Ibid.
62 Cited in Commission of Inquiry into the Sponsorship Program and Advertising Activities, 'Parliament and Financial Accountability,' in *Restoring Accountability: Research Studies*, vol. 1 (Ottawa: Minister of Public Works and Government Services, 2006), 82.
63 Interview with a former auditor general, Ottawa, ON, 26 October 2005.
64 Interview with a former top official, Privy Council Office, Ottawa, ON, 11 April 2006.

6. Fiscal Aggregates

1 Kevin Lynch, testimony before the Commission of Inquiry into the Sponsorship Program and Advertising Activities, Ottawa, ON, 6 October 2004.
2 Testimony as prime minister before the Commission of Inquiry into the Sponsorship Program and Advertising Activities, Ottawa, ON, 10 February 2005.
3 Quoted in 'Canadian Budget Calculator Could Use Some New Batteries,' IMF Study Suggests,' *Globe and Mail*, 8 April 2005, B11.
4 Milton Friedman, 'Why the Twin Deficits Are a Blessing,' *Wall Street Journal*, 14 December 1988, 1.
5 Interview with a senior official, Department of Finance, Ottawa, ON, 1 December 2004.
6 Paul Martin, testimony before the Commission of Inquiry into the Sponsorship Program and Advertising Activities.
7 Ibid.
8 Ibid.
9 Ibid.
10 For a description of the techniques used over a generation ago by the Department of Finance to hedge against the uncertainty inherent in revenue forecasting and in the costing of tax expenditures, see Good, *The Politics of Anticipation*, 13–19.
11 Interview with an assistant deputy minister, Department of Finance, Ottawa, ON, 27 October 2005.
12 Interview with a senior official, Department of Finance, Ottawa, ON, 1 December 2004.
13 Interview with an assistant deputy minister, Department of Finance, Ottawa, ON, 27 October 2005.

14 Tim O'Neill, *Review of Canadian Federal Fiscal Forecasting: Processes and Systems, June 2005*, retrieved September 2005 from www.fin.gc.ca/toce/2005/ONeil_e.html.

15 .International Monetary Fund, *Canada Selected Issues* (Washington, DC: International Monetary Fund, 2005), 82, available online from www.imf.org/external/pubs/ft/scr/2005/cro5116.pdf.

16 Interview with a senior official, Department of Finance, Ottawa, ON, 1 December 2004.

17 Madelaine Drohan, 'Secrets of Canada's Persistent Surplus Revealed,' *Globe and Mail*, 31 March 2005, A17.

18 For a comprehensive paper on Ottawa's recent experience with prudent economic and fiscal forecasting, see Mike Joyce, 'The Canadian Federal Government's Experience with Prudent Budget Planning,' draft working paper, Queen's University, School of Policy Studies, Kingston, ON, July 2006.

19 International Monetary Fund, *Canada Selected Issues*, 55.

20 In 2004 these four private sector economic forecasting organizations were Global Insight, the University of Toronto, the Conference Board of Canada, and the Centre for Spatial Economics. The Department of Finance is, however, worried about the 'declining expertise in macroeconomic forecasting in Canada' as the organizations 'are not making the necessary investments to update and improve their models and tools.' As a Finance assistant deputy minister explains, 'We need to ensure that they give us a reasonable forecast and that their numbers are not significantly wrong because in the end the Minister can not have a lot of difference between our forecast and theirs.' Interview, Ottawa, ON, 27 October 2005.

21 Since the rounding on the expenditure side is to $0.1 billion, some Finance officials quietly speak of the 'rounding reserve,' which affords flexibility for 'small imperatives' without concern that it will break the fiscal framework. Correspondence to author from a former senior official, Treasury Board Secretariat, 24 July 2006.

22 Interview with an assistant deputy minister, Department of Finance, Ottawa, ON, 27 October 2005.

23 Interview with a senior official, Department of Finance, Ottawa, ON, 1 December 2004.

24 Ibid.

25 Ibid.

26 Ibid.

27 While O'Neil in his study did not conclude a systematic bias by the Department of Finance in economic forecasting, he did report that Canada,

compared with other countries, was an 'outlier' when it came to the selection of more pessimistic economic assumptions. See O'Neil, *Review of Canadian Federal Fiscal Forecasting.*

28 Paul Martin, testimony before the Commission of Inquiry into the Sponsorship Program and Advertising Activities.

29 The Liberal Party of Canada, *Creating Opportunity* (Ottawa, September 1993), 20. The 3 per cent of GDP target for the deficit was justified on the grounds that is had been subscribed to by member states of the European Community in the Maastricht Treaty.

30 Paul Martin, testimony before the Commission of Inquiry into the Sponsorship Program and Advertising Activities.

31 Don Drummond, 'Do We Need Fiscal Rules?' in Christopher Ragan and William Watson, eds., *Is the Debt War Over? Dispatches from Canada's Fiscal Frontline* (Montreal: IRPP and McGill-Queen's University Press, 2004), 315.

32 Ibid, 316.

33 Interview with a senior official, Department of Finance, Ottawa, ON, 1 December 2004.

34 Interview with an assistant deputy minister, Department of Finance, Ottawa, ON, 27 October 2005.

35 Quoted in Bob Rae, *From Protest to Power: Personal Reflections on a Life in Politics* (Toronto: Viking, 1996), 194.

36 Drummond, 'Do We Need Fiscal Rules?' 318.

37 At the time of the 2005 budget, the debt to GDP ratio was continuing on its steady downward track from a peak of 68.4 per cent in 1995–6 to a level of 38.3 per cent in 2004–5.

38 Interview with a former senior adviser to a prime minister, Ottawa, ON, 18 November 2005.

39 For an explanation of the use of tax expenditures in support of persons with disabilities, including the general lack of visibility of the expenditure, see Michael Prince, 'Tax Policy as Social Policy: Canadian Tax Assistance for People with Disabilities,' *Canadian Public Policy* 27, no. 4, (2001), 487–501.

40 See 'Have Some Pity for the Taxpayer,' *Globe and Mail*, 26 February 2005, A16.

41 Interview with a former senior adviser to a prime minister, Ottawa, ON, 18 November 2005.

42 Interview with a senior official, Department of Finance, Ottawa, ON, 1 December 2004.

43 Jim Stanford, 'Federal Fiscal Forecasting Round 2: Post-Budget Update' (prepared for the House of Commons Standing Committee on Finance, 31 March 2005), 11.

44 Monty Solberg, 'Dithering, Not Delivering on Their Commitments,' Press Release, 24 February 2005.

45 The Honourable Ralph Goodale, Minister of Finance (Speech to the Regina and District Chamber of Commerce at the launch of pre-budget consultations, 12 January 2004).

46 Interview with a senior official, Department of Finance, Ottawa, ON, 1 December 2004. The official went on to note that 'we got a reservation from the Auditor General when we created the first foundation, the CFI [Canada Foundation for Innovation], because we had booked the expenditure but had not yet introduced the legislation.'

47 Auditor General of Canada, *Report of the Auditor General of Canada: Accountability of Foundations* (Ottawa: Public Works and Government Services Canada, 2005).

48 Herman Bakvis, 'The Knowledge Economy and Post-secondary Education: Federalism in Search of a Metaphor,' in H. Bakvis and G. Skogstad, eds., *Canadian Federalism: Performance, Effectiveness, and Legitimacy* (Don Mills, ON: Oxford University Press, forthcoming).

49 Ibid., and Peter Aucoin, 'Independent Foundations, Public Money and Public Accountability: Whither Ministerial Responsibility as Democratic Governance?' *Canadian Public Administration* 45, no. 1 (Spring 2003), 1–26.

50 Interview with an assistant deputy minister, Department of Finance, Ottawa, ON, 27 October 2005.

51 Ibid.

52 Ibid.

53 Ibid.

54 Ibid.

7. Budget Allocations

1 Kevin Lynch, testimony before the Commission of Inquiry into the Sponsorship Program and Advertising Activities.

2 Paul Martin, testimony before the Commission of Inquiry into the Sponsorship Program and Advertising Activities.

3 Kevin Lynch, testimony.

4 Paul Martin, testimony.

5 Genevieve Tellier, *Les dépenses des gouvernements provinciaux canadiens: L'influence des partis politiques, des élections, de l'opinion publique* (Quebec: Presses de l'Université Laval, 2005).

6 Interview with a senior official, Department of Finance, Ottawa, ON, 1 December 2004.

7 Interview with an assistant secretary, Treasury Board Secretariat, Ottawa, ON, 17 November 2005.

8 There is no evidence yet of a trend for 'big-budget fixes' to be made in separate decision-making processes outside the scope of the budget process. Although, some budget scholars are considering this as a distinct possibility. 'Many of the developments already underway as well as those in the future may remake budgeting into the dependent variable in government finance and policy. Rather than driving decisions on money and programs, budgeting may be swept away along by powerful tides. The budget will duly register what has been decided already or elsewhere whether by formula or by others, but it will not be the forum for making many of the decisions.' Allen Schick, 'Does Budgeting Have a Future?' 47.

9 Interview with an associate deputy minister, Department of Finance, Ottawa, ON, 18 November 2005.

10 Ibid.

11 Janice MacKinnon, former Saskatchewan finance minister in the Romanow government, in an interview about her book, *Minding the Public Purse: The Fiscal Crisis, Political Trade-offs and Canada's Future* (Montreal: McGill-Queen's University Press, 2003), expressed her strong concerns about major expenditure allocations to single priorities:

> The Romanow Commission is saying that we have a health care system that we are already struggling to fund and we are going to add on to it and we are not going to increase any taxes or find any other way to pay for it. Well, that's not possible except at a huge cost to everything else – it would mean taking every new dollar that comes to the federal government and putting it into healthcare which is obviously not wise public policy. It means that the Commission did not deal with the fundamental question – how do you pay for this? So, in that sense, I disagree fundamentally with it. You have to tell people how you are going to pay for it. (Retrieved October 2005 from www.fcpp.org/main/publication_detail.php?PubID=585)

12 Harriet Jackson and Alison McDermott, 'Health-care Spending: Prospects and Retrospect,' *Analytical Note* (Ottawa: Department of Finance, Economic and Fiscal Policy Branch, 2004).

13 Possible exceptions could be the establishment of the Canada Public Health Agency, a new Canada Learning Bond, and Goods and Services Tax relief for municipalities.

14 Steven Chase, 'Liberal Spending Blitz Hits $19.5 Billion,' *Globe and Mail*, 10 May 2005, A4.

15 Doern, Maslove, and Prince, *Public Budgeting in Canada*.

16 The five limited priorities were enacting the Federal Accountability Act; reducing the Goods and Services Tax; increasing penalties for crime; providing parents with direct cash assistance for child care; and establishing a patient wait times guarantee for health care.

17 Allen Schick, 'Does Budgeting Have a Future?' 31.

18 Under the related subtheme of 'innovation,' Industry Canada secured some limited funding for SchoolNet, the Community Access Program, and for the granting councils, but no other spending minister or department benefited from the budget.

19 Kevin Lynch, testimony before the Commission of Inquiry into the Sponsorship Program and Advertising Activities.

20 Interview with a former top official, Privy Council Office, Ottawa, ON, 11 April 2006.

21 Interview with a senior official, Department of Finance, Ottawa, ON, 1 December 2004.

22 Ibid.

23 Interview with an associate deputy minister, Department of Finance, Ottawa, ON, 18 November 2005.

24 Although this was called an 'Economic and Fiscal Update,' it had all the appearance of a budget since it contained a large number of big-ticket (as well as small) spending initiatives.

25 David A. Good, 'Promises and Pitfalls: Experience in Collaboration between the Canadian Federal Government and the Voluntary Sector,' *Policy Analysis and Management* 22, no. 1 (Winter 2003), 122–7.

26 For studies on the tax policy-making process, see Good, *The Politics of Anticipation*; Hartle, *The Revenue Budget Process of the Government of Canada*; and Hale, *The Politics of Taxation in Canada*. For studies on tax expenditures and the budgetary process, see G. Bruce Doern, 'Tax Expenditure Decisions and the Budgetary Decision Process,' in Neil Bruce, ed., *Tax Expenditures and Government Policy* (Kingston: John Deutsch Institute for the Study of Economic Policy, 1988), 105–22; Kenneth Woodside, 'The Political Economy of Policy Instruments: Tax Expenditures and Subsidies in Canada,' in Michael M. Atkinson and Marsha A. Chandler, eds., *The Politics of Canadian Public Policy* (Toronto: University of Toronto Press, 1983), 173–9, reprinted in Barbara Wake Carroll, David Siegel, and Mark Sproule-Jones, eds., *Classic Readings in Canadian Public Administration* (Don Mills, ON: Oxford University Press, 2005), 496–511; Aaron Wildavsky, 'Keeping Kosher: The Epistemology of Tax Expenditures,' *Journal of Public Policy* 5, no. 3 (1986), 413–31; John Wanna, 'Invisible Hands? The Non-Budgeting of Tax Expenditures in Australia and

Canada' (paper presented at the Australasian Political Science Association Conference, University of Tasmania, Hobart, Australia, 29 September
– 1 October 2003.

27 Good, *The Politics of Anticipation,* 190.

28 The formal titles to these three branches, which are classic guardians when
it comes to direct expenditures, are Economic Development and Corporate
Finance, Federal–Provincial Relations and Social Development, and International Trade and Finance.

29 Paul Martin, testimony before the Commission of Inquiry into the Sponsorship Program and Advertising Activities. One experienced senior budget
official suggests that this may be an 'unrealistic standard for expenditure
reductions,' and that, 'more practically, many governments would be quite
happy with an expenditure review outcome that made significant inroads
into the rate of growth of government spending, particularly if it could be
shown to have materially reduced the size of spending relative to GDP.'
Correspondence to author, 31 July 2006.

30 With respect to Transport Canada, it should be noted that many of the
expenditure reductions were the result of transferring responsibilities such
as airports, ports, and air navigation to other levels of government and
other organizational authorities. Aucoin and Savoie, eds., *Managing Strategic Change.*

31 Wildavsky, *Budgeting,* 23–68.

32 Paul Martin, testimony before the Commission of Inquiry into the Sponsorship Program and Advertising Activities.

33 Edward Greenspon and Anthony Wilson-Smith, *Double Vision: The Inside
Story of the Liberals in Power* (Toronto: Doubleday, 1996), 164.

34 Paul Martin, testimony before the Commission of Inquiry into the Sponsorship Program and Advertising Activities.

35 Organization for Economic Cooperation and Development, *Reallocation:
The Role of Budget Institutions* (Paris: OECD, 2005), 9.

36 The observation of a senior budget official in the Treasury Board Secretariat
suggests that there is no end to the game playing: 'I've always been a bit
sceptical of this as a budgeting strategy. The risks for departments in enter-
ing this "game" are sufficiently high (the identified cut will just be taken)
as to cause departments to think twice. And if they do, they probably have
considerable scope to pad the gross cost so that the allocation net of any
reduction (or reallocation) they agree to may be close to what their realistic
assessment of a more traditional claiming strategy might be. Whatever the
game playing, it still represents a net cost to the guardians.' Correspondence to author, 24 July 2006.

37 Interview with a former assistant deputy minister, Department of Defence, Ottawa, ON, 29 September 2005.
38 President of the Treasury Board, 'President of the Treasury Board Reports on Reallocation,' News Release, Ottawa, ON, 29 September 2003.
39 For an assessment of the state of financial and non-financial information in the Government of Canada and practical suggestions for improvement, see Andrew Graham, 'Integrating Financial and Other Performance Information: Striking the Right Balance of Usefulness, Relevance and Cost' (a paper prepared for the Conference Board of Canada's Financial Leadership and Management in Government Study, 2005).
40 Interview with a former top official, Privy Council Office, Ottawa, ON, 11 April 2006.

8. Budget Implementation

1 Paul Martin, testimony before the Commission of Inquiry into the Sponsorship Program and Advertising Activities.
2 Mike Joyce, Assistant Secretary of the Treasury Board, Expenditure Management Sector, testimony before the Commission of Inquiry into the Sponsorship Program and Advertising Activities, 20 September 2004.
3 Association of Professional Executives of the Public Service of Canada (APEX), *Improving Financial Management in the Government of Canada* (Ottawa, 30 January 2006), iii.
4 Despite significant concerns about the need for improving financial management, a survey of 1,100 executives in the summer of 2005 indicates that more than 80 per cent moderately or strongly agree that 'financial officer and executive accountabilities are clear and well documented.' See APEX, *Improving Financial Management in the Government of Canada*, 16.
5 In addition to the Financial Administration Act, departmental legislation and other acts like the Public Service Modernization Act assign powers directly to deputy ministers.
6 Good, *The Politics of Public Management*.
7 The expenditure level widely reported in the media, based on the reports of the Auditor General and others, appeared larger because it included total expenditures over a nine-year period. See 'Table 6: Summary by Year of SPS Contract Details for Agency Managed and Internally Managed Contracts,' Commission of Inquiry into the Sponsorship Program and Advertising Activities, *Who is Responsible? Forensic Audits* (Ottawa: Minister of Public Works and Government Services, 2005), 13.

8 Jim Judd, Secretary to the Treasury Board, testimony before the Commission of Inquiry into the Sponsorship Program and Advertising Activities, 20 September 2004.

9 The term chief financial officer (CFO) is associated to the changes in 2004 to re-establish in the Treasury Board Secretariat the Office of the Comptroller General of Canada. Prior to that time the most senior departmental finance official was referred to as the senior financial officer (SFO), and in those large departments where that position included other corporate responsibilities, the subordinate with exclusive financial responsibilities was referred to as the senior full-time financial officer (SFFO).

10 Interview with chief financial officers, Ottawa, ON, 17 and 29 June and 29 July 2005.

11 Interview with a chief financial officer, Ottawa, ON, 29 June 2005.

12 Interview with a chief financial officer, Ottawa, ON, 17 June 2005.

13 Interview with a chief financial officer, Ottawa, ON, 29 June 2005.

14 Interview with a senior official, Treasury Board Secretariat, Ottawa, ON, 17 November 2005.

15 Ibid.

16 Interview with a chief financial officer, Ottawa, ON, 17 June 2005.

17 Interview with a chief financial officer, Ottawa, ON, 12 July 2005.

18 Interview with a chief financial officer, Ottawa, ON, 17 June 2005.

19 Discussion with a former chief financial officer, Ottawa, ON, 12 January 2005.

20 For a recent comprehensive study of the changing role of chief financial officers and proposals for improvement, see The Conference Board of Canada, *From Stewardship to Strategy: Strengthening Financial Leadership and Management in the Public Sector* (Ottawa: Conference Board of Canada, 2006).

21 As studies have indicated, this has proved particularly difficult to achieve in practice. See, for example, Good, *The Politics of Public Management.*

22 The modern comptrollership movement first gathered momentum with the implementation of the Independent Review Panel on Modernization of Comptrollership in 1997. See Treasury Board Secretariat, *Background on Modern Comptrollership,* available online at www.tbs-sct.gc.ca/cmo_mfc/intro_e.asp.

23 Ian D. Clark and Harry Swain, 'Distinguishing the Real from the Surreal in Management Reform: Suggestions for Beleaguered Administrators in the Government of Canada,' *Canadian Public Administration* 48, no. 4 (Winter 2005), 453–76.

24 Interview with a chief financial officer, Ottawa, ON, June 2005.
25 Interview with a chief financial officer, Ottawa, ON, 29 June 2005.
26 Interview with a chief financial officer, Ottawa, ON, June 2005.
27 Interview with a chief financial officer, Ottawa, ON, 14 July 2005.
28 Interview with a chief financial officer, Ottawa, ON, July 2005.
29 Interview with a chief financial officer, Ottawa, ON, 12 July 2005.
30 Interview with a chief financial officer, Ottawa, ON, 17 June 2005.
31 Interview with a top level comptroller, Treasury Board Secretariat, Ottawa, ON, 18 November 2005.
32 Interview with a chief financial officer, Ottawa, ON, 14 July 2005.
33 The current Comptroller General has advocated that all CFOs have professional accounting designations.
34 Interview with a chief financial officer, Ottawa, ON, 14 July 2005.
35 Discussion with a former chief financial officer, Ottawa, ON, 21 July 2005.
36 Interview with a chief financial officer, Ottawa, ON, 29 July 2005.
37 Interview with a chief financial officer, Ottawa, ON, 29 July 2005.
38 Paul Martin, testimony before the Commission of Inquiry into the Sponsorship Program and Advertising Activities.
39 Auditor General of Canada, *Report of the Auditor General of Canada to the House of Commons for the Fiscal Year Ending March 31* (Ottawa: Minister of Supply and Services, 1976), 9.
40 Auditor General of Canada, 'Opening Statement,' November 2003 Report, Press Conference, Ottawa, ON, 10 February 2004.
41 'Interview with Charles-Antoine St-Jean,' *FMI Journal* 16, no. 3 (Spring/Summer 2005), 8.
42 Discussion with a former comptroller general, Ottawa, ON, 22 July 2005.
43 In 1980, one astute student of budgeting, reflecting on the sentiment of some departmental spenders, likened the Comptroller General to 'the "Man from Glad" … Like the famous seller of plastic bags, he is, on the one hand, interested in getting rid of waste and on the other hand he has a vested interest in producing more garbage!' See G. Bruce Doern, ed., *Spending Tax Dollars: Federal Expenditures, 1980–81* (Ottawa: School of Public Administration, Carleton University, 1980), 12.
44 Discussion with a former comptroller general, Ottawa, ON, 22 July 2005.
45 Interview with a senior official, Office of the Comptroller General, Ottawa, ON, 18 November 2005.
46 See, for example, the 3 March 2006 letter to Prime Minister Harper from private sector leaders, former officials in provincial and federal governments, and representatives of the voluntary sector advising him strongly not to implement a large number of the recommendations of the Gomery

Inquiry because they 'could do a good deal of harm.' See Canadian Association of Programs in Public Administration, 'Letter to the Prime Minister,' available online from http://cappa.ca/news/GomeryLetter.pdf.
On 14 December 2006, in a letter to Mr Sheldon Ehrenworth, the prime minister responded positively to the major concern raised in the letter of 23 March 2006. He stressed that, under the new Federal Accountability Act, deputy ministers are designated as accounting officers, responsible *before* parliamentary committees, but 'the fundamental accountability between a Minister and Parliament and between a Minister and his or her Deputy Minister have not been altered in any way.' Retrieved 30 December 2006 from www.gc.ca/grfx/docs/gomery_fromupm_e.pdf.
47 A.R. Elangovan and D. Shapiro, 'Betrayal of Trust in Organizations,' *Academy of Management Review* 23, no. 3 (1998), 547–66.

9. Parliament and Public Money

1 Commission of Inquiry into the Sponsorship Program and Advertising Activities (popularly known as the Gomery Inquiry), *Restoring Accountability: Recommendations* (Ottawa: Minister of Public Works and Government Services, 2006), 3.
2 Standing Committee on Government Operations and Estimates, *Meaningful Scrutiny: Practical Improvements to the Estimates Process* (Ottawa: Canada Communications Publishing, 2003), 19.
3 Carolyn Bennett, Deborah Grey, and Yves Morin, The *Parliament We Want: Parliamentarians' Views on Parliamentary Reform* (Ottawa: Library of Parliament, 2003), 7.
4 For an analysis of how these and other important differences in the circumstances, practices, and procedures in the Parliaments of Canada, Britain, Australia, and New Zealand shape the practice of accountability, see Peter Aucoin and Mark D. Jarvis, *Modernizing Government Accountability: A Framework for Reform* (Ottawa: Canada School of Public Service, 2005).
5 While all scholars and students emphasize the important role of Parliament in holding the government to account, they also list additional roles for Parliament. Savoie argues that 'the role of the government is to govern and that of the Commons is to subject political power to certain controls, to provide legitimacy to government action and activities, and to hold the executive to account.' See Donald J. Savoie, *Breaking the Bargain: Public Servants, Ministers, and Parliament* (Toronto: University of Toronto Press, 2003), 178. Dobell and Ulrich argue that there are three fundamental roles

of Parliament: empowering the government through legislation, scrutiny,
and representation. See Peter Dobell and Martin Ulrich, 'Parliament's Performance in the Budget Process: A Case Study,' *Policy Matters* 3, no. 5
(May 2002). Malloy argues that Parliament has four dimensions of activity
and influence: law making and the passage of legislation, holding the
government to account, the generation and discussion of policy ideas, and
determining party leadership – not in the ability to choose the leader, but
the ability to undermine them and force a leadership convention. See
Jonathan Malloy, 'The House of Commons Under the Chrétien Government,' in G. Bruce Doern, ed., *How Ottawa Spends, 2003–2004* (Don Mills,
ON: Oxford University Press, 2003). According to Malcolmson and
Myers, 'the primary purpose of the modern parliament is to make the cabinet accountable for its actions to the public.' See Patrick N. Malcolmson
and Richard Myers, *The Canadian Regime* (Peterborough, ON: Broadview
Press, 2002). Thomas states that 'constitutional theory places Parliament
at the centre of the Canadian policy process,' and he explains that Parliament's role is to approve legislation, hold ministers accountable for the
performance of government and their departments, and to scrutinize and
debate both political and administrative leadership. See Paul G. Thomas,
'The Past, Present and Future of Officers of Parliament,' *Canadian Public
Administration* 46, no. 3 (Fall 2003), 287–314.

6 Norman Ward, *The Public Purse: A Study of Canadian Democracy* (Toronto:
University of Toronto Press, 1962). For a recent review of the book, as part of
'Great Books Revisited,' see Audrey Doerr, 'Show Me the Money: Accountability of Government Expenditures,' *Canadian Public Administration* 46,
no. 2 (Summer 2003), 257–61.

7 In any budget there are two types of expenditures: those expenditures that
require the approval of Parliament on an annual basis and those expenditures that have ongoing legislative approval. The first expenditures, called
'voted appropriations,' require the annual approval of Parliament through
an annual appropriation bill. The second expenditures, called 'statutory,'
are those expenditures that Parliament has authorized on an ongoing basis
through enabling legislation.

In 1963, 'voted appropriations' represented 58 per cent of all expenditures
thereby giving parliamentarians, ministers, and public servants annual discretion over more than half of all expenditures. By 2004, the situation was
nearly reversed with 'voted expenditures' representing only 35 per cent
($65 billion) of total budgetary expenditures and statutory expenditures rep-
resenting 65 per cent ($118 billion). The annual discretion of Parliament, min-
isters, and public servants over expenditures has been greatly reduced over

the past forty years and, in turn, has affected the roles and relative influence of the Treasury Board Secretariat and the Department of Finance.

8 Ward, *The Public Purse*, 3–4.

9 Jonathan Malloy, 'The Standing Committee on Public Accounts,' Commission of Inquiry into the Sponsorship Program and Advertising Activities, *Restoring Accountability: Research Studies*, vol. 1 (Ottawa: Minister of Public Works and Government Services, 2006), 63–100.

10 When measured against the secrecy that has traditionally surrounded budget making, current budget consultations appear open. However, one senior Treasury Board official suggests, that by current standards for transparency and openness in government, the budget process continues to be considerably closed to outsiders: 'Finance's consultation process is pretty thin in terms of what most would consider substantive consultation, and the bulk of the budget development process still occurs in secrecy. I don't see the trial balloons and selective leaks that became routine with Martin as Minister of Finance as either a proxy for consultation or shedding the traditional veil of secrecy.' Correspondence to author, 31 July 2006.

11 OECD, *Budgeting in Canada*, 20th Annual Meeting of Senior Budget Officials, Public Management Committee (Paris: OECD, 1999) 9.

12 Hale, *The Politics of Taxation in Canada*.

13 House of Commons, *Report of the Standing Committee on Finance, Securing Our Future* (Ottawa, November 2001).

14 *The Hill Times*, No. 625, 'Legislative Process,' 18 February 2002. Robert Marleau was Clerk of the House of Commons from 1987 to January 2001.

15 Bennett, Grey, and Morin, The *Parliament We Want*; 'Meaningful Scrutiny'; and House of Commons, *The Business of Supply: Completing the Circle of Control*, Report of the Standing Committee on Procedure and House Affairs (Ottawa, December 1998).

16 Peter Dobell and Martin Ulrich, 'Building Better Relations,' Occasional Papers on Parliamentary Government, no. 13 (Ottawa: The Parliamentary Centre, 2002).

17 Gomery Inquiry, *Restoring Accountability: Recommendations*, and 'Parliament and Financial Accountability,' in *Restoring Accountability: Research Studies*, vol. 1.

18 'Report of the Royal Commission on the Civil Service,' Sessional Paper No. 29a (Ottawa: King's Printer, 1908), 2.

19 House of Commons, *Debates*, 1943, 5382–3.

20 W.F. Dawson, *Procedure in the Canadian House of Commons* (Toronto: University of Toronto Press, 1962), 211.

21 Ward, *The Public Purse*, 275.

22 House of Commons, Special Committee on Procedure, Third Report, 6 December 1968, 429–30.
23 Report of the Liaison Committee on Committee Effectiveness, *Parliamentary Government*, No. 43 (Ottawa, June 1993), 4.
24 Comments from J.R. Mallory citing a passage from the Lambert Commission Report in *First Sessional Report*, Meeting No. 8, November 30, 1995, 8:2.
25 House of Commons, *The Business of Supply*, 16.
26 Ibid.
27 Bennett, Grey, and Morin, The *Parliament We Want*, 13.
28 See Allen Schick, 'Can National Legislatures Regain an Effective Voice in Budget Policy?' *OECD Journal of Budgeting* 2, no. 3 (2002), 15–43.
29 Ibid.
30 Interview with a former director, Treasury Board Secretariat, Ottawa, ON, 1 December 2004.
31 Peter Dobell and Martin Ulrich, 'Parliament and Financial Accountability,' in Gomery Inquiry, *Restoring Accountability: Research Studies*, vol. 1, 24.
32 Correspondence to author, 16 November 2004. Twenty years later when the author was the assistant secretary, expenditure management in the Program Branch of the Treasury Board Secretariat, he had a near-identical experience with Treasury Board ministers.
33 Dobell and Ulrich, 'Parliament and Financial Accountability,' 23–61.
34 Treasury Board Secretariat, *Results for Canadians: A Management Framework for the Government of Canada* (Ottawa: President of the Treasury Board, 2000).
35 Ian D. Clark and Harry Swain, 'Distinguishing the Real from the Surreal in Management Reform: Suggestions for Beleaguered Administrators in the Government of Canada,' *Canadian Public Administration* 48, no. 4 (Winter 2005), 453–76.
36 Jacques Bourgault and Stéphanie Guindon, 'L'examen parlementaire des rapports de performance des ministères fédéraux: une étude empirique' (unpublished paper, 2005); and Jim McDavid, 'Using Performance Reports: Findings from the Legislator Uses of Performance Reports Project' (paper presented to the 25th Anniversary Conference of CCAF-FCVI, Ottawa, ON, 17–18 October 2005).
37 The following section is drawn from David A. Good, 'Parliament and Public Money: Players and Police,' *Canadian Parliamentary Review* 28, no. 1 (Spring 2005), 17–21.
38 See for example, Auditor General of Canada, *Annual Report to the House of Commons, 1993* (Ottawa: Minister of Public Works and Government Services Canada, 1993), 19.
39 Adrienne Clarkson, *Heart Matters* (Toronto: Penguin, 2006).

40 Office of the Secretary to the Governor General, *News Release*, 24 December 2004.

41 Gomery Inquiry, *Restoring Accountability: Recommendations*, 75.

42 Malloy, 'The Standing Committee on Public Accounts,' 63–100.

43 Cited in ibid., 77.

44 Ibid., 99–100.

45 Interview with an assistant auditor general, Ottawa, ON, 28 October 2005.

46 When the Public Accounts Committee reviewed the sponsorship scandal in 2003 and 2004 there were 76 substitute members of the committee, and in 2006 there were 102.

47 Gomery Inquiry, *Restoring Accountability: Recommendations*, 79.

10. Budget Reforms

1 Wildavsky, *The New Politics of the Budgetary Process*, 397.

2 Canada, Royal Commission on Government Organization, *Management of the Public Service* (Ottawa: Queen's Printer, 1962).

3 Canada, Royal Commission on Government Organization, *Management of the Public Service*, vol. 1, abridged version (Ottawa: Queen's Printer, 1962), 99.

4 For a perceptive account of the Planning Branch model from 1968–78, which the author labelled as 'BOISE (BOld Interference and Social Engineering),' see Rod Dobell, 'Evaluation and Entitlements: Hartle's Search for Rationality in Government,' in Richard M. Bird, Michael J. Trebilcock, and Thomas A. Wilson, eds., *Rationality in Public Policy: Retrospect and Prospect, A Tribute to Douglas G. Hartle* (Toronto: Canadian Tax Foundation, 1999), 79–107.

5 Treasury Board of Canada, *Planning Program Budgeting Guide* (Ottawa: Treasury Board of Canada, 1969). The key PPBS concepts were: the setting of program objectives; systematic analysis to clarify objectives and assess alternative ways to achieve them; framing the budgetary programs to achieve objectives; future projections of the costs of programs; plans for the year by year achievement of programs; and information by program to monitor achievement of program objectives, and to reassess objectives and programs. In addition, the Treasury Board Secretariat issued a guide to 'cost-benefit analysis' for use by departments and agencies in assessing existing programs and new proposals.

6 Specifically, over the period 1969–71:

  • expenditures were presented by departments on a program by program basis with a statement of objectives,
  • each program was broken down into activities and total costs were displayed in terms of objectives of expenditure,

- non-budgetary items (loans, investments, and advances) were individually displayed by program,
- estimates by program were presented for the coming year and were compared to the forecast of expenditures for the fiscal year just ending and to the actual expenditures of the previous year,
- grants and capital expenditures in excess of $5 million were segregated into separate votes,
- salary data were replaced by data on authorized and planned person-years (the equivalent of one person working full time for one year), and
- the number of standard objects of expenditure was reduced to twelve and included personnel; transportation and communications; information; professional and special services; rentals, purchased equipment and maintenance; utilities, material and supplies; acquisition of land; buildings and works; acquisition of machinery and equipment; transfer payments; public debt charges; and other subsidies and payments.

7 Treasury Board of Canada, *The Operational Performance Measurement System of the Government of Canada* (Ottawa: Treasury Board Canada, 1974).
8 See A.W. Johnson, 'The Treasury Board of Canada and the Machinery of Government in the 1970s,' *Canadian Journal of Political Science* 4, no. 3 (1971), 240–59; and 'Planning, Programming and Budgeting in Canada,' *Canadian Public Administration* 33, no. 24 (1973), 23–31.
9 By 1975, in the face of significantly rising inflation, the government established a broadly based regime of price-and-wage controls both within government and the private sector, and established the Anti-inflation Board for implementing the controls.
10 Canada, Auditor General of Canada, *Report of the Auditor General* (Ottawa: Minister of Supply and Services, 1976).
11 Royal Commission on Financial Management and Accountability, *Final Report* (Ottawa: Department of Supply and Services, 1979).
12 Department of Finance, *The New Expenditure Management System* (Ottawa: Department of Finance, 1979).
13 Privy Council Office, *The Policy and Expenditure Management System* (Ottawa: Privy Council Office, 1981). Lest anyone be sceptical about the scope and range of the policy and expenditure issues that were contemplated by the architects of the new Policy and Expenditure Management System, they only need to read the introduction of the Privy Council Office document:

> The 1970s has been a decade of increased uncertainty. The turbulence of the world environment and the rapidity of change have contributed to a sense of lost control. A sluggish economic climate has necessitated strict measures to cope with world-wide inflation and unemployment.

These economic difficulties have led to calls on all governments to restrain spending and to ensure that their expenditures are put to the most effective and efficient use.

The character of government has also changed, as the nation and the international context in which it lives have changed and as knowledge of what government can and cannot do has changed.

This change in the character of government needs to be understood and addressed in reforming the policy and financial machinery of government to meet the needs of the 1980s. There is a need not only to limit expenditures but also to increase choice.

The complexity and rapidity of change in Canadian society – and hence of the issues facing government – have meant that few problems can be contained within the span of a single department or responsibilities of a single Minister. As the number of government departments and agencies increases, in response to demands from the public for action in areas such as environmental protection, consumer affairs, and regional development, this situation becomes more serious. The need for mechanisms that provide for effective cross-departmental action and coordination becomes more urgent.

The speed of the events and the speed with which problems and policies are communicated added another dimension to the problem. It is no longer possible to formulate a solution to an issue in isolation, and then sort out at leisure the undesirable and unexpected side effects as they appear.

A government decision can have effects within hours on the lives, financial standing and prospects of individual Canadians. With equal speed, side effects can be transmitted through the complex interconnections of a modern industrial society into areas of national life seemingly quite divorced from the matter at hand.

These changes in the character of government and the structure of the environment within which it operates have drawn in their train an evolution in the thinking about how best to organize and manage government. The question of increasing concern today is not simply what to decide but how to decide.

How decisions are made – that is, the process of public decision-making – shapes what decisions are taken. The way in which the process is structured in terms of incentives and constraints determines how participants will interact in reaching public decisions. The process and hence the product (or decision) are influenced by who is consulted or ignored and when, what factors are considered, and who is accountable to whom.

It has become increasingly clear that changing the incentives, constraints and procedures in the decision-making process is fundamental to the effective management of government. It makes a difference whether policies are determined in isolation from, and at the expense of, resource considerations or whether expenditures are set without reference to policies and objectives.

It is also apparent that altering the way in which policy and expenditure decisions are made can be neither taken lightly nor accomplished easily. Experience in altering processes has taught us to treat such change with a healthy degree of circumspection.

The new policy and expenditure management system is not a panacea. Rather it is a conscious attempt to alter the decision-making process in a way which brings into sharper focus the key consideration of what the government wants to achieve with the resources available. It also recognizes that the current structure of federal expenditures is so rigid that fundamental change can be accomplished only in the longer term.

The often asked question of how much the government should spend depends on what the money is to be spent. Similarly, the question of where to spend depends upon how much there is to spend. Objectives shape the determination of resource limits and resource limits in turn shape objectives.

Government decision-making is often described as incremental: attention is focussed on change at the margin with little or no attempt to consider the base of ongoing policies and programs. In a period of lessening growth there is little opportunity for increase at the margin as the principal means for expanding choice. Not only must the government get credit for new initiatives but there must be a coordinated effort to ensure that the government and the public receive full value for the money that is now spent.

14 The budgetary envelopes define the financial resources that are available to a policy committee of cabinet for a particular policy sector.

15 Privy Council Office, *Policy and Expenditure Management System: Envelope Procedures and Rules* (Ottawa: Privy Council Office, 1980).

16 Correspondence to author from an anonymous reviewer of the manuscript, 16 August 2006.

17 Privy Council Office, Policy and Expenditure Management System. The essential 'rules of game' for PEMS were:

• The Cabinet Committee on Priorities and Planning, chaired by the prime minister, established the envelope levels (including policy reserves) on the basis of recommendations from the minister of finance on expenditure levels and, to a lesser extent, from cabinet policy committee chairpersons on sector priorities.

- The cabinet policy committees were responsible for making allocations from their policy reserves for new departmental initiatives and for reallocations across departments within their sectors.
- The Treasury Board was responsible for costing existing programs and for making allocations from the operating reserve to departments in order to maintain existing programs.
- The Department of Finance made provision within the government's overall expenditure framework for a central reserve in order to handle increases in statutory programs.
- Tax expenditures and off-budget financing (e.g., loans, loan guarantees, and advances) provided to departments and agencies were to be taken into account by the Department of Finance in recommending envelope levels.

18 Richard Van Loon, 'Ottawa's New Expenditure Process: Four Systems in Search of Co-ordination,' in G.B. Doern, ed., *How Ottawa Spends: The Liberals, the Opposition and Federal Priorities* (Toronto: James Lorimer, 1983), 93–120.

19 Treasury Board of Canada, Office of the Comptroller General, *Guide on the Program Evaluation Function* (Ottawa: Supply and Services, 1981).

20 For example, the decision on the controversial National Energy Program was made 'outside the system' by a small group of ministers including the ministers of energy and finance and the prime minister. See, for example, Don Johnston, *Up the Hill* (Montreal: Optimum, 1986).

21 See Wildavsky, *Budgeting*, chap. 14, 'Some Butterflies Were Caught, No Elephants Stopped: The Zero-Base Budget, a Precursor of PPBS,' 278–96.

22 Rod Dobell, 'Pressing the Envelope: The Significance of the New Top-down System of Expenditure Management in Ottawa,' *Policy Options* 2 (November-December 1981), 13–18.

23 Her name was Solange Denis and her message to Prime Minister Mulroney was that if 'you continue with this cut to senior's benefit, it's goodbye Charlie Brown,' which everyone understood meant the prime minister.

24 Interview with a senior official, Department of Finance, 1 December 2004.

25 Correspondence to author from a former deputy minister, 14 July 2006.

26 Task Force on Program Review, 'Program Review' (Ottawa, 1986).

27 For an analysis of why regional ministers are influential in any cabinet, and in particular the Mulroney and Trudeau cabinets, see Herman Bakvis, *Regional Ministers: Power and Influence in the Canadian Cabinet* (Toronto: University of Toronto Press, 1991).

28 In 1989 the government created five Special Operating Agencies (SOAs): Canada Communications Group, Consulting and Audit Canada, Training and Development Canada, Government Telecommunications and Informatics Services, and the Passport Office. By 2004 there were seventeen.
29 David Wright, *Special Operating Agencies – Autonomy, Accountability and Performance Measurement* (Ottawa: Canadian Centre for Management Development, 1995), vii.
30 Canada, *Public Service 2000: The Renewal of the Public Service of Canada* (Ottawa: Minister of Supply and Services, 1990).
31 John Edwards, *Looking Back from 2000 at Public Service 2000*. Report prepared for the Office of the Auditor General (Ottawa, September 2000), 8.
32 Treasury Board Secretariat, *Towards a Shared Management Agenda* (Ottawa: Treasury Board Secretariat, 1991).
33 On the stream of initiatives, see Ian D. Clark, 'Restraint, Renewal, and the Treasury Board Secretariat,' *Canadian Public Administration* 37, no. 2 (1994), 112–31.
34 Correspondence to author, 24 July 2006.
35 Kevin Lynch, 'The Virtuous Cycle: The Canadian Experience in a G7 Context,' *Policy Options* (October 2005), 63–7.
36 Treasury Board, *Getting Government Right: A Progress Report* (Ottawa: Treasury Board, 1996), and Treasury Board, *Getting Government Right: Governing for Canadians* (Ottawa: Treasury Board, 1997).
37 The five initial tests were:

   1 *Public Interest Test:* Does the program or activity continue to serve the public interest?
   2 *Role of Government Test:* Is there a legitimate and necessary role for government in this program area or activity?
   3 *Federalism Test:* Is the current role of the federal government appropriate, or is the program a candidate for realignment with the provinces?
   4 *Partnership Test:* What activities or programs should or could be transferred in whole or in part to the private or voluntary sector?
   5 *Efficiency Test:* If the program or activity continues, how could its efficiency be improved?

38 Correspondence to author, 14 July 2006.
39 One former senior public servant who had worked in the Treasury Board Secretariat in the mid-1970s observed Chrétien's behaviour thirty years later as prime minister was 'strongly reminiscent of his posture as president of the Treasury (1974–6), requiring that Ministers swallow within their department any financial implications following approval of a new program.' Correspondence to author, 24 July 2006.

40 One spending minister reflects on an event that crystallized for him the critical need for guardianship and fiscal restraint: 'For me one of the most telling moments of the revelation came from the deputy minister of finance, who told me, ashen-faced before a cabinet meeting in early 1994, that 30 minutes before a Government of Canada bond auction that morning there had been no bids.' See John Manley, 'How Canada Slayed the Deficit Dragon and Created the Surplus,' *Policy Options* (October 2005), 22.

41 Evert A. Lindquist, 'Citizens, Experts and Budgets: Evaluating Ottawa's Emerging Budget Process,' in Susan Phillips, ed., *How Ottawa Spends 1994– 95: Making Change* (Ottawa: Carleton University Press, 1994), 91–128.

42 Evert A. Lindquist, *Consultation and Budget Secrecy: Reforming the Process of Creating Revenue Budgets in the Canadian Federal Government* (Ottawa: Conference Board of Canada, 1985).

43 Treasury Board, *The New Expenditure Management System* (Ottawa: Treasury Board, 1995).

44 The principal features of the new expenditure management system included:

- Improved expenditure planning by requiring the review and reallocation of expenditures within the Budget process.
- Treasury Board changing its role from 'funder to banker' by reducing the size of its central 'operating reserves' to focus on departmental investments to yield future year savings or cost avoidance.
- Central 'policy reserves' were formally eliminated, with any new initiatives to require greater scrutiny and to be funded through reallocations.
- Departments were to focus on performance and program results with increased public accountability.
- Departmental business plans were established to focus on strategic changes in departmental programs and business to achieve the budget targets.
- Some increased administrative and budget flexibility was provided to departments to encourage more effective management and delivery of programs within significantly reduced resources.
- Departmental 'outlook' document were established to assist the House of Commons Standing Committees in reviewing departmental expenditure planning by focusing on future expenditure trends and priorities.
- The minister of finance published each fall an economic and fiscal update as the basis for setting fiscal and economic parameters and assumptions within which the spring budget was developed.

45 Evert A. Lindquist, 'How Ottawa Reviews Spending: Moving Beyond Adhocracy?' in G. Bruce Doern, ed., *How Ottawa Spends 2006–2007: In from*

the Cold, the Tory Rise and the Liberal Demise (Montreal: McGill-Queen's University Press, 2006), 185–207.

46 Joanne Kelly, 'Pursuit of an Elusive Ideal: Review and Reallocation under the Chrétien Government,' in G. Bruce Doern, ed., *How Ottawa Spends 2003–2004: Regime Change and Policy Shift* (Toronto: Oxford University Press, 2003), 118–33.

47 OECD, *Reallocation: The Role of Budget Institutions* (Paris: OECD, 2005), 9. The countries included in the comparative analysis were Canada, the Czech Republic, France, Germany, Italy, Mexico, the Netherlands, New Zealand, Sweden, the United Kingdom, and the United States.

48 These two tests were an expanded version of the tests used in the 1995 Program Review. The policy tests included the following questions:

- *Public Interest*: Does the program area or activity continue to serve the public interest?
- *Role of Government*: Is there a legitimate and necessary role for government in this program area or activity?
- *Federalism*: Is the current role of the federal government appropriate, or is the program a candidate for realignment with the provinces?
- *Partnership*: What activities or programs should or could be transferred in whole or in part to the private/voluntary sector?
- *Value-for-money*: Are Canadians getting value for their tax dollars?
- *Efficiency*: If the program or activity continues, how could its efficiency be improved?
- *Affordability*: Is the resultant package of programs and activities affordable? If not, what programs or activities would be abandoned?

The implementation tests included the following questions:

- *Achievability*: Are proposed expenditure reductions and time lines achievable and sustainable? How will their impacts be managed over time?
- *Future Cost*: Do the proposed changes avoid or create future cost or program pressures?
- *Capacity*: What is the effect of any proposed changes on policy and analytical capacity? On operational and delivery capacity?
- *Human Resource Management*: What is the effect of any proposed changes on human resource management, staffing levels, and compensation costs?
- *Program Integrity*: Do any proposed changes address existing operational and program integrity pressures? Do proposed changes ensure ongoing integrity of departmental corporate governance and comptrollership capacity, and information management systems?

- *Horizontal Implications*: Has the impact of any proposed changes on other departments been clearly specified? What is the effect of proposed changes on other levels of government, the private sector, and the voluntary sector? What is the effect of proposed changes on the departmental corporate risk profile, and what strategies does the department recommend to mitigate unacceptable risk? Does the proposal incorporate contingencies to address major risks associated with implementation of any changes proposed?

49 These areas included capital asset management ($47 billion in assets); public sector compensation and comparability ($25 billion); procurement and contracting ($13 billion); corporate and administrative services ($6.5 billion); professional services ($6.5 billion); use of information technology and its management ($5.2 billion); service delivery infrastructure ($3 billion); federal institutional governance ($3 billion in annual operations); and legal services ($700 million).

50 Interview with a former senior member, Privy Council Office Secretariat on Expenditure Reallocation, Ottawa, ON, 29 September 2005.

51 Department of Finance, *Government of Canada – Expenditure Review* (February 2005), retrieved May 2005 from www.expenditurereview-examendesdepenses.gc.ca/index_e.asp.

52 Department of Finance, 'Expenditure Review for Sound Financial Management,' *Budget 2005*, retrieved May 2005 from www.fin.gc.ca/budget05/booklets/bkexpe.htm.

53 Remarks at a public presentation, University of Victoria, 13 September 2005.

54 Interview with an associate deputy minister, Department of Finance, Ottawa, ON, 18 November 2005.

55 Arthur Kroeger, 'Speech to the Ontario Federal Council,' Toronto, ON, 8 December 2006.

56 Government of Canada, *Management in the Government of Canada: A Commitment to Continuous Change* (Ottawa: The President of the Treasury Board, 2005); Treasury Board Secretariat of Canada, *Review of the Responsibilities and Accountabilities of Ministers and Senior Officials* (Ottawa: The President of the Treasury Board, 2005); and Treasury Board Secretariat of Canada, *The Financial Administration Act: Responding to Non-Compliance* (Ottawa: The President of the Treasury Board, 2005).

57 The proposed changes, numbering forty-six pages, included some sixty individual items across thirteen areas of reform, ranging from the financing of political parties, to government appointments and parliamentary budget overview. See Conservative Party of Canada, *Stand Up for Canada*.

58 Michael Power, *The Audit Society: Rituals of Verification* (Oxford: Oxford University Press, 1977).

59 Of the nineteen recommendations put forward by Justice Gomery in his 1 February 2006 final report, the Harper Conservative government did not proceed with those which that reduced the scope and authority of the prime minister and the Clerk of the Privy Council. This included four recommendations, specifically:

- establishing a three-year minimum for deputy minister appointments,
- having members of the Public Accounts Committee serve on the committee for the duration of a Parliament,
- having deputy ministers no longer appointed by the prime minister on the recommendation of the Clerk of the Privy Council but rather by the specific minister, with appointments selected from a list of candidates screened by an internal government panel, with the choice endorsed by cabinet and with a provision for veto by the prime minister, and
- overhauling the position of the Clerk of the Privy Council, with the official title to be 'secretary to the cabinet' and the main role to be to represent the public service to the prime minister and cabinet, with the designations 'Clerk of the Privy Council' and 'Deputy Minister to the Prime Minister' to be abolished, with the Privy Council Office to become the 'Cabinet Secretariat,' and with the secretary of the Treasury Board to assume the title and function of 'Head of the Public Service.'

See Gomery Inquiry, *Restoring Accountability: Recommendations.*

60 The five new parliamentary watchdogs are the conflict of interest and ethics commissioner; the commissioner of lobbying; the parliamentary budget officer; the public sector integrity officer; and the director of public prosecutions. The four parliamentary watchdogs with increased legislature authority are the chief electoral officer; the privy commissioner; the information commissioner; and the public service agency. The three new internal, independent watchdogs are the public appointments commissioner within the prime minister's portfolio; the independent procurement auditor; and the chief audit executives with each department. The role of the existing Comptroller General is strengthened and deputy ministers have been designated as 'accounting officers,' accountable *before* Parliament for certain responsibilities.

61 The Federal Accountability Act received royal assent on 12 December 2006. With respect to the management of public money, the legislation was essentially the same as that which was proposed. The only major exception was that public servants would be rewarded for exposing wrongdoing.

62 Leger Marketing, *Professional Barometer Report*, 9 March 2006, 3.
63 Quote from Don Drummond, former associate deputy minister of Finance in, Steven Chase, 'Tories Risk Creating Dissenting Voice in New Budget Office,' *Globe and Mail*, 13 April 2006, A6.
64 The professional competence of the PBO should not be automatically assumed. In 2004 there were only four private-sector economic-forecasting organizations – Global Insight, the University of Toronto, the Conference Board of Canada, and the Centre for Spatial Economics – and the Department of Finance was worried about their 'declining expertise' as most 'are not making the necessary investment to update and improve their models and tools.' Interview with an assistant deputy minister, Department of Finance, Ottawa, ON, 27 October 2005.
65 Prime Minister Stephen Harper, 'Accountability and the Public Service' (speech to the public servants, Ottawa, ON, 23 March 2006).
66 See, for example, Good, *The Politics of Public Management*.
67 Interview with a former top official, Privy Council Office, Ottawa, ON, 6 April 2006.
68 David Zussman, 'The Accountability Act Should Also Account for Money Well Spent,' *Ottawa Citizen*, 24 April 2006, A13.
69 As a recent Clerk of the Privy Council has written, 'over the last 40 years ... the Public Service (has) tested various expenditure management and budgetary processes so that ministers were able to set political and fiscal priorities based on good information, strategic planning and empirical analysis.' Alex Himelfarb, *Tenth Annual Report to the Prime Minister on the Public Service of Canada* (Ottawa: Privy Council Office, 2003), 1.

11. Doing Better with Public Money?

1 Christopher Hood, 'Stabilization and Cutbacks: A Catastrophe for Government Growth Theory?' *Journal of Theoretical Politics* 3, no. 1 (1991), 37, citing Geoffrey Blainey, *The Causes of War* (London: Macmillan, 1973).
2 As Schick observes, 'during the high-growth era, incrementalism was the pre-eminent theory of budgeting. It offered the leading explanation about how the process works.' See Allen Schick, *The Capacity to Budget* (Washington, DC: Urban Institute Press, 1990), 24.
3 Wildavsky, *How to Limit Government Spending*.
4 Garrett Hardin, 'The Tragedy of the Commons,' *Science* 162 (1968), 1243–8.
5 Kelly and Wanna, 'Are Wildavsky's Guardians and Spenders Still Relevant?' 598–614.
6 Wildavsky, *The New Politics of the Budgetary Process*.

7 Michael Power, *The Audit Society: Rituals of Verification* (Oxford: Oxford University Press, 1997).

8 Allen Schick, 'From the Old Politics of Budgeting to the New.'

9 For an analysis of Mr Martin's 'perplexing and unsuccessful' role as prime minister, after having been 'the country's best finance minister since the Second World War,' see, Jeffrey Simpson, 'Why Mr Red Has the Blues,' *Globe and Mail*, 21 January 2006, F1, F4–F5.

10 Wanna, Jensen, and de Vries, eds., *Controlling Public Expenditure*.

11 Schick, *The Capacity to Budget*, 12.

12 Such 'scandals' have included sponsorships (extensively investigated by the Gomery Inquiry), the gun registry, Auberge Grande Mare, and the HRDC grants and contributions. Not all these turned out to be what they initially appeared. See, for example, Good, *The Politics of Public Management*.

13 See Aaron Wildavsky, 'A Budget for All Seasons? Why the Traditional Budget Lasts,' *Public Administration Review*, no. 6 (November/December 1978), 501–9.

14 See John Wanna and Stephen Bartos, '"Good Practice: Does It Work in Theory?" Australia's Quest for Better Outcomes,' in Wanna, Jensen, and de Vries, ed., *Controlling Public Expenditure*, 1–29.

15 Prime ministers who once were 'first among equals' are now 'first among un-equals.' See Savoie, *Governing from the Centre*.

16 The representation of certain ministers with responsibilities and interests in particular policy priorities will be important to prime ministers in reflecting and advancing the government's priorities in the budget-making process. For example, Prime Minister Trudeau in the period 1980–3 did not include his minister of national defence on the Cabinet Committee on Priorities and Planning. Instead, defence was 'represented' by the Secretary of State for External Affairs with the result that, when it came to budget allocations, defence received less priority relative to other priorities.

17 Interview with a former top official, Privy Council Office, Ottawa, ON, 11 April 2006.

18 Interview with a senior official, Treasury Board Secretariat, Ottawa, ON, 28 October 2005.

19 Interview with a senior official, Treasury Board Secretariat, Ottawa, ON, 17 November 2005.

Index

The Institute of Public Administration of Canada
Series in Public Management and Governance